AF521651

China's New Role in African Politics

China's rise to global power status in recent decades has been accompanied by deepening economic relationships with Africa, with the New Silk Road's extension to Sub-Saharan Africa as the latest step, leading to much academic debate about the influence of Chinese business in the continent. However, China's engagement with African states at the political and diplomatic level has received less attention in the literature. This book investigates the impact of Chinese policies on African politics, asking how China deals with political instability in Africa and in turn how Africans perceive China to be helping or hindering political stability.

While China officially operates with a foreign policy strategy which conceives of Africa as one integrated monolithic area (with the Forum on China–Africa Cooperation (FOCAC) the flagship of inter-continental cooperation), this book highlights the plurality of context-specific interaction patterns between China and African elites, demonstrating how China's role and relevance has differently evolved according to whether African countries are resource-rich and geostrategically important from the Chinese perspective or not. By looking comparatively at a range of different country cases, the book aims to promote a more thorough understanding of how China reacts to political stability and instability, and in which ways the country contributes to domestic political dynamics and stability within African states.

China's New Role in African Politics will be of interest to researchers from across Political Science, International Relations, International Law and Economy, Security Studies, and African and Chinese Studies.

Christof Hartmann is Professor of Political Science, in particular International Relations and African Politics, at the Department of Political Science, University Duisburg-Essen, Germany.

Nele Noesselt is Professor of Political Science with a special focus on China and East Asia at the University of Duisburg-Essen, Germany.

Routledge Global Cooperation Series

This series develops innovative approaches to understanding, explaining and answering one of the most pressing questions of our time – how can cooperation in a culturally diverse world of nine billion people succeed?

We are rapidly approaching our planet's limits, with trends such as advancing climate change and the destruction of biological diversity jeopardising our natural life support systems. Accelerated globalisation processes lead to an ever-growing interconnectedness of markets, states, societies, and individuals. Many of today's problems cannot be solved by nation states alone. Intensified cooperation at the local, national, international, and global level is needed to tackle current and looming global crises.

Series Editors:
Tobias Debiel, Dirk Messner, Sigrid Quack and Jan Aart Scholte are Co-Directors of the Käte Hamburger Kolleg/Centre for Global Cooperation Research, University of Duisburg-Essen, Germany. Their research areas are, among others, Global Governance, Climate Change, Peacebuilding and Cultural Diversity of Global Citizenship. The four Co-Directors are, at the same time, based in their home institutions, which participate in the Centre, namely the German Development Institute/Deutsches Institut für Entwicklungspolitik (DIE, Messner) in Bonn, the Institute for Development and Peace (INEF, Debiel) in Duisburg, the University of Duisburg-Essen (Quack), and the University of Gothenburg (Scholte) in Sweden.

www.routledge.com/Routledge-Global-Cooperation-Series/book-series/RGC

Titles:

Rethinking Governance in Europe and Northeast Asia
Multilateralism and Nationalism in International Society
Uwe Wissenbach

China's New Role in African Politics
From Non-Intervention towards Stabilization?
Edited by Christof Hartmann and Nele Noesselt

China's New Role in African Politics

From Non-Intervention towards Stabilization?

Edited by Christof Hartmann and Nele Noesselt

LONDON AND NEW YORK

First published 2020
by Routledge
2 Park Square, Milton Park, Abingdon, Oxon OX14 4RN

and by Routledge
52 Vanderbilt Avenue, New York, NY 10017

Routledge is an imprint of the Taylor & Francis Group, an informa business

British Library Cataloguing-in-Publication Data
A catalogue record for this book is available from the British Library

Library of Congress Cataloging-in-Publication Data
Names: Hartmann, Christof, editor, author. | Noesselt, Nele, editor, author.
Title: China's new role in African politics : from non-intervention towards stabilization? / edited by Christof Hartmann and Nele Noesselt.
Description: New York : Routledge, 2019. | Includes bibliographical references and index. Identifiers: LCCN 2019027830 (print) | LCCN 2019027831 (ebook) | ISBN 9781138392076 (hardback) | ISBN 9780429422393 (ebook)
Subjects: LCSH: Africa, Sub-Saharan–Foreign relations–China. | Africa, Sub-Saharan–Politics and government–21st century. | China–Politics and government–21st century. | China–Foreign relations–Africa, Sub-Saharan.
Classification: LCC DT38.9.C6 C47 2019 (print) | LCC DT38.9.C6 (ebook) | DDC 327.67051–dc23
LC record available at https://lccn.loc.gov/2019027830
LC ebook record available at https://lccn.loc.gov/2019027831

ISBN: 978-1-138-39207-6 (hbk)
ISBN: 978-0-429-42239-3 (ebk)

Typeset in Goudy
by Wearset Ltd, Boldon, Tyne and Wear

Printed in the United Kingdom
by Henry Ling Limited

Contents

PART II
Case studies 99

Contributors

Richard Aidoo is Associate Professor of Politics at Coastal Carolina University in South Carolina, USA where he also serves as Assistant Dean of the Thomas W. and Robin W. Edwards College of Humanities and Fine Arts. His research work on the political economy of Sub-Saharan Africa and China–Africa relations has appeared in journal articles, book chapters, and different media outlets including CNN, *Real Clear World*, *The Washington Post*, *The National Interest*, and *Yahoo News*. He is the co-author of *Charting the Roots of Anti-Chinese Populism in Africa* (2015), and the editor of *The Politics of Economic Reform in Ghana* published in 2019.

Lucy Corkin holds a PhD in Political Science from SOAS, University of London. Her doctoral work was published as *Uncovering African Agency: Angola's Management of China's Credit Lines* (2013) and has been translated into Portuguese. Although currently engaged in the private sector, she continues to write extensively and consults to a wide range of stakeholders on Africa–China relations. She speaks English, Portuguese, French, Afrikaans, and Mandarin Chinese.

Sven Grimm is Head of Research Programme on "Inter- and Transnational Cooperation" at the German Development Institute/Deutsches Institut für Entwicklungspolitik (DIE) in Bonn, Germany, and Extraordinary Professor of Stellenbosch University, South Africa. He is a political scientist with a strong interest in cooperation with African states. He has led research projects e.g. on emerging economies' African ventures and their implications for European international cooperation. He has published widely on both the European Union and on China's external relations (with Africa) and was director of the Centre for Chinese Studies at Stellenbosch University, South Africa, between 2010 and 2014.

Christine Hackenesch is Head of Research Programme on "Inter- and Transnational Cooperation" at the German Development Institute / Deutsches Institut für Entwicklungspolitik (DIE). Her research focuses on EU external relations, China-Africa cooperation, international development and democracy support as well as political regimes in Africa. She has recently published a monograph on the implications of China's rise for the EU's good governance support in Africa. The book "The EU and China in African authoritarian regimes. Domestic politics and governance reforms" is published with Palgrave Macmillan and available open access.

Christof Hartmann is Professor of Political Science, in particular International Relations and African Politics, at the Institute of Political Science at the University of Duisburg-Essen, Germany. He received his PhD from the University of Heidelberg (Germany) in 1997 and has been a Visiting Professor at the University of the Western Cape (South Africa). His main research interests are the change of political institutions in Sub-Saharan Africa, and its main driving domestic and international factors, as well as regionalism on the African continent. He has published and edited several books with Oxford University Press and Routledge, and contributed to a wide range of international academic journals.

Steve Hess is Assistant Professor of Political Science at Transylvania University. He is a graduate of Miami University (PhD in Political Science) and the University of Louisville (MA in Political Science). His research agenda focuses on the resilience of authoritarian regimes, democratic backsliding, and Sino-African relations. He is the author of over 20 research articles and the author of the book, *Authoritarian Landscapes: Popular Mobilization and the Institutional Sources of Resilience in Nondemocracies* (2013) and co-author of the book *Charting the Roots of Anti-Chinese Populism in Africa* (2015).

Georg Lammich is an Associated Researcher in International Relations and African Politics at the Institute of Political Science at the University of Duisburg-Essen, Germany and holds a diploma in East Asian Studies and a PhD in Political Science. His research focuses on interregionalism and China's impact on regional integration, development, and security in Africa. He has been a visiting research fellow at the Centre for Chinese Studies in Stellenbosch, South Africa and has conducted extensive fieldwork in China and various countries across the African continent.

Haifang Liu is Associate Professor in the School of International Studies, Peking University. She serves as Director of the Centre for African Studies, Peking University, and the Vice President of the Chinese Society of African Historical Studies. She previously worked for the Institute of West Asian and African Studies (IWAAS), the Chinese Academy of Social Sciences and as a visiting scholar at University of Oslo, the Institute of African Studies, Carleton University, Stellenbosch University (South Africa) and the Institute of Social Studies in The Hague. She has authored, edited, and translated numerous publications in English and Mandarin, including books such as *The Transformative Development of Africa & South-South Cooperation in Agriculture Sector* (both English and Chinese versions), *Beijing Forum 2017: Emerging trends in Sino-African Development Cooperation*, *Special Agricultural*

Foreign Direct Investment in Zambia (both English and Chinese versions), and *General History of Africa, Angola*. She has contributed chapters on aspects of China's comprehensive presence in Africa to several volumes published by Zed, Brill, Palgrave, Fahamu Publishing House, and Routledge. She also has contributed to international academic journals as both a reviewer and author. Her current research topics include New Migrants between China and Africa, Chinese company history in Africa, African perceptions of China and Chinese migrants, Chinese Aid, China–African relations, African sustainable development studies, and Contemporary Africa International Relations.

Nele Noesselt is Professor of Political Science with a special focus on China and East Asia at the Institute of Political Science and the Institute of East Asian Studies (IN-EAST) at the University of Duisburg-Essen, Germany. Since 2017, she is the speaker of the AREA Ruhr Graduate School 'Transnational Institution Building and Transnational Identities in East Asia' (joint PhD program of the University of Duisburg-Essen and the Ruhr University Bochum). Her research agenda ranges from general issues of comparative politics and domestic governance to world politics and theories of international relations.

Patricia Rinck is a Researcher at Käte Hamburger Kolleg/Centre for Global Cooperation Research, and a PhD candidate at the University of Duisburg-Essen, Germany. She has an MA in International Relations and Development Policy from the University of Duisburg-Essen. Her research interests include peacebuilding, statebuilding, feminist peace research, power sharing, and political settlements. Her doctoral research focuses on political settlements and post-conflict transformation in Sierra Leone, where she has carried out extensive field research.

Lloyd Sachikonye is Professor of Political Studies with particular reference to African Politics. He is based at the Centre for Applied Social Sciences at the University of Zimbabwe. He obtained his PhD from the University of Leeds (UK) in 1989. His main research interests relate to democratic processes in Africa, international relations in Southern Africa, and Zimbabwe's relations with China. He has published extensively in such journals as *Journal of African Elections*, *Review of African Political Economy*, and *Taiwan Journal of Democracy*.

Julia C. Strauss is Professor of Chinese and Comparative Politics at the School of Oriental and African Studies (SOAS), University of London, where she also served as Editor of *The China Quarterly* between 2002 and 2011. Her research interests span both sides of the Taiwan Straits and are focused on state building and institution building, governance, the performative dimensions of politics, and China's 'going out' policy toward the developing world, particularly with respect to Africa and Latin America. Her publications include the co-edited volumes *From the Great Wall to the New World: China and Latin American in the 21st Century* (2012), *China and Africa: Emerging*

Patterns in Globalization and Development (2009), and *Staging Politics: Power and Performance in Asia and Africa* (2007). Single-authored books include the edited volume *The History of the People's Republic of China* (2006), and the monograph *Strong Institutions in Weak Polities: State Building in Republican China, 1927-1940* (1998). Her new monograph, *State Formation in China and Taiwan: Bureaucracy, Campaign, and Performance* is forthcoming with Cambridge University Press in early 2020.

Efem N. Ubi is Senior Research Fellow and Head, Division of International Economic Relations with the Nigerian Institute of International Affairs (NIIA), Lagos, Nigeria. He is also a Visiting Scholar and Adjunct Research Fellow with the Center for Nigerian Studies (CNS) and the Institute of African Studies, Zhejiang Normal University, China. His research interests span International Economic Relations, China–Africa Studies, Political Economy, Development Studies, and International Territorial Conflict Management. He has published several articles and book chapters. His recent works include a co-edited book titled *Nigeria in Global Governance, Peace and Security* (2017); *Nigeria National Report: Nationhood Crisis and Violent Extremism as a Poverty Issue* (2017), A Report by the United Nations Development Programme (UNDP) and Humanitarian Dialogue (hd), and a co-authored book chapter titled *The Involvement of China in the Reconstruction of Nigeria's Transport Infrastructures* (2018).

Chun Zhang is Professor of the Institute of International Relations, Yunnan University and Adjunct Senior Researcher of Shanghai Institute for International Studies (SIIS). His research focuses on Sino-Africa relations, African politics and security, international relations theory, development studies, etc. He has published 7 monographs, more than 120 academic papers, more than 100 op-eds, both domestically and internationally. He was previously a Senior Research Fellow at Shanghai Institute for International Studies (SIIS) from 2005 to 2019, a Visiting Fellow to Chatham House London, UK, in 2009, to the South Africa Institute of International Affairs (SAIIA) based in Johannesburg in 2011, the Centre for Strategic and International Studies (CSIS) based in Washington, DC in 2011, the Foreign Service Institute (KFI) based in Nairobi, Kenya, in 2012, and to the Southern African Research and Documentation Centre (SARDC) based in Harare, Zimbabwe, in 2014.

Preface

The book is the outcome of a collective research endeavor that started with a workshop at the University Duisburg-Essen (Germany) in June 2017. Bringing together a variety of experts from Sub-Saharan Africa, China, and Europe, we wanted to better understand the political implications of China's growing economic presence on the African continent, and how these implications may vary across different countries. We were interested in understanding the specific perspectives of Chinese and African scholars, and their assessments of the agency of both sides in this dynamic relationship. While we offered some common guiding questions for all contributors to the project, we also considered it important to give space for quite contrasting research methodologies, interpretations, and narratives.

We are happy to present the results of our combined efforts as editors and authors in this volume, and would like to thank the people who made our cooperation over the last 2 years pleasant and productive. We thank our experts for their willingness to accept our research agenda, and for responding to many specific queries. We are also grateful to the additional colleagues whose constructive criticism enriched our workshop and our thinking about this important topic. We thank Tobias Debiel, Sigrid Quack, Dirk Messner, and Jan Aart Scholte for having accepted the book as part of the Routledge Global Cooperation Series, and Helena Hurd and Matthew Shobbrook from Routledge for their kind assistance and cooperation. Jonas Seyferth provided essential support in preparing the texts for publication. Georg Lammich and Elizaveta Priupolina assisted in the final editing process. Finally, we gratefully acknowledge financial support from the Fritz-Thyssen-Foundation for the organization of the 2017 workshop and thus for making this book possible.

Preface

1 China's new role in African politics

From non-intervention towards stabilization?

Christof Hartmann and Nele Noesselt

'A continent of hope and promise' – these were the terms used for praising Africa when Xi Jinping, as then newly appointed state president of the People's Republic of China (PRC), visited Tanzania and offered win–win cooperation as opposed to policy-based development lending offered by the 'West.' Five years later, in July 2018, Xi went again on a presidential trip to Senegal and Rwanda – before attending the Brazil, Russia, India, China, South Africa (BRICS) summit in Johannesburg (South Africa). Between 2013 and 2018, the PRC's Africa approach had witnessed a tremendous deepening of cooperation in terms of scale and scope: it is not only investing in major infrastructure projects, but has also silently started to adjust its position on issues of stability and security in other world regions. For the first time in Chinese history, the country provided 'combat troops' for peacekeeping operations in Mali. Chinese mediators diplomatically intervened in a civil war in South Sudan; and, finally, Beijing is seeking to strengthen its ties with the African Union and expresses its hopes that the Union might become a major stabilizing regional security player. Beijing's Africa strategy is clearly driven by a complex economy–security nexus: Due to the going global campaign, further added by the Chinese New Silk Road initiative (also known as One Belt, One Road (OBOR) or Belt and Road Initiative (BRI)), Chinese companies, banks, and financial institutions have expanded to the African market and opened local overseas branches. Furthermore, major Chinese state companies are the main architects of connectivity projects (transportation, electrification, communication) spanning the African continent. At the same time, the transcontinental and transregional dimensions of China's New Silk Road increase the vulnerability of the Chinese economy resulting from local conflicts and security dilemmas in Africa. Xi Jinping's speech at the BRICS Business Forum in July 2018 highlighted the potential of cooperation in fields of green and inclusive development – hence indirectly presenting the Chinese modernization path as a blueprint for the emerging economies:

> Africa has more development potential than any other region in the world. We should strengthen cooperation with Africa, support its development and make BRICS-Africa cooperation a model for South-South cooperation. We should actively carry out cooperation with African countries in such

> areas as poverty reduction, food security, innovation, infrastructure development and industrialization in a way compatible with their national conditions. We should help African countries develop their economic structure, contribute to the implementation of Agenda 2063 of the African Union and thus enable Africa, an ancient continent, to gain strong vitality.
>
> (Xi 2018)

The PRC is constantly 'learning' and adapting its foreign strategy. It maintains bilateral ties with African countries and pays special attention to those states that it identifies as strategic gateways to African subregions or specific groups of states or networks (such as the Arabic communities in Africa). At the same time, it supports regional organizations that follow an agenda compatible with Chinese interests. The call for multilateralism and criticism of unilateral intervention – referred to as violation of 'collectively adopted international rules' – responded to the reorientation of the US before the backdrop of Trump's 'America first' strategy. Beijing's statements at the BRICS Summit 2018 are hence in line with Xi Jinping's earlier statement that China would insist on global free trade, warning against the negative effects the US new strategy might have for emerging and catching-up economies.

While most analyses of the relationship between Africa and China have focused on Beijing's strategy (as opposed to the Washington Consensus and conditionality-based development cooperation), African agency has only very recently become the object of research. African interest in stronger economic relationships with China is often taken for granted, but African opposition parties or non-governmental advocacy organizations might have more mixed assessments of the growing political and security role of China, and also a more varied set of strategies to deal with it. Given the existing cleavages and tensions inside the BRICS – especially between China and India – as well as between the PRC and the US, some African states can certainly make strategic choices and pursue a strategic triangular approach to avoid falling in the next debt and dependency trap. This edited volume seeks to sketch the emerging plurality and diversity of Beijing's Africa strategy and to assess the strategic actions and responses by African actors.

The growing complexity of academic debates

Following the visible rise of China to global power status, research on the PRC's foreign relations has been dominated by the tantalizing question whether the PRC would act as an assertive game changer or as a responsible great power complying with international norms and standards. Given the PRC's thirst for raw materials and energy imports, the deepening relationship between China and Africa has raised concern among international observers. This has resulted in an ever-growing number of publications on trade relations between China and the African continent. In the past few years, the PRC has started to adjust its foreign strategy and to professionalize its foreign diplomacy. Simultaneously, the perception of China's international role and its activities in Africa has changed tremendously. With the more important role that the PRC has assumed in many African states, new questions and puzzles regarding geopolitical and security cooperation and their political implications have emerged that have not been sufficiently explored so far in the literature and require both further theoretical reflection and empirical analysis.

Within research on the PRC's African policies, emphasis has been put on tracing changes in the perception and strategies vis-à-vis the African continent as a whole. This is also true for the increasing research on Chinese contributions to peace and security on the continent. While there is a growing number of edited volumes exclusively dedicated to the analysis of Sino-African relations (inter alia Rotberg 2008; Men and Barton 2011; Adem 2013; Li 2013; Alden and Large 2018), recently published textbooks on Chinese foreign policy do often not pay too much attention to the African case(s). These studies primarily concentrate on the changing patterns of Sino-US and Sino-Russian relations or deal with basic structures and instruments of Chinese foreign relations as such (Ross and Bekkevold 2016; Zheng 2016). Studies on China's foreign strategy display a strong focus on the assumed struggle for hegemony between China and the US, one of the few exceptions being the conference volume edited by Kitissou on Africa's role in China's global strategy (Kitissou 2007, cf. also Xu 2017). Many scholars have argued that leadership changes do not impact on the PRC's foreign behavior as they are orchestrated as a smooth passing of the baton from one leadership generation to the other (Noesselt 2015; see also the special issue of *Journal of Chinese Political Science* on China's Leadership Transition and Chinese Foreign Policy, volume 20, issue 1, March 2015). Nevertheless, China's foreign strategy is dynamically evolving: The PRC's One Belt, One Road initiative launched in 2013 that seeks to build a transregional transportation network – a 'New Silk Road' – constructs 'Africa' as one nodal point of Beijing's new global network. The integration of Africa into China's global strategy is a quite recent event and thus has not yet been systematically examined. The PRC's official White Papers on the country's relations with the continent neither reflect the variety of the political regime types in Africa nor discuss the plurality of actors involved in China's interactions with Africa (i.e., ministries; banks; state-owned and private companies).

Within research on China's foreign policy the relationships to Sub-Saharan Africa are an excellent arena to analyze the tensions between the self-perception of China as a non-colonial 'Southern' power, respecting the principles of non-intervention into the domestic affairs of other sovereign states, and growing African perceptions of China as a rather hegemonic power, major investor, and dominant trade partner. If the 'Going Global Strategy' leads to a heavier Chinese footprint in the economies and politics of African states, does this imply a questioning of the 'Beijing Consensus' in the long run? Discrepancies and tensions between role claims and role articulations by China and competing role ascriptions by African states might vary across the continent depending on the specific context of China's economic and political involvement. There is an obvious gap between the PRC's self-proclaimed role identity as a developing country and advocate of the 'Global South' and the roles attributed to China by Beijing's strategic cooperation partners on the African continent (on China's national role conflicts, see also Noesselt 2014). The analysis of role identities and conflicts is still an under-researched domain of International Relations that we want to address in the volume through contributions by African, European and Chinese scholars. Furthermore, the analysis of selected relationships between China and African states allows insights into the hidden processes of role contestation occurring inside the Chinese Communist Party as well as among Chinese academic elites.

While China officially operates with a foreign policy strategy, which conceives of Africa as one integrated monolithic area (the Forum on China–Africa Cooperation (FOCAC) being the flagship of inter-continental cooperation), in practice it seems rather perceiving Sub-Saharan Africa as a 'fragmented' continent with specific contexts, and with different Chinese actors having different relevance in these settings. Competition between Chinese ministries and banks for market access in Africa has increased and stands in sharp contrast to the PRC's 'unified' Africa strategy (Corkin 2011). Chinese politics vis-à-vis resource-rich countries (Angola, Zambia, Sudan, the Democratic Republic of Congo (DRC), Nigeria) and in geostrategic important countries (Djibouti) differ from the strategies coined for relations with those African states without strategic resources – but the PRC's stability and security concerns might be similar. China has engaged itself also in countries such as Rwanda, Zimbabwe, or Mali, which are neither resource-rich nor geostrategically particularly important. These partner countries, however, have different regime trajectories and also displayed huge differences in political and regime stability. One of the book's core objectives is thus to investigate to what extent these differences in political stability, understood both as stability of state apparatus and regime/government stability, across the continent are taken into account at the strategic level and in the evolving bilateral relationships between China and African states, how the evolving 'pluralism' of Chinese foreign policy actors is strategically coordinated in such contexts, and which practical relevance China attributes to non-state actors.

The discussion of China's impact on African politics and economies has been so far dominated by similarly sweeping assumptions about equal partnership, neocolonialism, or the emulation of the Beijing model – i.e., operating with stereotype assumptions regarding the global ambitions of 'socialist' great powers. Over the last decade, there has been a growing body of literature dealing with the general developmental aspects of Sino-African relations, with Alden et al. (2008), Bräutigam (2009), Taylor (2009), and Sun (2014) as – very different – attempts of major synthesis. The edited volumes by Ampiah and Naidu (2008) and by Cheru and Obi (2010) brought together many prominent African scholars with several important case studies analyzing the bilateral African–Chinese relationships, but these volumes cannot reflect the developments of the last decade (for recent more case-specific contributions Benabdallah 2016, Kamwengo 2017). More recently, the genuine political and security role of China on the African continent has started to feature in academic publications, whether in case studies (Cabestan 2018), or from a more general perspective, such as Benabdallah and Large (2018) or Alden et al. (2018), who combine case studies of peacekeeping with a broader reflection about changing Chinese security strategies on the Africa continent.

A third strand of academic literature deals with the role of international factors for the domestic regime dynamics and state formation in Africa. This literature has traditionally focused on the formative role of the international system and colonial powers in the creation of the African state system (Clapham 1996) and specific state structures (Fatton 1992; Mamdani 1996). Much research has continued to perceive African states and domestic political dynamics as shaped by a variety of external actors and factors, by the leverage of global powers (Whitaker 2010), the liberal peacebuilding approach of the United Nations, international diffusion and linkage (Levitsky and Way 2010) as well as the growing importance of regional and continental actors and norms (Hartmann 2016). Bayart (1989) framed the concept of 'extraversion' to describe the active role played by transnational networks of African actors in mobilizing international support for domestic political competition. This legacy has been carried on with the heavy influence of economic and political conditionalities and the resulting quite limited policy space (Mkandawire and Soludo 1999; Englebert and Peiffer 2012). France's direct role in the governance of many former colonies has been thoroughly criticized and analyzed (Chafer 2002). From such a perspective China's emergence as a major power on the continent is not only a welcomed alternative to policy-based development lending by Western donors. It might be also more than an alternative model of governance (Beijing Consensus), which is emulated by the more authoritarian regimes on the continent (Fourie 2015). Despite all intentions to keep out of domestic politics, Chinese companies, banks, and ambassadors are drawn into the domestic power game. They might become the target of populist campaigns, are perceived to support incumbent parties in electoral campaigns, or to assist illegitimate governments to quell 'legitimate' domestic grievances. Some recent publications have started to highlight the diverse some African reactions to this growing Chinese presence. While the edited volume by Gadzala (2015) discusses the role of a variety of non-state actors in shaping and reacting to Chinese presence in their countries, the monograph by Aidoo and Hess (2015) is an analysis of how domestic political dynamics influences different forms of anti-Chinese popular protest.

The book's agenda

Political stability has been defined in the literature in a variety of ways. It might be equated with the absence of violence, with the existence of a legitimate constitutional order, with the duration of a given government, or with the absence of revolution or structural changes, meaning a capacity to maintain its basic structural arrangements against external and internal pressures (Hurwitz 1973). Social scientists might agree that the absence of violence is the least plausible definition, because the stability of a system would rest on whether it can cope with violent events, and not on the frequency of their occurrence (Dowding and Kimber 1983, 230). Yet it seems that Chinese understandings of (African) instability are mostly based on the occurence of different types of violence, which endanger the physical security of Chinese residents and the continued operation of economic activities. Such violence might indeed also be an indicator of broader systemic failure to cope with challenges to the state monopoly of violence.

If we turn to those definitions of stability that share the idea of some form of enduring, continuous, or persistent order, this might refer to the stability of a government, or those of the regime, broader settlement, or authority patterns at national level. In the non-democratic states of Africa, both types of instability converge, as governments (or presidential terms of rule) do not end in line with constitutional provisions. Only in the more democratic states it might be relevant to look at governmental instability and electoral cycles.

'The problem of "stability" in Africa has been the weakness not of physical control (…) but rather of social control (the capacity to create the forms of authority needed to secure voluntary obedience)' (Clapham 2008, 365). But if this is so, and the sources of violence actually reside in the instability of authority patterns or regimes, more stable forms of governance will not necessarily be obtained by China 'respecting the national sovereignty' of African partner states. Open military or political interventions are risky, but no interventions might further trigger the destabilization of African regimes and state institutions and thus threaten Chinese interests.

Since 2009, the PRC has started its own anti-piracy mission in the Gulf of Aden, a mission that might challenge the axiomatic patterns of Chinese foreign policy, i.e., the Five Principles of Peaceful Coexistence (especially the principle of non-interference) and the official rejection of interventions in other world regions. In 2011, the PRC's People's Liberation Army coordinated the evacuation of Chinese citizens from Libya – a mission later on justified by the 2013 White Paper on the 'Diversified Employment of China's Armed Forces.' This was followed by the 2015 White Paper on the PRC's 'Military Strategy.' These two papers published after the ascent of the so-called fifth generation of Chinese leaders headed by Xi Jinping document a new awareness among Chinese political elites and their advisers concerning the increased vulnerability deriving from the PRC's embeddedness in the global economy and cross-regional trade flows. Since 2012/2013 China's official foreign strategy and its global role claims have silently been reconfigured and adapted to the new development and security needs. This also includes a more refined approach to the African continent.

The dominant view among scholars of Chinese–African policies has been to argue that China has tried to be pragmatic in dealing with all these situations, working mainly with authoritarian governments, but also building up contacts with opposition forces (Aidoo and Hess 2015, Holslag 2011).

As the book is not only interested in understanding changing Chinese dynamics and perceptions, we intend to also enhance the general understanding of how the growing role of China becomes part of the domestic political competition and quest for stability within African states. We thus want to see whether China's promotion of stability is different to how US military support, French party politics or, more generally, Western political conditionalities have (supposedly) shaped domestic political dynamics and stability within African states.

We offer a new perspective to this existing literature by focusing on three questions and empirical puzzles:

1 Mapping and decrypting China's Africa strategy: What are the main drivers and triggers of China's engagement in Africa? Is China pursuing any kind of 'great strategy'? How does China (re-)define its role on the global stage and its Africa strategy in the shadow of shifting global power constellations?
2 Assessing China's role and the perception of Chinese engagement in Africa: How has China perceived stability in African countries and how might Chinese assessments of stability or instability have changed over time? Are there any Chinese strategies, policies, or specific policy decisions, which might have directly or indirectly affected the political stability? Is China treated as a new type of actor or seen as a neocolonial power?
3 Identifying and understanding African agency: To what extent do African actors (governments, opposition parties, civil society actors, media, or private companies) mobilize, influence, or manipulate Chinese actors on the ground? To what extent have Chinese actors become part of a domestic political settlement or peace agreement?

By bringing together researchers both from China and Africa it is the book's main objective to investigate the emerging patterns of Chinese–African relationships in different contexts and scenarios of instability and to undertake a systematic mapping of the PRC's 'new' role as global player.

Structure and chapters

The volume opens with a general overview of the PRC's foreign policy readjustments and strategic reorientations vis-à-vis Africa before the background of the Belt and Road Initiative (BRI), formally launched in 2013 (Chapter 2). Based on official documents, Chinese think tank publications, as well as data sets mapping the global activities of Chinese companies, Nele Noesselt assesses the economy–security nexus determining Beijing's strategic calculations. She sketches the PRC's increased involvement in United Nations (UN) peacekeeping missions and support for regional security initiatives, mainly focusing on the African Union. Looking at select case studies, she postulates that the growing economic and financial interdependencies could finally imply that the PRC will, contrary to expectations, insist on the setting-up of checks-and-balances as well as transparent governance structures in order to secure its large-scale infrastructure projects across Africa and to create a stable and safe environment for Chinese investment. This finding ultimately empirically devalues the assumption that the PRC would tend to support (neo)authoritarian systems and undermine African states' transition towards rule of law and liberal–democratic system features. Nonetheless, as this chapter also underlines, the PRC did not internalize the existing 'Western' patterns of good governance but put forward its own concepts and notions on peace, security, and stability (and ways to achieve them).

Julia C. Strauss (Chapter 3) examines the changes in China's official rhetoric on its approach towards and activities in Africa since the mid-1950s. She identifies a transition in official statements from China's self-proclaimed role as being a supporter of national liberation movements in Africa, added by its upholding of the principle of non-interference, towards a novel narrative focusing on 'win–win' collaboration and, since the launching of the BRI, 'common development.' She convincingly argues that Beijing did not substitute the frames and narratives coined during the Maoist period, but has continuously adapted its Africa strategy by adding additional frames and layers. Looking at the responses of select African states and their domestic civil societies to the frames underlying Beijing's BRI charm offensive, Julia C. Strauss brings in an often-overlooked dimension of Afro-Sino cooperation. While Western media reflect the emergence of a new South–South axis, Julia C. Strauss' assessment of the tensions between Chinese role claims, role enactment, and role ascriptions by African states reveal the persisting fragmentation, frictions, and diversity of interaction between Chinese and African players on the bilateral, regional as well as global level.

China's Africa strategy has certainly evolved with regard to a growing inclusion of continental and regional organizations as direct counterparts, as Georg Lammich argues in Chapter 4. As security threats to Chinese interests have become more important from the Chinese perspective since the Africa policy was first fully defined in 2006, the African Union with her Peace and Security Architecture was fully recognized with the 2015 White Paper and officially accepted as FOCAC member. While the material support to African peacebuilding has remained at a low level compared to the traditional Western backers of African-led peacekeeping missions, China perceives the African Union (AU) as an ally in the attempt to establish alternative international norms about peacebuilding defying the dominant liberal model. China continues to entertain bilateral relationships with nearly all African states. An even stronger prioritization of multilateral channels of cooperation remains so far restricted, due not only to Chinese skepticism about the capacity of the AU to provide stability, but also because of African interest in continued bilateral security cooperation, and a lack of African consensus concerning the actual role of the AU in tackling transnational security challenges on the continent.

Haifang Liu (Chapter 5) follows up on the perceived plurality and diversity of actors by analyzing the role of Chinese actors involved in business activities across the African continent for African stability and security. She shifts the focus from the intergovernmental level of transactions towards the micro-level of Chinese traders and their local associations. Based on fieldwork observations and interviews with the leaders of these Chinese associations in Africa, she outlines these players' strategic positioning in issues of human security. These local associations, as her empirical data evidence, are cooperating with local police branches and seeking to establish robust consultative relationships with local governments across Africa. In addition, these associations are engaged in soft power activities to generate trust and sympathy for Chinese businessmen among the people in Africa. While most analyses on China's role in issues of African security and peacebuilding focus on the PRC's participation in UN missions or mediation efforts, Haifang Liu persuasively argues that the self-interest of Chinese overseas communities in securing a stable and peaceful environment for their activities makes them contribute to (often informal) local security initiatives.

Chapter 6 by Christof Hartmann looks at the evolution of China–Africa relationships from the perspective of African agency. The question of how African actors shape the relationships with a variety of Chinese actors has recently received more interest from researchers. One analytical challenge in using the concept is that agency remains closely related to the structural environment, which both enables and restricts such agency. In discussing African agency vis-à-vis China the chapter argues that the domestic political environment of African states offers strongly varying contexts for state elites to exert agency. African states and regimes have followed different paths, either moving in a liberal–democratic trajectory, sticking to a more neopatrimonial and clientelist form of governance, or opting for a developmentalist authoritarianism. African elites will thus rely on traditional strategies of extraversion to secure short-term benefits derived from Chinese infrastructure in the neopatrimonial trajectory. In the democratic model, political accountability will create incentives for elected leaders to take into account legitimate or more populist grievances against Chinese living in the country, while in the authoritarian–developmental model, China will serve as a source of emulation and legitimization.

Lucy Corkin (Chapter 7) takes a closer look at the impact of Chinese credit lines on the stability of post-war Angola. She argues that the political elites were strategically playing the China card, i.e., using the credit lines offered by the China EXIM Bank, to stabilize the regime in the early post-war years, as the Chinese bank became a significant financier of the Angolan Government's Public Investment Program. As her evaluation of the Movimento Popular de Libertação de Angola (MPLA) succession shows, the Chinese side did not try to convert its monetary power into political influence. She argues that, despite ongoing domestic restructuring processes, the Angolan elites will most likely continue to pursue strong external relations with Beijing. Access to loans and credit lines is regarded as a crucial determinant of Angola's post-war national reconstruction and regime robustness.

In analyzing China's role for the political trajectory of Ethiopia, Steve Hess (Chapter 8) highlights the benefits that Ethiopia's leadership could draw from developing intense economic relationships with the US, the European Union (EU), and with China. Ethiopia positioned itself as China's main ideational ally and spokesperson on the African continent. Parliamentary elections in 2005 led to a surprising oppositional breakthrough, and the regime seemed to lose control of the capital city Addis Ababa. The crackdown of the regime met with strong criticism from Western allies. Given Ethiopia's strategic location in the US-led global fight against Islamist terrorism, Western states were unlikely to cut down official development assistance (ODA) budgets, but China's engagement with Ethiopia strengthened the bargaining position of the ruling party, and facilitated authoritarian backsliding. Hess argues that, despite their conventionally weak power position in relation to established and emerging great powers, leaders in Ethiopia and other African states are taking advantage of an increasingly multipolar international system to improve their bargaining position and pursue their particular foreign and domestic interests.

Zambia features prominently among those African cases where Chinese economic investment has led to anti-Chinese populism. Richard Aidoo (Chapter 9) looks more closely at the impact of China on the fragile democracy in the country. In his account, the Zambian public, notwithstanding repeated malpractices in Chinese-owned mines and the increasing Chinese control of local markets, has maintained a quite positive attitude towards China. At the same time, in a context of political competition the mobilization of anti-Chinese populism might be a rewarding strategy, although it is difficult to tell how important it was in securing electoral victory by the opposition. From a more general perspective, Aidoo argues that China's enormous economic influence necessarily shapes expectations of voters about developmental effects, and will affect policy-making in a context of economic scarcity and high dependency on global copper prices.

Chun Zhang (Chapter 10) investigates the conceptual underpinnings of China's efforts in stabilizing Sudan and South Sudan. Concentrating on the Chinese notion of 'developmental peace,' he stresses that the PRC continues to rely on the principle of non-interference and proposes conflict solutions without any military intervention by external powers. The general idea, also in line with the narratives surrounding the BRI, is that access to development is the necessary prerequisite for stability and security, and the only powerful weapon against the spread of religious extremism. Chun Zhang also outlines how the global criticism of China's positioning in the Darfur crisis somehow served as a turning point in China's Africa strategy. As an immediate response to the reputational losses, the PRC started to engage in mediation efforts among the conflict parties. In addition, the Chinese side increased its engagement in infrastructure-building and development-related projects. Chun Zhang argues that the latter is in line with the idea of 'developmental peace,' hence opposing the 'Western' declassification of China's Africa strategy as being merely focusing on securing access to resources and the expansion of the Chinese sphere of (economic and financial) influence.

Rwanda represents another specific and challenging partner for the PRC. As in Ethiopia, scarcity of resources has forced Rwanda's elite to develop a cohesive authoritarian state with a strong commitment to developmental social transformation. Both Rwanda and China are strong states with relatively stable, authoritarian regimes. Sven Grimm and Christine Hackenesch (Chapter 11) argue that business interests do not feature prominently in the bilateral relationship, and China's engagement with Rwanda is driven by political, strategic, and aid-policy interests. China does not provide more assistance than Western actors and does not engage in sectors or through aid modalities that would have a more regime-stabilizing effect than aid provided by other actors. China's impact on regime survival is thus limited in the case of Rwanda. President Kagame's economic and political aspirations to regional leadership have rather prevented the government from getting too close to Beijing. Grimm and Hackenesch also point out that meeting an equally development-oriented government in Kigali makes bilateral discussions particularly difficult, as both Rwanda and China are first and foremost concerned with their respective national developments.

Lloyd Sachikonye (Chapter 12) sheds light on the controversial relationship of Zimbabwe's regime and long-time President Robert Mugabe to China. While the PRC's policies were dictated by economic investments, for Zimbabwe's rulers the political support and continued economic cooperation proved to be essential when Western governments enacted sanctions in the wake of disputed and violent elections. China's policy of 'non-interference' in internal matters reaped economic dividends in Zimbabwe, as China became one of the leading investors in mining, agriculture, energy as well as infrastructure, and one of the country's principal trading partners. However, the succession crisis, factional politics, and economic nationalist measures in recent years, which directly affected some of the Chinese mining interests, illustrated the Chinese dilemmas in a regime, which could neither guarantee political nor economic stability. China proved first unwilling to provide additional loans when the economic and debt crisis hit the country hard since 2015 and Zimbabwe had not been able to service previous Chinese loans. The 'coup' that removed Mugabe from power in 2017 was also at least implicitly supported by China, but Sachikonye cautions that both factionalism within the ruling party, weak legitimacy, and economic crisis, do not bode well for a more stable political settlement.

Nigeria's relations with China are the subject of the chapter by Efem N. Ubi (Chapter 13). He is particularly interested in China's potential contribution towards building peace within Nigeria, as the country has been plagued by a number of violent conflicts both in the oil-producing regions in the South, and, during the last years, in the North with the rise of Boko Haram. As one of Africa's most powerful states, with regard to population and army size and oil income, Nigeria has been keen to avoid external intervention in the management of its conflicts. It has accepted Chinese military training and weapons, which proved important when Western countries were hesitant to support Nigeria's strategy to fight the Islamist rebels. According to Ubi, Nigeria also welcomed the Chinese understanding of 'developmental peace.' Yet, ultimately, and because China refrained from joining any more formal alliance in fighting Boko Haram, its contribution towards solving Nigeria's multiple security challenges (including those which affect its own citizens and investments) consists in the prospect that economic growth and development would somehow solve these conflicts.

The Sierra Leone chapter by Patricia Rinck (Chapter 14) deals with the recent controversy around Chinese 'interference' into the presidential electoral campaign in the West African country. This is another case where the Chinese supposedly sovereignty-based cooperation with incumbent governments was locally interpreted as a quite blatant support to one party in contested elections. China clearly had an interest in a continued working relationship with the incumbent government, and the victorious opposition candidate immediately cancelled a controversial major infrastructure deal with China. The episode is, however, particularly illustrative as a case study of how African actors try to politically benefit from the massive Chinese presence in the country. Interestingly, both government and opposition mobilized voters by making reference to how China was instrumental for continued developmental success (incumbent) and to how China was responsible for opaque and corrupt deals, and even directly financing the ruling party (opposition).

In the concluding chapter, the editors provide an assessment on how the chapters have contributed towards clarifying the book's three puzzles about how China (re-)defines its Africa strategy in the shadow of shifting global power constellations, about China's perception of and contribution to political stability in Africa, and about identifying and understanding African agency in the quest for stable political settlements within Africa–China relationships.

References

Adem, S. (ed.) (2013) *China's Diplomacy in Eastern and Southern Africa*, Ashgate, Farnham.

Aidoo, R. and Hess, S. (2015) *Charting the Roots of Anti-Chinese Populism*, Springer, Heidelberg.

Alden, C., Alao, C., Chun, Z. and Barber, L. (eds) (2018) *China and Africa. Building Peace and Security Cooperation on the Continent*, Palgrave Macmillan, London.

Alden, C. and Large, D. (eds) (2018) *New Directions in Africa–China Studies*, Routledge, London/New York.

Alden, C., Large, D. and Soares de Oliveria, R. (2008) *China Returns to Africa: A Rising Power and a Continent Embrace*, Columbia University Press, New York.

Ampiah, K. and Naidu, S. (eds) (2008) *Crouching Tiger, Hidden Dragon? Africa and China*. University of Kwazulu-Natal Press, Scottsville.

Bayart, J. (1989) *L'état en Afrique. La politique du ventre*, Fayart, Paris.

Benabdallah, L. (2016) 'China's Peace and Security Strategies in Africa: Building Capacity is Building Peace?', *African Studies Quarterly*, 16(3–4), 17–34.

Benabdallah, L. and Large, D. (2018) 'China and African Security', in C. Alden and D. Large (eds) *New Directions in Africa-China Studies*, Routledge, London, 312–325.

Bräutigam, D. (2009) *The Dragon's Gift: The Real Story of China in Africa*, Oxford University Press, Oxford.

Cabestan, J.-P. (2018) 'China's Involvement in Africa's Security: The Case of China's Participation in the UN Mission to Stabilize Mali', *The China Quarterly*, 235, 713–734.

Chafer, T. (2002) 'Franco-African Relations: No Longer So Exceptional?', *African Affairs*, 101(404), 343–363.

Cheru, F. and Obi, C. (eds) (2010) *The Rise of China and India in Africa*, Zed Books, London.

Clapham, C. (1996) *Africa and the International System: The Politics of State Survival*, Cambridge University Press, Cambridge.

Clapham, C. (2008) 'Fitting China In', in C. Alden, D. Large and R. Soares de Oliveira (eds) *China Returns to Africa: A Rising Power and a Continent Embrace*, Hurst, Columbia, 361–369.

Corkin, L. (2011) 'Redefining Foreign Policy Impulses toward Africa: The Roles of the MFA, the MOFCOM and China Exim Bank', *Journal of Current Chinese Affairs*, 40(4), 61–90.

Dowding, K. M. and Kimber, R. (1983) 'The Meaning and Use of Political Stability', *European Journal of Political Research*, 11(3), 229–243.

Englebert, P. and Peiffer, C. (2012) 'Extraversion, Vulnerability to donors, and political liberalization in Africa', *African Affairs*, 111(444), 355–378.

Fatton, R. (1992) *Predatory Rule: State and Civil Society in Africa*. Lynne Rienner, Boulder.

Fourie, E. (2015) 'China's Example for Meles' Ethiopia: When Development "Models" Land', *The Journal of Modern African Studies*, 53(3), 289–316.

Gadzala, A. (ed.) (2015) *Africa and China: How Africans and Their Governments are Shaping Relations with China*, Rowman and Littlefield, Lanham.

Hartmann, C. (2016) 'Leverage and Linkage: How Regionalism Shapes Regime Dynamics in Africa', *Zeitschrift für vergleichende Politikwissenschaft*, 10(S1), 79–98.

Holslag, J. (2011) 'China and the Coups. Coping with Political Instability in Africa', *African Affairs*, 110(440), 367–386.

Hurwitz, L. (1973) 'Contemporary Approaches to Political Stability', *Comparative Politics*, 5(3), 449–463.

Kamwengo, C. M. (2017) 'China and Brazil as Southern Africa's Non-Interfering Development Partners: Rhetoric or Reality?', *Journal of Southern African Studies*, 43(5), 1087–1101.

Kitissou, M. (ed.) (2007) *Africa in China's Global Strategy*, Adonis & Abbey, London.

Levitsky, S. and Way, L. (2010) *Competitive Authoritarianism. Hybrid Regimes After the Cold War*, Cambridge University Press, New York.

Li, X. (ed.) (2013) *China-Africa Relations in an Era of Great Transformations*, Ashgate, Farnham.

Mamdani, M. (1996) *Citizen and Subject. Contemporary Africa and the Legacy of Late Colonialism*, Princeton University Press, Princeton.

Men, J. and Barton, B. (eds) (2011) *China and the European Union in Africa: Partners or competitors?*, Ashgate, Farnham.

Mkandawire, T. and Soludo, C. (1999) 'The Adjustment Experience', in T. Mkandawire and C. Soludo (eds) *Our Continent, Our Future. African Perspectives on Structural Adjustment*, Africa World Press, Trenton.

Noesselt, N. (2014) 'China's Contradictory role(s) in World Politics: Decrypting China's North Korea Strategy', *Third World Quarterly*, 35(7), 1307–1325.

Noesselt, N. (2015) 'China's Foreign Strategy after the 18th Party Congress: Business as Asual?', *Journal of Chinese Political Science*, 20(1), 17–33.

Ross, R. S. and Bekkevold, J. I. (eds) (2016) *China in the Era of Xi Jinping: Domestic and Foreign Policy Challenges*, Georgetown University Press, Washington, DC.

Rotberg, R. I. (ed.) (2008) *China into Africa: Trade, Aid, and Influence*, Brookings Institution Press, Washington, DC.

Sun, Y. (2014) *Africa in China's Foreign Policy*, Brookings Institution Press, Washington, DC.

Taylor, I. (2009) *China's New Role in Africa*, Lynne Rienner, Boulder.

Whitaker, B. (2010) 'Soft Balancing among Weak States? Evidence from Africa', *International Affairs*, 86(5), 1109–1127.

Xi, J. (2018) *Full text of Chinese president's speech at BRICS Business Forum in South Africa* (www.xinhuanet.com/english/2018-07/26/c_129920686.htm), accessed 15 June 2019.

Xu, Y. (2017) *China, Africa, and Responsible International Engagement*, Routledge, Oxford.

Zheng, Y. (2016) *China's Foreign Policy: Challenges and Prospects*, Singapore: World Scientific.

Part I

Patterns, discources, and practices

2 China's African dream

Assessing China's new strategy

Nele Noesselt

Introduction

The 'Chinese Dream' as outlined by Xi Jinping promises the realization of a prosperous, well-off society (*xiaokang shehui*) at the very end of a high-speed catch-up and transformation process initiated and top-down coordinated by the Chinese Communist Party (CCP). Due to the upgrading of socio-ecological production standards in China and the formal shift to sustainable development, Chinese companies have started to outsource parts of the production chain to Africa. In addition, via the Belt(s) and Road(s) Initiative (BRI) – also known under the name of 'New Silk Road' – the Chinese government has commenced to conclude bilateral investment deals with African governments to secure contracts for Chinese infrastructure-building sector and to export-related overcapacities.

Global investment and transregional economic activities by Chinese state-owned banks as well as private entrepreneurs in countries and regions characterized by fragile statehood and instability, however, have forced the government in Beijing to rethink its approach to peacekeeping and conflict settlement. Moreover, securing a safe and stable environment for Chinese infrastructure and investment projects implies that the Chinese side has to calculate and evaluate the potential impact of shifting local actor constellations as resulting from unexpected *coup d'états* or regular (competitive) elections.

Nonetheless, the PRC's two policy papers on Africa do not pay too much attention to the plurality and diversity of socio-economic and political conditions across the African continent. While the first Chinese policy paper on relations with Africa (2006) contained only a rather abstract commitment to cooperation, the second version, released under Xi Jinping in 2015, included already one full sub-chapter on 'peace and security' in Africa, signaling an increased awareness of local developments and potential destabilizing spill-over effects of local upheavals and conflicts. From late June to early July 2018, the Chinese Ministry of National Defense hosted the first China–Africa Defense and Security Forum. This 2-week spanning conference assessed the current security constellations in Africa and discussed future options of military cooperation between China and Africa (*Africa Times* 2018). A couple of months later, in September 2018, the Forum on China–Africa Cooperation (FOCAC) was held in Beijing with Xi Jinping strongly pointing at the need to increase peace and security in Africa by strengthening African regional organizations and initiatives (Xinhua 2018a).

Before this backdrop of a visible active positioning of the Chinese government in issues of African security, which, at a first glance, seems to signal a major deviation from the PRC's axiomatic principle of non-intervention, this chapter looks at the readjustment and diversification of China's approach to Africa since the formal launching of the BRI. It argues that – in connection with this initiative – security and stability in Africa have become a major concern for Chinese political leaders, as local turbulences might all too easily exert spill-over effects on core partners along China's New Silk Road corridors. In the long run, this implies that the PRC is not only engaged in the stabilization of resource-rich countries in Africa but is highly alerted by reported transborder activities of non-state actors and the spread of religious extremism and terrorism. Given the emergence of powerful networks of actors apart from national governments and heads of state, Chinese players operating in Africa might be involved in bargaining with powerful local elites to protect their interests – hence deviating from Beijing's state-centric approach to global politics. Business activities, including arms sales to Africa by China's globally expanding weapon industry, might, if not centrally coordinated, increase the security dilemma Chinese people are facing on the African continent.

China's BRI: fostering global connectivity

Xi Jinping's report to the 19th Party Congress (2017) set the BRI as an anchor concept of China's finetuned foreign strategy in the twenty-first century. Xi's report focused on the PRC's domestic development strategy that seeks to secure economic growth via the building of powerful metropolitan clusters, connected further with regional markets and supply chains via the BRI trade corridors. But he also elaborated on the further provision of global connectivity through the wider expansion of the BRI, ascribing China the role of a promoter of 'win–win'-based global development:

> China champions the development of a community with a shared future for mankind, and has encouraged the evolution of the global governance system. With this we have seen a further rise in China's international influence, ability to inspire, and power to shape; and China has made great new contributions to global peace and development.
>
> (Xi, quoted from Xinhua 2017b)

Xi's report leaves no doubt that the PRC is currently redefining China's role as a global player. Along the corridors of the New Silk Road, Beijing is bargaining bilateral agreements to build (and finance) large-scale infrastructure projects.

While this is officially framed as a contribution to 'global peace and development,' the main starting point of China's BRI activities is the perceived interconnectedness between China and the world economy. To fuel its economy, the PRC heavily depends on the import of energy resources and raw materials. It has undertaken efforts to reduce its reliance on conventional energy resources by investing in the development of green technologies and is generally trying to transform China from being a producer of cheap consumer goods and subcontractor of international companies to becoming a center of global technological innovation. This is partly due to the fact that China's economic model has entered a new stage: The introduction of higher socio-ecological production standards and the beginning aging of China's population forces Chinese companies to open production sites in less developed world regions with a surplus of cheap labor forces; parts of China's textile and shoe manufacturing, and even car production, have been outsourced to Africa.

In addition to (private) entrepreneurial migration to the African continent, the BRI secures contracts for China's state-owned companies from the fields of infrastructure-building and allows Chinese banks to reinvest their currency reserves or to further strengthen the internationalization of the Chinese currency by offering loans and credit lines in renminbi. As Bräutigam and Tang outline (2014), China's discovery of Africa as a strategic trade partner and potential export market for Chinese-manufactured products speeded up in the mid-1990s. Starting in 1994, two additional banks were formed: The Chinese Export–Import (EXIM) Bank and the China Development Bank (CDB). While the latter was originally designed for facilitating investment in China's domestic infrastructure-building, over time, both of them have become key players in financing Chinese activities across the African continent (Bräutigam and Tang 2014, 803).

While the starting point of Chinese trade relations with Africa might have been the exploration of export market for (relatively cheap) Chinese-manufactured goods as well as access to raw materials and energy resources, the finetuning of China's domestic development model might have long-term implications for business relations with Africa. Africa's rising economies are thinking of ways to further integrate their markets and to form trading blocs able to participate in global competition, which opens a strategic window of opportunity for China to advance its 'win–win' infrastructure investment deals.

Framing China's BRI: countering nightmare scenarios

In official diplomatic speeches during state visits by Chinese politicians to Africa, bilateral interactions are framed as 'South–South cooperation' and 'win–win solutions,' with China highlighting its role identity as a development country and socialist state. It actively shapes a storyline of joint and shared development and heavily refutes any comparisons to the resource extraction and exploitation by the former 'Western' colonial powers in Africa (see Chapter 3 by Julia C. Strauss).

In 2018, 5 years after the formal launching of China's New Silk Road, international evaluations of the project's implications for the targeted countries documented the risk of new financial bubbles and debt traps. Sri Lanka was unable to repay its debts and thus finally had to sublet parts of its strategic (port) infrastructure to its Chinese investors (Hurley at al. 2018). These alarming reports and the spread of anti-Chinese sentiments, such as in Zambia (Huynh and Park 2019, 162), have, however, caused an increased awareness among some recipients of Chinese infrastructure investment in Africa about unexpected side effects of China's charm offensive, and, unexpectedly, resulted in the cancellation of already existing airport and harbor deals.

Given the spreading negative reports about BRI-triggered debt traps, it is hardly surprising that Beijing used the 3rd FOCAC Summit to announce additional foreign aid packages as well as interest-free loans for large-scale infrastructure projects in Africa – instead of interest-bearing conditional loans. In addition, Xi Jinping, hosting the FOCAC meeting in Beijing, announced eight major initiatives in the fields of industrial promotion, infrastructure connectivity, trade facilitation, green development, capacity-building, healthcare, people-to-people exchange, as well as peace and security. With regard to the latter Xi stated that the PRC would set up a China–Africa peace and security fund, support peacebuilding activities of the AU, and contribute to UN peacekeeping missions and joint efforts in fighting terrorism and piracy (Xinhua 2018b). In his opening speech, Xi Jinping further highlighted the win–win patterns and the focus on joint development as a key pattern of Sino-African relations:

> Let us build a China-Africa community with a shared future that pursues win-win cooperation. We could both seize the opportunity created by the complementarity between our respective development strategies and the major opportunities presented by the Belt and Road Initiative. We need to see to it that the Belt and Road Initiative and the AU Agenda 2063, the UN 2030 Agenda for Sustainable Development and the development programs of African countries better complement each other …
>
> (Xi, quoted from Xinhua 2018a)

Instead of imposing a Chinese development blueprint on its African partners, the PRC officially seeks to create synergies between both sides' domestic (and/or regional) development agendas. Sustainable development ranks high on the UN and the African Union (AU) roadmaps for Africa. The BRI, by contrast, has rather been discussed by outside observers as a resource-intense infrastructure initiative triggering a race to the bottom of socio-ecological norms and standards. As Xi's FOCAC signature speech evidences, the Chinese side opposes these views by framing the BRI as a green and sustainable global connectivity initiative in line with international development principles. The Asian Infrastructure Development Bank (AIIB), launched in connection with the PRC's development and connectivity initiative for Asia, brands itself as 'lean, clean, green' (AIIB 2017). Quite a number of financial transactions and deals concluded with African governments include the development of green energies and sustainable urbanization projects.

Chinese increased investment in BRI-related projects in Africa as well as the opening of local branches of private Chinese companies has visible effects on Beijing's perception of issues of peace, security, and stability across the African continent. Political instability, local rebellions, religious extremism, and terrorism do, as Chinese scholars stress, not only have an impact on China's domestic energy and resource security but also pose a severe challenge to Chinese companies and banking institutions maintaining local branches, especially those in African states characterized by fragile political institutions and legal insecurity (Wang 2018, 107).

While China's past infrastructure-building focused on select major cities or strategic partners, the future plans include the construction of a high-speed railroad network spanning the whole African continent. Civil wars, local rebellions, and guerilla movements, as well as religious terrorism, have thus to be included into the official risk calculation of Beijing's BRI expansion plans. To protect Chinese overseas interests in Africa, the Chinese side has to calculate the risks resulting from internal developments in African states, transnational security threats (including religious extremism, piracy and maritime terrorism), as well as the positions taken by other external players – the US, Europe, Japan, and India. Elections and leadership changes are regarded as a potential threat to Chinese overseas interests – as the incoming coalitions might alter their position towards Chinese outward foreign direct investment (OFDI) or business activities by private and state-owned Chinese companies operating in the region (Zhang and Ren 2018, 65).

The PRC's concern about peace and security in Africa did, however, not just arise after the proclamation of the expansion of the BRI towards Africa. Already in 2012, at the Fourth FOCAC Summit, Chinese President Hu Jintao voiced the idea of building a 'China-Africa strategic partnership for peace and security cooperation' (Zhang 2017, 115). To reduce costs and potential losses, Beijing formally highlights African agency and autonomy, stressing the role of the AU in regional conflict solutions. The Chinese idea centers on the idea of strengthening Africa's peacekeeping and conflict-solving capacities by assisting in the training and financing of national and regional peacekeeping structures (Zhang 2017, 117; Alden and Zheng 2019, 56). The focus on African agency and African sovereignty had also been emphasized during Xi Jinping's first official state visit to Tanzania in 2013 (Yuan 2014, 69). At the already mentioned 3rd FOCAC Summit, Xi Jinping once again confirmed:

> China champions a new vision of security featuring common, comprehensive, cooperative and sustainable security. We firmly support African countries and the African Union as well as other regional organizations in Africa in solving African issues in the African way, and we support the African initiative of 'Silence the Guns in Africa'. China is ready to play a constructive role in promoting peace and stability in Africa and will

> support African countries to strengthen their independent capacity for safeguarding stability and peace.
>
> (Xi, quoted from Xinhua 2018a)

While this statement seems to be generally in line with the PRC's 'five no' policy for Africa – underlying the principle of non-interference into African domestic affairs – the Chinese side has reportedly commenced monitoring the positions and official views held by the elected governments of their African counterparts, hence taking internal developments and election campaigns into account. While (civil) wars pose a severe threat to Chinese activities in the region, anti-Chinese sentiments might all too easily fuel upheavals and attacks on Chinese managers or workers. The nightmare scenario of a second wave of (neo)colonialism and the exploitation of African states by Chinese investors and enterprises served as a powerful tool in political elections. In May 2018, Nelson Chamisa, presidential candidate of Zimbabwe's political opposition party, promised to 'call the Chinese and tell them the deals they signed are unacceptable and they should return to their country' (BBC 2018). These statements indirectly referred to the dark episode of labor disputes and strikes erupting in the Zambian mining sector, reaching their peak with the Chinese side opening the fire against the mass of protesters (Hess and Aidoo 2014, 137). Since 2015, the Republican Progressive Party, a comparatively weak grouping of the Zambian opposition movement led by James Lukuku, had repeatedly voiced its concerns regarding Chinese investment and entrepreneurial activities under the slogan of '#say no 2 China' (Rosen 2018). Also, in 2015, protests against President Kabila's attempt to extend his mandate without formal elections had resulted in violent riots against Chinese merchants operating in the Democratic Republic of Congo (AFP 2015).

Given the rising number of civil protests against Chinese-financed port and railway construction projects in Africa, Chinese scholars have stressed the need to pay more attention to the socio-ecological dimensions in Chinese construction plans in order to defuse opposition campaigns by local civil society actors, and to engage in dialogue with influential societal actor groups (Sun 2018, 77).

Farewell to the principle of non-interference?

The case of Zimbabwe

In 2017/2018, the PRC's long all-weather friendship with Mugabe came to an abrupt end; rumors spread that the coup dethroning Mugabe had been backed, if not prepared, by China: Given that China's support for the ZANU PF government also included military-to-military exchange, the visit of Zimbabwe's army leader Gen Chiwenga and his meeting with the Chinese defense minister prior to the coup in Harare did, at first, not catch major attention. Some international analysts, however, argue that, in retrospect, these meetings paved the way for the ousting of Mugabe and the promotion of the formerly demoted

Vice President Emmerson Mnangagwa, who is said to have strong ideological ties to China due to his (military and political) training in China during the 1960s as part of the PRC's support for African liberation movements (Tisdall 2017; Asuelime 2018, 18). Earlier already, Chinese analysts had documented that – although Chinese farmers reportedly had profited from the seizure of formerly white farms in Zimbabwe and agreed to take over large-scale agricultural production – a feeling of unease and uncertainty regarding the reliability of promised land-use rights had started to spread among local Chinese groups. The closure of Chinese diamond-mining companies in 2016, as part of the enforcement of Mugabe's indigenization law, and the mismanagement of the Zimbabwean economy finally, according to Wang Xinsong (2016), made Beijing look for alternative political partners among the Zimbabwean elites.

If that was the case, this would mark a radical departure from Beijing's principle of non-interference and it's 'five no' strategy for interactions with African countries. In Chinese academic journal publications, the dethroning of Mugabe is generally referred to as a 'positive' development, without any reference made to a potential involvement of Chinese actors in the related *coup d'état* (inter alia Zhang and Ren 2018, 58). Yuan, in line with the majority of Chinese scholars, generally insists that the principle of non-interference into other states' internal affairs is still valid and further explains that China's participation in UN missions to Africa would be in line with the basic axiomatic principles of Chinese foreign policy as defined after 1949 (Yuan 2014, 78).

Sudan/South Sudan

When the Darfur conflict escalated, Beijing's relationship with Khartoum and rumors about the delivery of weapons, disregarding international conventions and the imposed sanctions, caused a severe decline of the PRC's reputation as a responsible great power in the eyes of the international community. In February 2007, the PRC finally seemed to bow to international pressure, as Hu Jintao, during his state visit to Sudan, directly voiced China's concern over the crisis and asked Sudan's President al-Bashir to allow the deployment of UN peacekeepers to Darfur (Large 2007, 60). Jonathan Holslag, however, sees China's strategic positioning as the outcome of three combined aspects: the risks of a potential spill-over of the Darfur crisis to the Southern regions, which would have interrupted the supply of the Chinese economy with Sudanese oil; the expectations voiced by the AU to permit a joint AU/UN mission in Darfur; the pressure exerted by the government in Chad, which had just started to become an additional strategic oil supplier for the PRC, asking for a robust intervention to stop refugee streams (Holslag 2008, 74–75). A closer look at the official statements by China's ambassador to the UN as well as background analyses by Chinese clearly evidences that the PRC never overtly opposed any conflict solution in Darfur, but continued to stress the principle of non-interference and opposed the formal imposing of economic sanctions on Khartoum. Already in 2004, China's non-vetoing of UN resolutions on Sudan generally opened the way for the deployment of a hybrid AU/UN peacekeeping unit – which was rejected by Khartoum. After several rounds of informal meetings, finally, in 2007, UN Resolution 1769, backed by Beijing, approved an official peacekeeping mission (Chen 2016, 690).

However, due to the PRC's heavy dependence on oil imports, Beijing shifted its attention towards stable relations with the Southern regions of Sudan. In January 2005, a peace agreement was signed between Sudan and the the Sudan People's Liberation Movement (SPLM/A), which was followed by further steps of South Sudan to position itself as an independent state. In July 2007, President Kiir sought to intensify ties with Beijing; a few months later, in September 2008, a Chinese consulate was opened in Juba. Briefly after the referendum on South Sudan's independence, the PRC granted the country official diplomatic recognition (Large 2016, 37).

Mali

South Sudan and Mali are the only UN peacekeeping missions backed by Chinese combat forces. While the PRC's engagement in the Sudanese case could have been driven by the country's interests in securing access to oil resources, landlocked Mali is neither known for its resources nor for its strategic relevance as export market for Chinese products. However, a destabilization of Mali would have undesirable side-effects for its neighboring states – essential corner stones and resource suppliers for China's global rise. The transnational activities of religious extremists and the transcontinental formation of the Islamic State (IS) also targeted Chinese companies and delegations. Members of Chinese railway companies died during the IS' Radisson Blue attack in Bamako (Mali) (Du Plessis 2019, 323).

In addition, subdivisions of the IS were also reported of having sought to recruit followers among the more liberal Muslim minorities in China. China's contribution to the war against religious terrorism and fanatism is hence mainly driven by 'domestic' security concerns. The government in Beijing formally proclaims to take measures to increase the security of Chinese citizens operating in Africa and, simultaneously, to prevent any spill-over of religious extremism or mass movements such as the Arab Spring to China (see also, Hess 2013).

Yao Le observes a general transformation of China from being a rule-taker and passive member of the international society to becoming a rule-shaping power, promoting modifications and readjustment of the basic patterns of peacekeeping missions. Questioning the idea of 'liberal peace' and peace-enforcement via international interventions, the Chinese side prioritizes conflict prevention measures based on the idea of 'developmental peace' (Yao 2018, 135). China's active positioning in issues of African peace and security could, according to Yuan, become a cornerstone of China's self-proclaimed role as a 'responsible great power' and ultimately help to counterbalance the omnipresent 'China threat' debate (Wang 2012, 37–38; Yuan 2014, 76) – if communicated in a convincing way.

According to data compiled by the Stockholm International Peace Research Institute (SIPRI), the PRC has become the world's fifth-largest exporting country of weapons and military equipment (Wezeman et al. 2018). Nonetheless, the PRC remains alerted to the proliferation of weapons across Africa. It has signed and ratified the protocols linked to the African Nuclear Weapon Free Zone Treaty (signed in 1996, formally activated in 2009) and supports measures of disarmament and dialogue-based conflict resolution in Africa (Wang 2012, 32–33).

Maritime Silk Road and strategic ports

Responding to the threat of maritime terrorism and piracy, the PRC has started to engage in multilateral operations in the Gulf of Aden and has opened a Chinese logistical base in Djibouti. These actions are not pursued unilaterally, but via the collaboration with already existing international missions (Information Office of the State Council 2013). Liu and He, assessing the maritime risks in the waters close to African, recommend considering the establishment of a 'China-Africa Maritime Security Community' and to closely cooperate with other international powers engaged in Africa (Liu and He 2017, 117).

Beyond the logistic base for China's anti-piracy mission in Djibouti, Chinese state-owned companies – predominantly COSCO and China Merchant – are investing in port facilities considered crucial for the realization of China's Silk Road dreams. In June 2017, the PRC's National Development and Reform Commission and the State Oceanic Administration published a paper on the further building of China's maritime BRI corridors entitled 'Vision for Maritime Cooperation under the Belt and Road Initiative.' The vision plan included the construction of three maritime passages: the 'China-Indian Ocean-Africa-Mediterranean Sea blue economic passage,' the 'China-Oceania-South Pacific passage,' and a third passage reaching out to the Arctic Ocean (Xinhua 2017a).

One of the signature projects of China's connectivity initiatives in Africa is the construction of the railway connection between Kenya's capital Nairobi and its coastal port city Mombasa. In 2013, during Xi Jinping's first stop of his visit to Africa, Tanzania's President, Jakaya Kikwete, and Xi signed an agreement on constructing a major port in the small fishing village of Bagamoyo, located in the close vicinity of Dar es Salaam, jointly financed by Oman's State General Reserve Fund and the Chinese EXIM Bank. The project, to be realized by China Merchants Holdings International, would not be limited to the construction of Africa's largest container port but – similar to the naval base in Djibouti – also come with the installment of a special economic and industrial zone (Reuters 2019).

China's 'export' model(s): safe and smart cities

China's pilot special economic zone in Shenzhen (Servant 2019) is referred to as a blueprint for modernization by some African states (Alden 2019). In 1978, the first Chinese pilot zone was established in Shenzhen (located in Guangdong Province) to allow local experimentation with market elements and capitalist patterns. Overall, these special economic zones permitted an incremental resteering of the Chinese economy without any formal farewell to the paramount idea of socialism. In retrospect, they are now regarded as incubators of China's high-speed economic growth catapulting the country to the top echelons of global capitalist trade and finance (second, only, to the US). While the PRC formally does not seek to export its specific system patterns and interacts with other systems based on the principles of peaceful coexistence and non-interference into other countries' domestic affairs, it is offering best practice-inspired development solutions, mirroring features of China's domestic modernization roadmap. Chun Zhang generally predicts an increased interested among African heads of states to look 'towards the East' and to learn from China's opening-up and reform process. He notes that African states have entered a new stage of state-building and might hence commence to pursue a development model independent from 'Western' blueprints (Zhang 2018, 7).

Beijing's bilateral BRI deals with African countries include the setting-up of telecommunication networks and artificial intelligence (AI)-based urban governance solutions. A huge number of these infrastructure projects are run by 'private' Chinese companies (Huawei; ZTE) (Gagliardone and Geall 2014). The heated trade war of the US under President Donald Trump (reaching its peak in mid-2019) targeting China's telecommunication companies might thus develop (negative) spill-over effects on Africa. The US' decision to cut Huawei off from access to Google and to end the delivery of US chips and electronics might have an severe impact on Chinese companies' market shares in Africa, where 70 percent of all 4G commercial telecommunication networks have been built by Chinese IT companies, which started their local service around the year 1999. Pilot 5G projects have been launched in cooperation with local telecommunication companies in South Africa. In 2019, during the World Mobile Congress in Spain, the South African mobile network operator Rain concluded an official partnership agreement with Huawei (Huawei 2019a). A crackdown on Chinese IT companies would potentially render large parts of Africa's Internet and communication infrastructure dysfunctional, causing severe economic damages.

Chinese AI-based governance solutions are reported to have caught the attention of non-democratic governments in Africa; tools and instruments of controlling (and steering) social media have found their way to the African continent. In addition, Chinese companies have sold surveillance technologies and AI-based facial recognition to neoauthoritarian African states such as Zimbabwe and are cooperating with local enterprises in setting-up 'smart city' solutions, with a strong focus on surveillance camera networks. Urban security is obviously at the center of all major AI-projects designed by Chinese telecommunication giants in collaboration with international and/or African IT companies. This includes, inter alia, Huawei's contribution to Marrakesh's 'Safe City' project (Huawei 2019b), and Egypt's smart city initiatives, coordinated by the Talaat Mostafa Group – with plans to expand the joint smart city solutions towards the Middle East (InvestGate 2019). Kenya started its 'Safe City' program in Nairobi and Mombasa, seeking to combat crime and street violence. According to Huawei reports, video surveillance established throughout these cities helped to reduce crime by almost 50 percent (Huawei 2019c) (given that the company is programming these AI solutions, these reports, must, however, be treated with caution).

Accusations and suspicions have been voiced by the US and Australia (and some international analysts) regarding potential cyber espionage or the collection of sensible data via cloud systems and servers provided by Chinese companies, including related projects in African countries. In some African states, in cases of local civil rebellions and upheavals, the Internet got temporarily shut down – reminding observers of the instruments of Internet regulation in the PRC and refueling the debate about autocracy promotion by 'China' (Griffiths 2019).

Chinese companies are also seeking to win the ongoing bidding process for building 5G connectivity across Africa, which would enable Chinese companies to expand services such as autonomous driving and more sophisticated AI-based modes of urban governance to Africa.

Conclusion: traditional and non-traditional security challenges

The positive framing and branding of China's Africa strategy under Xi Jinping is closely linked to the witnessed negative effects of reputational losses and threat perceptions fueled by dark predictions of an increasingly aggressive positioning of the PRC in regional and global affairs.

Negative reports about China's reluctance to intervene in the case of Darfur did damage China's reputation not only in the 'West' – where they seemed to confirm the perception of the government in Beijing as being a supporter of rogue states and authoritarian rulers – but also among African actors. The PRC's constructive voting behavior on UN peacekeeping missions in Africa – i.e., by not playing its veto power as a permanent member of the UN Security Council – is hence not necessarily a result of 'Western' pressure on China and compliance with international human rights, but might ultimately be a response to the perceived deterioration of China's image in Africa and a bowing to the demands put but forward by the AU, and, in select cases, the Arab League.

The PRC is reportedly seeking to strengthen its soft power capacities via promoting cultural exchange and offering Chinese language classes, scholarships for African students to study in China, and by investing in the financing of stadiums, libraries, or schools. Even the BRI activities are part of this soft power strategy, as they are presented as offering development opportunities for less developed and underfinanced African states. In this vein, although the PRC is officially not exporting any 'Chinese Model' and not demanding any compliance with Chinese norms and values when granting loans and credits, it is referring to the Chinese growth model as a potential blueprint for catch-up modernization of transformation economies. The most obvious sector where this export dimension materializes are urbanization projects relying on AI-based smart city (surveillance) solutions developed and sold by Chinese IT companies.

Chinese investment and trade activities in Africa comprise a huge variety of players, ranging from state-owned companies and banks to joint ventures, private enterprises, and individual Chinese (street) vendors.

The Chinese government's official call, addressing Chinese companies, to 'go global' and to explore new markets in connection with BRI infrastructure deals, bargained by Beijing, have caused an unexpected spill-over of BRI programs from trade and finance to the fields of security. Chinese companies have started to contract private security firms to protect Chinese managers and workers based in Africa (Ghiselli 2018).

Moreover, the high amount of travel activities and trade connections between Africa and China has increased Beijing's awareness about the threat of importing diseases and epidemics. While the transcontinental expansion of diseases is usually associated with tourist flows, in the Chinese case, the main issue seems to be the employment of unvaccinated Chinese workers in large-scale BRI infrastructure-building across the African continent. In 2016, the first cases of Yellow Fever imported to China via workers and employees formerly based in Angola were officially reported (Wilder-Smith and Leong 2017). China's generous offering of e-health solutions and support in setting up a working healthcare system in Africa is hence ultimately motivated by the perceived transglobal threat of pandemics – and, as a side effect, also offers new market shares for China's globally expanding healthcare companies. It fits, nonetheless, also quite nicely into the PRC's master narrative of 'South–South' cooperation and 'win–win'-based joint development.

The final outcome of Beijing's more differentiated global risk assessment and non-traditional security calculations is a more active engagement in issues of global governance, including the provision of local solutions. The 'going global' dimension of China's economic development roadmap hence seems to finally compel the government in Beijing to contribute to multilateral solutions, as the inclusion of more players reduces costs and allows burden-sharing. So far, given that the PRC is still focusing on domestic development and stability, an overt overthrow of the existing international institutions and regulations providing stability and security is rather unlikely to happen. By contrast, in the long run, China's rise along the lines of global capitalism implies that the Chinese side has an increased interest in securing long-term stable investment environments and thus, potentially, might be grudgingly willing to promote the transition (of African states) towards transparent, accountable, and rule-based governance patterns.

References

AFP (2015) *Chinese become targets in DR Congo anti-government riots*, (www.dailymail.co.uk/wires/afp/article-2925241/Chinese-targets-DR-Congo-anti-government-riots.html), accessed 10 January 2019.

Africa Times (2018) *China-Africa Security Forum concludes in Beijing*, (https://africatimes.com/2018/07/11/china-africa-security-forum-concludes-in-beijing/), accessed 10 January 2019.

AIIB (2017) *Opening address meeting of the AIIB Board of Governors*, (www.aiib.org/en/news-events/news/2017/20170616_002.html), accessed 28 August 2018.

Alden, C. (2019) 'A Chinese Model for Africa: Problem-Solving, Learning, and Limits', in C. Alden and D. Large (eds) *New Directions in Africa-China Studies*, Routledge, London/New York, 279–289.

Alden, C. and Zheng, Y. (2019) 'China's Changing Role in Peace and Security in Africa', in C. Alden, C. Alao, C. Zhang, and L. Barber (eds) *China and Africa: Building Peace and Security Cooperation on the Continent*, Routledge, London/New York, 39–66.

Asuelime, L. E. (2018) 'A Coup or Not a Coup: That is the Question in Zimbabwe', *Journal of African Foreign Affairs*, 5(1), 5–24.

BBC (2018) *Zimbabwe opposition MDC 'will expel Chinese investors'*, (www.bbc.com/news/world-africa-43973908), accessed 10 January 2019.

Bräutigam, D. and Tang, X. (2014) '"Going Global in Groups": Structural Transformation and China's Special Economic Zones Overseas', *World Development*, 63, 78–91.

Chen, Z. (2016) 'China and the Responsibility to Protect', *Journal of Contemporary China*, 25(101), 686–700.

Du Plessis, R. (2019) 'Comparing China's Approach to Security in the Shanghai Cooperation Organization and in Africa: Shifting Approaches, Practices and Motivations', in C. Alden, C. Alao, C. Zhang, and L. Barber (eds) *China and Africa: Building Peace and Security Cooperation on the Continent*, Routledge, London/New York, 311–331.

Gagliardone, I. and Geall, S. (2014) 'China in Africa's Media and Telecommunications: Cooperation, Connectivity, and Control', *NOREF Expert Analysis* (April 2014).

Ghiselli, A. (2018) 'Market Opportunities and Political Responsibilities: The Difficult Development of Chinese Private Security Companies Abroad', *Armed Forces & Society*, online first: DOI: 10.1177/0095327X18806517.

Griffiths, J. (2019) *Democratic Republic of Congo Internet shutdown shows how Chinese censorship tactics are spreading*, (www.cnn.com/2019/01/02/africa/congo-internet-shutdown-china-intl/index.html), accessed 15 March 2019.

Hess, S. (2013) 'From the Arab Spring to the Chinese Winter: The Institutional Sources of Authoritarian Vulnerability and Resilience in Egypt, Tunisia, and China', *International Political Science Review*, 34(3), 254–272.

Hess, S. and Aidoo, R. (2014) 'Charting the Roots of Anti-Chinese Populism in Africa: A Comparison of Zambia and Ghana', *Journal of Asian and African Studies*, 49(2), 129–147.

Holslag, J. (2008) 'China's Diplomatic Manoeuvring on the Question of Darfur', *Journal of Contemporary China*, 17(54), 71–84.

Huawei (2019a) *Rain and Huawei jointly launch the first 5G commercial network in South Africa*, (www.huawei.com/en/press-events/news/2019/2/rain-huawei-first-5g-commercial-network-south-africa), accessed 15 March 2019.

Huawei (2019b) *Marrakesh: Safe city*, (https://e.huawei.com/en/videos/industries/2018/201812060902), accessed 15 June 2019.

Huawei (2019c) *Safe city: Kenya*, (https://e.huawei.com/en/videos/global/2018/201804101038), accessed 15 June 2019.

Hurley, J., Morris, S., and Portelance, G. (2018) *Examining the Debt Implications of the Belt and Road Initiative from a Policy Perspective*, CGD Policy Paper 121.

Huynh, T. T. and Park, Y. J. (2019) 'Role of Race in China–Africa Relations', in C. Alden and D. Large (eds) *New Directions in Africa–China Studies*, Routledge, London/New York, 158–172.

Information Office of the State Council (2013) *The diversified employment of China's armed forces*, (http://english.gov.cn/archive/white_paper/2014/08/23/content_281474982986506.htm), accessed 10 January 2019.

InvestGate (2019) *TMG holding Inks MoU with Huawei for Smart Cities Services*, (https://invest-gate.me/news/tmg-holding-inks-mou-with-huawei-for-smart-cities-services/), accessed 15 March 2019.

Large, D. (2007) 'China and the Changing Context of Development in Sudan', *Development*, 50(3), 57–62.

Large, D. (2016) 'China and South Sudan's Civil War, 2013–2015', *African Studies Quarterly*, 16(3–4), 35–54.

Liu, L. and He, J. (2017) 'Yidai, yilu changyi xia de Zhong-Fei haishang anqian hezuo' (On China-Africa Maritime Security Cooperation From the Perspective of the Belt and Road Initiative)', *Guoji Anquan Yanjiu* (Journal of International Security Studies), 1, 98–117.

Reuters (2019) *Why Tanzania, China's $10 billion port project has just stalled*, (www.cnbcafrica.com/zdnl-mc/2019/05/23/why-tanzania-chinas-10-billion-port-project-has-just-stalled/), accessed 10 June 2019.

Rosen, J. W. (2018) *'China Must Be Stopped': Zambia debates the threat of 'debt-trap' diplomacy*, (www.worldpoliticsreview.com/insights/27027/china-must-be-stopped-zambia-debates-the-threat-of-debt-trap-diplomacy), accessed 10 January 2019.

Servant, J. (2019) *Will a new port make Tanzania 'Africa's Dubai'?*, (www.thenation.com/article/tanzania-china-bagamoyo-port/), accessed 12 June 2019.

Sun, H. (2018) 'Zhongguo canyu Feizhou hangkou fazhan: Xingshi fenxi yu fengxian guankong' (China's Participation in African Ports Project: Progress and Risk Controls), *Taipingyang Xuebao* (Pacific Journal), 10, 67–78.

Tisdall, S. (2017) 'Zimbabwe: Was Mugabe's Fall a Result of China Flexing Its Muscle?', *Guardian*, (www.theguardian.com/world/2017/nov/17/zimbabwe-was-mugabes-fall-a-result-of-china-flexing-its-muscle), accessed 10 January 2019.

Wang, H. (2018) 'Feizhou anquan xin tiaozhan jiqi dui Zhong-Fei hezuo de yingxiang' (New Security Challenges in Africa: Implications for China-Africa Cooperation), *Guoji Wenti Yanjiu* (International Studies), 4, 99–111.

Wang, X. (2012) 'Zhongguo canyu Feizhou heping yu anquan jianshe de huigu yu sikao' (Retrospect View and Reflections on China's Participation in the Construction of Peace and Security in Africa), *Guoji Wenti Yanjiu* (International Studies), 1, 29–42.

Wang, X. (2016) 'China's Zimbabwe Risk', *Guardian*, December 7, (https://thediplomat.com/2016/12/chinas-zimbabwe-risk/), accessed 10 January 2019.

Wezeman, P. D., Fleurant, A., Kuimova, A., Tian, N., and Wezeman, S. T. (2018) 'Trend in International Arms Transfers, 2017', *SIPRI Fact Sheet* (March 2018), (www.sipri.org/sites/default/files/2018-03/fssipri_at2017_0.pdf), accessed 10 January 2019.

Wilder-Smith, A. and Leong, W. Y. (2017) 'Importation of Yellow Fever Into China: Assessing Travel Patterns', *Journal of Travel Medicine*, 24, https://doi.org/10.1093/jtm/tax008, accessed 10 January 2019.

Xinhua (2017a) *China proposes 'Blue Economic Passages' for maritime*, (www.chinadaily.com.cn/business/2017-06/21/content_29825517.htm), accessed 10 January 2019.

Xinhua (2017b) *Secure a decisive victory in building a moderately prosperous society in all respects and strive for the great success of socialism with Chinese characteristics for a new era* (Speech by Xi Jinping at the 19th Party Congress), (www.xinhuanet.com/english/special/2017-11/03/c_136725942.htm), accessed 10 January 2019.

Xinhua (2018a) *Full text of Chinese President Xi Jinping's Speech at Opening Ceremony of 2018 FOCAC Beijing Summit*, (www.xinhuanet.com/english/2018-09/03/c_137441987.htm), accessed 10 January 2019.

Xinhua (2018b) *Xi says China to implement eight major initiatives with African Countries*, (www.xinhuanet.com/english/2018-09/03/c_137441563.htm), accessed 10 January 2019.

Yao, L. (2018) 'Xin shidai Zhongguo Feizhou anquan zhili juese yanjin: Yi weihe xindong wei lie' (The Evolution of China's Role in African Security Governance in the New Era: A Case Study of Peacekeeping Operations), *Guoji Guanxi Yanjiu* (Journal of International Relations), 3, 119–138.

Yuan, W. (2014) 'Tuijin Feizhou de heping yu anquan: Zhongguo de renzhi, zuoyong yu tiaozhan' (Enhancing Peace and Security in Africa: China's View, Role, and Challenges), *XiYa Feizhou* (West Asia and Africa), 4, 64–80.

Zhang, C. (2017) 'Feizhou anquan zhili kunjing yu Zhong-Fei heping anquan hezuo' (Dilemmas of African Security Governance and China-Africa Peace and Security Cooperation), *Alabo Shijie Yanjiu* (Arab World Studies), 5, 102–117.

Zhang, C. (2018) 'Feizhou keyi jiejian Zhongguo de zhiguo lizheng jingyan' (Africa Can Use Chinese Governance Patterns as a Blueprint), *Xiandai Guoji Guanxi* (Contemporary International Relations), 8, 4–7.

Zhang, Z. and Ren, H. (2018) 'Haiwai liyi weihu shijiao de Feizhou fazhan yu anquan dongtai huigu yu fazhan' (Development and Security in Africa: Retrospect and Prospect From the Perspective of Protecting Overseas Interests), *Shijie jingji yu zhengzhi luntan* (Forum of World Economics and Politics), 4, 54–73.

3 Layered rhetorics and multiple realities

China and Africa

Julia C. Strauss

Introduction

One of the most common questions about the burgeoning complex of relationships between China and Africa is simple to ask and difficult to answer: what is China doing in Africa? The immediate if often unstated corollary that often follows is: what are China's intentions in (doing whatever it is doing) Africa? These questions, repeated endlessly in Western press and by Western policy-making think tanks, may reveal far more about the structure of Western press and the preoccupations of Western policy-makers than they do about China, Africa, or the increasingly complex and multilayered set of interactions between the two. Rather than focusing on one element, sector, or specific bilateral relationship, this chapter proposes a broad view that takes seriously what 'official China' (government organizations, state-owned enterprises, and their spokespeople) have claimed its intentions in Africa to be, and then engages in brief excursion into the range of African voices that respond to both these intentions and the inevitable gaps between intention and reality that ensue. In so doing, this chapter draws on and updates my earlier work on China's official rhetoric for Africa (Strauss 2009) and the extension of the rhetoric to Latin America several years later (Strauss 2012).

To reiterate the caveats first articulated 7 and nearly 10 years ago, I do not suggest by any means that China's self-image as a development actor, that the rhetoric in support of its developmental claims are somehow 'true,' or that they do not need to be treated skeptically. I suggest only that the gap between most states' official claims (whether to benevolence, democracy, human rights, or to 'win–win' development) and their actions is often quite large, and that the Chinese state is no more or less devious than any other state if it seeks to explain its motivations and activities in the best possible light. Insofar as one can separate claims from reality, with all the slippage and legitimate different interpretations that engaging in critical analysis inevitably entails, paying attention to the rhetoric makes it possible to understand the broad framing, the basic assumptions, and also the pitch that the entity we call 'China' is making to the entity we call 'Africa.' How different African actors respond to the rhetoric – and its inevitable departure from realit(ies) – is surely more important than how Western press and think tanks respond to the same rhetoric and departures from realit(ies), but that does not mean that Western press, think tanks, and academia are absolved from making the effort. This chapter suggests that China's official rhetoric seldom, if ever, actively repudiates earlier iterations. Rather, as time goes on and circumstances dictate different responses to new questions, layers of rhetoric accrete without ever fully fading away. While typically the newest overlays of official rhetoric are what is most visibly deployed in response to the policy concerns of the moment, older, more foundational components of official rhetoric can be and are revealed either in response to a crisis, sometimes supporting and on other occasions remaining in uneasy juxtaposition with the new. For their part, the African voices that respond to China are multivocal, varying by country, sector, and specific immediate context.

All states make grand claims about the principles and rightness of their international actions that are often contradicted by reality: the United States' historic claims to be a beacon of democracy and its support for human rights are frequently belied by its realpolitik support for authoritarian and often brutal regimes. China's rhetorical justification and claims are different, but also generate tensions and contradictions. China claims solidarity and fraternity with Africa, but now stands accused of putting key countries – including those in Africa such as Kenya and Djibouti – into 'debt traps' (Peralta 2018). It continues to distinguish its approach to development as untainted by colonialism and hegemonism, but in 2017 the China Merchant Ports Holding Company took a 70 percent stake and a 99-year lease on the Hambantota Port in Sri Lanka when the government could not pay back the loans it had taken out. Sri Lanka is not a stand in for Africa, but the China Merchant Ports Holding Company's precedent shattering takeover of the Habantota Port must raise concerns for heavily indebted countries in Africa, and, for those who know their history, a 99-year lease on the port is exactly what was imposed on China with the 99-year lease of the New Territories in Hong Kong – a marker of colonially imposed national humiliation until Hong Kong's retrocession to China in 1997. China insists on non-interference and respect for sovereignty, but has come to play an increasingly interventionist role in Sudan and South Sudan, most clearly in 2008, when it responded to the Darfur crisis by playing a large role in organizing peacekeeping by the United Nations and when it established a consulate in Juba in anticipation of the independence of South Sudan, where it continues its attempts to ensure security for its personnel and broker agreements between the warring factions (ICG 2017). For all, events and national interests often, even typically, undermine principled rhetoric. But that does not mean that the rhetoric is meaningless, or that the rhetoric might not contain its own internal tensions and contradictions.

The foundational rhetoric of 'Five + Eight': thirteen principles for imagined solidarity

Chinese official rhetoric on its foreign relations with the developing world has as its foundation two sets of principles it claims to be unchanging and eternal.

The first of these is the Five Principles of Peaceful Co-existence. Almost as old as the People's Republic of China (PRC) itself, they were formulated in 1954, when the PRC was militarily secure, had just fought the world's superpower to a standstill in Korea, and was domestically strong in pushing through its programs of revolutionary transformation. It was against this background of relative strength and regional security that the young PRC negotiated an agreement with Nehru government in India that incorporated the Five Principles as a way of dampening down tensions between China and India over their contested border in the Himalayas.[1] The Five Principles were a product of its time and circumstances: two large Asian states emerging from (semi-) colonialism with a strong desire to secure their borders and establish their national sovereignty, but also pitched to be broadly acceptable to other developing nations as a wider non-aligned movement gathered pace, culminating in the Bandung Conference of April, 1955. As such the Five Principles perfectly replicated the standards of a post-Westphalian state with a soupçon of Wilsonian pacifist idealism: the supreme sanctity of territorial integrity and state sovereignty, mutual non-aggression, mutual non-interference in domestic affairs, equality and mutual benefit, and peaceful coexistence.

The Eight Principles for Foreign and Economic Aid were announced some 10 years later, when then Premier Zhou Enlai was on a multi-country tour to Africa in January 1964. This timing also coincided with a period of relative moderation, as China sought to recover from the mass starvation that resulted from the Great Leap Forward of the late 1950s and early 1960s. In this iteration of eternal principles, revolutionary China went further in staking out its claim to be different and presumptively better than its then rivals – the West and the Soviet Union – in the way it approached aid and assistance to other developing countries. The Eight Principles stressed equality, mutual benefit rather than aid, the repudiation of conditionality and strict respect for sovereignty, reduction of crippling indebtedness through low-interest loans, no interest loans, extension of rescheduling of loan repayments when necessary, and, critically, the goal of helping recipient countries to become self-reliant (Zhou 1964). Not unlike the Five Principles of Peaceful Co-existence, the Eight Principles failed its immediate acid test: not only was China's bid to lead the non-aligned movement at Bandung the following year unsuccessful, only a year after that the PRC was itself consumed by the domestic conflagration of the Cultural Revolution.

Given how each of these sets of presumptively unchanging principles failed to accomplish its immediate and medium term goals and were developed in a revolutionary, mobilizational context that has all but been repudiated by the developmentalist authoritarianism of the Chinese party-state since 1980, it is worth asking why these two, such old texts continue to exert such power. There are, I suspect, two answers to this question. First, educated Chinese elites – including political elites – are deeply attached to history, and the further a foundational principle can be pushed back into the past, the more legitimating resonance it has in the present.[2] But second, and more importantly, the Five Principles (of Coexistence) in combination with the Eight Principles (for Foreign and Economic Aid) reflect Chinese norms and practices emblematic of the Mao period that are still at the beating heart of what Chinese political and business elites imagine to be at the core of their own success: nationalist developmentalism, self-reliance, and a fierce dedication to what C. K. Lee labels 'collective asceticism' through the trope of 'eating bitterness' (*chi ku* 吃苦) (Lee 2018).

Taken together, the Five and the Eight reflect a world view of China's place in the world and of development in general that can claim to be *different* from and *better* than its competitors – the West (and, after the late 1950s, the 'revisionist' Soviet Union): 'we – like developing countries in Africa – are ourselves a developing country itself untainted by colonialism, principled in our distaste for moralistic name calling and inappropriately imposed conditionalities.' In addition, the Five and the Eight together are predicated on ideals of development and self-reliance that are in turn based on what I call 'modified fractal replication.' Drawing from mathematical notions, the fractal is a fundamentally self-replicating model or shape that is 'self-similar across different scales … made by repeating a similar process' (The Fractal Foundation n.d.). As applied to China and Africa, this modality of modified fractal replication relies on a profoundly Maoist set of ideas: that development requires hard work, struggle, collective sacrifice, and the self-reliance of the unit in question. In Mao's own words, 'On what basis should our policies rest? It should rest on our own strength, and that means regeneration through our own efforts. We are not alone … nevertheless we stress regeneration through our own efforts' (Mao 1945). Within China under Mao, the unit of self-reliance in daily life was the work unit, the collective, or the commune. But for the central economic plan it was a geographical unit (the county, city, or province depending on what level of the plan was under consideration), each of which was to fulfil its part in the plan on the basis of local materials and local initiative. And like the countries of Africa (or the countries of the developing world more generally), different regions within China – whether at the provincial, county, or municipal levels – varied dramatically in size, positionality, natural resource endowments, education of the population, climate, and so on. Thus, despite the obvious differences between Africa and revolutionary China (Africa was clearly not part of a unitary state that insisted on a central economic plan), and within Africa itself, the Mao-era insistence on self-reliance simply exported what already made sense within China (replication of centrally mandated models on the basis of self-reliance and local adaptation), to foreign environments. Thus from the mid-1950s onward, the revolutionary Chinese state's overtures to the developing world were predicated on both an imagined commonality and ideologically inflected notions of what worked well domestically within China itself: 'we, China, are a country that stood up to the imperialist West, developed only somewhat before you, and present a model that you can adapt in the light of your own circumstances. In the distant past, our ships came with Zheng He to make contact and trade, after which we left, unlike the Western powers that came and stayed to exploit; we understand you and your challenges because we have suffered from underdevelopment, poverty, and the indignities of a colonial West, too. Our technicians do not live in remote compounds, we live plainly and simply, and we work and sweat alongside with you.'

The second layer: from imagined commonality to globalized division of labor and comparative advantage

From the 1980s to the present, the post-Mao reform era has sharply reversed the Chinese state's autarchic and egalitarian approach to its domestic development. While initially keeping the central plan, it brought in domestic markets, decollectivized agriculture, tolerated concentrations of wealth generation in already favored areas on the grounds that it was permissible for some to get rich faster than others and established incentives for local cadres to prioritize economic growth. It also, critically for the model of its relations with Africa, invited in foreign direct investment as a way of rapidly catching up with other rapid developers in East Asia in terms of technology transfer, shifted to globalization on the basis of specialization and comparative advantage, and quashed political dissent and social organizations it could not directly control in order to maintain 'stability' – as evidenced by the continuation of single-party rule. These policies, enacted piecemeal over the course of the next 30 years, ushered in an explosion of corruption and environmental damage, but equally did succeed in raising incomes, sustained very high rates of growth of the gross domestic product (GDP) averaging 10 percent a year in the 1990s and 2000s, and lifted hundreds of millions out of absolute poverty (Riskin 2004; Baidu Baike 2019). The Chinese Communist Party (CCP) is, not unreasonably, proud of its role in presiding over China's leap up into the ranks of middle-income countries, reduction of poverty, and displays of shiny 'advanced' modernity through high-speed rail networks, skyscrapers, and big dams.

It is not surprising that when it turned back to engagement with Africa in the early 2000s, China's official rhetorics of engagement would feature exactly those elements that its state elites themselves consider so fundamental to its success: hard work in a globalized context of division of labor that ultimately benefits everyone to best pursue development. The older fractal logic of commonality and fraternity still continues to frame the preambles to high-level official pronouncements: China's First African Policy Paper of 2006 opines that 'Sharing similar historical experience, China and Africa have all along sympathized with and supported each other in the struggle for national liberation and forged a profound friendship' (State Council 2006) – a statement that would not have been out of place in 1956 or 1976. The African Policy Paper of 2006, and all summits of the Forum on China–Africa Cooperation (FOCAC) from 2002 onward also open by noting that China is the largest developing country in the world and Africa is the continent with the largest number of developing countries. This otherwise unremarkable statement is by itself ambiguous in its nods to both old and newer rhetorics: does it suggest that China provides a model for the many African developing states to emulate and adapt to suit (the old fractal logic), or that China (one unitary state) and Africa (many smaller states) are complementary by virtue of different geographical scales and different stages of development?

Other official content makes clear that the current developmental logic is one of complementarity. Take, for example, this telling quote from FOCAC 2002 by Zhu Rongji:

> Africa, on the one hand, boasts talented and hard-working people, abundant in natural resources, and great market and development potentials [*sic*]. China, on the other hand, has got considerable economic strength, a promising market and a wealth of commodities, managerial expertise and production technologies suitable for African countries.
>
> (Zhu 2002)

Thus, when China began its serious re-engagement with Africa in the late 1990s and early 2000s, its rhetoric stressed how the complementary differences of Africa (lots of people, natural resources, market and development potential) fit like hand and glove with China's more advanced economic strength, promising market, commodities, expertise, and technology. Zhu does not explicitly frame the China–Africa relationship as one of 'win–win,' buttressed by resource-backed loans structured to ensure 'giving and getting' but the logic of complementarity in a globalized division of labor certainly lays the necessary groundwork for so doing. Other official pronouncements are more open about this logic. In the African Policy Paper 'China will establish and develop a new type of strategic partnership with Africa which features *political equality* and mutual trust, *economic win-win* [*jingji gongying*] cooperation and cultural exchange' (State Council 2006, italics added). It is important to point out that the original Chinese '*gongying*' (共赢) is invariably slightly mistranslated into English as 'win–win' – a locution with an explicitly transactional, often American business dealing inflected tone. '*Gongying*' in Chinese is more collaborative and collective in connotation, meaning literally 'common winning' or 'winning in common.' Nevertheless, '*gongying*' is nearly always paired with either grand pronouncement or as a legitimating principle for business deals between Chinese entities, typically state-owned enterprises (SOEs), and African governments that is dependent on globalized economic complementarity. This fundamental update of older fractal notions of replication and adaptation based on essential sameness still adheres to one of the core Five Principles – that of political equality and mutual benefit, now in practice reframed as the equality of states to decide which contracts they wish to make and loans they wish to take out in a globalized world of trade for profit.

Needless to say, there are any number of practical problems with China's upbeat and continually reiterated slogan of economic 'win–win.' In aggregate, Africa may well have 'won' more than China over the past two decades of increased trade and deal making. As Table 3.1 makes clear, in only 6 of the 15 years between 2002 and 2017 were Chinese exports to Africa greater than its imports from Africa, and in three of those years (2002, 2003, and 2009) the gaps between imports and exports were very small.

Table 3.1 China–Africa trade relations 2002–2017

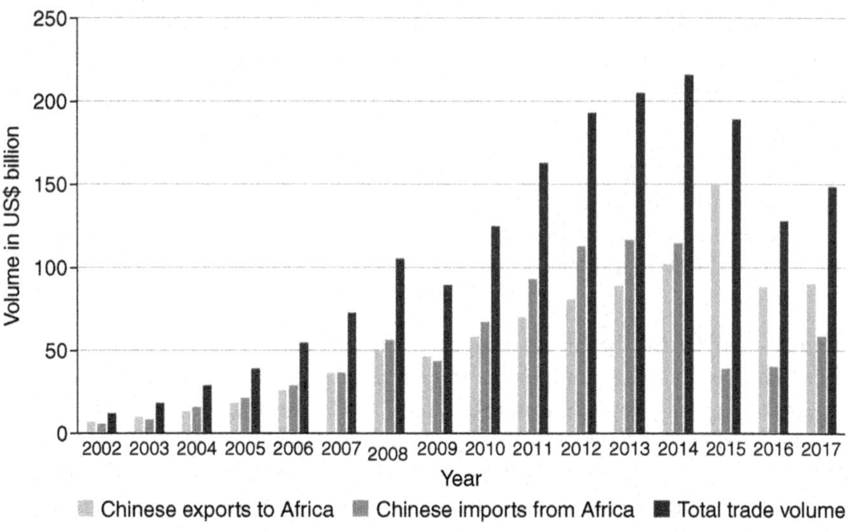

Source: China Africa Research Initiative, www.sais-cari.org/data-china-africa-trade.

Aggregate numbers, however, often gloss more than they reveal. Trade between China and Africa – as well as between China and the rest of the developing world – is often deeply and problematically skewed by country and by sector. The simplifying but not inaccurate slogan of 'win–win' begs a series of important political as well as economic questions: who wins, over what kind of time scale, and with what consequences that are not included in what is being measured? Are the winners African consumers, who benefit from lower prices on consumer goods? African political elites and their networks, who now have additional resources to tap? Chinese SOEs, for whom tied infrastructure deals guarantee profit? Resource-rich African states (Angola, the Democratic Republic of Congo, Nigeria, South Sudan) rather than resource-poor ones (Malawi, Chad, Senegal), or those sitting on prime real estate (Djibouti) rather than those that are landlocked (Malawi, the Central African Republic)? Those with important historic and public relationships with China (Tanzania, Zambia, Sudan, Ethiopia, Zimbabwe) rather than those of relative historical unimportance (Malawi, Chad, Madagascar)? Given a historic pattern of trade of African raw materials and commodities in exchange for either investment in infrastructure or the import of cheap consumer goods, is 'win–win' something that only obtains when the prices for commodities are relatively high, only to crash when prices for commodities decline, as they inevitably do in response to either oversupply or reduced demand?[3] And what about the potential mismatch of different sectors across different temporal scales? A win in investment, roads built, increase in GDP, cushion against future rises in commodity prices may well be another's loss in terms of forced sale of land or timber over which communities had customary right of use, medium term environmental degradation, or interest repayments that cannot be met. A win in terms of profit may come at the cost of labor rights, casualization, and bad local publicity. These considerations are, of course, elided in the smooth rhetoric of 'win–win,' but they are very much a part of what Chinese diplomats, SOEs, and managers deal with every day in Africa.

The third layer: from 'win–win' to 'common development'

Perhaps in implicit recognition of the limitations suggested by the transactional language of 'economic win–win,' China's official rhetoric on China and Africa has quickly come to add to 'win–win' the softening ideal of 'common development' (*gongtong fazhan*), without, however, jettisoning its fundamental commitment to the pursuit of comparative advantage in a globalized division of labor. In the Second Africa Policy Paper (*China Daily* 2015), the presumptions of formal equality, friendship, and complementarity for development are as pronounced as they ever were.

> Over the past five decades and more, they [China and Africa] have always been *good friends who stand together through thick and thin, good partners who share weal and woe, and good brothers who fully trust each other* despite changes in the international landscape … The development strategies of China and Africa are *highly compatible*. Given their respective strengths, China and Africa *need each other* for cooperation and development. Rare historic opportunities for *mutually beneficial* cooperation and *common development* have emerged. *China's comparative advantages in development experience, applied technology, funds and market can help Africa* overcome the two major bottlenecks constraining its development – backward infrastructure and inadequate professional and skilled personnel. They can also help Africa translate its natural and human resources advantages and potential into a driving force for development and benefits for people's livelihoods, thereby speeding up industrialization and agricultural modernization, and *doing a better job in pursuing economic independence as well as self-reliant and sustainable development* and achieving lasting peace and stability.
>
> (*China Daily* 2015, italics added)

Let us consider this paragraph. Even when one factors in that such broad policy statements on important topics are invariably written by committee, as recently as 2015, the official updated paper on China's Africa strategy displays elements of each of these three layers of China's rhetoric on Africa. The foundational base of amity and friendship, predicated on Mao-era notions of economic independence and self-reliance (the fractal based on a gendered commonality), is prominent. The paper reiterates China's principles of non-interference and respect for sovereignty that stand in implicit contrast to the West:

> China respects African countries' independent choice of the way to development ... China has always sincerely supported Africa's development. It never interferes in African countries' internal affairs, never imposes its will on them, and attaches no political strings when providing aid to Africa.
>
> (*China Daily* 2015)

The Second Africa Policy Paper then goes on to stress the second rhetorical layer of 'win–win' predicated on ideals of China's comparative advantage; complementarity and mutual benefit between China and Africa, now with nods to the more inclusive language of common development and sustainable development.

> The core principle is to connect assistance to developing countries, including those in Africa, for their independent and sustainable development with China's own development, achieve win-win cooperation and common development, and promote more balanced, inclusive and sustainable development of the world at large.
>
> (*China Daily* 2015)

The third section of the Africa Policy Paper explicitly points to what China means by 'deepening economic and trade cooperation':

- investing in Africa's industrialization 'to promote industrial alignment and capacity cooperation between China and African countries in an orderly fashion' (*China Daily* 2015);
- boosting Africa's agricultural modernization;
- participating in Africa's infrastructure modernization;
- strengthening China–Africa financial cooperation;
- promoting China–Africa trade and investment;
- bolstering resource and energy cooperation;
- expanding cooperating on the marine economy.

While this laundry list of aspirational promises is unlikely to ever be met in full, the list is itself important for what it reflects about China's ideals in terms of China–Africa policy (and indeed policy towards the developing world more generally): exporting much of China's own domestic experiences of the distant and recent past in catapulting state investment into market based high-speed growth. In the Africa Policy Paper vision, China's support for Africa's industrialization means promoting special economic zones (SEZs), industrial parks, and science and technology parks: one of China's first departures from the Maoist autarkic economy was to promote foreign direct investment through SEZs.

Agricultural modernization through the application of scientific techniques predates the establishment of the PRC and has been a constant in China's domestic development ever since. The stress on infrastructure mirrors China's own domestic growth (and current problems with excess capacity) and is directly attributable to campaign style state investment in infrastructural projects: roads, high-speed rail, port development, airports, and telecommunications. Investment in and production of green technology such as solar and wind energy have made China the world's top exporter of clean energy (Buckley et al. 2018).

More recently still, the Beijing Declaration that opened the FOCAC in Beijing in September 2018 (FOCAC 2018) imagines China and Africa as a joint community through continued 'common winning,' now backed up by China's pledge to invest another US$60 billion in key priority areas, now including such new frontiers as connectivity, capacity-building, and peace and security, as well as returning to one of China's previous strengths in Africa – health care (Xi 2018).

The outer wrapper: the Belt and Road Initiative and new imaginaries

The most recent, and most remarked upon, layer of China's formal rhetoric on Africa (and its outward-bound development policy more generally) is the enormous publicity given to what is now known as the Belt and Road Initiative (BRI). Previously translated directly and accurately into English from the Chinese '*yidai yilu*' (一帶一路) as 'One Belt–One Road' (OBOR), the BRI is a mega-strategy for the comprehensive export of China's distinctive approach to external development: complete upgrading of hard and soft infrastructure (roads, ports, railroads, energy generation, and communications) for the facilitation of trade and local development from China, softened by the organizing concepts of policy coordination, facilities connectivity, unimpeded trade, financial integration, and people-to-people bonds.

The original formulation for BRI consisted of land routes west through Central Asia to Europe and south to Pakistan, and overseas through a 'string of pearls'; building and upgrading ports from the South China Sea through to Venice. Launched in 2013, the sheer scale of BRI – with amounts notionally pledged in the trillions to seventy-one states accounting for more than half the world's population – would by itself attract enormous attention from investors and foreign policy analysts. Much is rhetorically claimed for BRI. As a Xi Jinping-mandated signature policy that is important enough to have been enshrined in the CCP's most recent constitution in 2017, BRI is a profoundly political project domestically in China as it stakes part of Xi's legitimacy on its implementation, thus setting up powerful incentives for officials to rapidly conclude deals that can be trumpeted as successful. The contours of BRI are unclear in two major respects. First, there has been ambiguity in the ideational and conceptual construction of BRI. Originally conceived as an economic "Belt" across Eurasia and a (Maritime Silk) "Road" across the Pacific and Indian Oceans up through the

Red Sea towards Suez and Europe, BRI is now beginning to be promoted with a very different imaginary, a fundamentally global reach of 'wings' to the east (Latin America) and west (Europe, Africa) that complements a main 'axis' from Asia to Australia with China at the center (Deloitte Insights 2018). This imaginary could hardly be more important, as it recenters China as a benevolent and modern source of global development and wealth generation with its own institutions of finance, its own models of development, and its own rhetorics of friendship, non-intervention, and complementarity.

For Africa, the difference in these two conceptions is profound. When following the lines of the Economic 'Belt' and the Maritime Silk 'Road' China's extension of BRI to Africa is focused on the Indian Ocean ports (and additional infrastructure to serve those ports) in Tanzania, Kenya, and Djibouti, omitting the rest of the continent. The new imaginary of the 'axis' and enveloping 'wings' points to the inclusion of all of Africa as a 'west wing,' with more potential spots for investment than any other region on the globe.[4] Senegal – a state that by no sleight of hand could be considered as part of the original Belt or Road – has now been reimagined as a 'key extension of the BRI' (MOFA 2018). At the same time, BRI is invoked in the opposite geographical direction, south and east across the Pacific: Ecuador and China signed a document to jointly pursue BRI in December 2018 (Mo 2018); some 5 months later Peru announced that it is set to join BRI as well (Galinda 2019). Second, it is unclear how much of BRI is simply putting the veneer of a unified plan on a range of initiatives that either were already underway or would likely have been concluded without the BRI label. For example, in July 2018 the memorandum of understanding for BRI states that Senegal simply 'formalizes pre-existing cooperation on infrastructure,' notably in a road linking the capital with Senegal's second city of Touba, and the development of an industrial park (Tiezzi 2018). A quick perusal of China's official BRI website encompasses everything from bilateral deals for loans, official diplomatic communiques, sports tourism, the contents of BRICS summits, Confucius Institutes, Sino-African art exchange exhibits, and the full content of FOCAC.

Thus, how much of BRI is new, how much is simply repackaged under a putatively unified program, and how much is down to investors and Chinese officials rushing to propose projects in order to pursue funding streams or demonstrate compliance with targets is at present uncertain. No one knows where the boundaries of BRI are. What is clear is that that, ambitious as it is, the BRI wrapper encompasses the earlier layers of rhetoric: insistence on national sovereignty, amity and equality (the fractal), 'win–win' based on globalized division of labor and wealth generation, and common development. And although it is profoundly uncertain what newer planks of BRI such as financial integration and connectivity might eventually mean for these older rhetorics, for the time being at least, participation in BRI is no impediment to the strong articulation of earlier, familiar rhetorics. For example, Ismail Omar Guelleh, President of Djibouti for nearly 20 years, has invited in Chinese investment for big infrastructure (the Doraleh Port, the Djibouti International Free Trade

Zone, a water pipeline from Ethiopia, and the Djibouti–Addis rail line), taken out loans in excess of US$1.4 billion, concluded a strategic partnership in 2017, and agreed to a Chinese naval facility that is, depending on one's perspective, either a logistics and supply station or a full-fledged naval base. Because of its location and long-term friendliness to China, Djibouti is perhaps the country in Africa most obviously tied to the BRI; if one were to find evidence of newer BRI-inflected rhetorics in Africa, Djibouti would be the place to look for it. Indeed, as befits an old friend of China, Guelleh frequently comes to China's public defense, particularly when it is accused of debt diplomacy. But instead of pointing to anything new in terms of BRI claims, Guelleh repeatedly reflects the long-standing official rhetoric of win–win cooperation and mutual benefits [*sic*] noting 'that the history of cooperation between China and Africa was based on win-win cooperation and mutual respect, in contrast to the defaming by some external powers' (Luo 2018).

African voices and responses

While most of Western press and think tanks are agnostic to actively critical of China's actions in Africa, it is of course much more important to get to grips with what Africans themselves think of China. And here Miles' Law – 'where you stand depends on where you sit' – is pertinent. On the whole, the political elites of African countries, particularly when they are in charge of the state, have tended to be very welcoming of China. They appreciate China's stress on sovereignty, its stated principles of non-interference, and its willingness to provide the critically needed transport and communications infrastructure that Western donors and businesses have either not placed in their remit (for the former) or deemed to be sufficiently profitable (for the latter). It is true that autocrats and narrow political elites (e. g. Angola, Equatorial Guinea) in resource-rich countries have continued to enrich themselves through Chinese deals, and it is little wonder that these leaders publicly support China's continued investment and presence. As but one illustrative example, as recently as January 2019, Teodoro Obiang Nguema Mbasogo, President of Equatorial Guinea and one of the most politically repressive in Africa, met with Xi Jinping's special representative and lauded China as 'an important cooperation partner' (Xinhua 2019) stating that

> [Equatorial Guinea] appreciates the Chinese side's long-term and strong support and assistance, welcomes more Chinese enterprises to invest and start business in Equatorial Guinea, and is ready to further reinforce mutually beneficial cooperation with the Chinese side in jointly building the Belt and Road Initiative and implementing the eight major initiatives. The Equatorial Guinean side will continuously enhance communication and coordination with the Chinese side on international and regional affairs.
>
> (MOFA 2019)

Given the highly repressive political environment and official cult of personality around Obiang, what most in Equatorial Guinea think of the Chinese presence, or indeed any topic, is as unknowable as what most in the PRC thought in the latter Mao years. But even in relatively open and democratic environments, African leaders and political elites are often effusive in their praise of China and consciously or otherwise mirror Chinese rhetorics. For example, when Ghanaian President Nana Akufo-Addo made a state visit to China several days ahead of the 2018 FOCAC meeting in Beijing, Chinese CCTV reported that Akufo-Addo stated:

> the Ghana-China friendship forged by the two countries' older generations of leaders is unbreakable. Ghana cast its vote in support of the People's Republic of China taking its rightful seat in the UN and has been upholding the one-China principle. Ghana is willing to deepen bilateral relations, actively participate in the Belt and Road construction, and inject new vitality into bilateral cooperation. Marching on the road of socialism with Chinese characteristics, China plays an important role in world peace and development. China provides an important opportunity for Africa's stability and revitalization. Ghana will always be China's trustworthy friend in Africa.
>
> (CCTV 2018)

Mirroring rhetoric such as this certainly suggests that the Ghanaian political elite either believes, or at least pretends to believe, in the vision that China has in Africa: old friendship, the one-China principle, a proper role in world peace and development. Although 'win–win' based on comparative advantage is not explicitly invoked, it is implicitly present, as this official visit was accompanied by the signing of a US$2 billion deal between the Ghanaian government and Sinohydro to swap infrastructure-building for refined bauxite – the key mineral used in producing aluminum that Ghana as yet does not have the capacity to refine. Ghanaian citizens, on the other hand, possess a range of vibrant views about China and their own government's trustworthiness in managing Chinese projects. Those resettled by the Bui Dam, a megaproject concluded between Sinohydro and the government, were promised compensation and training by a newly created Ghanaian body, the Bui Power Authority, have complained in no uncertain terms about reduced farm yields, skyrocketing prices for the foodstuffs that they can no longer grow, and decreased access to forest products and fishing – to mention nothing of the gap between projected power generation and actual power generation (Yankson et al. 2018). While Ghanaians appear to be more distrustful of their own government's capacity to make decisions and follow through on the common good for the country than on China per se, there is a good deal of open criticism of a government that apes China's rhetoric in concluding deals, its lack of transparency, the terms of the deals themselves, and the poverty and youth unemployment that is omnipresent even as a minority get rich from these deals (Pilling 2018; Yen News 2018).

Conclusion

How China's rhetoric on Africa evolves, and how it will or will not take hold among a multitude of African voices remains to be seen. But, given what has and has not changed over the past decade, I would venture these concluding propositions. First, Chinese rhetoric will be unlikely to shift very substantially. New layers may well be added, but if the past 60 years of China–Africa interaction serves as a guide, a bedrock of amity, friendship, equality, and fractal replication, a second layer of differentiation and 'win–win,' a softening third level of 'common development' and what is at present an outer wrapper of globalized BRI will remain in place unrepudiated and ready to be drawn upon as circumstances dictate. Second, Western reporting on China and Africa may well become more nuanced and less overtly critical, but the incentives within Western reporting, its notions of what a story is, and the ways in which Western journalists are socialized and rewarded all suggest that Western press will continue to focus on the critical, the hidden costs, and the individual stories of loss and transformation that are seldom reflected in the official rhetoric. Unless there is dramatic regime change in the PRC, all the present indications within China are that Chinese press will become increasingly market-savvy, but will toe an ever closer domestically determined line of positive coverage on China and Africa and China and BRI. And finally, within Africa itself, the combination of diversity, growth, the spread of Internet connectivity, and ever more vibrant civil societies will convey ever wider platforms for the really important, and likely increasingly diverse and sophisticated, voices to be heard.

Notes

1 Ironically for a policy so tightly clung to for the subsequent 65 years, within five years the Principles proved not fit for purpose, when border clashes between China and India broke out in 1959 and a full-scale border war in 1962.
2 The creation of Confucius Institutes by a one-party state that claims to be the dictatorship of the proletariat is but the most obvious example of this kind of historically legitimating branding. See the preface to Justin Yifu Lin and Yan Wang's conclusion of their influential book, *Going Beyond Aid: Development Cooperation for Structural Transformation*, explicitly invokes quotes from Confucius and Mencius as a way to link China's glorious past with the promising model it offers to the developing world at present (Lin and Wang 2017, 167).
3 This concern features prominently in the current discussions around China's 'debt diplomacy' and the risks inherent to highly indebted countries, many of them in Africa.
4 A Deloitte Insights report offers apt visualization of these conceptualizations, https://www2.deloitte.com/insights/us/en/economy/asia-pacific/china-belt-and-road-initiative.html.

References

Baidu Baike (2019) *Zhongguo GDP (China's GDP)*, (www.baike.com/wiki/%E4%B8%AD%E5%9B%BDGDP), accessed 11 January 2019.

Buckley, T., Nicholas, S. and Brown, M. (2018) *China 2017 Review: World's Second-Biggest Economy Continues to Drive Global Trends in Energy Investment*, Institute for Energy Economics and Financial Analysis, Cleveland.

CCTV (2018) *China, Ghana to further enrich relations*, (www.youtube.com/watch?v=JxZL5TJg60Q), accessed 18 March 2019.

China Daily (2015) *Full text: China's Second Africa policy paper*, (www.chinadaily.com.cn/world/XiattendsParisclimateconference/2015-12/05/content_22632874.htm), accessed 11 January 2019.

Deloitte Insights (2018) *Embracing the BRI ecosystem in 2018: Navigating pitfalls and seizing opportunities*, (https://www2.deloitte.com/insights/us/en/economy/asia-pacific/china-belt-and-road-initiative.html), accessed 4 November 2018.

FOCAC (Forum on China–Africa Cooperation) (2018) *Beijing Declaration-Toward an even stronger China-Africa community with a shared future*, (https://focacsummit.mfa.gov.cn/eng/hyqk_1/t1594324.htm), accessed 5 January 2019.

Galinda, J. (2019) *Peru to join China's Belt and Road Initiative*, (https://theglobalamericans.org/2019/05/just-the-facts-peru-to-join-chinas-belt-and-road-initiative/), accessed 7 May 2019.

ICG (International Crisis Group) (2017) *China's Foreign Policy Experiment in South Sudan*, Asia Report no. 288, International Crisis Group, Brussels.

Lee, C. K. (2018) *The Specter of Global China: Politics, Labor and Foreign Investment in Africa*, University of Chicago Press, Chicago.

Lin, J. Y. and Wang, Y. (2017) *Going Beyond Aid: Development Cooperation for Structural Transformation*, Cambridge University Press, Cambridge.

Luo, J. (2018) *Commentary: China-Africa win-win partnership won't be derailed by false claims*, (http://english.xiongan.gov.cn/2018-09/05/c_129947658.htm), accessed 7 May 2019.

Mao, Z. (1945) *The situation and our policy after the victory in the War of Resistance against Japan*, (www.marxists.org/reference//archive/mao/works/red-book/ch21.htm), accessed 8 December 2018.

Mo, J. (2018) *Xi welcomes Ecuador to help build Belt, Road*, (https://eng.yidaiyilu.gov.cn/qwyw/rdxw/74589.htm), accessed 16 January 2019.

MOFA (Ministry of Foreign Affairs of the People's Republic of China) (2018) *Foreign Ministry spokesperson Geng Shuang's regular press conference on July 23, 2018*, (www.fmprc.gov.cn/mfa_eng/xwfw_665399/s2510_665401/2511_665403/t1579567.shtml), accessed 16 January 2019.

MOFA (Ministry of Foreign Affairs of the People's Republic of China) (2019) *Yang Jiechi meets with President Teodoro Obiang Nguema Mbasogo of Equatorial Guinea*, (www.fmprc.gov.cn/mfa_eng/zxxx_662805/t1631000.shtml), accessed 20 March 2019.

Peralta, E. (2018) *A new Chinese-funded railway in Kenya sparks debt-trap fears*, (www.npr.org/2018/10/08/641625157/a-new-chinese-funded-railway-in-kenya-sparks-debt-trap-fears), accessed 11 May 2019.

Pilling, D. (2018) *Ghana relations with China raise the emotional heat: Funds for infrastructure projects are welcome but many high-profile ventures have become headaches for Accra*, (www.ft.com/content/bdb7c066-c1ad-11e8-84cd-9e601db069b8), accessed 17 March 2019.

Riskin, C. (2004) *The Fall in Chinese Poverty: Issues of Measurement, Incidence and Cause*, paper for the 'Keith Griffin Festschrift Conference', Amherst, 23–24 April.

State Council (2006) *China's African policy*, (www.gov.cn/misc/2006-01/12/content_156490.htm), accessed 11 January 2019.

Strauss, J. C. (2009) 'The Past in the Present: Historical and Rhetorical Lineages in China's Relations with Africa', in J. C. Strauss and M. Saavedra (eds) *China and*

Africa: Emerging Patterns of Globalization and Development, Cambridge University Press, Cambridge, 227–245.

Strauss, J. C. (2012) 'Framing and Claiming: Contemporary Globalization and "Going Out" in China's Rhetoric towards Latin America', in J. C. Strauss and A. C. Armony (eds) *From the Great Wall to the New World: China and Latin America in the 21st Century*, Cambridge University Press, Cambridge, 134–156.

The Fractal Foundation (n.d.) *What is a fractal?* (https://fractalfoundation.org/fractivities/WhatIsaFractal-1pager.pdf), accessed 11 December 2018.

Tiezzi, S. (2018) *China's Belt and Road makes inroads in Africa*, (https://thediplomat.com/2018/07/chinas-belt-and-road-makes-inroads-in-africa/), accessed 12 January 2019.

Xi, J. (2018) *Full text of Chinese President Xi Jinping's speech at opening ceremony of 2018 FOCAC Beijing Summit*, (www.xinhuanet.com/english/2018-09/03/c_129946189.htm), accessed 11 January 2019.

Xinhua (2019) *China, Equatorial Guinea pledge to strengthen cooperation*, (www.xinhuanet.com/english/2019-01/18/c_137754446.htm), accessed 20 March 2019.

Yankson, P. W. K., Asiedu, A., Owusu, K., Urban, F. and Siciliano, G. (2018) 'The Livelihood Challenges of Resettled Communities of the Bui Dam Project in Chana and the Role of Chinese Dam Builders', *Development Policy Review*, 36(supplement 1), 476–494.

Yen News (2018) *Ghana News Today: Ghana-China agreement – Ghanaians reaction*, (www.youtube.com/watch?v=oa0qa033308), accessed 20 March 2019.

Zhou, E. (1964) *The Chinese government's Eight Principles for economic aid and technical assistance to other countries*, (https://digitalarchive.wilsoncenter.org/document/121560.pdf?v=7842ff83b1fa6e84a7b0e483012dfe15), accessed 10 December 2019.

Zhu, R. (2002) *Strengthen solidarity, enhance co-operation, and pursue common development*, (www.china.org.cn/english/features/focac/184410.htm), accessed 7 January 2019.

4 China and regional security in Africa

Georg Lammich

Introduction

Until a few years ago, China had no specific policy to engage regional organizations in Africa and focused on advancing its bilateral relations with the states on the continent. In recent years, however, China started to integrate a regional dimension in its African strategy, and new forms of cooperation with different regional and subregional actors in various thematic areas have been established. There are several reasons for China's policy shift and increasing willingness to include new partners in its relationship with the African continent and extend its traditional state-to-state approach to a multilateral and regional level. While many of these factors relate to Africa's special relevance for China's foreign policy and growing investments on the continent, the move towards a more regionalized cooperation in Africa should not be seen in isolation but in context of an overall policy shift in China. This chapter investigates China's emergence as a regional security actor in Africa considering not only the changing security objectives on the continent but also domestic and global drivers of China's foreign policy. The chapter starts by outlining how China's African Policy has moved away from a predominantly bilateral approach to a more nuanced policy which includes growing interactions with the African Union (AU). The second part of the chapter focusses on China's regional security interests in Africa in context of current developments in China's foreign policy. The final part of the chapter assesses the configuration and emerging institutional structure of China's security cooperation with the AU.

While the rise of China in Africa has received a lot of attention, China's engagement in multilateral and interregional dialogues on the continent is mostly uncharted.[1] Van Hoeymissen (2011) sketched the role of regional organizations in China's security strategy for Africa, and in the last few years, some scholars (Benabdallah 2015; Verhoeven 2016; Alden et al. 2018) have highlighted certain other aspects of the regional dimension of Sino-African cooperation and China's increasing linkages with the AU. The aim of this chapter is to complement extant scholarship by assessing China's various motives for expanding its regional security engagement in Africa and providing an overview of China–AU security cooperation.

The regional dimension of Sino-African cooperation

In the early 2000s, China maintained an indifferent position towards regional organizations in Africa and focused on advancing its bilateral relations with African states focusing on resources, political influence, and the disclosure of new markets guided by the principle of non-interference. The Forum on China–Africa Cooperation (FOCAC) served as the main instrument to foster this new relationship between China and the respective national governments. At this point the recognition of African regional or subregional organizations by the Chinese side happened out of deference to some African actors that were supporting regional integration on the continent, but these organizations were otherwise not taken into account. In the FOCAC Declaration from 2000, China mentioned the 'efforts made by the African continent to enhance sub-regional cooperation' and recognized the founding of the AU, but no further claims for support were made (FOCAC 2000). The passive stance of China towards the Organization of African Unity (OAU) respectively AU is also a result of the timing of the FOCAC summit a mere month after the adoption of the Sirte Declaration announcing the founding of the AU. When the structure of FOCAC was defined, the still existing OAU was dissolving and thus hardly relevant for future cooperation, with the AU as designated successor not yet functional. During that period of transition from the OAU to the AU the Chinese government, with its nascent interest in regional cooperation, as well as the African states, had no persuasive reasons to strengthen the role of regional organizations within the context of FOCAC (Barton 2009, 14; Ikome 2010, 202).

Three years later, referring to the New Partnership for Africa's Development (NEPAD), China cited the 'progress of NEPAD implementation and African regional cooperation' (FOCAC 2003), but all assistance offered was still strictly limited to bilateral channels. The turning point of China's official strategy came with the introduction of China's African Policy in early 2006, which has shaped the course of Chinese cooperation in Africa ever since. The allegiance with these organizations was regarded as one way for China to foster peaceful development without breaking with its tenet of non-interference. With the consolidation of the AU, the founding of NEPAD, and the slow emergence of a viable regional and subregional framework in Africa, the structural preconditions for China's regional endeavor in Africa were sufficient, and Beijing announced its motivation to increasingly use regional and multilateral channels to deal with Africa and expand its relations with regional organizations in its 2006 African Policy (State Council 2006).

In an albeit short but meaningful passage at the end of its 2006 African Policy, China

> appreciates the significant role of the AU in safeguarding peace and stability in the region and promoting African solidarity and development and further … supports the positive role of Africa's subregional organizations in promoting political stability, economic development and integration in

their own regions and stands ready to enhance its amicable cooperation with those organizations.

(State Council 2006)

This official recognition of African regionalism and pronouncement of support was the starting point for a new Chinese emphasis on facilitating regional integration in Africa and the establishment of new forms of cooperation with the AU and various subregional organizations.

In line with its increasingly flexible geopolitical approach, China has extended its engagement in Africa to a regional dimension without diminishing its established bilateral ties. Based on the predominantly positive experiences China has made in dealing with the Association of Southeast Asian Nations and the European Union (EU), Beijing regards regional organizations to a certain extent as expedient partners that can be utilized to promote Chinese interests. This new approach is based on Beijing's realization that a supplementary regional policy in Africa might be beneficial for economic development and is the logical continuation of its long-term strategy on the continent. As will be outlined in the following sections, the promotion of development and the protection of Chinese investments in Africa face transnational economic and security threats that have to be addressed on a multilateral basis. The AU and various subregional organizations are therefore seen as instruments for creating a better setting for Chinese investments and for furthering the strategic goals of China on the continent.

China–African Union relations

While China initially tried to engage with all regional and subregional organizations in Africa, many of these attempts came to nothing and were suspended or are simmering at a very low level. The ongoing interlocutions, usually termed as dialogues or forums in the official wording, with the Southern African Development Community (SADC), the Economic Community of West African States, and the East African Community are mostly concerned with commercial and developmental issues rather than targeting security or geopolitical topics. These frameworks have a consultative character and are based on an irregular conference schedule without any permanent structures. The institutional concessions on the Chinese side are in most cases limited to installing a Chinese diplomat operating in the respective subregion as an official representative to the Regional Economic Communities (RECs) and the financial support given to these organizations is erratic and scant (Alden 2014, 6). Therefore, despite continuing attempts on both sides to strengthen the ties between China and the RECs, the continent-wide schemes have gained the most attention.

With the AU and NEPAD, two counterparts to China's regional quest have emerged that tackle some of Beijing's most pressing issues, have a measurable impact and are easier to engage than the various subregional organizations.

> Thanks to the concerted efforts of African countries and the Organization of African Unity (OAU)/the African Union (AU), the political situation in Africa has been stable on the whole, regional conflicts are being gradually resolved and economy has been growing for years. The New Partnership for Africa's Development (NEPAD) has drawn up an encouraging picture of African rejuvenation and development.
>
> (State Council 2006)

China has shown a clear preference for these two organizations and several new dialogue mechanisms and mutual initiatives have been established.

After the general policy formulation towards an engagement with regional organizations in Africa in the 2006 White Paper, China specified this strategy at the third FOCAC meeting 4 months later in Beijing and announced its support for a new AU convention center in Addis Ababa (FOCAC 2006, section 2.5). Apart from offering moral and technical support, China also lauded 'the AU's leading role in resolving African issues' and announced that it would 'take an active part in UN peacekeeping operations in Africa' (FOCAC 2006, section 2.5.2). The recognition of the AU as an important security actor in Africa and its active involvement in peacekeeping on the continent show a more flexible approach by Beijing towards its principles of national sovereignty and non-interference and paved the way for China to play an active role in African security.

Shortly after the 2006 FOCAC III meeting in Beijing, a formal strategic dialogue mechanism between China and the AU was implemented in 2007. The first meeting was held at the AU headquarters in Addis Ababa. Zhai Jun, then vice-secretary of foreign affairs, and Jean Ping, then head of the African Union Commission (AUC), discussed general topics of Sino-AU cooperation but also concrete problems in Darfur, Zimbabwe, DR Congo, and Somalia (Taylor 2011, 78). The second strategic dialogue took place in September 2009 in Beijing with Yang Jiechi, the Minister of Foreign Affairs at the time, in attendance. The talks focused on Chinese support of the AU's peacekeeping missions and future projects for capacity-building at the AU level (Thomashausen 2010). Meetings on an ad hoc basis to discuss recent international developments with a special focus on security-related issues supplement the annual meetings. In the FOCAC Action Plan (2013–2015), the establishment of several subcommittees on various topics of Sino-African relations was also envisioned and mostly implemented in the following years. In these smaller frameworks targeting specific topics ranging from cultural exchange to security, different strategies adjusted to the respective regions can be discussed and complemented by periodic continental FOCAC summits. Although this mechanism is no novelty in China's foreign policy – comparable dialogues exist with South Africa, the US, India, and others – it highlights the Chinese perception of the AU as a relevant actor in Africa and the willingness to integrate the AU and the AUC as the organization's permanent representative further into its hitherto state-centric African strategy. Apart from the establishment of new dialogue platforms, the number of high-level exchanges between the AU and the People's Republic of China (PRC) has increased in the last few years culminating in FOCAC 2018, the largest diplomatic event to ever be hosted by China (*China Daily* 2018). Representatives from fifty-three African countries and the AU, including forty presidents, ten prime ministers, and the chairperson of the AUC, attended the Beijing FOCAC summit leaving – according to an African news agency – the African continent briefly bereft of leaders (*Africa News* 2018). Though the summit still followed mostly a Chinese agenda, the role of the AU was lauded by Xi Jinping and the AU and its various initiatives featured prominently in the Beijing Declaration and FOCAC Action Plan: 'China appreciates the positive role of the African Union Commission since joining the FOCAC, and welcomes the establishment of an African Union Representative Mission in Beijing' (FOCAC 2018b; see also FOCAC 2018a).

Beijing is in favor of proactive involvement of the AU in the various existing bilateral dialogue frameworks with the FOCAC being the most prominent one. In the fifth Action Plan (2013–2015), the first after the elevation of the AU to a full member of FOCAC, a whole passage was dedicated to the expansion of China–AU relations with a focus on security, development, and regional integration. The document states:

> The two sides recognized the important role of the African Union in safeguarding Africa's peace and stability, promoting Africa's development and advancing the African integration process, and support a bigger role and greater influence of the African Union in international and regional affairs. (FOCAC 2012)

Although the inclusion of regional organizations in the Sino-African dialogue strengthens the bargaining power of the African side compared to a bilateral setting, China expects several advantages in including regional organizations (see also Alden 2005). Engaging the AU as an aggregator for African interests would greatly reduce the complexity of negotiation costs compared to maintaining fifty-four bilateral dialogues and would legitimize China's engagement with Africa on a continental level.

On the eve of the 2015 FOCAC Johannesburg summit, China published its second policy document on its overall African Policy. While the two types of documents – Declarations and Action Plans – adopted at the FOCAC summits cover a 3-year period, the overall policy sets the long-time framework of China's policy on the continent (Wekesa 2015). The new policy document is not just significantly longer and more specific on projects and commitments of China in Africa than the previous Policy Paper from 2006; it also encompasses elements of the FOCAC Declaration and Action Plan. The document sets the broad parameters for the future direction of FOCAC ensuring that FOCAC declarations should essentially align with the Africa Policy Paper (Mthembu 2016, 2). In its core framework for China's bilateral relations with the continent, it provides some references to regional development and security cooperation and dedicates a few lines to China's relations with African regional organizations. In its last paragraph the document states:

> China values and supports the AU's leadership in building a united and strong Africa and promoting African integration, its centrality in safeguarding peace and security in Africa, as well as a bigger role for the organization in regional and international affairs.
>
> (China Internet Information Center 2015)

While the enhancement of the AU is in line with the 2006 document and the operationalization of this policy in the last FOCAC Declaration, the new policy also refers to the African Union's Agenda 2063. Though the recognition of the Agenda underlines China's support for a holistic development strategy for Africa, the general outline of the document is less accommodating to a broad pan-African vision. Industrialization and agricultural modernization, two areas that China is mostly engaging on a bilateral level, are the main focus in its cooperation with Africa (China Internet Information Center 2015, part III).

China's new African Policy and the increasing cooperation with the AU is not only an attempt to further China's strategic goals on the continent and gain organizational advantages for FOCAC and other areas of interaction, it is also mirroring a broader political reorientation under Xi Jinping. As Wekesa (2015) points out, the new policy is an extension of a shift in Beijing's national development strategy and an adaptation to the 'new normal' (新常态) of economic restructuring in China. The policy transfers Xi Jinping's vision of the 'Chinese Dream' (中国梦) to Africa as a template for development and modernization and links the Chinese Belt and Road Initiative (BRI) to the African Union Agenda 2063 (Zhang and Kangombe 2016, 77). Africa was initially not included in China's BRI as a vision of a major global development strategy, but an increasing number of Chinese-funded projects are now labeled as part of the initiative (Ehizuelen and Abdi 2017, 295). While the majority of these projects are related to transport infrastructure – including the AU's plans for a continental transport link – China is now also introducing a security dimension to the African part of its BRI: 'Fifty security assistance programs will be launched to advance China-Africa cooperation under the Belt and Road Initiative, and in areas of law and order, UN peacekeeping missions, fighting piracy and combating terrorism' (FOCAC 2018b). The restructuring of China's domestic and foreign policy in the era of Xi also comprises a 'global vision of [a] national security policy' (全球思维谋篇布局), which, in combination with the development objectives outlined in the Chinese African Policy, has a significant impact on China's role as a security actor in Africa. Chinese official discourse asserts that on the one hand China's key interests increasingly face threats that emerge in other world regions and that on the other hand economic development needs to be prioritized as a prerequisite for building a peaceful society (Benabdallah 2016, 20; Huotari et al. 2017, 27). The long-standing policy of Beijing that domestic and international security can only be achieved in combination with development was reinforced under Xi Jinping: 'development is the foundation of security and security is the condition for development (发展是安全的基础, 安全是发展的条件)' (Xinhua 2014). Under Xi development and peacebuilding efforts became a cohesive part of China's Africa strategy and are treated as interrelated concepts (Benabdallah 2016, 22). The linkage between development and security with special regard to the role of African regional organizations has also been a key theme of various policy documents: 'China will continue to support the leading role of the African Union and Africa's subregional organizations in peacemaking, peacebuilding and post conflict reconstruction initiatives, … achieving lasting peace and common prosperity' (FOCAC 2018b).

China's engagement with the AU also has a global dimension and is sparked by Xi Jinping's ambitions to transform China into 'a mighty force' (Xi 2017) that could lead the world on political, economic, military, and environmental issues and challenge Western dominance in several discourses. While Africa might not be the center stage of world politics, it is a perfect platform to build China's leadership role and image in the international community and to externalize Beijing's normative concepts (Yun 2014). By creating a 'favorable interpretative community' (Paltiel 2007, 205) with the AU, China is looking for support in shaping the international debate in several sensitive areas. China presumes a normative consensus or at least normative overlap with the AU on issues ranging from national sovereignty over views on multilateralism and multipolarity to human rights making the AU a possible ally against a Western exegesis of these topics.

> The recognition of the strategic character of the formation and implementation of international norms pushes China to assertively promote its own alternative project, which by no means negates basic universal humanitarian values but implies the principle of the 'right balance between justice and interest' (正确义利观).
>
> (Kozyrev 2016, 329)

Two key areas in this normative debate – conflict management and Responsibility to Protect (R2P) – are renegotiated at the African example with the AU as China's witness for a conflict resolution model that respects national sovereignty (Van Hoeymissen 2011, 109). The R2P concept that gained rapid popularity at the beginning of the new millennium challenged China's traditional emphasis on non-interference and was first seen quite critically in the Chinese discourse (Chen 2016, 688). After its initial phase of opposition, China quickly came to terms with the basic concept of R2P and articulated – in the wake of the Darfur crisis in 2005 – its own albeit very restricted interpretation of the right to intervene in other states in times of extreme domestic crisis (Cabestan 2018, 714). In its favorable vote on the United Nations Security Council (UNSC) resolution 1769 (2007) on the establishment of the United Nations (UN) and AU hybrid operation in Darfur China recalled that the 'the Peace and Security Council of the African Union urgently requested the Security Council of the United Nations to urgently authorize the deployment of the African Union/United Nations hybrid operation' (UNSC 2007, 11). China stressed the constructive role of the AU 'in spite of the serious financial and logistical constraints.' According to the Chinese representative Wang Guangya the Chinese consent was based on the 'consensus reached by the United Nations/African Union/Sudan tripartite dialogue mechanism on the hybrid operation' (UNSC 2007, 10).

In contrast to some pivotal Northern countries that saw the 'protection of civilians' (POC) as their top priority, China emphasized state sovereignty as a means to achieve human protection. Beijing favored state-level early warning systems and a greater consideration of the position of relevant regional organizations in the UNSC decision-making process. To better account for local circumstances and regional sensitivities, these organizations should agree to any imposed measures and play a supportive role (Fung 2016, 3). In the UNSC China supported a greater involvement of African regional organizations for conflict resolution in the case of Libya, Côte d'Ivoire, and South Sudan (all in 2011), Mali (2012), and Somalia (2014) (Huotari et al. 2017, 92).

This position matches with the AU who on the one hand is entrusted to defend the sovereignty, territorial integrity, and independence of its member states and on the other hand has the responsibility of promoting peace, security, and stability on the continent as laid down in article three of its Constitutive Act. The AU is supportive of the R2P concept but wary towards external interventions and advocates African agency to address security issues on the continent (Bah 2017, 148). While the AU recognizes its lack of resources and military capacities to conduct independent peacekeeping missions and thus accepts the practical need to include the UN, this partnership 'is often characterized by legitimacy struggles over whether the UN or the AU should call the shots in deciding how to respond to Africa's peace and security crises' (Williams and Boutellis 2014, 257). African representatives in the UNSC have criticized that the UNSC 'seems to disregard full consideration of the position and/or recommendations of the AU or its organs' and called for a set of principles clarifying the AU–UNSC relationship support for African ownership and priority-setting (UNSC 2012, 9).

While the reasons of China and African actors to promote a stronger role of regional organizations might differ, as China seeks a compromise between non-interference and humanitarian intervention, whereas the African side welcomes protection against Western dominance, they both enhance the ability of these organizations – in particular the AU – to influence the norms for international interventions in Africa.

China–AU security cooperation

Despite China's heavy involvement in UN peacekeeping on the African continent – China is currently the ninth-largest contributor to peacekeeping operations and the leading contributor among permanent members of the UN Security Council – several potential problems remain regarding Beijing's multilateral approach. The UN and the UN Security Council are suspected of being dominated by Western ideas, and calls for interventions based on the responsibility to protect are still regarded by many members of Beijing's political elite as a violation of China's sacrosanct principle of non-interference.

China's new military presence on the continent has strengthened voices accusing China of neocolonialism, an allegation that China, the self-declared vanguard of the developing world, tries to avoid at all costs. Though the idea that China is influencing regime change in Africa became popular in the wake of the events that ended Robert Mugabe's 37-year rule in Zimbabwe, there is no conclusive evidence that China instigated the military coup. China issued a forceful denial calling media reports linking them to events in Zimbabwe illogical, inconsistent, 'and filled with evil intentions' (cited in IOL News 2017; see also Sachikonye, Chapter 12 in this volume). China is wary of any accusations that it fosters regime change either through military interventions or through clandestinely supporting the opposition. A regime change sanctioned or even supported by China could not just spark allegations of neoimperialism and weaken Beijing's influence in the respective country but also cause dismay among other non-democratic rulers across the continent (van der Putten 2015, 16).

To counter these potential risks to China's influence and reputation close collaboration with the AU and other African subregional organizations that are clearly non-Western actors and seen as mostly independent from US influence offers a viable solution. The partial alignment of China's policies with those of the AU in areas that are either less important or in line with the Chinese security and foreign policy strategy is, on the one hand, deflecting neocolonial criticism, and on the other, balancing the interventionist position of the West. Although China's stance towards international intervention is far more passive than the principles of mandatory intervention articulated in article four of the Constitutive Act of the AU and the Chinese concept of non-interference clashes with the AU's notion of non-indifference, both have shown many similarities in their position on national sovereignty and interstate conflicts. China is highlighting those cases where the views of the AU and key African players converge with its own positions and is using them as reference points for military engagement or the absence thereof on the continent (Van Hoeymissen 2011, 102). Thus, in 2008, Beijing justified its criticism of international sanctions against Zimbabwe arguing the Chinese position was in line with that of the AU and the SADC which both opposed sanctions and were regarded by China as the expression of the consensus of African countries on the current situation (United Nations 2008, Van Hoeymissen 2011, 100).

Apart from the rhetorical level, there is a growing appreciation of the AU as a capable actor in conflict resolution, and China has emphasized its willingness to take concrete measures to help Africa reinforce its collective security mechanism. Hence, the PRC has supported the AU in various areas related to peace and security, particularly the African Union Mission in Somalia (AMISOM) and the hybrid UN–AU Mission in Darfur (UNAMID), provided military aid, and conducted several training courses for AU troops and security personnel at the Peace and Security Department in China (Woldemichael 2012, iii).

In the case of AMISOM that was established by the AU in 2007 to replace the IGAD Peace Support Mission to Somalia, China advocated support or even complete takeover of the mission through the UN. 'An important factor behind China's position was that the African Peace and Security Council for a long time had pushed for a UN takeover of the AU mission in Somalia' (Olsen 2015, 8). In terms of direct financial or technical support, China's contribution was rather declarative and included sporadic financial assistance and the contribution of some equipment:[2] in 2009 China provided AMISOM with US$300,000 and added logistic support to the AMISOM contingents from Burundi and Uganda. In 2010, China pledged CN¥30 million for equipment and material, which was paid the following year. The next significant contribution was only in 2015 with a commitment over US$2.2 million for the enhancement of the operational conditions of AMISOM and the building of an arms depot for the Somali National Armed Forces (SNAF). In 2016 China donated again some equipment to AMSIOM and the SNAF including three soup kitchens, sleeping backs, and helmets (Chinese Embassy in Ethiopia 2009; African Union 2015; AMISOM 2017; Dreher et al. 2017). However, in international comparison, China's financial and technical contribution is barely perceptible, the EU, next to the US and the United Kingdom, one of the largest supporters of AMSIOM, has contributed about US$2 billion from 2007–2017 (Williams 2017).

The AU Mission in Sudan established in 2006 received US$3.5 million as a one-time support from China contributing about 0.75 percent to the yearly budget of the mission (Van Hoeymissen 2011, 100; Ayenagbo et al. 2012, 29). While China's support for peacekeeping missions in Sudan continued in the following years, the hybrid character of the UNAMID and the opaque declaration of funding by China does not allow for an estimation of support to the AU.

Even if the total amount China has contributed to these missions seems insignificant compared to other international donors, China's direct support is an acknowledgment of the AU's role as a security actor in Africa, as stated in China's African Policy Paper:

> China supports the positive efforts by the AU and other African regional organizations and African countries concerned to settle regional conflicts and will provide assistance within our own capacity. It will urge the UN Security Council to pay attention to and help resolve regional conflicts in Africa. It will continue its support for and participation in UN peacekeeping operations in Africa.
>
> (State Council 2006)

A decade after this proclamation the different arrangements in the field of security in the context of the China–AU partnership stretch from soft confidence-building measures and preemptive diplomacy to the development of specific conflict solution mechanisms and direct military support.

The security-related dialogue and consulting mechanisms between China and the AU headquarters in Addis Ababa have evolved and several regular exchange formats have been created. Besides the 2008-established strategic dialogue mechanism that deals with 'major international and regional issues of common concern' (MOFA 2011), the AUC is also participating in the Initiative on China–Africa Cooperative Partnership for Peace and Security (ICACPPS), China's regular exchange with the African foreign secretaries (Huang 2011, 264–265; Zhang 2016). China sees the AU as the 'premier pan-African institutional actor in relation to peace and security matters' (Ukeje and Tariku 2018, 304) and is increasingly institutionalizing the relationship with the AUC and deepening the interregional linkages. The China Africa Defense and Security Forum (CADSF) inaugurated in September 2018 in Beijing with delegations from forty-nine African countries and the AU attending is yet another example for the institutionalization (and militarization) of the Sino-African security cooperation. The CADSF, chaired by Hu Changming, head of the international military cooperation office of the People's Liberation Army's (PLA) Central Military Commission discussed regional security and military cooperation and is expected to become a permanent fixture of the Sino-African dialogue structure that could be tied to the tri-annual meeting schedule of the FOCAC summits (Kovrig 2018; Xinhua 2018).

One of the goals of the fifth FOCAC ministerial conference held in Beijing in July 2012, which the AU attended for the first time as a full member, was to strengthen cooperation on African peace and security between China and the AU. The action plan adopted at the conference determined that China would launch the ICACPPS, provide financial support for AU peacekeeping missions in Africa and the development of the African Standby Force (ASF), and train more AU peacekeepers and officials in peace and security affairs. In September 2015, President Xi announced that China would provide free military aid of a total of US$100 million over 4 years to the AU to support the building of the ASF and the African Capacity for Immediate Response to Crisis (Xi 2015). Three months later, at the 2015 FOCAC summit in Johannesburg, China confirmed its commitment to supporting the AU's capacity for peacekeeping and promised an additional US$60 million in grants to the ASF and the African Capacity for the Immediate Response to Crisis (FOCAC 2015). In addition to direct financial and logistic support to AU peace missions, China is also contributing indirectly to the AU's military capacity by tying its bilateral military aid to African countries' contributions to AU missions. Several countries, including South Africa, Tanzania, Nigeria, Burundi, and Uganda, have thus received additional military aid justified by China by their contribution to regional security schemes (Shinn 2008).

The AU has become a major pillar of China's security strategy in Africa, and it seems that despite the mixed results of AU missions in Africa, China will continue its support for regional African security solutions. China has shown its willingness to support regional initiatives in Africa despite other multilateral or even bilateral solutions that might for the time being also serve its interests on the continent. Whether the AU can also establish itself as the premier partner for peace and security and related issues (terrorism, climate change, piracy, migration, to name a few) will depend first and foremost on the ability of the AU to mobilize a broad pan-African consensus on these matters (Ukeje and Tariku 2018, 307).

China's support for the AU and African security in general is not based on any specific program and leaves a great amount of latitude in its long-term commitments (Van Hoeymissen 2011, 100). Technical and financial support often reflects current issues of China's foreign policy priorities or comes in the wake of big events like the FOCAC summit or top-level visits from China. The contribution to the AU mission in Darfur can thus be interpreted as a reaction to international criticism of the close ties between Beijing and Khartoum just as the contribution to AMISOM can be considered as a move to protect international trade routes (Shichor 2007). This flexibility creates some uncertainty on the African side and prevents the reliable long-term inclusion of Chinese support for capacity development in Africa's security sector.

Conclusion

When China formulated its African Policy in 2006, the issue of regional security and fighting international terrorist groups was not of great concern to Beijing, even less it was envisioned that the PLA would play an active fighting role in peacekeeping on the African continent. The evolution of China's role in African security and its gradual convergence towards multilateral and regional security measures is as much influenced by the emergence of new international threats and ad hoc responses to a changing local environment as it is part of a long-term security strategy. Additionally, domestic power shifts, leadership change, and institutional competition between the PLA and civil actors have to be taken into account when analyzing China's evolution from bilateral support to multilateral force protection. The Chinese approach to security in Africa is a combination of reactive and adaptive measures and an elaborate foreign policy strategy with the intent of protecting Chinese interests in Africa but also of shaping future norms in international conflict resolution.

The bilateral approach favored by China for many years is now slowly being replaced by a double-track strategy where regional organizations are gaining importance as a political counterpart in Africa. Conflicts and unstable regimes are endangering the success of Chinese investments in Africa and are forcing China into a more active role in order to protect its interests. The AU as a major actor in conflict resolution and peacebuilding is seen as an instrument for creating a better setting for Chinese investments. Additionally, interregional arrangements are one tool in Beijing's foreign policy kit for allaying the fears of other actors about its proactive international behavior. The notion that 'security ventures should be proposed, agreed and led by Africa' (Large 2016) can be viewed as a concession to the principle of non-interference that in its pure form no longer complies with China's growing need to control political uncertainty in Africa.

Due to structural deficits, a lack of coordination between the different levels and insufficient institutional capacities at the AU level, as well as the preference of African states for national solutions instead of a joint African approach, China has not fully embraced the AU as a cooperation partner in many areas. There are still concerns on the Chinese side as to whether the AU can live up to its claim of regional leadership against the national interests of its member countries and curb the effort to coordinate the implementation of regional projects. On the side of the AU, China's increased recognition as a negotiating partner gives the AU leverage to extend its influence in the region and establish itself as an envoy for Africa's external relations. Therefore, the AU has prioritized the expansion of its cooperation with China in several areas.

Notes

1 Interregionalism as defined by Hänggi (2000) can either refer to relations between regional groupings (pure interregionalism), arrangements where states from different regions participate in an individual capacity (transregionalism), or relations between regional groupings and single powers (hybrid interregionalism). In this chapter interregionalism is synonymous with state-to-region relations.

2 Indirectly, China also supported AMISOM by contributing to the UN support mission to AMISOM (DFS Factsheet 2014).

References

Africa News (2018) *Handful African presidents not attending 2018 FOCAC summit in China*, (www.africanews.com/2018/09/03/handful-african-presidents-not-attending-2018-focac-summit-in-china/), accessed 20 May 2019.

African Union (2015) *The People's Republic of China extends financial support to the African Union Mission in Somalia*, (www.peaceau.org/en/article/the-people-s-republic-of-china-extends-financial-support-to-the-african-union-mission-in-somalia), accessed 19 April 2019.

Alden, C. (2005) *Leveraging the dragon: Toward 'An Africa that can say no'*, (https://yaleglobal.yale.edu/content/leveraging-dragon-toward-africa-can-say-no), accessed 20 May 2019.

Alden, C. (2014) *Seeking security in Africa: China's evolving approach to the African Peace and Security Architecture*, NOREF Report March 2014, Norwegian Peacebuilding Resource Centre, Oslo.

Alden, C., Alao, A., Chun Z. and Barber, L. (eds) (2018) *China and Africa. Building Peace and Security Cooperation on the Continent*, Palgrave Macmillan, Basingstoke.

AMISOM (African Union Mission in Somalia) (2017) *AMISOM hands over part of the Chinese donated equipment to the Somali National Army*, (http://amisom-au.org/2017/05/amisom-hands-over-part-of-the-chinese-donated-equipment-to-the-somali-national-army-sna/), accessed 19 April 2019.

Ayenagbo, K., Njobvu, T., Sossou, J. V. and Tozun, B. K. (2012) 'China's Peacekeeping Operations in Africa: From Unwilling Participation to Responsible Contribution', *African Journal of Political Science and International Relations*, 6(2), 22–32.

Bah, A. B. (2017) 'African Agency in New Humanitarianism and Responsible Governance', in A. B. Bah (ed.) *International Security and Peacebuilding*, Indiana University Press, Bloomington, 148–169.

Barton, B. (2009) 'EU-China, Africa Trichotomy: The Normative Power Concept on the African Continent', *EU-China Observer*, (3), 12–17.

Benabdallah, L. (2015) 'AU-China Peace and Security Cooperation: RECs, CSOs, and Think Tanks for the Win', *African East-Asian Affairs*, (1), 50–75.

Benabdallah, L. (2016) 'China's Peace and Security Strategies in Africa: Building Capacity is Building Peace?', *African Studies Quarterly*, 16(3–4), 17–34.

Cabestan, J. (2018) 'The Case of China's Participation in the UN Mission to Stabilize Mali', *The China Quarterly*, 235, 713–734.

Chen, Z. (2016) 'China and the Responsibility to Protect', *Journal of Contemporary China*, 25(101), 686–707.

China Daily (2018) *Visiting leaders hail success of* FOCAC *summit*, (www.chinadaily.com.cn/a/201809/07/WS5b921208a31033b4f4654d9c.html), accessed 20 May 2019.

China Internet Information Center (2015) *China's second Africa policy paper*, (www.china.org.cn/world/2015-12/05/content_37241677.htm), accessed 20 May 2019.

Chinese Embassy in Ethiopia (2009) *China supports* AMISOM *mission*, (http://et.china-embassy.org/eng/zgxx/zgxw/t531472.htm), accessed 19 April 2019.

DFS Factsheet (2014) *Field support fact sheet, key facts and figures for the United Nations Department of Field Support*, (www.unic.or.jp/files/DFS_Factsheet_Draft_150106.pdf), accessed 20 May 2019.

Dreher, A., Fuchs, A., Parks, B. C., Strange, A. M. and Tierney, M. J. (2017) *Aid, China, and Growth: Evidence from a New Global Development Finance Datatset*, AidData Working Paper no. 46., AidData, Williamsburg.

Ehizuelen, M. M. O. and Abdi, H. O. (2017) 'Sustaining China-Africa Relations: Slotting Africa into China's One Belt, One Road Initiative Makes Economic Sense', *Asian Journal of Comparative Politics*, 3(4), 285–310.

FOCAC (Forum on China–Africa Cooperation) (2000) *Beijing Declaration of the Forum on China–Africa Cooperation*, (www.focac.org/eng/zywx_1/zywj/t606796.htm), accessed 20 May 2019.

FOCAC (Forum on China–Africa Cooperation) (2003) *Forum on China–Africa Cooperation Addis Ababa Action Plan 2004–2006*, (www.focac.org/eng/zywx_1/zywj/t606801.htm), accessed 20 May 2019.

FOCAC (Forum on China–Africa Cooperation) (2006) *Forum on China–Africa Cooperation Beijing Action Plan, 2007–2009*, (www.focac.org/eng/ltda/dscbzjhy/DOC32009/t280369.htm), accessed 20 May 2019.

FOCAC (Forum on China–Africa Cooperation) (2012) *Forum on China–Africa Cooperation Beijing Action Plan, 2013–2015*, (www.focac.org/eng/zywx_1/zywj/t954620.htm), accessed 20 May 2019.

FOCAC (Forum on China–Africa Cooperation) (2015) *Declaration of the Johannesburg Summit of the Forum on China-Africa Cooperation*, (www.focac.org/eng/ltda/dwjbzjjhys_1/hywj/t1327960.htm), accessed 20 May 2019.

FOCAC (Forum on China–Africa Cooperation) (2018a) *Beijing Declaration – toward an even stronger China–Africa community with a shared future*, (www.focac.org/eng/zywx_1/zywj/t1594324.htm), accessed 20 May 2019.

FOCAC (Forum on China–Africa Cooperation) (2018b) *Forum on China–Africa Cooperation Beijing Action Plan, 2019–2021*, (www.focac.org/eng/zywx_1/zywj/t1594297.htm), accessed 20 May 2019.

Fung, C. (2016) *China and the Responsibility to Protect. From Opposition to Advocacy*, Peace Brief no. 205, United States Institute of Peace, Washington, DC.

Hänggi, H. (2000) *Interregionalism: Empirical and Theoretical Perspectives*, paper for the workshop 'Dollars, Democracy and Trade: External Influence on Economic Integration in the Americas', Los Angeles, 18 May.

Huang, C. H. (2011) 'Principles and Praxis of China's Peacekeeping', *International Peacekeeping*, 18(3), 257–270.

Huotari, M., Gaspers, J., Eder, T., Legarda, H. and Mokry, S. (2017) *China's Emergence as a Global Security Actor. Strategies for Europe*, MERICS Papers on China no. 4, Mercator Institute for China Studies, Berlin.

Ikome, F. (2010) 'The Role and Place of the African Union in the Emerging China–Africa Partnership', in A. Harneit-Sievers, S. Marks and S. Naidu (eds) *Chinese and African Perspectives on China in Africa*, Pambazuka Press, Oxford, Cape Town, 201–211.

IOL News (2017) *Ulterior motives behind linking China to Zimbabwe political crisis*, (www.iol.co.za/news/africa/ulterior-motives-behind-linking-china-to-zimbabwe-political-crisis-12083946), accessed 19 April 2019.

Kovrig, M. (2018) *China expands its peace and security footprint in Africa*, (www.crisisgroup.org/asia/north-east-asia/china/china-expands-its-peace-and-security-footprint-africa), accessed 18 April 2019.

Kozyrev, V. (2016) 'Harmonizing 'Responsibility to Protect': China's Vision of a Post-Sovereign World',*International Relations*, 30(3), 328–345.

Large, D. (2016) *China's changing involvement in African security*, (www.friendsofeurope.org/security-europe/chinas-changing-involvement-african-security), accessed 18 April 2019.

MOFA (Ministry of Foreign Affairs of the People's Republic of China) (2011) *China, AU hold the Fourth Strategic Dialogue*, (http://rw.china-embassy.org/eng/gnzyxw/t820459.htm), accessed 20 May 2019.

Mthembu, P. (2016) *Reflecting on the Johannesburg Summit of the Forum on China-Africa Cooperation (FOCAC): Where To from Here?*, Global Insight no. 125, Institute for Global Dialogue, Pretoria.

Olsen, G. R. (2015) *Providing Security in a Liberal World Order: The Only Tool Left for European Union in Africa?*, paper prepared for the EUSA 'Fourteenth Biennial Conference', Boston, 5–7 March.

Paltiel, J. (2007) *The Empire's New Clothes Cultural Particularism and Universal Value in China's Quest for Global Status*, Palgrave Macmillan, London.

Shichor, Y. (2007) 'China's Darfur Policy', *China Brief*, 7(7), 5–8.

Shinn, D. (2008) 'Military and Security Relations: China, Africa, and the Rest of the World', in R. Rotberg (ed.) *China into Africa: Trade, Aid, and Influence*, Brookings Institution, Washington, DC, 155–196.

State Council (2006) *China's African Policy*, (www.gov.cn/misc/2006-01/12/content_156490.htm#1), accessed 18 April 2019.

Taylor, I. (2011) *The Forum on China–Africa Cooperation (FOCAC)*, Routledge, Oxford.

Thomashausen, A. (2010) 'China is Filling the Gap Left by Nepad's Failure', *Independent*, 20 June.

Ukeje, C. and Tariku, Y. (2018) 'Beyond Symbolism: China and the African Union', in C. Alden, A. Alao, Z. Chun and L. Barber (eds) *China in Africa: African Peace and Security*, Palgrave Macmillan, Basingstoke, 289–309.

United Nations (2008) *Security Council fails to adopt sanctions against Zimbabwe as two permanent members cast negative votes*, (www.un.org/press/en/2008/sc9396.doc.htm), accessed 20 May 2019.

UNSC (United Nations Security Council) (2007) *Provisional record of the Security Council*, 5727th meeting, 31 July, New York.

UNSC (United Nations Security Council) (2012) *Provisional record of the Security Council*, 6702nd meeting, 12 January, New York.

van der Putten, F. P. (2015) *China's Evolving Role in Peacekeeping and African Security. The Deployment of Chinese Troops for UN Force Protection in Mali*, Clingendael Report September 2015, Netherlands Institute of International Relations, The Hague.

Van Hoeymissen, S. (2011) 'Regional Organizations in China's Security Strategy for Africa: The Sense of Supporting "African Solutions to African Problems"', *Journal of Current Chinese Affairs*, 40(4), 91–118.

Verhoeven, H. (2016) *From trade partner to custodian of African security: Why China will increasingly intervene in Africa*, (www.friendsofeurope.org/security-europe/trade-partner-custodian-african-security-china-will-increasingly-intervene-africa), accessed 18 April 2019.

Wekesa, B. (2015) *China's Africa Policy 2015: New policy for new circumstances*, (http://africachinareporting.co.za/2015/12/chinas-africa-policy-2015-new-policy-for-new-circumstances/), accessed 20 May 2019.

Williams, P. D. (2017) *Paying for AMISOM: Are politics and bureaucracy undermining the AU's largest peace operation?*, (https://theglobalobservatory.org/2017/01/amisom-african-union-peacekeeping-financing/), accessed 20 May 2019.

Williams, P. D. and Boutellis, A. (2014) 'Partnership Peacekeeping: Challenges and Opportunities in the United Nations–African Union Relationship', *African Affairs*, 113(451), 254–278.

Woldemichael, D. (2012) *Sino-African Union Cooperation in Peace and Security in Africa*, conference report from the ISS Coonference 'Sino-African Union Cooperation in Peace and Security in Africa', Addis Ababa, 22 May.

Xi, J. (2015) *'China is here for peace', remarks by H.E. Xi Jinping President of the People's Republic of China at the United Nations Peacekeeping Summit, 28 September 2015*, (www.fmprc.gov.cn/mfa_eng/wjdt_665385/zyjh_665391/t1302562.shtml), accessed 20 May 2019.

Xi, J. (2017) *Secure a decisive victory in building a moderately prosperous society in all respects and strive for the great success of socialism with Chinese characteristics for a new era*, (www.shine.cn/news/nation/1711136310/), accessed 20 May 2019.

Xinhua (2014) 习近平: 坚持总体国家安全观 **走中国特色国家安全道路** (*Xi Jinping: Adhere to the National Security Concept as a way to National Security with Chinese Characteristics*) (www.xinhuanet.com//politics/2014-04/15/c_1110253910.htm), accessed 20 May 2019.

Xinhua (2018) *China-Africa defense, security forum opens in Beijing*, (http://eng.chinamil.com.cn/view/2018-06/27/content_8071089.htm), accessed 19 April 2019.

Yun, S. (2014) *Xi Jinping's Africa policy: The first year*, (www.brookings.edu/blog/africa-in-focus/2014/04/14/xi-jinpings-africa-policy-the-first-year/), accessed 20 May 2019.

Zhang, C. (2016) *Thinking strategically on China-Africa peace and security*, (www.friendsofeurope.org/security-europe/thinking-strategically-china-africa-peace-security), accessed 19 April 2019.

Zhang, Q. and Kangombe, A. (2016) 'Chinese Investment in Africa: How the New Normal can Leverage Agenda 2063 for Sustainable Economic Co-operation', *African East Asian Affairs*, (3), 62–95.

5 Coping with security challenges in African society

The role of overseas Chinese associations in protecting new Chinese migrants in Africa

Haifang Liu

Introduction

A new wave of Chinese outbound migrants occurred with China's opening-up and reform process. After 1986, thanks to the relaxation of the previously rigid control system that was replaced by a new flexible mobility regime – with the ID card policy – aiming to turn Chinese nationals into 'mobile subjects' (Xiang 2007a), a new tide of Chinese people migrating as individuals arose – including some going to Africa. With the relaxation of the regimentation of its citizens by the Chinese government, the so-called governmental persons – those who had ever traveled to or stayed in Africa as diplomats and implementers of governmental aid projects (in all sectors, ranging from infrastructure, industry, and agriculture to medical service, education, and research) – became the first batch of new Chinese migrants: they either directly quit their positions in public institutions (including state-owned enterprises, SOEs) to start private businesses, or they returned to Africa after finishing their domestic official duties.

Another important source of these new migrants were those coastal city dwellers who could easily smell the business opportunities at hand, as well as the leading fashions. Shanghai people, for example, were very much motivated by the popular words *chu guo* ('going abroad') floating in the air and the 'last-bus sentiment' driving the rush to go somewhere new so as to grab the 'first barrel of gold.' Many of them only took Africa as their middle point between China and the United States or Europe, places that had automatically been more important destinations for these new migrants since the middle of the 1980s (members of the Southern Africa Shanghai Industrial and Commercial Liaison Association (SASICLA) and of the Zimbabwe Chinese Business Association (ZCBA), interviews, August 28, 2014). They only decided to stay in Africa after some years there, with a strong attachment formed to the great climate conditions and rich opportunities (Liu 2018).

According to pioneering scholars' observations, it is very likely that Chinese nationals have scattered in almost every country of Africa following the niche markets that they were able to identify for selling rather affordable Chinese goods to local societies – including in those ones that have not established formal diplomatic relations with China (Park 2009; Li, A. S. 2018). São Tomé and Principe as well as Burkina Faso – two countries that only re-established a diplomatic relationship with China in 2017 and 2018 respectively – are good examples. In the former, a business consulate was established several years ago, while Mainland China has become the largest exporter to the latter since 2005 due to the presence of over 600 Chinese traders there (Li, A. S. 2018).

The unprecedented speed and scale of these new Chinese migrants flooding the whole world have been regarded as symbolic of one significant aspect of 'China's rise' on the international stage in recent years. This is especially true in Africa, where they have been explained as an instrument of the Chinese government for establishing its sphere of influence – or empire, more precisely. This has been termed 'the human activity, migration, that provides the most striking parallels with imperial patterns of the past' (French 2014, 218).[1]

This huge myth came out of a conventional research paradigm approach to China studies, namely the state-centered perspective that suggests the existence of a monolithic China. While French (2014) did gather many individuals' stories, he however somewhat believed that the Chinese government could instrumentalize all these people so as to realize its dream of an empire. To close the research gap on Chinese nationals in Africa, this chapter will take a meso-level perspective to look at those associations self-organized by these new migrants from Mainland China. These associations occupy a position between the state (both the sending and the receiving one) and each individual migrant, and thus examining them provides a basic understanding of this newly emerging migration phenomenon in Africa. This contribution specifically investigates how associations have agency to help the new migrants adapt to the host environments, and to respond to different kinds of complicated security challenge on the ground in respective African countries.

New type of association catalyzed by crisis

Self-organized societies, Chinese-language media, and education provided in Chinese have been widely accepted as 'three pillars' of Chinese communities, indicating their 'maturity' within host societies. In most African countries, only recently have there started to be some public accounts serving the Chinese communities by providing news and necessary information. This is thanks to the latest digital developments and the widespread access to and use of Chinese social media platforms (such as WeChat); there still tends to be lack of education provided in Chinese however (Liu 2018). Diversified societies have become quite common among Chinese migrants in Africa.

Why do people organize themselves in this or that way? There could be many reasons. Kinship, geography (based on both original places and current locations), religion, business, and goods-related relationships – the so-called five bonds – have been used by Chinese scholars to explain why traditionally the overseas Chinese gathered together (Lin 1995). Mutual support has been the number one reason for Chinese migrants collaborating, such as when Johannesburg was emerging as a new city in the late nineteenth century and people started flooding into this 'new gold mountain,' with the Chinese also beginning to move into South Africa. There has been a tradition of organizing associations so as to unite fellow Chinese people, to provide mutual assistance, and to accommodate the new fortune-seekers with basic living needs. Due to the existence of these organizations, 'there has never been a Chinese beggar' in the city proudly noted the leaders of the oldest such Chinese society way back in 1904 (members of the Chinese Association Gauteng, interviews, September 2014).[2] Worldwide, all the old Chinese migrants tended to join either kinship or geographical associations; a typical feature of this kind of older association lay in its function of holding ritual ceremonies. After the end of World War II, the older style of association started to shrink away; now there are few people attending the ones established by their earlier predecessors. There have, however, been mushrooming associations self-organized by the new Chinese migrants wherever they have moved to around the world, including in Africa (Zhang 2018, 14).

For these new Chinese migrants in Africa, the formalization of associations has often been catalyzed by a number of emergent issues. In Zimbabwe, for example, new Chinese migrants first began to move in from the beginning of the 1990s, and since the year 2000 they have increased rapidly to about 10,000 people in number. The aforementioned ZCBA, one such organization of new Chinese immigrants to Africa, was literally born out of the need to survive a particular crisis. The policy was suddenly announced to increase import taxes around 50 to 100 times in 2004 by Zimbabwe Customs, which would bring about serious losses – as more than 300 containers holding goods with a value of US$80 million would be affected. A 'Containers Salvation Committee' was quickly organized among the Chinese community to join hands and rescue their business. First communicating with the Chinese embassy and second working with the media (especially the Chinese media, like Xinhua News Agency), the association started to appeal for its members' rights so as to protect their joint interests. The Zimbabwe government eventually postponed the new policy for 2 months, which gave enough time for the Chinese traders to finish clearing port.

In many of the African countries that the author has investigated, the aforementioned bottom-up approach is a quite common feature of most organic Chinese communities, being catalyzed, as noted, by emergent issues. These pressing problems initiate self-organization into formal associations with clear missions, lead to constitutions to regulate the responsibilities of their president, their governing board, as well as the whole election process, and also generate mutual assistance and a reaching out to society with a clear sense of 'we.' Besides via formal channels, to be able to 'save fellow Chinese' in any emergency that may arise normally means that leadership of the association is given to those who could have or have had a close relationship with the host government. The reaction by the association in the face of an emergency can amount to public marches or protests, as a way to send strong signals about being for or against something. This often takes place in those rather mature Chinese communities like the ones in South Africa, for instance holding public marches against xenophobia in 2015.

The General Chamber of Tanzania Chinese Business (GCTCB) was another such typical case. Facing a rapidly increasing number of household robberies, break-ins by armed people, and also incidents of harassment by immigration officers, the Chinese community in Tanzania – with businessmen playing a leading role – decided to establish an association in 2006 to pressurize the Chinese embassy to on the one hand coordinate with the Tanzanian police force to bring justice, and on the other to request the Tanzanian Immigration Office, Customs and Tax Department to provide an enabling business environment. Since then, the chamber has become an important platform for Chinese businessmen in the country to make their voices heard (GCTCB, interview, July 20, 2014). In 2011 twelve Chinese nationals were killed by robbers in Tanzania; Mrs. Zhu, wife of the then president of the chamber, was robbed and killed; the Chinese community was furious, and the subsequent ceremony of condolence turned into a mass demonstration – with thousands of cars assembled on the road to show the solidarity of the Chinese community. Up until 2014, the time when the research investigation here began, there were over 40,000 Chinese in Tanzania already; with the association's intervention, the acute security challenges that the Chinese community there faced were obviously ameliorated.

There are also less-organized community needs urgently calling for Chinese nationals coming together. For instance, with newly arrived and less-experienced Chinese traders operating in the very busy Kariakoo commercial area of Dar es Salaam – where fierce competition occurs quite often, alongside a growing number of Chinese traders, cheaper Chinese goods, and the products' quality being questioned – significant hatred was aroused among local traders. So much so that, in 2012, the Tanzania Traders' Union started to try to kick Chinese business people out. The Chinese ambassador at the time, Dr. Lv Youqing, encouraged Chinese traders to organize a chamber among themselves to regulate and stimulate their activities – taking the form of the newly established Chinese Chamber of Commerce (CCC). In Kariakoo, the CCC launched 'Quality Month' – one of the most important serial campaigns – to improve the images of both Chinese traders and of Chinese products. In total, over 400 Chinese traders registered in this area, with nearly half of that number joining the new organization. Later interviewed, Ambassador Lv was very proud of the achievement of organizing these 'straggling Chinese traders' together to educate and also to protect themselves; 'in Tanzania there were over 40,000 illegal foreign traders deported in the first half year of 2014, [but] only less than ten Chinese' are involved (Lv Youqing, Chinese Ambassador to Tanzania, interviewed by Ning Er, August 2014).

Associations as daily 'de-territorialized nation-states'

Many associations established in Southern Africa have an obvious identity as a 'Southern African Overseas Chinese Community' due to the erstwhile white regimes' segregation policies in South Africa and Zimbabwe. The Chinese historically often had to play sports only among themselves across the region, instead of with other races from the same colonies. This helped with keeping their 'Chinese-ness,' with China's position as the motherland consequently rising in prominence. This carefully preserved Chinese-ness obviously looms larger as the attachment of the Chinese community to China grows stronger. Indeed, recently these transnational associations have been operating in their mission similar to a homeland outside of the state of origin – as a 'de-territorialized nation-state,' an imagined entity embracing the ethnic Chinese (Kuhn 2009, 367–368). They not only symbolically represent the government that these new Chinese migrants used to belong to, but also function as the most immediate governing body to look after their welfare as well as to help them face difficulties such as robbery, traffic accident, disease, and death.

New Chinese migrants from Mainland China arrived in South Africa in the 1980s, long before the establishment of official diplomatic relations between the two countries. In 1997 the first two associations for new migrants from the Chinese mainland were established, namely the Southern Africa Fujian Overseas Chinese Association (SAFOCA) and the aforementioned SASICLA. Under the guidance of the Overseas Chinese Affairs Office of the State Council, they took part in the preparations for the celebration of the establishment of formal diplomatic relations in 1998 (Si Hai, Chairman of SASICLA, interview, September 5, 2014; Yang Tianchi, Chairman of SAFOCA, interview, September 6, 2014).

Up until now, the two societies – and especially SAFOCA – have continuously worked on behalf of the Chinese government. This they have done to bring together overseas Chinese in South Africa to celebrate China's National Day, Spring Festival, Mid-Autumn Festival, and similar. They have also helped spread news of China's new policies to its expatriates, as well as guided members on how to be good citizens in their host country (Yang Tianchi, Chairman of SAFOCA, interview, September 6, 2014).

Likewise, after the crisis of survival that helped to deliver the birth of its committee, ZCBA was formally established to carry on this special heritage. It strives to protect on a daily basis the interests of all Chinese living in Zimbabwe (regarded as natural members of the association, according to the leader interviewed). Besides educating its members on how to be good citizens, abiding by the law, controlling the quality of their goods, avoiding cut-throat competition, reaching out with helping hands to local society to become more closely connected while respecting native culture and customs, the association also functions as a body to look after all its members regarding security issues (Li Manjuan, General Secretary of ZCBA, interview, January 6, 2019).[3]

In Ghana meanwhile, Chinese formal community building first started in the 1960s. Since the beginning of the 1990s, the number of Chinese there has rapidly increased from less than 1,000 originally to 30,000 by 2010 (Xinhua 2010). The very first association – named the Ghana Chinese Chamber of Commerce (GCCC) – was organized in 1997, a time when the idea of 'Greater China' was looming large. Zhu Yinian from Hong Kong was the first voluntary leader of the

Chinese community in Ghana, and he encouraged Chinese from all backgrounds to stick together. This helped to build up the shared identity of a Chinese community across all traditional divides – old and new, Taiwan, Hong Kong, Mainland China. This is clearly indicated by the origins of the eight batches of leaders: two from Hong Kong, one from Taiwan, and the rest from Mainland China.

As the most trustworthy organization among the Chinese community in Ghana, GCCC provides both shelter and opportunities for any ethnic Chinese newcomer. At the same time, it works to unite the Chinese community so as to protect their common interests – especially if there are urgent situations at hand. From 2012 the Ghanaian government started to react to the swarming in of Chinese traders by chasing them out of local markets, even imprisoning some (Xiao Bo, Vice President of GCCC, interview by Liu Shaonan, August 2014). Like ZCBA in facing its crisis of survival, GCCC immediately reacted by making its voice heard prominently in Ghana. It negotiated on more than ten separate occasions with the Ministry of Commerce and Industry, and ultimately managed to stop this persecution by the Ghanaian government. Regarding illegal Chinese gold miners and the initiatives by the Ghanaian government in 2013, the chamber did not complain however. Rather it donated large amounts of medicine, food, and clothes via the Accra Bureau of Immigration – to be delivered to these imprisoned fellow Chinese (Xiao Bo, Vice President of GCCC, interview by Liu Shaonan, August 2014).

To unify all ethnic Chinese is already to project one common identity to the host country, and to deliberately present a cohesive cultural image – for example through Chinese festivals, martial arts, traditional Chinese medicine, and table tennis training. These have also become pertinent activities for GCCC and for other Chinese associations in other countries too, as part of building up better mutual understanding and winning the hearts of host societies. For China, these associations also play a role as 'resident cultural ambassadors' that aid the promotion of bilateral friendship between peoples at the grassroots level. The Spring Festival, for example, is normally celebrated for such purposes. Since 2005, the year after its establishment, ZCBA has picked up the torch of the old Chinese community and thus renewed this tradition. In Tanzania meanwhile, 'Happy Chinese New Year' is now a brand with 10 years of history behind it (Liu Dong, Cultural Counselor of the Chinese Embassy in Tanzania, interview, July 14, 2010).

Closing gaps between the state and non-state spheres

To exaggerate the role of these Chinese associations is, however, quite risky. To suggest that they perform a role as de-territorialized nation-states requires a proper understanding of the relationship between these associations and the motherland – and the Chinese embassies in particular. Normally – though equally providing consular services to private businesses and individual Chinese nationals abroad alike – Chinese embassies are supposed to directly take on greater leadership, and therefore offer more protection on behalf of the government to Chinese SOEs abroad (Lin Zhiyong, Chinese representative of the business and trade consulate in Tanzania, interview).[4]

How the embassy – and the ambassador in particular – finds ways to close the conventional gap between SOE staff and private businessmen as well as individual small traders, and to act or react on their behalf so as to create a sense of solidarity, is the most important question here. Like in other African countries that have similar challenges of hostile public opinions towards Chinese businesspeople, the Chinese embassy in Tanzania started to offer guidance on how to behave in accordance with the law and how to be good corporate citizens. The establishment of a Chinese Contractors Association, including both private and public construction companies, was encouraged to ensure better coordination and collaboration among those concerned. Later, as part of its efforts to help mitigate cut-throat competition, this association publicized a blacklist intended to drive bad companies out of the Tanzania market, and also directly communicated with the host country to recommend qualified ones to participate in the bidding system for projects.

After 2014 Ambassador Lv started to publicly express his view that 'China's image is the biggest national interest.'[5] Ambassador Lv strongly believes that China's image has been greatly ruined by 'some shameless Chinese in Tanzania,' and this has been among the main reasons for the insecurity that the Chinese community there now faces. For China to have a sustainable presence in Africa, the solution can only be to educate nationals on 'upholding China's fame'; he even publicly warned every Chinese not to expect any protection from the embassy if there is a record of going to the casino to gamble (Lv Youqing, Chinese Ambassador to Tanzania, interview, July 2016).

In the domestic Chinese context, Tanzania by then had only one meaning – namely, the best among the close African friends of China. There was almost no media reportage about those daily complaints regarding the quality of both Chinese goods and Chinese construction projects, or the emerging negative images of China among Tanzanian people – let alone about the fact that similar anti-Chinese sentiment had been seen in many other countries worldwide too (Hess and Aidoo 2014).[6] Thanks to the bravery and the frankness of Ambassador Lv, the downside of this bilateral relationship was finally brought to the Chinese public's attention and a series of measures of public diplomacy followed – such as the launch of the China Global Television Network Africa in Nairobi – targeting the critical issue of African public opinion towards China. At the same time, the importance of making sure that the inclusive benefits of economic cooperation were felt by a wider range of African people was given due recognition by Chinese policy-makers. Chinese leaders advised Chinese companies to encourage 'benevolence' (*ren*) and 'righteousness' (*yi*) before profit; this was seen, for instance, in the remarks that Xi Jinping delivered in 2013 in Tanzania, immediately after he became the president of China (Xi 2014).

Ambassador Lv's concerns about China's image among Tanzanian society, existing within a 'harsh environment,' as well as his benevolent and fatherly way of engaging with and managing both SOEs and the private Chinese community via social organizations is certainly not a common approach shared by Chinese diplomats in other African countries (Lv Youqing, Chinese Ambassador to Tanzania, interview, July 2016). Other ambassadors may not share the understanding of one's image being a security concern, but rather easily take the harshness for granted if they happened to have ever worked in the US or Europe before – where such public opinion struggles have been regarded as quite normal (Yang Youming, Chinese Ambassador to Zambia, interview, December 2018). This necessitates the establishment of certain institutionalized mechanisms between Chinese associations and embassies so as to guarantee communication at the most basic levels, especially given the emerging security challenges. Specifically, given the conventional differentiation between SOEs and the private individual – as well as typical complaints from Chinese migrants in some African countries that they are still in a secondary position as compared to those who work for the Chinese government.

The recent literature has refuted the older discourse of China 'propping up' rogue states in Africa by suggesting instead that, regardless of whether the target country's political regime is authoritarian or democratic, China's overarching strategy is eminently pragmatic, aimed at forging positive working relations (Aidoo and Hess 2015). This is not necessarily an erroneous conclusion, but obviously rather a simplification of the state-centered research paradigm.

Instead of setting a foundational governmental agenda and waiting for people to take up the torch, investigations on the ground often reveal one of two scenarios. First, that Chinese official representatives are firefighters, saving the day after non-governmental actors have made trouble in local contexts – as with the case of Chinese traders in Kariakoo. Or, second, non-government associations of Chinese migrants help diplomats from the motherland to understand the host country better, and sometimes can even bring solutions to a stalemate thanks to their much longer stay and deeper entanglement locally.

In 2000 Ghana's newly elected New Patriotic Party was very unhappy about being previously ignored by the Chinese government, so it refused to accept the letter of credence of the newly appointed Chinese ambassador when he arrived there. Six months later, it was said that GCCC found a channel via which to influence President John Kufuor to finally change this hostile attitude (Xiao Bo, Vice President of GCCC, interview by Liu Shaonan, August 2014). Having been in Ghana for a much longer time, the association's leaders had developed a very good relationship with Ghanaian elites and thus could serve as a bridge for the Chinese embassy to renew diplomatic relations no matter which party came to power. Indeed, as Xiang Biao suggested, 'the movement of people is only part of migration; the movements of documents, money and information, and the enactment of various kinds of social relations and technologies sheds light on how migrations and larger socio-political institutions such as nation-states co-constitute' (Xiang 2007b).

As China ascends to the position of great power globally, and the Chinese government increasingly perfects the regime of emigration management (Xiang

2015), a much more intense trend among these Chinese new migrants has been to internalize the 'national interests' of the remote motherland. This can, for example, be seen from their reaction in organizing donations and sending money back to China whenever there is a significant tragedy like the earthquakes in Sichuan or Qinghai. Another interesting dimension to these new migrants concerns their automatic position to enhance the 'reunification of the motherland' and to reinforce the 'One-China Policy' (Li. A. S. 2018). In January 2017, immediately after South Africa's Solly Msimanga – the newly elected Democratic Alliance (DA) leader and deputy mayor of Tshwane municipal government – traveled to Taiwan, 106 Chinese organizations jointly published an open letter to DA leaders and the mayor of Tshwane requesting a formal apology for this visit (Si Hai, Chairman of SASICLA, interview, January 31, 2017; see also, Molewa 2017). Organizing peaceful marches against xenophobia and participation in Nelson Mandela's funeral ceremony are also types of behavior normalized by these active Chinese associations; a conscious or subconscious sense of intertwined national security, ethnic security, and personal interests is obvious.

Create institutions to deal with security challenges

The dispatching of peacekeepers to many African countries via the United Nations has generated much naïve speculation about China's intention to protect its business interests. However the more prominent role in UN peacekeeping missions arises from the burgeoning of China's international profile instead of from narrow bilateral relations with host countries, even if the latter is often also an accompanying positive outcome hereof (Benabdallah and Large 2018).

When the (Chinese) state (represented by the embassy) fails to immediately respond to an emergency (conflict, violence, robbery, killing, xenophobia attack, etc.), then the Chinese community needs to find more bottom-up approaches. The Chinese Community Police Forum (CPF), innovatively set up by the Chinese community in tandem with the South African police force in 2004, is one such innovation.[7] It took the Chinese CPF's founders a long time to convince the South African police force of the necessity of having such an initiative – one based on the Chinese community being able to help chase out the criminal elements also from within its own ranks (Si Hai, Chairman of SASICLA, and Chen Wenbing, interviews, September 5, 2014).

The mission of the Chinese CPF is to receive calls from the Chinese community on a daily basis, to work together with the local police in tracking down criminals, to provide translation assistance to Chinese victims, and to help the Chinese embassy in offering consular services. Chinese community members, and especially members of the board, jointly pay the necessary administration fees for the forum – covering also the salaries of three professionals hired for overseeing the CPF's operations and services. These board members are often people very successful in terms of their own businesses, and individuals who have already served as leaders in other associations before. The Chinese CPF turned out to be a very effective mechanism, especially in terms of cleaning up the criminal elements within Chinese society in the period of time shortly after its creation (Si Hai, Chairman of SASICLA, and Chen Wenbing, interview, September 5, 2014).

Later on, the widely recognized success of the model would bring branches of the Chinese CPF to all provinces of South Africa;[8] to reward its contributions, the Chinese embassy started to provide some financial support for its operations – to pay for rent and the hiring of staff to man 24-hour hotlines and provide qualified translation services. The mechanism has been introduced in other countries where the Chinese government also feels pressure to provide consular protection to rapidly increasing numbers of its nationals – such as in Angola, Lesotho, and Tanzania, as well as beyond the African continent (like in some European countries).

In other countries, similar security challenges have also arisen and so the Chinese associations there have explored suitable ways to confront these acute pressures. In 2005, after some fellow Chinese continuously suffered from serious attack or being robbed, ZCBA coordinated with the Chinese embassy to pressurize the Zimbabwe Ministry of Security into tracking down the criminals responsible and providing necessary protection to the Chinese community. To work together more directly, a Chinese Desk was set up within the police force to regularly hold meetings with the Chinese community – with the Chinese embassy also in attendance. On the one hand the Chinese community was now able to raise concerns about ad hoc issues to the police, and on the other to receive timely news of Zimbabwe's new laws or regulations.

This two-way conduit mechanism has helped both sides in handling presenting issues, smoothening the relationship as well as solving the security concerns of the Chinese community in Zimbabwe. In 2015, the time when the research investigation there took place, the ZCBA leadership was feeling the limitations of this communication mechanism however, as the new personnel are less responsive than previously; a more efficient mechanism is yet to be born without severe challenges emerging (members of ZCBA, interviews, August 28, 2014). At the same time, thanks to continuous philanthropy efforts vis-à-vis local society by this self-organized association, a better image of Chinese businesses and fewer security challenges have since been witnessed by the Chinese community in Zimbabwe (Li Manjuan, General Secretary of ZCBA, interview, January 2019).

With many Chinese businessmen suddenly flowing into Angola after the peace accord signed in 2002, the Chinese Business Association in Angola – led by Xu Ning, one of the first of a number of Chinese migrants coming to the country in the 1990s – was established. This was done to avoid cut-throat competition among Chinese businessmen, to help regulate Chinese behavior so as to keep the commercial environment healthy and in order, and to protect common interests from unexpected destructive local forces (such as robbery, blackmail). It was also a way to reinforce the whole competitive strength of Chinese businesses confronting an ever-increasing number of competitors from other parts of world, such as the 'dreadful Western African businessmen' (Xu Ning, interview, March 2009).

From the second half of 2014, the Angolan economy, reliant on oil, started to suffer from the commodity's steep fall in price on the global market. With this, the security challenges faced by the Chinese community gradually started to increase as local people began to feel the effects hereof. As members of that community were perceived to travel around with significant amounts of cash in their pockets, they were the first to bear the brunt of national economic decline. As one after another robbery and murder case involving Chinese people took place, the very cautious Chinese official media (like Xinhua News and China Central Television) started to report on the worsening security environment in Angola, where over 200,000 Chinese nationals were faced with a grave situation on the ground. In June of 2016, after testing small-scale joint defense and patrol maneuvers around the most important areas home to frequent Chinese activity, a nationwide Chinese Committee of Joint Defense for Public Security in Angola was established. Its aim is to network and coordinate previously rather fragmented smaller-level patrol and defense associations tackling security issues, and to offer protection to every ethnic Chinese in Angola. The new committee stands for the building up of a holistic safety net for the whole Chinese community in the country, taking on board the advantages of communications as well as anti-crime technologies. This is so as to be able to quickly react to emergencies, and to help one another first before communicating with the Chinese embassy and the Angolan police force regarding further protection (China African Business Council 2016).

At the same time, an institutionalized dialogue forum on security was also officially launched in tandem with the Angolan Ministry of Interior – so as to raise greater awareness among the Angolan government of these issues, leading to them thereafter taking Chinese nationals' security more seriously. As a formal communication mechanism, the Chinese ambassador must attend this forum together with representatives from both the SOEs and private business associations. It is worth mentioning that there is strong solidarity and sincere cooperation between the two, something rarely found in other African countries. Beyond any differentiation between SOEs and private companies, one mechanism that has been built (and proved effective) to help Chinese nationals potentially being robbed or kidnapped as they drive along is the 'safe houses system.' This is an initiative of thirty-five Chinese enterprises voluntarily providing access to their well-equipped mansions and other buildings for any one in need (Chinese in Angola Network 2017). From Zimbabwe to South Africa to Angola, the experiences on the ground make clear that to efficiently face security challenges the Chinese community first requests the creation of institutionalized communication and cooperation mechanisms with the host state. The focus of all these mechanisms highlights effective communication being a prerequisite for further collaboration with host countries.

From the point of view of the *new* Chinese migrants in Africa, there are some inherent characteristics that explain this. First, like their predecessors, they are peaceful migrants coming of their own volition rather than being brought there by government incentives – as was the case with white settlers a century ago; they have a strong transnational character, as they may never claim citizenship or even permanent residence cards of the host countries even if they stay there for many years; they may migrate on to a third country to seek a new market for their businesses or better educational opportunities for their offspring (Li, A. S. 2018).

Second, partially as a phenomenon of globalization from below, the majority of them did not come with large capital reserves but rather started out with only very small businesses. In this way, unlike nationals from other countries, the new Chinese migrants are more exposed to local society, and thus more vulnerable to the envy of people engaging in the same level of business dealings. Third, miscommunication happens on a daily basis due to a lack of basic linguistic skills and cultural understanding – both in the working field of Chinese companies and in other business environments too (Hess and Aidoo 2014).

Conclusion: security management, shifting from state to individual

'Development' has been a concept taking unquestionable priority for a number of decades in China now, and lately its relationship with security has come to fore in the debates among Chinese scholars (see, for example, Li 2019). This of course brings with it another, more important issue: namely, what are the connotations of 'security' in the Chinese context, and how have Chinese perceptions of it been evolving in different spatial and temporal contexts, both domestically and abroad? Specifically, as China's interests seemingly increase in Africa, what are the Chinese views – from official attitudes to those of individual people on the ground – regarding security challenges on that continent? And, how these have been translated into new security cooperation policies moving from the margins to the center in the wide-ranging Chinese government action plans that followed the 2015 Johannesburg Summit of the Forum on China–Africa Cooperation? At the same time, how have the actions and reactions of the Chinese communities living and experiencing security challenges in Africa on a daily basis also contributed to changes in Chinese government policy?

This chapter has sought to capture this emerging trend of giving more attention to security issues related to China–Africa cooperation, and to theorize the role that overseas Chinese associations play in coping with them. As early as 1983, at the first session of the 6th National People's Congress, 'national security' was already mentioned for the first time in the accompanying government report. In the one of the 14th National Congress of the Communist Party of China in 1992 meanwhile, the term was repeated again – there was a lack of precise definition hereof, but it was implicitly equated to 'stability and solidarity' or 'social political security.' This was interpreted by Chinese scholars as a time period when, even though as a dimension of government work the issue had been raised, security was still not regarded as that important when compared to the prioritization of development; the two issues were very much considered separate ones (Li 2019).

It was only in 2006, when the National Defense White Paper was published, that the idea 'to integrate development and security' was included for the first time in an official document. Thereafter, both in the 2007 and 2012 reports, the relevance of the two issues to each other was emphasized – even if security was still regarded as less important, with it merely serving the goal of development. This finally changed in 2014, when the first meeting of the National Security Council was held and security started to be prioritized as a key dimension of government work – and it was hence categorized into eleven kinds thereof in the 'Overall National Security Outlook.'[9]

In the report of the 19th Party Congress (2017), 'to integrate development and security' was even highlighted as the overriding principle of the party in governing the country. For some Chinese scholars, continued focus on political security is, however, still obvious, which as a tradition highlights that unthreatened sovereignty and domestic stability can even be traced back to the Spring and Autumn periods of Chinese history (Wang, J. 2018). The rather recently formalized term 'human security,' circulating since the 1990s as part of a new international focus in Security Studies, has, as one Chinese scholar suggested, caused the debate about human rights versus sovereignty to rage more furiously (Yang 2001). The Chinese government's attitude, similar to that of other developing countries, has been a very cautious one; Algerian President Abdelaziz Bouteflika, for example, gave a speech to the UN General Assembly in 1999 in which he warned that to use human rights to violate sovereignty is dangerous – as the latter is the last line of defense for developing countries used to suffering so much from external intervention (Wang, J. 2018).

To summarize briefly the evolution of the concept of security in China suggests that it is a state-centric view, has a political orientation, came, at least originally, with a lack of understanding of the correlation with development, and that there is an absence herein of individual and social perspectives. However, the philosophy of China – to diagnose the security challenges of the contemporary world, and to address their root cause – also connects to development, as the country has emphasized for so long now that security challenges lie in limited development and that the current international world order needs to 'enlarge the cake' to offer everyone a bigger piece for a better life. This of course would be a state-led solution, even for the individual's development, using a state-mobilization approach – including the Belt and Road Initiative (Benabdallah and Large 2018).

Recently, Chinese scholars have debated extensively the multiple security challenges in Africa and their impacts on long-term China–Africa cooperation. An example is one analysis starting from the 'great retreat of Chinese nationals from Libya,' focusing on current deterrents to high-level economic cooperation there in the form of industrialization, in-depth integration, the stable supply of resources, and investor confidence. The focus is also on distorted public opinion in Libya, as deliberately whipped up by certain Western media outlets (Wang, H. 2018). Beyond terrorism, infectious diseases, and domestic conflicts, the conventional dimensions that Chinese scholars normally focus on as the sources of African security challenges (Liu 2016), Wang Hongyi emphasizes public security as a more pressing challenge – pointing out that African security has deteriorated since the financial crisis of 2008, with rapid demographic increases, urbanization coupling with deindustrialization in some countries, and inequality continuing to grow. Wang makes an important point here, with it being a perspective more reflective of the situation on the ground in Africa as experienced by Chinese nationals there, and particularly the new migrants at the heart of this chapter.

At the same time, there are many Chinese think tanks also acknowledging the pressing threats to public security vis-à-vis Chinese nationals in Africa. Herein they focus on the discourse of the 'need to protect China's overseas interests' so as to appeal to the national government to help address these challenges (Liu 2018),[10] thereby equating nationals' public security with those national interests.[11] This preference for state-centered solutions does not necessarily mean denying rights to individual nationals, but rather is representative of a different mindset in understanding China's presence in Africa – and of the different measures used in terms of necessary interventions when SOEs, in the name of national interests, are put ahead of individuals in priority.

As the author's own investigations in many different African countries have revealed, rarely do the security challenges that the Chinese communities face there come from the state level, nor are they generally caused by the traditional tensions or conflicts between states. Rather, they exist as what the UN has categorized as personal security (physical violence, crime, terrorism, domestic violence, child labor) and community security (interethnic, religious, and other identity-based tensions) issues either directly or indirectly resulting from migration from China to Africa (United Nations Human Security Unit 2009). This chapter has shown that the interests of the Chinese state, as embodied by its embassies, and of individual Chinese migrants having a transnational status do not necessarily clash with each other; on the contrary, in fact, they are even strongly interconnected with each other. As the case of Tanzania reveals, indeed, 'China's image is its biggest national interest,' and each individual is supposed to be responsible for upholding it.

On the ground, we have seen how the state itself often is not the first to respond to this perceived national interest, due to conventional state-oriented thinking and ignorance of 'human security' as connected to the community and personal levels; often the Chinese communities have to organize themselves when faced with pressure. As the process unfolds, the relationship between the state and individual Chinese migrants also becomes dynamic – from one-way hierarchy to two-way mutual reliance, while the lines between state-owned business and private business also blur as a common sense of being Chinese grows stronger. Certainly, in different African countries Chinese association-driven management has encountered varying scenarios and discovered different ways to work with the respective host countries. This diversity is due also to the objective local conditions as well as the heterogeneous interactions between the

Chinese and the African sides across countries. There might be literally a million scenarios possible, and so human creativity is the thing most needed – be it to face security challenges, or anything else besides.

As new Chinese migrants are strangers to African society, largely being traders but also even street vendors and manual laborers, they can easily arouse anger from local people perceiving them as job-stealers. To demonize the Chinese community and spread rumors based on cultural misunderstandings is probably the simplest outlet for local people's anger. It is astounding that Zambian newspaper *Kachepa* published front-page news about Chinese products including canned human flesh in 2016; what should really be asked, though, is why there are a significant number of people who even buy into these kinds of rumors. Even in a society like South Africa, that has been home to ethnic Chinese for over a century now, such negative images still invariably exist. The instinct to combat these unfavorable images has, for example, pushed ZCBA to directly communicate with Zimbabwean local media (such as *Daily News*), so as to dissipate anti-Chinese rumor (such as Chinese labors being prisoners, or exaggerated eating habits). When face-to-face communication fails to convince local media not to relay erroneous information, the ZCBA leadership said that they are ready to bring rumor-spreading media outlets to court for defamation (members of ZCBA, interviews, August 2014). In 2017 the same impulse also drove the old Chinese community of South Africa, the so-called South African-born Chinese, to mobilize against anti-Chinese sentiment in that country, which had been whipped up on local social media platforms in relation to the globally reported Chinese demand for donkey and their 'brutal way of slaughtering animals.' Working in whichever ways necessary to uphold a positive collective image, this battle will be a long one. Chinese associations can serve exactly this purpose, and that on a daily basis, by helping addressing the need

> to stabilize the unease between migrants and the host societies, [being] irreplaceable by other forces either from the sending country or from the hosting country given the composition of these people (predominantly contract laborers and traders), their businesses (penetrating from urban environments into rural areas), and their capacities (linguistically and culturally) to autonomously adapt to different host countries' environments.
>
> (Liu 2018)

To deconstruct the monolithic image of China using its 1 million migrants as an instrument of empire-building, this chapter has revealed instead an often vulnerable Chinese presence in Africa. Further, it has illustrated how representatives of China's state power need to 'downgrade' the traditional concept of security based on national interests to a human-centered perspective, and how Chinese associations as community-grown agency have shown greater innovation in networking with one another to provide mutual assistance to members. These associations also reach out to and engage with local society so as to present a benevolent and positive cultural image of China, as well as to work together with both officials in the motherland and those in host countries to institutionalize mechanisms for dealing with endemic security challenges.

Notes

1 This very politicized 'China-making-Empire-in-Africa' discourse has, according to Li Anshan (Li 2016), been in the air ever since 2005, with Howard French's book (2014) being nothing more than just a summary of this series of empire discourses.
2 The Chinese Association of Gauteng, formerly known as the Transvaal Chinese Association, is the oldest Chinese association, celebrating its 110th anniversary at the time of visit.
3 Li Manjuan was one of the organizers of these subgroups.
4 Lin Zhiyong confirmed that providing only leadership (and therefore also protection) on behalf of the Chinese government to SOEs (and thus not to private businesses) and their staff is a clearly defined mandate (Ning 2014).
5 It is worthwhile to mention that his voice was made heard via an interview with a domestically based Chinese journalist, who was sponsored by a special foundation in China to travel around Tanzania for many days; it was published in the flagship newspaper *Southern Metropolis Daily*. Later this reportage was featured many times elsewhere by different kinds of media. Available online at: http://epaper.oeeee.com/epaper/A/html/2014-07/13/content_3277446.htm, (accessed June 6, 2019).
6 Of course this is not to say that nobody knows anything about the situation on the ground. The author of this chapter, together with a Ghanaian colleague, was entrusted in 2013 by the Joint Research and Exchange Initiative of the Forum on China–Africa Cooperation to conduct an investigation in Ghana, Kenya, Nigeria, and Tanzania on the perceptions of Africans towards Chinese businesses.
7 For further information, please refer to the website of the organization: http://chinesecpf.com/.
8 Ironically, such a mechanism also arouses greater speculation and suspicion – such as when a popular female Kenyan Internet celebrity, Dr. Mumbi Seraki-Boers, even circulated through social media the rumor of China dispatching policemen to all South African provinces to take over sovereignty in a certain way (Seraki-Boers 2018).
9 These categories comprise political, territorial, military, economic, cultural, social, technological, informational, ecological, resource, and nuclear security.
10 In March 2017 a conference co-organized by the Ford Foundation and Chinese African Business Council, focusing on comparative China–US practices in term of their overseas interests' protection in Africa, was attended by high-ranking officials from the Chinese Ministries of Defense and Foreign Affairs, American representatives from think tanks, large Chinese SOEs, and by Chinese bankers.
11 One indicator is to use the search term 'overseas interest protection + Africa' in Peking University's library databases; there are 113 journal or newspaper articles, essays, and academic papers that come up. The majority of these were published after 2008; the Arab Spring of 2011 and China's setbacks in Libya were obvious watershed moments that stimulated heating debates regarding this discourse.

References

Aidoo, R. and Hess, S. (2015) 'Non-Interference 2.0: China's Evolving Foreign Policy towards a Changing Africa', *Journal of Current Chinese Affairs*, 44(1), 107–138.

Benabdallah, L. and Large, D. (2018) 'China's Evolving Security Engagement in Africa', in C. Alden and D. Large (eds) *New Directions in in Africa-China Studies*, Routledge, New York, 312–326.

China African Business Council (2016) *Chinese Joint Committee of Joint Defence for Public Security in Angola formally launched*, (www.qdsabc.com/index.php/post/166), accessed 24 July 2018.

Chinese in Angola Network (2017) *Chinese fellows escaped from being robbed, sheltered by the safety houses under the Joint Committee of Joint Defense for Security System*, (https://mp.weixin.qq.com/s/NQO0pMhx5FZ3FjCTsRkgLQ), accessed 24 January 2019.

French, H. (2014) *The Second Continent of China: How a Million Migrants are Building a New Empire in Africa*, Knopf, New York.

Hess, S. and Aidoo, R. (2014) 'Charting the Roots of Anti-Chinese Populism in Africa: A Comparison of Zambia and Ghana', *Journal of Asian and African Studies*, 49(2), 129–147.

Kuhn, P. (2009) *Chinese among Others: Emigration in Modern Times*, Rowman & Littlefield Publishers, Lanham.

Li, A. S. (2016) 'Chinese Immigrants in International Political Discourse: A Case Study of Africa', *West Asian and African Studies*, 1, 76–97.

Li, A. S. (2018) 'A Second Discussion of Chinese New Migrants: A Case Study of Africa', *Asian and African Studies*, (1), 3–20.

Li, W. (2019) *40 years of reform and opening up: Changes in the relationship between development and security*, (www.toutiao.com/i6649510293032403459/?tt_from=weixin&utm_campaign=client_share&wxshare_count=3&from=timeline×tamp=1548210757&app=news_article&utm_source=weixin&isappinstalled=0&iid=58568812242&utm_medium=toutiao_android&group_id=6649510293032403459&pbid=6647807092592821773), accessed 21 April 2019.

Lin, Q. Y. (1995) 'Five-Bonds Culture and Global Chinese Entrepreneur Network', *Economics Review*, 3, 49–53.

Liu, H. F. (2018) 'Associations as Social Capital of "New Chinese Migrants" in Africa: Empirical Investigations of Ghana, Zimbabwe, Tanzania and South Africa', in S. Cornelissen and Y. Mine (eds) *Migration and Agency in a Globalizing World: Afro-Asian Encounters*, Palgrave Macmillan, London, 69–90.

Liu, Q. (2016) *The latest situation of African security development*, (https://mp.weixin.qq.com/s/ZrNL7VWcMI_DsWtyBiIgGg), accessed 21 April 2019.

Molewa, E. (2017) *Basic lessons in diplomacy – in case the DA is confused over Taipei*, www.businesslive.co.za/bd/opinion/2017-01-16-basic-lessons-in-diplomacy--in-case-the-da-is-confused-over-taipei/, accessed 28 August 2019.

Ning, E. (2014) *Making fortune in Africa, between money and reproaches*, (http://money.163.com/14/0818/15/A3UJJP9600253B0H.html#from=relevant#xwwzy_35_bottomnewskwd), accessed 5 May 2017.

Park, Y. J. (2009) 'Chinese Migration in Africa', Occasional Paper, No.24, China in Africa Project, SAIIA, January, p. 4.

Seraki-Boers, M. (2018) *Chinese colonization of African nations*, (https://tvclip.biz/video/PfDRTg9d8aQ/dr-mumbi-seraki-boers-chinese-colonization-of-african-nations-live.html?nsukey=DjewDChdhONGkW8%2F4TSwsrFMezfEfQ7L6ziA1iyVH6xVEaDwDMwyEyKAVA8poa0jD1LGQm7RC1HW7NX9R0oiHWUoOOpmYMM%2B2zvNKL84R6MmT1O6JfiiZ0jMjWlvJ9elvBS2RlbAFEoxi2Ea7NiRxBDuzktG8GB8%2FApbB%2Fv3V02UvoNtAvWhzOMI9QG3O%2F3XF0Gu%2F79otS0Iw8%2BaGoNPnw%3D%3D), accessed 21 April 2019.

United Nations Human Security Unit (2009), *Human Security in Theory and Practice*, United Nations, New York.

Wang, H. (2018) *The new challenges of African securities*, (https://mp.weixin.qq.com/s/hW3srh6rEruuYKx6mRmq-A), accessed 21 April 2019.

Wang, J. (2018) *The Final Goals of World Politics*, China CITIC Press, Beijing.

Xi, J. (2014), *Keynote remarks on the celebration of 60 anniversary of Five Principles of Peaceful Coexistence*, (http://cpc.people.com.cn/n/2014/0629/c64094-25214154.html), accessed 21 April 2019.

Xiang, B. (2007a) 'The Making of Mobile Subjects: How Migration and Institutional Reform Intersect in Northeast China', *Development*, 50(4), 69–74.

Xiang, B. (2007b) *A New Mobility Regime in the Making: What Does a Mobile China Mean to the World?*, Idées pour Le Debat 10/2017, Institut du developpement durable et des relations internationals, Paris.

Xiang, B. (2015) 'Beyond Methodological Nationalism and Epistemological Behaviouralism: Drawing Illustrations from Migrations within and from China', *Population Space and Place*, 22(7), 669–680.

Xinhua (2010) *Overseas Chinese celebrated lantern festival in Ghana*, (http://news.xinhuanet.com/world/2010-02/28/content_13070448.htm), accessed 1 May 2017.

Yang, C. (2001) 'Sovereignty is the last Protective Screen of Developing Countries', *International Studies*, 2, 1–3.

Zhang, Y. (2018) *Report on Overseas Cantonese Associations' Development*, Jinan University Publishing House, Guangzhou.

6 China's contribution to African governance

Some conceptual thoughts

Christof Hartmann

Economic interests were the starting point of China's more recent outreach into Sub-Saharan Africa. Chinese state companies invested in many African countries, markets were conquered, trade and cooperation agreements were concluded both bilaterally, and since the early 2000s, also multilaterally within the Forum on China Africa Cooperation (FOCAC). Politics seemed to be absent from this massive intervention of Chinese companies and business, but also from the inflow of an estimated 1 million Chinese across the continent (French 2014). This Chinese immigration or the political rights of Chinese within the polities of Africa never became an issue, probably both due to the quite informal migration regimes of many African countries and because the Chinese preferred a more informal accommodation of their interests through personal networks with ruling elites. The dominant 'political' strategy consisted rather in emphasizing 'sovereignty' and in providing almost unconditional support for a given state's 'existing political order, and indeed in many cases for the individual ruler who currently controls it' (Clapham 2008, 365), a strategy that the US and the Soviet Union had used in the past as well, during the Cold War. China was flexible enough to adapt even to the military coups that toppled cooperating governments and to find new arrangements with successor regimes (Holslag 2011).

With growing investments and increasing numbers of uncontrolled migration, and given the precarious authority that some African governments claim over parts of their territory, it was unavoidable that this political strategy could not be effective in actually protecting investments and own citizens. Chinese became objects of terrorist attacks, potential hostages, or victims of violent populist mobilization. Chinese economic investments and activities had to be given up as in Libya or suspended as in South Sudan. Political stability therefore slowly emerged as a key concern of Chinese policy-makers. In the absence of an explicit 'stabilization policy,' China had to modify and stretch its traditional policy stance, especially as instability was increasingly perceived to emanate from transnational sources, such as terrorism, refugee flows, or piracy.

Making sense of the changing rationales or motivations of Chinese policies in Africa, and discussing whether non-interference is still the building block or not, is the task of other chapters in this book. In the following, we will instead turn to the question of how African actors perceive and use the influence of

China within their own countries in their strategies to establish or maintain stable forms of governance. Looking at China–Africa relations from the perspective of African actors situates the argument within the growing debate about African agency, and the first part of the chapter will thus distinguish different ways to conceptualize African agency. In a second step, our discussion of governance within Africa engages with some assumptions from the extant literature, but moves beyond this in distinguishing between different types of governance trajectories, which result in different challenges for external actors. How China fits into these different scenarios and what follows for African agency will be the subject of the final section. The analytical perspective taken is thus drawn from comparative politics, in acknowledging the many differences between African contexts, and in framing China as an external actor among others who becomes relevant in shaping domestic politics.

African agency and extraversion within the China–Africa debate

The massive presence of China on the African continent and the resulting complex web of relationships between different African and Chinese actors have, without any doubt, been major drivers of the new interest in a better understanding of various forms of 'African agency.' A growing number of publications claimed that African agency needs to be considered within the study of relationships between China and Africa, or better between Africa and China. This debate started from the assumption that the first decade of writing about Chinese–African relationships had been heavily shaped by an interest in understanding the rationale and objectives of Chinese foreign policy, or of international competition between China and Western actors over influence on the African continent. Within these dichotomous and mostly normative assessments of China's influence Africans were either seen as beneficiaries of Chinese largesse or as victims of a new wave of 'colonization.' African states, their governments, or its people seemed to matter little for understanding trends, patterns, or lending decisions. Mohan and Lampert (2013) or the volume edited by Gadzala (2015), on the contrary, were interested in understanding how and in what ways African actors were shaping the relations with China.

The debate about African agency had started earlier, with a broader interest in Africa's role within global governance as a site of 'interaction, rather than one-way domination' by powerful external actors (Brown and Harman 2013, 2). This strand of literature was interested in the capacity of African governments to defend their interests in multilateral institutions, and in asking how collective agency might increase the policy space within institutions shaped and dominated by global actors. A different body of literature was instead concerned with 'the ways in which African states leverage their assumed strategic value to major powers – mainly Western states, but also the former USSR and, increasingly, China – to secure resources, influence, or favor which might otherwise be unavailable to them' (Fisher 2018, 6). Bayart (1989) framed the concept of 'extraversion' to describe the active role played by transnational networks of African actors in mobilizing international support for strengthening and consolidating their regimes, but also for supporting specific interests within domestic political competition. According to this radical and controversial hypothesis, African ruling elites consciously employ their dependent relationship with the external world to appropriate resources and authority in order to establish or reinforce their power over domestic competitors. Such strategies of extraversion included the domestic instrumentalization by some African elites of slavery, colonization, development aid, commodity exports, or structural adjustment programs (Bayart 2000). In this literature Agency was focused on securing of short term, strategic goals in a context of structural dependency. Lucy Corkin (2013, see also her Chapter 7 in this book) had been the first, especially within the literature on Africa–China relationships, to link the agency debate to Bayart's concept of extraversion.

Agency came to be defined quite differently in these studies and was applied to vastly different situations ranging from African states driving and reframing key international agendas and norms, to the cynical manipulation of international donors and investors, and to everyday examples of choice, resilience, or resistance (Fisher 2018). While a number of studies used the concept as largely synonymous to influence or power, authors relying on a more explicit definition of the concept, mostly referred to the work by IR scholar Colin Wight.

Wight (1999) started from the assumption that agency combines three dimensions. The first and most constitutive dimension refers to the idea of agency as capacity of doing something intentionally, and based on the exercise of subjective freedom of action, which also means that action is never fully determined by the social environment. At the same time, for Wight, such capacity of meaningful and intentional acting remains embedded in the context from which agency emerges. The second dimension thus refers to the way in which agency 'becomes an agent of something and this something refers to the socio-cultural system into which persons are born and develop' (Wight 1999, 133). It highlights the enabling and constraining factors constituting and shaping the power of agents, and makes clear that 'not all agents are equally placed and positioned' (ibid.) within a given (international) structure. According to Wight, agents are, third, positioned within particular roles such as a diplomat, which do not result from meaningful and intentional acting, but will still empower or constrain their choices. Invocations of agency thus make reference to these three dimensions of roles and subjectivity ultimately shaped by a given social context.

In his seminal discussion of African agency, Brown suggested two main tasks for further research. To analyze the scope of agency in terms of the ability to exercise subjective freedom of action, and to account for the social and political content of that agency with regard to the roles being filled and the social context within which agency arises, that is the identification of those factors that constrain or enable such agency (Brown 2012, 1899). Some studies, which have tackled the argument of African agency vis-à-vis China, have indeed taken up this research agenda.

For Taylor 'agency implies that individuals ("agents") are capable of directing their *structurally formed capabilities* in ways that are imaginative and inventive, for personal or communal advancement' (Taylor 2015, 28; *my emphasis*). Mohan and Lampert (2012, 95) argued that African agency will be critically shaped by national and local circumstances. While not using the concept of Agency, Aidoo and Hess (2015) in their analysis of anti-Chinese populism in Africa, selected a specific aspect of African agency, the growing recognition of different violent or non-violent manifestations of anti-Chinese sentiment. They linked different modalities of African agency to the varying nature of domestic political competition. Within Africa–China relations, the enabling and restricting conditions for agency are thus indeed varied and 'the room for manouver available to African actors is dependent on rather particular configurations of power and interest internationally' (Brown 2012, 1903).

One critical aspect repeatedly highlighted in these debates is the related need to move beyond the earlier emphasis on the agency of states. Wight was very clear in arguing that the state can act only through individual agents (Wight 1999, 127). Taking Agency seriously thus requires to move beyond 'win–win' or 'unequal exchange' in describing Chinese–African interactions. In the light of the 'embeddedness' of mutual political and economic ties' between China and African countries, Mohan and Lambert (2012) asked to move beyond statist, elite dialogues, while Benabdallah and Large claimed that with the increased relevance of Africa's Peace and Security Architecture, 'our conceptualization of Agency should include or even prioritize the activities of regional actors and institutions' (Benabdallah and Large 2019, 315)

The chapter seeks to explain the different patterns of interaction, which have emerged between China and African countries in shaping African governance. It is our contention that systematic differences in governance structures differently shape African agency towards Chinese policies. While we do compare African countries we nevertheless do not analyze the agency of African states, but to the contrary, analyze how different elite actors are likely to engage with China, and make use of their Agency.

China's emergence as a major power on the continent has been a welcomed alternative to Bretton-Woods conditionalities by Western donors. While the vulnerability of African states and likelihood of extraversion strongly varies (Peiffer and Englebert 2012), China's arrival has neither reduced the structural dependence nor the leverage that external actors have over policies. This leverage, however, is a structural feature, and needs to be 'activated.' Different external actors might have different ideas about how to influence domestic politics and economics or they might opt not to interfere.

Given the long history of extraversion, it is however not surprising that Chinese actors (i.e., companies, ambassadors, etc.) are drawn into the domestic power game, as being perceived to be allies of one or the other political party, to favor particular ethnic groups or to assist illegitimate governments to quell 'legitimate' domestic grievances. From the perspective of African ruling elites concerned with maintaining the stability of their governments and regimes or with their own survival at the helm of the state, China is one external actor among others who might directly affect the domestic legitimacy, resource basis and strategic interactions of ruling elites. African actors will thus try to use Chinese influence for their own political advantage even if China claims to keep a low profile in governance matters. Within a context of structural dependency, there is thus space for agency.

Our argument, which will be further elaborated in the next two sections, is that the 'particular configurations of power and interest' which enable and restrict African agency do not only reside in the varying insertion of African economies into the international economic system and the ensuing economic interest which China might have in investment. Agency is also shaped by the regime dynamics within Africa, and the evolution of distinct trajectories of state development over the last three decades, which offer different opportunities for China to engage or to be 'fitted in.'

The diversity of African state and governance trajectories

Many studies dealing with China's non-interference policy seem to suggest that Sub-Saharan Africa is a continent either with authoritarian regimes, which are tired of being exposed to political conditionalities because of human rights violations and non-competitive elections, or with failed states that go through protracted civil wars. Africa then seems to be a combination of Zimbabwe and South Sudan. Ian Taylor, in various publications, has made a strong argument about the African predicament for China. In his view, most African regimes have a decisively neopatrimonial character.

> Of course, in China the party is the government, and the government is the state: there is a blur between the interests of the Communist Party of China (CPC) and the Chinese state. This is the de facto situation in parts of Africa where the interests of the ruling clique are conflated with those of the state. Thus, the concept of politics in China is very similar to that in many African countries, and the Chinese have been accused of personalizing their political engagement with African leaders, hence reifying the extant neo-patrimonial regimes.
>
> (Taylor 2019, 2)

In an earlier statement of this position, Clapham had already argued that China would fit in 'neatly into the familiar patterns of rentier statehood and politics with which Africa's rulers have been accustomed to maintain themselves' (Clapham 2008, 364). Should China's approach to African politics then consist in a strategy of official non-interference coupled with a de facto support of clientelist regimes?

Such descriptions of African politics hardly capture the different political dynamics on the continent. It is true that the major changes in the domestic politics of many African states over the last 25 years have been interpreted as the attempt of astute elites to adapt their domestic regimes to the new democratic Zeitgeist without substantially altering the rules of political participation and competition (Bayart 2000). A controlled and ultimately fictitious 'democratization' would then indeed be an exercise of extraversion, i.e., an attempt to use a democratic rent to strengthen fragile states and the control of specific elite segments over the state and resources. Yet, whatever our understanding of democracy or appropriate instruments of empirical democracy measurements are, few scholars would contest the diversity of political regimes on the continent, which grant basic freedoms, meaningful political participation, and fair political competition to highest offices in quite varying intensity (Gyimah-Boadi 2004; Whitfield and Mustapha 2009; Cheeseman 2015).

There has been a consequent request by many scholars to better reflect this diversity of political trajectories in analyzing China–Africa relationships, as China's engagement would certainly be influenced 'in tone and texture by the recipient country with which it engages' (Dittgen et al. 2016, 2). Mohan and Lampert pointed out that the extant literature had increased their understanding of how China might adapt strategies to suit the particular histories and geographies of the African states with which they engage, but still failed to 'capture the more dynamic interactions between China and a differentiated landscape of African politics' (Mohan and Lampert 2013, 94).

How should we then capture this differentiated landscape of African politics best? One obvious starting point is the nature of the postcolonial state. In some places, former colonizers or white settlers remained in control and built a settler state, based on the denial of citizenship rights to Africans. Where African elites took over power, they still made different decisions regarding how to deal with the colonial past. They could continue with some form of 'indirect rule' by guaranteeing political stability through accepting ethno-regional elites as intermediaries, or they could provide stability through more centralizing institutions such as the construction of strong single parties and/or a national army apparatus (Mamdani 1996; Cooper 2002; Nugent 2002; Young 2012). Strengthening of authoritarian rule was the common denominator, with only single states such as Botswana or Mauritius maintaining their democratic regimes. The different size and location of states, but also their varying economic resource basis (and consequential type of economic interaction with global actors) mattered as well for the specific regime dynamics.

The end of the 1980s and early 1990s represented a critical juncture for the political dynamics on the continent. The settler states came finally to an end. Protracted conflicts maintained through global rivalry as in Mozambique were solved, but the end of the global East–West conflict, which had triggered the militarization of the continent and propped up dictatorships, also further weakened many regimes already stressed by structural adjustment programs imposed by the international financial institutions.

A wave of political protests swept through most of the continent, and many regimes were forced to introduce some elements of political liberalization. Pluralistic elections were held, which led to the defeat of long-ruling incumbent presidents such as Kaunda in Zambia or Kerekou in Benin. Donors started to reorient their aid portfolios and to reward democratically governed countries. While this wave of political liberalization did not alter the economic structure of African countries, the massive increase of economic globalization became possible only in the changed global political environment of the 1990s. The downfall of long-ruling dictators also led to the emergence of protracted domestic violent conflicts in Somalia or the Democratic Republic of Congo (DRC).

With the risk of simplifying a complex variety of developments and leaving out the few cases of collapsed states (Somalia, Central African Republic), I would argue that during this critical juncture three alternative pathways of further political development emerged, and that most African states proved quite stable in following one of these paths.

The political opening led to substantial democratization in some cases, to the strengthening of the rule of law and effective political accountability. Governments in these countries rely on the support of voters, and several parties effectively compete for power. Civil society is not harassed, and there is space for non-state agency. Examples would be Cape Verde, Ghana, Mauritius, Botswana, Namibia, and South Africa (although the latter three have a dominant party, which has never been defeated in elections since independence or the demise of Apartheid). A couple of other states such as Benin or Senegal have also followed the liberal script, introduced and maintained open competition for political office, and respected the autonomy of civil society actors. In the absence of more institutionalized parties and with lower levels of state capacity, democracy and the rule of law seem, however, less institutionalized, as seen in the case of Mali, which had been considered as belonging to this category until the 2012 coup and the ensuing military conflict.

In a second group of countries, democratization might have been the official agenda, but was actually never seriously introduced. Elections are regularly organized but have no importance for deciding who rules the country and how it is ruled. Political stability remains linked to the continuing rent, which is derived from extraction of resources with high demand on the world market, and governance is shaped through clientelistic linkages. In many ways, these regimes try to perpetuate the model of governance, which existed during the single-party era. Examples would be Gabon, Angola, Cameroon, Chad, DRC or South Sudan. Some resource-based states such as Zambia or Nigeria have moved away from the neopatrimonial model, but democratic institutions remain quite fragile.

There is a third and distinct trajectory of state-building, where rebel or armed liberation movements, often with a leftist and populist orientation, took power, and decided to introduce a centralist and autocratic form of government by claiming a superior legitimacy for their state-building project. This legitimacy resulted from the liberation of their countries through armed struggle from colonial rule, Apartheid, or previous corrupt or nefarious regimes. While Rwanda or

Ethiopia seem to be the obvious candidates, Museveni's Uganda was actually the template of this model, which takes up the centralist legacy of the single-party era, but is linked to a strong output-legitimacy and the attempt to steer social and developmental transformation top-down. Museveni had banned political parties for the first 10 years of his government, and built up a participatory but no-party local governance system, allowing him to consolidate his power before more competitive elections were held at some point. Stability in these countries is maintained through the undisputed rule of an often charismatic president who manages to bring together able technocrats within government, but ultimately needs the backing of the military leadership. Non-state actors have very little space for agency. Uganda (as also Zimbabwe) serve as examples that countries that started as developmental-authoritarian states, might in the long run also display characteristics of more neopatrimonial governance (on Zimbabwe see Chapter 12 by Sachikonye in this volume).

From the binary discourse about China's non-intervention policies and Western political conditionalities, one should expect that Western development interventions have been mostly concentrated on those countries that are aligned to the 'liberal script.' But this is far from true. While the international financial institutions such as World Bank or International Monetary Fund, in any case, work with any type of regime, the autocratic developmental states such as Uganda, Rwanda, or Ethiopia have been – against all odds – the primary targets of Western development aid (and military assistance). Development cooperation has also been continued in countries as DRC or South Sudan, to the extent that civil war made this possible at all. In many of the 'neopatrimonial' states, financial investments by Western companies are certainly more important than Official Development Assistance flows, as Western countries remain interested in access to mineral resources (although some of the companies are nowadays Chinese or Malaysian). But generally there are very few cases in Africa where Western donors cut or suspended development funding (such as Zimbabwe), and where it happened it was mostly not related to the nature of the political regime, but to corruption scandals (Malawi, Mozambique).

But what do these different trajectories of political development signify for China's role on the continent? While China defines its African strategy according to geopolitical or economic interests, and might have tackled governance issues so far only as a response to actual crises (military coups, civil war), different African elite segments might have specific interests in engaging with China and different types of interaction are likely to emerge within the three paths outlined.

Neopatrimonial governance

The idea of neopatrimonial governance consists in a fusion of different types of authority where ruling through personalistic and clientelist networks invades a principally rational bureaucratic state based on the application of universalist formal rules (Pitcher et al. 2009). Over time, the dominance of clientelist networks has been complemented by nepotism at the helm of the state with fathers handing over power to their sons or massively recruiting family members to cabinet. Restrictions of this personal rule do not result from rules but from the power of competing actors and networks, and governance in such countries therefore 'is more a matter of seamanship and less one of navigation – that is, staying afloat rather than going somewhere' (Jackson and Rosberg 1982, 18). The stability of elite contracts with the ruler are typically acquired through the joint consumption of the 'national cake,' but as formal rules are bent, might also result in a lot of unpredictable behavior which is a major challenge for international cooperation partners or investors. Chinese actors officially engage with a sovereign state, manifested in flags, borders, or embassies, but these symbols might hide a different form of governance, which follows a different logic.

> This has proven a problem for Beijing as it has attempted to construct coherent, long-term developmental relationships according to its stated foreign policy goals in Africa (although short-term commercial exchanges of mutual benefit to the African elite and Chinese corporations are eminently possible).
>
> (Taylor 2019, 3)

The African agency exercised by the state elites of such neopatrimonial systems will consist in strategies to seek short-term material and other resources to maintain personalistic networks and ultimately the survival of the ruling group. In fact, Bayart (2000) used Cameroon or Gabon as main empirical examples when introducing the concept of extraversion, although by then the reference was to the interaction with Western donors and investors. Corkin (2013) selected Angola for her case study of how African leaders use strategies of extraversion for dealing with Chinese actors. Leaders of neopatrimonial regimes will leverage their main strategic value, the control of resource extraction, to China to secure immediate financial and political advantages. As neopatrimonial leaders are interested in the direct benefits of economic and diplomatic interactions they will not hesitate to arrange barter deals, where the state's income from resource extraction (and accompanying tax income) over several decades are exchanged against short-term infrastructure which might be needed to maintain some minimum level of popular support (Marysee and Geenen 2009). The activities of Chinese construction companies in building presidential palaces or national stadiums might make sense from the perspective of Chinese economic diplomacy, and also be understood as a reference to symbols of state sovereignty. It is however also of direct political benefit to African presidents if the Chinese engagement is not geared towards poverty reduction but to the construction of prestige buildings, which will have no relevance for tackling developmental challenges but might still impress the urban part of the population. Chinese actors might appreciate that negotiations with Congolese leadership over acquisition of mines are held in secrecy, no journalists are asking critical questions, and no space for public debate exists. But Chinese leaders might still have been surprised of being 'accused of seeking to exploit the personalization and informalization that are the hallmarks of politics in many African states' (Taylor 2019, 3).

The even bigger risk from a Chinese perspective is a scenario where African governments lose control over their own territory and population, and Chinese companies might be forced, as happened in the South of Nigeria, to deal with a variety of local actors (traditional authorities or even criminal gangs). The erosion of state monopoly of violence might in some cases be the direct result of external arms supplies, where China occupies a prominent role among the leading global suppliers. The worst scenario, however, happened in South Sudan, where the state broke down entirely and a civil war paralyzed oil production and blocked other related Chinese investments. According to Large, after independence,

> China was engaging a kleptocratic petro-state underpinned by military rule and a national security system, governed by the imperatives of political necessity, not competence. Power lay in the hands of men with guns. The patronage system underpinning the new state was financed by oil (and the prospect of oil revenues).
>
> (Large 2016, 38)

Chinese leadership came to realize that increasing the coercive capacity of the South Sudanese state could not guarantee the security of Chinese investments, as leaders in a neopatrimonial setting will not and cannot have an interest in building up a professional and neutral security apparatus (or a developmental state). While African elites were certainly not involved in developing the new Chinese narrative about developmental peace as a strategy of conflict resolution, they would certainly not disagree, insofar it promises continuing short-term investments in infrastructure even to regimes that might have already lost the control of their populations, without a need to address the root causes of conflict.

The liberal–democratic trajectory

As the broader population and their concerns become important in a democratic state, popular perceptions of the Chinese presence and activities in the country might gain relevance, and it is not only the government or different factions within government but also other actors who will engage with China. In Zambia, opposition parties and candidates built a whole electoral campaign around prevailing anti-Chinese sentiments, unifying an otherwise divided opposition. When Sata had been elected president he was able to make peace with the Chinese government (Aidoo, Chapter 9 in this volume). It seems that Chinese officials still have to learn to deal with such open criticism in the domestic public sphere. Western donors have more routine in being publicly accused of following their own interests; but they have also clearly accepted the uselessness of claiming to be neutral in such an asymmetrical and dependent relationship.

The democratic environment in Ghana offered the spaces for a variety of agents to engage with China. A combination of strong civil society actors and a democratically elected government makes sure that principles of transparency and openness are adhered to in the agreements with China. Advocacy organizations are openly criticizing the terms of planned infrastructure deals with China, including a government-initiated change to a key bill that would allow 70 percent of oil revenues to be used as collateral for infrastructure loans (Chipaike and Bischoff 2018). Trade unions also enforced the implementation of Ghanaian laws allowing trade union activities in large Chinese investment projects such as Bui Dam.

But even ruling elites might face different contextual conditions for exercising their agency as seen in the violent escalation of conflicts about Chinese small-scale miners in Ghana. There is a long-standing tradition of artisanal gold mining in Ghana, called *galamsey*, which is regulated by law, and reserved to Ghanaian citizens, although there have always been a majority of unregistered and some isolated non-Ghanaian miners active. With the hike in global gold prices in the 2000s a massive invasion of several thousand Chinese gold miners occurred, which both led to the introduction of superior and more efficient techniques for alluvial gold mining and to conflicts with the existing group of estimated 250,000 local miners. When these conflicts turned violent from mid-2012 onwards, and after an uproar in the local media about the impossibility of thousands of Chinese miners being active where the law reserves mining for Ghanaians, the government acted, and in May 2013 sent the military into the region to drive out the illegal Chinese miners. Of an estimated up to 50,000, 4,592 Chinese nationals were eventually deported. A quite unusual public intervention of the Chinese ambassador in January 2013 asked the Ghanaian government to 'guide the media,' to cover the Chinese galamsey issue more 'objectively' or risk damaging the 'environment for further development of our bilateral exchanges and co-operation' (Fick 2017).

It is clear that the newly elected Ghanaian president had to reply that China had a responsibility for making sure that its citizens do not breach the laws of the country, although technically, most illegal Chinese miners seem to have benefitted from informal coverage of registered Ghanaian galamseys and traditional chiefs (Crawford and Botchwey 2017). The government had, however, in a parallel move, to negotiate with the Chinese government over the further disbursement of a US$3 billion infrastructure in the gas sector, agreed upon in 2012. While the Ghanaian government had technical reasons to discontinue the loan, it also faced, in the midst of the Galamsey affair, strong popular pressures not to increase further dependence on China. The government eventually agreed with the IMF about a US$1 billion loan to finance part of the initially planned infrastructure projects (Aidoo 2016).

Emulating the Chinese model?

The authoritarian–developmental states should finally represent again a different context for African agency. China becomes the object of particular strategies of extraversion, because some of these leaders perceive their countries as ideologically similar to China, and would claim to actively emulate the Chinese model of political and economic governance (Davies 2008; Fourie 2015). It remains an empirical question for further research to what extent these states have actually tried to emulate the Chinese model (cf. Chapter 8 by Hess in this volume), and to what extent the historical context and frame conditions in most Sub-Saharan African countries make such emulation feasible at all. Typically, their elites should represent the ideal counterparts for China, as one might assume that it is here, and not in the neopatrimonial states, where China finds negotiation partners who share a governance model of strong economic growth with a development-oriented leadership, and high levels of social control and capacity of political repression.

When China came to Africa it seemed not interested in actively selling its own mode of governance to other countries. This would also have contradicted its general position of non-interference in the politics of other countries. Chinese policies were supposed to follow business interests ignoring the regime type in investment and cooperation decisions. More recently, the Chinese leadership under Xi Jinping seems however to be more confident that the Chinese governance model could and should indeed serve as a model for other countries worldwide (Zhao 2017).

The Beijing model is an alternative option of developmental intervention, which has enabled African agency in offering policy-makers the possibility to avoid IMF conditions, or to bargain for a lower level of conditions (Hernandez 2017). But this holds independently of whether regimes have themselves tried to follow the Chinese way. The core question is whether successful emulation of the model can be considered an additional leverage in bargaining with China, especially if the PRC could consider broadcasting it more openly. Threats to regime stability could then be reframed as an attempt to question the Chinese governance model, and even lead to an obligation of China to defend its alternative model of governance in Africa. So far, emulation seems however not to consist in a strategy to garner material support, but rather result from the need to legitimize quite repressive regimes by making reference to the success of China.

Ethiopia is a good example here, insofar as this country, with a huge domestic market but few mineral resources, under the long-term leader Meles Zenawi, early on lobbied for Chinese investment. Zenawi offered Ethiopia as the first African venue for FOCAC (II) in 2003, and following the controversial 2005 elections, openly declared that China offered a more appropriate model for African states to adopt in comparison with the Western liberal–democratic template (Fourie 2015, Hess, Chapter 8 this volume). Robert Mugabe, at one point, proposed to make the learning of Mandarin a compulsory element for all academic programs in Zimbabwe, a policy never implemented (*The Herald* 2015). We might exclude that this reflected pressures from China to do so, and would rather see here as well a manifestation of African agency.

Conclusion

In this chapter an attempt was made to provide a typology of institutional contexts that might shape the agency of African elites in negotiating governance with Chinese actors. The proposition might be considered audacious insofar the Chinese negate to be involved in the political affairs of African countries. Yet, as a long debate about extraversion and agency has shown, within contexts of structural dependency, even a policy of non-interference will be interpreted as a de facto support for specific elite segments in their rivalry with others, or as legitimation of a specific type of state-building. There is plenty of evidence from different cases about how African elites try to make use of different aspects of Chinese presence in Africa to pursue their own interests.

While China's rise has empowered collective African agency, the specific domestic political contexts that shape the possibilities for the exertion of agency vary in line with path-dependent trajectories of regime and state development. The initial question of how African actors perceive and use the influence of China within their own countries in their struggle to establish or maintain stable forms of governance, needs thus to be answered with three different models. In the neopatrimonial model, African elites will rely on traditional strategies of extraversion to secure short-term benefits derived from Chinese infrastructure; in the democratic model, political accountability will create incentives for elected leaders to take into account legitimate or more populist grievances against Chinese living in the country, while in the authoritarian–developmental model, China will serve as a source of emulation and legitimization.

References

Aidoo, R. (2016) 'The Political Economy of Galamsey and Anti-Chinese Sentiment in Ghana', *African Studies Quarterly*, 16 (3–4), 55–72.

Aidoo, R. and Hess, S. (2015) *Charting the Roots of Anti-Chinese Populism*, Springer, Heidelberg.

Bayart, J.-F. (1989) *L'état en Afrique. La politique du ventre*, Fayard, Paris.

Bayart, J-F. (2000) 'Africa in the World: A History of Extraversion', *African Affairs*, 99(935), 217–267.

Benabdallah, L. and Large, D. (2019) 'China and African Security', in C. Alden and D. Large (eds) *New Directions in Africa-China Studies*, Routledge, Abingdon, 312–325.

Brown, W. (2012) 'A Question of Agency: Africa in International Politics', *Third World Quarterly*, 33(10), 1889–1908.

Brown, W. and Harman, S. (2013) 'African Agency in International Politics', in W. Brown and S. Harman (eds) *African Agency in International Politics*, Routledge, Abingdon, 1–15.

Cheeseman, N. (2015) *Democracy in Africa. Successes, Failures, and the Struggle for Political Reform*, Cambridge University Press, Cambridge.

Chipaike, R. and Bischoff, P. H. (2018) 'A Challenge to Conventional Wisdom: Locating Agency in Angola's and Ghana's Economic Engagements with China', *Journal of Asian and African Studies*, 53(7), 1002–1017.

Clapham, C. (2008) 'Fitting China In', in C. Alden, D. Large and R. Soares de Oliveira (eds) *China Returns to Africa: A Rising Power and a Continent Embrace*, Hurst, Columbia, 361–369.

Cooper, F. (2002) *Africa since 1940: The Past of the Present*, Cambridge University Press, Cambridge.

Corkin, L. (2013) *Uncovering African Agency: Angola's Management of China's Credit Lines*, Ashgate, Farnham.

Crawford, G. and Botchwey, G. (2017) 'Conflict, Collusion and Corruption in Small-scale Gold Mining: Chinese Miners and the State in Ghana', *Commonwealth & Comparative Politics*, 55(4), 444–470.

Davies, M. (2008) 'China's Developmental Model Comes to Africa', *Review of African Political Economy*, 35(1), 134–137.

Dittgen, R., Lalbahadur, A., Sidiropoulos, E. and Wu, Y.-S. (2016) *On Becoming A Responsible Great Power: Contextualizing China's Foray into Human Rights and Peace & Security in Africa*, South African Institute of International Affairs, Johannesburg.

Fick, M. (2017) 'Ghana Crackdown on Illegal Gold Mining Inflames Tensions with Beijing', *Financial Times*, 1 May 2017.

Fisher, J. (2018) 'African Agency in International Politics', in N. Cheeseman (ed.) *Oxford Research Encyclopedia of Politics*, Oxford University Press, Oxford.

Fourie, E. (2015) 'China's Example for Meles' Ethiopia: When Development "Models" Land', *The Journal of Modern African Studies*, 53(3), 289–316.

French, H. W. (2014) *China's Second Continent: How a Million Migrants are Building a New Empire in Africa*, Alfred A. Knopf, New York.

Gadzala, A. W. (ed.) (2015) *Africa and China: How Africans and Their Governments are Shaping Relations with China*, Rowman and Littlefield, Lanham.

Gyimah-Boadi, E. (ed.) (2004) *Democratic Reform in Africa. The Quality of Progress*, Lynne Rienner, Boulder.

Hernandez, D. (2017) 'Are "New" Donors Challenging World Bank Conditionality?', *World Development*, 96, 529–549.

Holslag, J. (2011) 'China and the Coups: Coping with Political Instability in Africa', *African Affairs*, 110(440), 367–386.

Jackson, R. H. and Rosberg, C. G. (1982) *Personal Rule in Black Africa*, University of California Press, Berkeley.

Large, D. (2016) 'China and South Sudan's Civil War, 2013–2015', *African Studies Quarterly*, 16(3–4), 35–54.

Mamdani, M. (1996) *Citizen and Subject. Contemporary Africa and the Legacy of Late Colonialism*, Princeton University Press, Princeton.

Marysee, S. and Geenen, S. (2009) 'Win-win or Unequal Exchange? The Case of the Sino-Congolese Cooperation Agreements', *Journal of Modern African Studies*, 47(3), 371–396.

Mohan, G. and Lampert, B. (2013) 'Negotiating China: Reinserting African Agency into China–Africa relations', *African Affairs*, 112(446), 92–110.

Nugent, P. (2002) *Africa Since Independence*, Palgrave Macmillan, London.

Peiffer, C. and Englebert, P. (2012) 'Extraversion, Vulnerability to Donors, and Political Liberalization in Africa', *African Affairs*, 111(444), 355–378.

Pitcher, A., Moran, M. H. and Johnston, M. (2009) 'Rethinking Patrimonialism and Neopatrimonialism in Africa', *African Studies Review*, 52(1), 125–156.

Taylor, I. (2015) 'The Good, the Bad, and the Ugly: Agency-as-Corruption and the Sino-Nigerian Relationship', in A. W. Gadzala (ed.) *Africa and China: How Africans and Their Governments are Shaping Relations with China*, Rowman & Littlefield, Lanham, 27–44.

Taylor, I. (2019) 'China and Political Governance in Africa', in N. Cheeseman (ed.) *Oxford Research Encyclopedia of Politics*, Oxford University Press, Oxford.

The Herald (2015) 'Government Changes Education Syllabus', 11 May 2015, accessed 14 May 2019.

Whitfield, L. and Mustapha, A. R. (eds) (2009) *Turning Points in African Democracy*, James Currey, London.

Wight, C. (1999) 'They Shoot Dead Horses Don't They? Locating Agency in the Agent-Structure Problematique', *European Journal of International Relations*, 5(1), 109– 142.

Young, C. (2012) *The Postcolonial State in Africa. Fifty Years of Independence, 1960–2010*, University of Wisconsin Press, Madison.

Zhao, S. (2017) 'Whither the China Model: Revisiting the Debate', *Journal of Contemporary China*, 26(103), 1–17.

Part II
Case studies

7 Financing regime stability?

The role of Chinese credit lines in post-war Angola

Lucy Corkin

Introduction

In 2004, China Export–Import (China Exim) Bank extended a US$2 billion oil-backed loan to the Angolan government to fund post-war reconstruction.[1] The loan has been extended repeatedly and is widely reported to be several times the original facility ceiling.[2] As I will argue here, the Angolan political elite has used the China Exim Bank credit line to strengthen its hold on power in the critical period immediately following the end of the country's protracted civil conflict, effectively adopting a strategy of 'extraversion,'[3] adapting to Angola's shifting political context in a post-war era. This chapter draws on fieldwork and research conducted between 2006 and 2011, which focused on the years immediately following the cessation of Angola's civil war in 2002, and the phenomenon of relations with China being subverted and utilized as a mechanism to bolster regime stability without Beijing's explicit intention of so doing. The Angolan case of the ruling party Movimento Popular para a Libertação de Angola (MPLA) utilizing relations with China and the subsequent credit lines from Chinese state-owned banks to operationalize a discourse of national reconstruction is explored. The intention of Angolan political elites was to bolster regime legitimacy, presented as political stability.

This chapter begins by tracing the origins of the political class that has dominated Angola's state structures since before the country's independence from Portugal in 1975. Angola's characteristics as a 'strong' weak state are then outlined, examining how this determines regime stability in this context, and the method through which Angola's political elites continue to pursue it – largely the subversion of external relations, among them China. The chapter then briefly outlines the body of public work that the original China Exim Bank loan tranches sought to finance. The chapter concludes by demonstrating how the Angolan political elite channeled China Exim Bank financing into supporting a discourse of national reconstruction that was important in the ruling party's consolidation of political power in the run-up to parliamentary elections in 2008. Finally, the chapter considers how these dynamics have played out in Angola's most recent leadership transition, some 10 years later.

The origins of Angola's ruling political elite

To fully appreciate the interplay between political legitimacy and regime stability, a brief historical context of Angola's political incumbents is required. The consolidation of political power of the MPLA – Angola's de facto[4] ruling party since independence in 1975 – has largely occurred within the context of protracted civil war. The Afro-Portuguese, who continue to be the backbone of the MPLA, have a history of political dominance in Angola pre-dating independence, as outlined by Heywood (2000) and Chabal (2007, 5). The MPLA founding fathers, under the influence of Soviet-style Marxism–Leninism saw themselves as a kind of 'vanguard party' representing the Angolan masses. However, ultimately the MPLA assumed control of the colonial bureaucracy rather than fundamentally transforming it. The structure of the colonial state has remained largely intact by design, retaining the economy's international dependency. A substantial disconnect has emerged and merely widened between the MPLA elite and the proletariat they have claimed to represent.[5]

Such differences were successfully employed by the MPLA's political opponents during the party's early years to prevent the MPLA's appeal from expanding beyond its urban strong hold in Luanda. However, by 1976, the MPLA was in a dominant position by virtue of force and control of Luanda, the country's political and economic capital. This persisted throughout the country's civil war, which raged from the declaration of independence from Portugal in late 1975 until 2002, following the death in combat of Jonas Savimbi, leader of the opposition movement. Claiming the importance of consolidating the country's newly won peace, the MPLA procrastinated until 2008 to hold the promised post-war parliamentary elections, presumably to consolidate political power so as to secure victory at the ballot box (Croese 2013, 2). The 2008 parliamentary elections saw the MPLA win a landslide victory of 191 from 220 parliamentary seats, representing an 87 percent majority. Angola's political reality at this point thus was a deeply entrenched political incumbent whose ability to retain the status quo of power appeared to ensure regime stability, positioned as political stability, in a country newly emerged from protracted civil war.

However, the MPLA, in power since Angola's independence since 1975, has faced constant threats to its monopoly of political power and internal legitimacy, namely: intra-party factionalism, rural resistance within Angola – (galvanized by the movements Frente Nacional de Libertação de Angola (FNLA) and União para a Independência Total de Angola (UNITA) during the civil war) – and intervention from foreign powers. Such challenges to the regime point to weak legitimacy, which in many instances have only been countered by intervention solicited from external actors, further eroding the regime's domestic legitimacy (Clapham 1996, 21). In keeping with this pattern, the ruling MPLA has utilized relations with China and the subsequent credit lines from Chinese state-owned banks to operationalize a discourse of national reconstruction to bolster regime legitimacy, presented as political stability in Angola's post-civil war period. The next section examines dynamics of regime stability in Angola in more detail.

Conceptualizing state strength and regime stability

It is important at this point to note that there is a conceptual difference between 'state' and 'regime'; 'state' defined here as the permanent structures of government and 'regime' as the organization of powers in these structures (Fischer 1990, 428). Angola's political reality is a product of the way the state has been organized and power exercised, hence a function of the regime. However, as demonstrated earlier, the MPLA has been in power since Angola's independence, and the country retained the same head of state from 1979 to 2017. Restricted political participation has led to the growth of an entrenched political elite far removed from the rest of society (Malaquias 2000, 109). In order to preserve its status, the political elite has successfully collapsed the division between the state and their ruling party's regime (Orre 2010, 8). The intertwined nature of state and regime in the context of Angola renders the concepts virtually interchangeable.

Despite the political preponderance of its ruling party, I argue that Angola is a weak state internally because the economic and political power of the elites is dependent on external relations that allow them to cling to a fragile domestic legitimacy. Thus, the management of relations with China, and specifically the credit lines extended by state-owned financial institutions, notably China Exim Bank, have been governed by the executive so as to mitigate the risks inherent in continued political power and to foster regime stability.

Migdal (1988, 4) defines the strong state as having the ability to penetrate society, regulate social relationships, extract resources, and appropriate them. He assesses state strength in the context of the relationship between the state and society and the relative strength of these sets of institutions in comparison to each other (Migdal 1988, 35). In this case, Angola could be construed as a strong state, as the state has a very dominant relationship with society. However, the Angolan presidency uses tactics Migdal (1988, 214) terms the 'politics of survival' in order to retain a grip on power, indicating the very tenuousness of this grip and demonstrating the simultaneous weakness of the regime.

Characterizing Angola as a 'weak state' may seem as being at odds with the argument that the Angolan government displays considerable agency in efforts to consolidate its own internal political position. However, this is perfectly aligned to Clapham's (1985, 42) definition of a weak state, meaning fragile internal political legitimacy – applicable to MPLA. He distinguishes lack of legitimacy from lack of capacity (considered a characteristic of a 'strong state'), pointing out that an inherent feature of the so-called Third World postcolonial state is to be both 'strong' and 'fragile' or weak (Clapham 1985, 39).

Thus, despite the Angolan political elite's outward show of power, the presidency demonstrates several key characteristics of so-called 'weak states' as defined by Migdal (1988, 214) in that former President Dos Santos for almost four decades prioritized regime survival over the growth of the country. The contradiction of Angola displaying at once signs of a strong and weak state has been commented on several times, leading to the description of a 'successful failed state' being liberally applied to Angola (Soares de Oliveira 2007a; Sogge 2009).

Former President Dos Santos, having centralized power around his position and personality over the course of several decades, faced the constant dilemma of balancing political stability and economic growth as described by Migdal (1988, 236). Migdal (1988, 226) argues that political elites' tactics to retain control of political power does not mean that political elites have never had a social or developmental agenda, merely that the imperative to remain in power has superseded any plans for development.

This has a very tangible link to the manner in which external relations are conducted. Retention of political power and recognition hereof by the outside world affords political elites access to state monopoly on economic rents such as international trade, establishment of official exchange rates, and import licenses among others (Clapham 1999, 527). As Kremenyuk (1991, 23) notes, the main currency in international negotiations is sovereignty. Indeed, political elites define their role by brokering internal resources and striking further bargains in the international arena. They thus marshal external support and resources to maintain domestic control through their monopoly of foreign relations (Clapham 1996, 62). Putnam's (1988) concept of 'two-level games' posits that the interplay of both domestic and international factors in dynamic interaction influences international bargaining. This 'dynamic interaction' (Evans 1993, 397) is very much in evidence in terms of the MPLA's (and other Cold War proxies) use of superpower agendas to serve their own domestic needs (Krauss 1993, 291) and is equally valid in Angola's new set of interactions with China. Because the power of the political elites is tied to external relations, domestic and foreign policy are inextricably linked (Clapham 1985, 113). In this way, elites have effectively subverted formal sovereignty as the right of people to govern themselves (accorded African states during decolonization) as a mechanism to maintain internal control (Clapham 1996, 268).

In this manner sovereignty conferred on states gave political elites the right to represent their people and act as intermediaries for them with the international community, regardless of whether the government in question was in fact legitimately representative of the people. Clapham (1999, 530) argues that using sovereignty garnered in this way as an ideology for state power is fragile, dependent as it is on the tacit acceptance of both the international community and that of domestic constituencies. A paucity of internal legitimacy inevitably leads to an overreliance on external legitimacy. This simultaneous dependence on and subversion of external forces is best encapsulated by Bayart's (1993, 74) concept of 'extraversion,' whereby the monopoly of access to foreign influence and capital is used as a tool to maintain internal power.

While the end of the Cold War removed African countries' strategic position vis-à-vis the superpowers, China's commercial challenge to Western interests in Africa has renewed African governments' potential to leverage their position (Taylor 2006, 12). Clapham's (2008, 366) assertion that China will merely become the next in a long line of actors to be channeled by African elites for their own political agendas is particularly true in the case of Angola.

The Angolan political elite, primarily the presidency, has seized the opportunities presented by engagement with China to strengthen and reinforce mechanisms through which it retains power. These mechanisms are those used by weak states engaging in 'survival politics' (Migdal 1988, 214). As Macdonald and Woolcock (2007, 66) argue, national interests are defined by governments that serve their most powerful interests.

As has been alluded to previously, the power structure of the political elite in Angola has to a large extent been defined by former President Dos Santos, who served as head of government for almost four decades. This conforms to the classic case of a political elite as described by Putnam (1976, 22) as a small, autonomous (in that they are not accountable to those at the 'bottom' of the pyramid of power), interlinked, and privileged group with a shared commitment to the political status quo. Their support was vital for the former President Dos Santos' continued political control, both in terms of retaining a monopoly of force (through control of the army) and economic rents (ensuring that all business is linked to his patronage). Thus, legitimacy stems from control of rents for distribution[6] (Chabal and Daloz 1999, 15) and ensures a shared commitment of clients to the system (Putnam 1976, 116). Essentially, Dos Santos typically allowed public services to be used as privileged access to goods for the elite[7] (Ostheimer 2000, 120). As Hibou (1999, 72) notes, this extends to more than just the cessation of public enterprises to private actors. It can include the acquisition, the creation, or the conquest of markets by various means by persons linked to those in power but operating in a personal capacity as has extended to the mechanisms managing the Chinese credit lines. Thus, only a select group had access to the economic gains to be made from the largely Chinese-funded reconstruction process.

As a result of these patronage networks, political and economic power was concentrated into the hands of a select few. Economic opportunity was a function of political access and the elites thus fundamentally relied on Dos Santos, as he was the source of this wealth and power. Their fortunes were bound to his, just as he relied on them for support to remain in power, rendering a classic example of the neopatrimonial state.[8]

It is important to note here that I am not arguing that China Exim Bank loans exclusively propped up the incumbent regime. Rather it is an example of how the ruling party subverted the mechanism to strengthen its hold on power, using a discourse of national (physical) reconstruction to consolidate political stability. Within this context, it is to the China Exim Banks loans and the infrastructure projects they financed that we now turn.

Chinese-funded infrastructure projects

China Exim Bank's role as a significant financier of the Angolan government's Public Investment Program only took shape following the end of the Cold War and the cessations of Angola's own civil conflict. After the death of Jonas Savimbi and the collapse of UNITA armed resistance in 2002, the MPLA government needed to access financing to rebuild the country after the war. The end of the Cold War had lost Angola its earlier geostrategic significance resulting in a lack of interest by the parties that had previously been so involved in Angola's political landscape. President Dos Santos wrote to the International Monetary Fund (IMF) in June 2001 requesting additional assistance following the conclusion of an IMF economic monitoring program (Afrodad 2008, 10). The IMF, however, while prepared to offer loans, was insistent on increased transparency and a macro-economic stabilization policy, aimed at reducing inflation by cutting public expenditure and reducing borrowing. Angola refused to cut back on expensive oil-backed commercial financing which also prevented Luanda from satisfactorily explaining where its oil revenues went[9] (Global Witness 2004, 2011; Bräutigam 2009, 275). Furthermore, under IMF constraints, any large-scale infrastructure reconstruction program would have to wait until Angola had achieved a healthier fiscal situation (Lee and Shalmon 2008, 124).[10] Neither condition was acceptable to Angola, so in 2002 President Dos Santos appealed to China (diplomat, Chinese Ministry of Foreign Affairs, interview, October 28, 2009).[11]

The loans extended by China Exim Bank are targeted specifically towards facilitating public investment in Angola and are officially managed by the Angolan Ministry of Finance (Burke et al. 2007; Vines et al. 2009), specifically the department 'Gabinete de Apoio Técnico' known as GAT,[12] previously under Madalena Ramalho.[13] According to the terms of the loan, Chinese companies are largely contracted to undertake required projects. Although in principle China Exim Bank loans require that all projects that it finances are undertaken by a Chinese company, with a minimum of 50 percent of the procurement value sourced from China, in the Angolan case it was negotiated that 30 percent of contract value was to be allocated to the Angolan private sector, to encourage Angolan participation in the reconstruction process (Corkin 2011b). This was reportedly the maximum concession that China Exim Bank would allow (staff member, Angolan Ministry of Finance, interview, July 6, 2010). Once the projects have been satisfactorily completed, the contractors may present their invoices to the Angolan Ministry of Finance, which then requests China Exim Bank to disburse the funds.

The scope of the projects was wide-ranging, covering the sectors of agriculture, education, health, energy and water provision, transport, and public works. Projects financed in the first two phases of the China Exim Bank disbursements exclusively focused on the construction and rehabilitation of facilities (schools, hospitals and clinics); the provision of equipment (fishing vessels and agricultural equipment), utilities refurbishment (water treatment and grid networks), as well as major arterial road and railway construction.[14]

While an impressive array of infrastructure has been completed since 2004, the execution of these projects has not been without its challenges. The main hurdles are bureaucratic capacity, poor understanding of the operating environment on the part of the Chinese companies, and supply bottlenecks (Corkin 2008). This is unlikely to improve in the short term, although it is expected that contracted Chinese companies will learn to be less ambitious in setting their projected project completion targets. There are also fears that the massive infrastructural spending planned by the government will be misdirected if it is not complemented by capacity-building and training programs to improve Angola's ability to absorb investment of such magnitude. The problem is compounded by the fact that due to a lack of local capacity and short supply, most construction materials, and often the technical expertise, need to be imported (Corkin and Burke 2006, 37; for more details see also Corkin 2011a).

According to a respondent from China Exim Bank, phase I started disbursements in 2005 (US$1 billion); phase II started in 2007 (also US$1 billion), as has largely been disbursed (staff member, China Exim Bank, interview, December 9, 2009). As of December 2008, GAT appears to have thus accounted for most of the first loan package of US$2 billion (phase I and II); with plans drawn up for the US$500 million loan as well as phase III, the first tranche of the US$2 billion loan signed in September 2007.

The discourse of national reconstruction

The arrangement of Chinese financing has in the past been promoted as crucial for rapid national reconstruction, the project of rebuilding the country physically after so many decades of civil war (Corkin 2013, 122). Through the rhetoric of the Angolan government, it took on a political spirit, intended to galvanize nationwide popular support for the regime in Luanda. But as Clapham (1985, 120) notes cynically 'nationalism is not, save in the rhetoric of leaders, the united feeling of a single people.' It is instead the demands put forward by a dominant group within the state. The completion of many of the public works carried out for national reconstruction were timed to coincide with electioneering in 2008 and have gratuitously been used primarily as a campaign drive to combat abysmal service delivery. National (physical) reconstruction was advanced rhetorically as an urgent priority by the Angolan government, not only as a short-term election campaign promise, but also in order to bolster long-term regime legitimacy.

It is important to note that the mechanism through which this reconstruction has been pursued focused only on the projects themselves as constitutive of the physical rebuilding of the country's infrastructure.[15] The Angolan government, while portraying the Chinese credit line as crucial for 'national reconstruction,' has not focused on rebuilding 'soft' infrastructure, such as the requisite concurrent institution- and capacity-building through local participation (Marques de Morais 2011, 70).[16] This averted the rise of independent entrepreneurs operating outside of the central patronage networks and ensured regime and patronage network stability (Bayart 1993, 91).[17] To use Migdal's concept of a balancing act between political stability and economic growth, it is clear that (short-term) political status quo prevailed over the, ironically, more stable political legitimacy that could be cultivated over time through the facilitation of economic growth. A contradictory policy environment ensured that only the politically connected benefitted from the reconstruction process, thus reinforcing the political and economic status quo maintained by patronage.[18] In this way, the political elite adapted the patronage system to serve in peace time, or instrumentalized the post-war environment, as suggested by De Beer and Gamba (2000). This is described by Soares de Oliveira (2007b, 148) as having 'adapted its grip to a peace-time gear.'

With regards to the Angolan government's domestic role in the economy, it is clear that the MPLA government has rhetorically upheld national reconstruction as a priority since the end of the civil war. It was targeted at bolstering the Angolan government's internal legitimacy, particularly in the run-up to legislative elections that were finally held in 2008. However, despite claiming to promote national reconstruction 'for the people,' Angola's population has been kept largely separated from the process. Marques de Morais, one of the MPLA's more outspoken critics in this regard, characterizes the Chinese credit line as a new avenue for elite enrichment under the guise of national reconstruction. Marques de Morais argues:

> [s]uch economic arrangements have insulated the Dos Santos regime from the will of the Angolan people, who remain economically and politically irrelevant. China's new prominence is part of an effort by the ruling elite to keep them that way by excluding society at large from the task of national reconstruction.
>
> (Marques de Morais 2011, 73)

The lack of broad-based participation in the China Exim Bank process, due largely to tied procurement policies and unenforced local quotas (see Corkin 2013, 99–122) means that the implementation of the construction projects has not historically rendered as much benefit to local industries as it could have. The Angolan state has approached national reconstruction rather as a provision of services by a paternalistic government in order to reinforce the government as the source of all public goods. National reconstruction has thus been portrayed as the delivery of a turnkey product rather than an interactive process required to re-establish a connection between the rulers and the ruled. Furthermore, it is increasingly a paid for service, outsourced to foreigners with no provision for Angolans to maintain or even organically expand on what external contractors provide.

In rebuttal, Chinese commentators have pointed out that the onus is not on China to develop Africa; rather this is the responsibility of African governments themselves (Yu 2009). It is unlikely that Angola's development or lack thereof is a result of genuine lack of capacity. It is far more due to a lack of political will and institutions weakened by design. Moreover, I have argued elsewhere (Corkin 2013) that the lack of support for broader-based local participation in the national reconstruction process is a conscious strategy to prevent the creation of economic growth independent of the patronage linkages of the political elite.

Some of the infrastructure projects have had genuine developmental benefits for Angolan citizens.[19] With an eye on the impending national elections, which eventually took place in 2008, the ruling party saw the political dividends of public investment in infrastructure. An Angolan researcher commented that there were many 'hidden motives' (university researcher, Catholic University of Angola, interview, August 28, 2010). As is so often the case in ruling party politics, many of the works were presented as MPLA achievements, rather than government achievements, once again blurring the distinction between the party and the state. This calculated merging of ruling party and state institutions allowed the MPLA to benefit from the successful delivery of such public works. These were particularly important in rural areas where infrastructure was not only sorely needed, but MPLA image required bolstering.

It is important to point out that while I argue that China's engagement with Angola has been a factor in the regime's continued existence, I do not subscribe to the body of literature that asserts that China is actively propping up 'rogue regimes.' To do so is to once again deny agency on the part of the Angolan actors. I conversely argue that Angolan elites have actively developed and structured relations in order to consolidate their position. Nevertheless, the same elites are astute in employing rhetorical language to their own advantage (Chabal and Daloz 1999, 117).[20]

Regime stability and extraversion: placing relations with China in context

Accepting loans from China was politically expedient for the Angolan political elite for two reasons. First, Angola had been experiencing difficulties securing other sources of capital on conditions acceptable to the Dos Santos regime. Particularly since 2005, on the back of stronger oil prices and Angola's debt normalization, Luanda has been approved an increasing number of credit lines from a number of countries as noted above. Aside from the material assistance that China's Exim Bank loans have provided, the provision of funds seems to have acted in part as a kind of financial catalyst for other flows of financing (senior diplomat, Angolan embassy, interview, October 28, 2009).

Second, such developments led to a considerable thawing of relations between Angola and the international financial institutions. Recall that in 2002, negotiations with the IMF had collapsed over the loans' conditionalities, leading Angola to turn to China for financing. It appears that the World Bank has pursued a different approach in order to avoid marginalization by other emerging financiers. The Bank has also been mollified by the Angolan government's policy of debt normalization in an attempt to move away from using oil as collateral for commercial loans. Interestingly, the IMF followed suit and, in 2009, made provisions for a standby loan of US$1.4 billion for Angola. Indeed, far from alienating financial institutions such as IMF and the World Bank as some have claimed (Soares de Oliveira 2007b, 295), one could argue that Angola has actively courted them, in order to balance China's influence in the country. Angola, therefore, despite international concerns, particularly in the context of strengthening China–Angola relations, will strongly resist becoming or being perceived as a client state of any other country and will continue to engage with all international actors. Indeed, Martins (2010, 1) describes Angola as having a 'multi-vector' foreign policy, managing 'to keep a balance of interests regarding foreign intervention in its domestic markets.'

Conclusion

On the domestic front, in the early years following the end of the civil war, China Exim Bank's loans provided the means to begin physical national reconstruction. Aside from its practical necessity following the destruction of the civil war, the MPLA government has utilized Chinese financial assistance to kick-start a state-building process through which the government, controlled by the ruling party, could consolidate political and economic power. It also lent credence to the narrative of national reconstruction employed by the government. This was essential from the perspective of political survival and proved successful, given the MPLA's landslide victory in the legislative elections of 2008. This is what Hodges (2004, 169) calls 'manufactured legitimacy.'

This chapter has demonstrated the political adaptability of the Angolan regime to navigate its internal and external weaknesses with remarkable 'behavioural power' (Habeeb 1988, 34). The leadership transition in 2017, only the second since Angola's independence in 1975, is momentous in the country's political history but not necessarily a break with the past. MPLA presidential successor João Manuel Gonçalves Lourenço, despite being handpicked by his predecessor Dos Santos, has made sweeping political changes early on in his term, most notably removing the former president's daughter and son from prominent positions, respectively chairman of the state-owned oil company Sonangol and Angola's sovereign wealth fund. However, a clear distinction must be made between the dismantling of a predecessor's patronage networks, and fundamental structural reform required to bolster internal regime legitimacy. The beginning of Lourenço's administration has set a promising precedent, but is as yet indistinct in its actions from a new regime seeking to consolidate the position of the ruling clique.

Furthermore, the MPLA government is adept at making incremental changes that do not fundamentally alter the country's political economy. Instead, these 'easy' reforms act as a release valve for potential dissension and obfuscate the actual lack of reform occurring (van de Walle, 2001, 37), what Migdal (1988, 242) calls 'tokenism.' Lourenço's 2017 campaign with its lumbering slogan 'improve what's good and correct what's bad,'[21] may well have merely been the latest example of this. By distancing both himself and the MPLA from the influence of the former first family, he renders Dos Santos an implicit scapegoat,[22] without addressing the more deep-seated political reform required within the party itself.

There is no evidence to suggest that Chinese actors had a hand in the MPLA succession. However, regardless of the Lourenço's domestic policy changes, little looks set to change as regards Luanda's external relations with Beijing and international partners whose influence is sought to counter China's. This balancing act continues in the Lourenço era, having become ever more critical over the last few years, as Angola's need for credit has increased in the context of a low oil price.[23] Within a year of ascending to the presidency, Lourenço has visited China twice,[24] securing an additional US$11 billion credit line from various Chinese institutions (Eisenhammer 2018; Vines 2018). In counterpoint, Angola sold more than US$3 billion in sovereign bonds, and continued to re-engage the IMF over a financial service support program (Vines 2018). Thus, given the MPLA's propensity for optical reforms, it is likely that Lourenço will continue to craft external relations, among them those with China, to prioritize the MPLA regime's political survival over above all else.

Notes

1 'National Reconstruction' refers here to the physical rebuilding of the country's hard infrastructure. Whereas it is acknowledged that the spiritual and psychological rebuilding of a nation that has been at war for decades is critically important, physical reconstruction is the focus of this chapter due to importance placed on it by the ruling party itself to bolster post-war regime legitimacy.

2 The quantum of Chinese debt (albeit not exclusively from China Exim Bank) was reported in *Africa Times* (2018) as US$23 billion.

3 'Extraversion' was first coined by Bayart (1993) who describes the process whereby the monopoly of access to foreign influence and capital is used as a tool to maintain internal power.

4 Although MPLA fought a protracted civil war with rival political movement União para a Independência Total de Angola (UNITA) from 1975 to 2002, the MPLA, controlled the political capital, Luanda, and Angola's oil reserves.

5 This is a well-worn pattern in communist and communist-influenced states as recognized by Putnam (1976, 209) in his comparative study of elites.

6 Cillliers (2000, 5) and De Beer and Gamba (2000), in line with Chabal and Daloz's (1999) concept of the 'instrumentalisation of disorder' argue that prolonging the war in Angola was in fact a calculated agenda to reap more benefits than peace would allow as the lack of accountability in war is not possible during peace time. However, Malaquias (2000, 95) points out that describing Angola as purely a 'resource war' is accurate but overly reductionist.

7 Shaxson (2007, 52) relates how during the war, only politically connected Angolans had access to purchasing US currency at the official rate and then selling it on the black market (twenty times the official rate in early 1994).

8 A full analysis of the nature of the neopatrimonial oil-state is beyond the scope of this work. For in-depth analysis see Hodges (2004), Soares de Oliveira (2007b), and Shaxson (2007).

9 According to Bräutigam (2009, 274), Angola had by the end of the civil war taken out forty-eight commercial oil-backed loans.

10 In fact, according to Bräutigam (2009, 275), Germany 'broke ranks' with the Paris club decision not to lend more money to Angola before its overdue loans were settled. Berlin drew up a debt reduction agreement in 2003 allowing German companies access to Angola's market and the extension of further German export credits.

11 According to one respondent, President Dos Santos had previously studied the rise of China (university professor, interview, August 18, 2010).
12 GAT was created in September 2004 by executive decree specifically to manage the Chinese credit lines (Angop 2004).
13 Madalena Ramalho was, according to a respondent, side-lined from GAT in early 2011 (journalist, interview, February 2, 2010).
14 For full details of the projects approved and scheduled between 2004 and 2008, please refer to Corkin (2013).
15 Soares de Oliveira (2007b, 121) describes the 'privatisation' of oil states whereby essential services and public goods are effectively outsourced to non-governmental organizations or private firms' Corporate Social Responsibility programs. In the case of national reconstruction, a lack of indigenous human resources and industrial inputs have, it could be argued, necessitated the Angolan state 'outsourcing' the national reconstruction projects' financing and implementation to Chinese companies.
16 See also Corkin (2013) which details the projects funded by China Exim Bank and demonstrates that only hard, tangible infrastructure was funded.
17 Soares de Oliveira (2007b, 91) details how Sonangol's expansion into non-oil sectors and services has 'crowded out other entrepreneurs as Sonangol not only commands greater resources, but also demands that international firms form joint ventures with its own subsidiaries, thus making market entry and/or technological transfer opportunities for other fledging Angolan businesses hard to access.'
18 This is an example of elites using the market as a policy instrument in order to accrue policy-generated rents (Staniland 1985, 59). As Bayart (1993, 266) notes, 'networks founded on inequality perpetuate inequality.'
19 According to the African Development Bank, 80 percent of Angola's transport infrastructure was not operational in 2009 (BMI 2009, 6), thus funds directed at remediating this situation were of critical importance.
20 The Angolan government specifically employed a well-oiled public relations campaign throughout the civil war, successfully demonizing Savimbi for the international community, and continually managing to convince an exhausted and marginalized domestic population that the war was 'almost won' for more than a decade (Messiant 2008, 259). The argument is not that Savimbi was unjustifiably vilified, but that he was successfully painted as the villain while the MPLA's own transgressions were left unchecked during the civil war. It thus characterizes Angolan society as suffering from MPLA repression, rather than Savimbi's tyranny (Messiant 2008, 244).
21 Translated from the Portuguese 'Melhorar o que está bem e corrigir o que está mal,' as reported by Voice of America (2017), the slogan appears to be a rare and tacit concession that the ruling party needs to be taken in hand. There are echoes of the Deng Xiaoping era pronouncement that Mao was '70 percent correct and 30 percent wrong' (Kristof 1989).
22 Tellingly, the former president secured a seat on the Council of the Republic, a presidential advisory body whose members enjoy immunity from prosecution (Kazeem 2017), thus precluding any further action against him.
23 Angola's debt burden has increased significantly, estimated to be 71 percent of its gross domestic product, excluding that of parastatal Sonangol (Vines 2018). Bilateral loans from China account for 56 percent of this debt (US$23 billion).
24 Lourenço attended the Forum on China–Africa Co-operation Summit in Beijing in September 2018 and returned for a state visit little more than a month later.

References

Africa Times (2018) *Angola's Lourenço announces $2 billion Chinese loan*, (https://africatimes.com/2018/10/10/lourenco-announces-2-billion-chinese-loan-for-angola/), accessed 4 March 2019.

Afrodad (African Forum and Network on Debt and Development) (2008) *Mapping Chinese Development Assistance in Africa: An Analysis of the experiences of Angola, Mozambique, Zambia and Zimbabwe*, African Forum and Network on Debt and Development, Harare.

Angop (2004) *Criado gabinete de apoio a gestão da linha de crédito com a instituição chinesa*, (www.angonoticias.com/full_headlines.php?id=2331), accessed 29 May 2019.

Bayart, J. F. (1993) *The State of Africa: The Politics of the Belly*, Longman Group UK, London.

BMI (Business Monitor International) (2009) *Angola Infrastructure Report Q2 2009*, March.

Bräutigam, D. (2009) *The Dragon's Gift: The Real Story of China in Africa*, Oxford University Press, Oxford.

Burke, C., Corkin, L. and Tay, N. (2007) *China's Engagement of Africa: Preliminary Scoping of African Case Studies: A Scoping Exercise Evaluating China's Engagement of Six African Case Studies*, Centre for Chinese Studies, Stellenbosch.

Chabal, P. (2007) 'E Pluribus Unum: Transitions in Angola', in P. Chabal and N. Vidal (eds) *Angola: The Weight of History*, Hurst Publishers, London, 1–18.

Chabal, P. and Daloz, J.-P. (1999) *Africa Works: Disorder as a Political Instrument*, James Curry, Oxford.

Cilliers, J. (2000) 'Resource Wars – A New Type of Insurgency', in J. Cilliers and C. Dietrich (eds) *Angola's War Economy: The Role of Oil and Diamonds*, Institute for Security Studies, Pretoria, 1–20.

Clapham, C. (1985) *Third World Politics: An Introduction*, Croom and Helm, London.

Clapham, C. (1996) *Africa and the International System: The Politics of Survival*, Cambridge University Press, Cambridge.

Clapham, C. (1999) 'Sovereignty and the Third World State', *Political Studies*, 47(3), 522–537.

Clapham, C. (2008) 'Fitting China In', in C. Alden, D. Large and R. Soares de Oliveira (eds) *China Returns to Africa: A Superpower and a Continent Embrace*, Hurst Publishers, London, 361–370.

Corkin, L. (2008) *AERC Scoping Exercise on China-Africa Relations: The Case of Angola*, Centre for Chinese Studies, Stellenbosch.

Corkin, L. (2011a) *Chinese Construction Companies in Angola: A Local Linkages Perspective*, Making the Most of Commodities Programme Discussion paper no. 2, University of Cape Town and Open University, Cape Town.

Corkin, L. (2011b) 'Uneasy Allies: China's Evolving Relations with Angola', *Journal of Contemporary African Studies*, 29(2), 169–180.

Corkin, L. (2013) *Uncovering African Agency: Angola's Management of China's Credit Lines*, Ashgate, Farnham.

Corkin, L. and Burke, C. (2006) *China's Interest and Activity in Africa's Construction and Infrastructure Sectors. A Research Undertaking Evaluating China's Involvement in Africa's Construction and Infrastructure Sector Prepared for DFID China*, Centre for Chinese Studies, Stellenbosch.

Croese, S. (2013) *Angola: Chronicle of an Unfulfilled Promise*, Friedrich Ebert Stiftung occasional paper, Friedrich-Ebert-Stiftung, Berlin.

De Beer, H. and Gamba, V. (2000) 'The Arms Dilemma: Resources for Arms or Arms for Resources', in J. Cilliers and C. Dietrich (eds) *Angola's War Economy: The Role of Oil and Diamonds*, Institute for Security Studies, Pretoria, 69–94.

Eisenhammer, S. (2018) *What you need to know about Angola securing a $2 billion infrastructure financing from China*, (www.cnbcafrica.com/news/special-report/2018/10/11/what-you-need-to-know-about-angola-securing-a-2-billion-infrastructure-financing-from-chi%E2%80%A6), accessed 4 March 2019.

Evans, P. (1993) 'Building an Integrative Approach to International and Domestic Politics: Reflections and Projections', in P. Evans, H. K. Jacobson and R. D. Putnam (eds) *Double-edged Diplomacy: International Bargaining and Domestic Politics*, University of California Press, Berkeley, 397–430.

Fischer, R. (1990) 'Review: Rethinking State and Regime: Southern Europe's Transition to Democracy', *World Politics*, 42(3), 422–440.

Global Witness (2004) *Time for Transparency: Coming Clean on Oil, Mining and Gas Revenues*, Global Witness Report March 2004, Washington, DC.

Global Witness (2011) *Oil Revenues in Angola: Much More Information, but Not Enough Transparency*, Global Witness and Open Society Initiative for Southern Africa-Angola, London.

Habeeb, W. (1988) *Power and Tactics in International Negotiation: How Weak Nations Bargain with Strong Nations*, Johns Hopkins University Press, Baltimore.

Heywood, L. (2000) *Contested Power in Angola: 1840s to the Present*, University of Rochester Press, Rochester.

Hibou, B. (1999) 'The "Social Capital" of the State as an Agent of Deception', in J. F. Bayart, S. Ellis and B. Hibou (eds) *The Criminalisation of the State in Africa*, James Curry, Oxford, 69–113.

Hodges, T. (2004) *Angola: Anatomy of an Oil State*, James Curry, London.

Kazeem, Y. (2017) *Africa's richest woman has been fired from Angola's state oil firm by the new president*, (https://qz.com/1130420/africas-richest-woman-has-been-fired-from-angolas-state-oil-firm-by-the-new-president/), accessed 19 April 2019.

Krauss, E. (1993) 'U.S.-Japan Negotiations on Construction and Semiconductors, 1985–1988: Building Friction and Relation-chips', in P. Evans, H. K. Jacobson and R. D. Putnam (eds) *Double-edged Diplomacy: International Bargaining and Domestic Politics*, University of California Press, Berkeley, 265–301.

Kremenyuk, V. A. (1991) 'The Emerging System of International Negotiation', in V. A. Kremenyuk (ed.) *International Negotiation. Analysis, Approaches, Issues*, Jossey-Bass Publishers, San Francisco, 22–39.

Kristof, N. (1989) *Legacy of Mao called 'Great Disaster'*, (www.nytimes.com/1989/02/07/world/legacy-of-mao-called-great-disaster.html), accessed 26 February 2019.

Lee, H. and Shalmon, D. (2008) 'Searching for Oil: China's Oil Strategies in Africa', in R. I. Rotberg (ed.) *China into Africa: Trade, Aid and Influence*, Brookings Institution Press, Washington, DC, 109–136.

Macdonald, K. and Woolcock, S. (2007) 'State Actors in Economic Diplomacy', in N. Bayne and S. Woolcock (eds) *The New Economic Diplomacy: Decision-making and Negotiation in International Economic Relations*, Ashgate, Aldershot, 63–76.

Malaquias, A. (2000) 'Ethnicity and Conflict in Angola: Prospects for Reconciliation', in J. Cilliers and C. Dietrich (eds) *Angola's War Economy: The Role of Oil and Diamonds*, Institute for Security Studies, Pretoria, 95–114.

Marques de Morais, R. (2011) 'The New Imperialism: China in Angola', *World Affairs Journal*, 173(6), 67–74.

Martins, V. (2010) *Keeping Business In and Politics Out: Angola's Multi-vector Foreign Policy*, IPRIS Viewpoints no. 22, Portuguese Institute of International Relations and Security, Lisbon.

Messiant, C. (2008) *L'Angola postcolonial: Guerre et paix sans democratization*, Karthala, Paris.

Migdal, J. S. (1988) *Strong Societies and Weak States*, Princeton University Press, Princeton.

Orre, A. (2010) *Who's to Challenge the Party-State in Angola? Political Space & Opposition in Parties and Civil Society*, paper presented at the CMI and IESE conference 'Election processes, liberation movements and democratic change in Africa', Maputo, 8–11 April.

Ostheimer, A. (2000) 'Aid Agencies: Providers of Essential Resources?', in J. Cilliers and C. Dietrich (eds) *Angola's War Economy: The Role of Oil and Diamonds*, Institute for Security Studies, Pretoria, 115–140.

Putnam, R. D. (1976) *The Comparative Study of Political Elites*, Prentice Hall, Englewood Cliffs.

Putnam, R. D. (1988) 'Diplomacy and Domestic Politics: The Logic of Two-level Games', *International Organization*, 42(3), 427–460.

Shaxson, N. (2007) *Poisoned Wells: The Dirty Politics of African Oil*, Palgrave Macmillan, New York.

Soares de Oliveira, R. (2007a) 'Business Success, Angola-style: Post-colonial Politics and the Rise and Rise of Sonangol' *Journal of Modern African Studies*, 45(4), 595–619.

Soares de Oliveira, R. (2007b) *Oil and Politics in the Gulf of Guinea*, Hurst Publishers, London.

Sogge, D. (2009) *Angola: 'Failed' yet 'Successful'*, FRIDE Working Paper no. 81, Fundación par alas Relaciones Internacionales y el Diálogo Exterior, Madrid.

Staniland, M. (1985) *What is Political Economy: A Study of Social Theory and Underdevelopment*, Yale University Press, New Haven.

Taylor, I. (2006) *China and Africa: Engagement and Compromise*, Routledge, London.

van de Walle, N. (2001) *African Economies and the Politics of Permanent Crisis*, Cambridge University Press, Cambridge.

Vines, A. (2018) *Lourenço's first year: Angola's transitional politics*, (https://mg.co.za/article/2018-09-26-lourencos-first-year-angolas-transitional-politics), accessed 14 November 2018.

Vines, A., Wong, L., Weimer, M. and Campos, I. (2009) *Thirst for African Oil: Asian National Oil Companies in Nigeria and Angola*, Chatham House Report, Royal Institute of International Affairs, London.

Voice of America (2017) *João Lourenço: 'Melhorar o que está bem e corrigir o que está mal'*, (www.voaportugues.com/a/joao-lourenco-melhorar-o-que-esta-bem-corrigir-mal/4017873.html), accessed 26 February 2019.

Yu, V. (2009) *China Outbound: Investing in Africa and Latin America*, presentation at American Chamber of Commerce Event, Shanghai, 16 September.

8 The role of China and asymmetric bargaining in Ethiopia's authoritarian backsliding

Steve Hess

Introduction

Scholars and activists have warned of an extended 'democratic recession' that has taken place since the year 2006 (Diamond 2015, 141–155). Diamond (2015) contends that this trend is driven by an overall increased rate of democratic breakdown, a decline in the stability and quality of democracy in 'swing states' such as Turkey, Thailand, Venezuela, and Ethiopia, the strengthening of authoritarianism in large and powerful states such as Russia and China, and a weakening and loss of confidence in powerful Western democracies such as the United States, Britain, and France (Diamond 2015, 143–153).

Nancy Bermeo (2016) defines backsliding as 'the state-led debilitation or elimination of any of the political institutions that sustain an existing democracy' (Bermeo 2016, 5). However, Dresden and Howard (2015), note that backsliding frequently occurs not only in genuine democracies but in hybrid regimes, where the competitiveness of elections are already limited by restrictions that favor ruling parties over the opposition (Dresden and Howard 2015, 1–2). In such regimes – too often deterministically cast as regimes 'in transition' to democracy (Diamond 2002, 23) – incumbent leaders make the strategic choice to bring about 'a decrease in the competitiveness (or potential for competitiveness) of the electoral playing field due to increasing concentration of power in the hands of the incumbent executive, relative to other actors' (Dresden and Howard 2015, 2). Because backsliding involves a degree of political risk and could trigger international condemnations and sanctions, reputational losses, and/or elite or popular backlashes, incumbents are unlikely to engage in this activity if their interests are adequately served by the political status quo (Dresden and Howard 2015, 10).

The following chapter thus investigates the question of why incumbent executives engage in backsliding behaviors, namely the weakening of formal constraints on executive power, tilting of the electoral playing field in favor of the incumbent party, and erosion of civil liberties, particularly limits on free speech and assembly (Levitsky and Way 2010, 5–16; Dresden and Howard 2015, 5–10; Bermeo 2016, 10–14). Previous research suggests that authoritarian backsliding is driven by shifts in the international environment, namely the weakening linkage and leverage of powerful democratic states relative to authoritarian 'black knights,' and domestic changes – either a rapid economic decline that weakens the position of an incumbent and threatens his or her discretionary control of the economy or the growing strength of the opposition relative to the incumbent regime (Huntington 1991, 17–18; Levitsky and Way 2010, 17–23; Dresden and Howard 2015, 11–12).

To investigate forces driving authoritarian backsliding, this chapter presents a case study of post-Derg Ethiopia (1991 to the present), giving particular attention to the country's intensifying relationships with China. Ethiopia itself represents an important case of examination. It has a hybrid political regime characterized by nominally democratic but flawed elections and civil liberties protections and a fluid, often uneven political playing field. Ethiopia stands as Sub-Saharan Africa's second most populous country and has had one of Sub-Saharan Africa's fastest growing economies over the last decade (World Bank 2017, 20). In a more global context, Ethiopia represents a test case for how larger shifts in the international environment influence the political development of regimes in the developing world. Scholars including Bunce and Wolchik (2009, 99–100) and Levitsky and Way (2010, 40–46) have described how democratizing pressure from powerful Western states and institutions in the late Cold War and post-Cold War era has contributed to the breakdown of autocratic regimes as well as liberalizing reforms within hybrid regimes. Conversely, counterhegemonic powers such as the Soviet Union/Russia and, more recently, China have served to counter Western democratizing pressure with diplomatic, economic and political support (Levitsky and Way 2010, 41). Considering the well-documented expansion of Chinese influence across Sub-Saharan Africa over the last decade, more research is needed to examine how and when Beijing's engagement may be impacting political development within its African partner states.

Ethiopia offers an excellent vantage point to observe the local impact of a contemporary international order characterized by power contestation between established, status quo players such as the United States and its Western allies and increasingly assertive revisionist powers such as China. Ethiopia is Africa's leading recipient of Official Development Assistance (ODA) from the Organization for Economic Co-operation and Development (OECD) Development Assistance Committee (DAC), receiving US$3.23 billion in 2015, and is also the second-largest recipient of infrastructure financing from China on the continent (Bräutigam and Hwang 2017; OECD 2017). Moreover, Ethiopia has long-established trade linkages to Western powers in Europe and the United States, which have more recently been supplanted by rapidly intensifying links to China and other Global South trading partners (Simoes and Hidalgo 2017). Finally, Ethiopia's strategic location on the Horn of Africa has led to deepened security relationships with both the United States and China. The United States has valued Ethiopia's partnership in counterterrorism efforts against al-Shabaab, its contributions to regional United Nations (UN) peacekeeping missions, and its role in stabilizing civil conflict in South Sudan (Obama and Hailemariam 2015). China has also prioritized its security relations with Ethiopia, providing military assistance, deploying peacekeepers to UN missions in neighboring South Sudan and Darfur, and in the interest of protecting valuable sea lanes along the Gulf of Aden, establishing its first overseas military base in neighboring Djibouti (along with American, French, and Japanese facilities) (United Nations 2016; Ministry of National Defense of the People's Republic of China 2017). In short, Ethiopia is a country with established economic and security connections to democratizing powers, the United States and Europe, that has increasingly deepened its ties to a counterhegemonic power in China.

The following case study finds that Chinese engagement has had a significant, if complex, impact on Ethiopia's political development. During the 1990s and early 2000s, the Ethiopian People's Revolutionary Democratic Front (EPRDF) maintained an effective monopoly on political power. But seeking Western trade and development assistance, its leadership implemented liberalizing reforms that opened the political system to greater political competition. However, as Chinese trade and assistance came to complement Ethiopia's foreign economic relations in the early 2000s, this change deleveraged Western donors and reduced democratizing pressure on the EPRDF. In its asymmetrical negotiations with strong Western powers, Ethiopia's leadership thus 'borrowed power' from China (Zartman 1997), using the new availability of alternative trade and assistance to improve its bargaining position. Thus, when Ethiopia faced harsh international criticism in the wake of its hotly contested 2005 national elections, this borrowed power helped enable it to weather the storm and resist Western pressure. Moreover, recent research has indicated that after the 2005 elections, Meles Zenawi and other leading officials in Ethiopia 'engaged in a conscious and voluntary attempt to emulate aspects of China's perceived developmental successes' now perceiving that China provided an alternative and possibly superior developmental pathway than that provided by advanced liberal democracies (Fourie 2015, 289).

Of course, China's appearance as an alternative governance model and source of foreign assistance seems to have worked in cooperation with other factors in deleveraging Western influence, namely Ethiopia's important role as a regional security bulwark. Deteriorating regional stability and security in the Horn of Africa increased Ethiopia's importance as a regional security ally to Western partners, creating competing foreign policy objectives. The country's repositioning as a bastion of regional stability and contributor to counterterrorism operations, only further weakened Western pressure on the country to advance liberalizing reforms. The EPRDF leadership, realizing its increasingly crucial security role, calculated (correctly) that Western partners could not afford to deny it military and development assistance needed to stabilize the regime and combat terrorism, meaning they would ultimately overlook backsliding actions and crackdowns on the political opposition. Consequently, when the ruling party was challenged by a relatively better organized political opposition in the 2005 national elections, the regime responded by publicly confronting now deleveraged Western partners and rapidly closing the political system through backsliding actions. This culminated in the emergence of a de facto single-party autocracy in 2010 and 2015 elections. The case suggests that Chinese influence can have an impact on the political development of its African partner states, but this impact is compounded by other factors, such as the competing foreign policy objectives of Western powers, which deleverages their democratizing pressure, and the strength of the local political opposition, which motivates incumbent executives to gamble on backsliding actions designed to preserve their grip on power.

Backsliding in Ethiopia

After the fall of the Derg in 1991, the EPRDF established a legal framework for a multiparty democratic system but faced little organized competition in the parliamentary elections of 1995 and 2000 (Arriola 2008, 118). Opposition parties boycotted the 1995 elections and, in 2000, fielded candidates in only half of Ethiopia's electoral districts. However, prior to 2005 elections, Ethiopian opposition parties formed two competing opposition coalitions: the Coalition for Unity and Democracy (CUD) and the United Ethiopian Democratic Forces (UEDF). During the 2005 parliamentary elections, the CUD and UEDF aggressively campaigned against the EPRDF, ultimately winning a combined 174 of 547 seats in parliament. After the results were announced, the opposition parties accused the EPRDF of stealing the election through widespread vote rigging and organized large anti-government demonstrations. The government responded by violently dispersing protests, arresting tens of thousands of demonstrators and opposition activists, and suppressing civil society organizations (Abbink 2006, 176).

In local elections in 2008 and national elections in 2010, the EPRDF rolled back the 'unprecedented level of openness ... observed' in the run-up to the 2005 parliamentary contest (Aalen and Tronvoll 2008, 112). The CUD and most other splinter opposition parties faced recurrent intimidation, harassment, and restrictions on their ability to run candidates and ultimately refused to participate in the 2008 local elections (Aalen and Tronvoll 2008, 112–117). In the run-up to the 2010 national contest, the EPRDF used arrests, surveillance, intimidation, and legal restrictions to silence opposition party organizations and activists, critical non-governmental organizations (NGOs), independent election monitors, and independent media outlets. Moreover, government offices and public resources were used to aggressively support EPRDF candidates and churn out pro-regime voters. Ultimately, these efforts proved effective. Voter turnout was reported at 93.4 percent, and the EPRDF won a Soviet-style 99.6 percent of the seats in the parliament (Tronvoll 2011, 121–122). With unchallenged authority at the local and national level, an electoral playing field severely tilted towards the ruling party, and heavy restrictions on opposition forces and independent civil society, the EPRDF had effectively 'reestablish[ed] the one-party state' (Tronvoll 2011).

Sino-Ethiopian relations

Since the inception of the EPRDF regime in 1991, Ethiopia has expanded and deepened its relationship with China. Soon after coming to power, Ethiopia's Meles Zenawi aggressively courted Western powers, particularly the United States, and international financial institutions for development aid and assistance needed to rebuild the country's damaged infrastructure and address its underdeveloped economy. This effort proved successful, as the total ODA received by Ethiopia exceeded US$1 billion (in current US dollars) from 1991 to 1994, making Ethiopia one of the world's leading recipients of foreign ODA at the time (World Bank 2018).

As early as 1995, officials in Ethiopia's leadership circles began to express concern with the country's overdependence on Western donors and trade partners, which had begun to place pressure on Ethiopia to improve its human rights record and implement democratizing reforms (DOS 1996). In the face of such pressures, Meles had agreed to partially adopt political and economic reforms requested by Western donor states. At the same time, he maneuvered to maintain his control over a party-state riddled by ethnic and factional divisions (Fourie 2015, 297). In an attempt to maintain the unity of the EPRDF and prevent the outbreak of new ethnic wars, Meles backed the establishment of Ethiopia as a multiethnic federal state, in which recognized ethnic groups or 'nationalities' would enjoy regional self-determination and self-government, even the constitutional right to secession (Aalen 2006, 243). Despite these efforts, the EPRDF struggled with serious factional and ethnic disunity within the party structure. The Tigray People's Liberation Front (TPLF), of which Meles was a member, continued to dominate positions of power within EPRDF coalition, leading many non-Tigrayan members of the EPRDF and opposition parties to worry that the state was favoring Tigrayans and giving them a disproportionate share of national power and resources. Additionally, Ethiopia continued to function in practice as a centralized single-party state, meaning non-Tigrayan ethnic groups and nationalities saw little benefit from the 'federal bargain' promised in the state's constitutional framework, which presumably would have guaranteed a greater degree of autonomy for the regions (Aalen 2006, 250). Meles also struggled to balance the need to implement liberalizing economic and political reforms expected of Western donor states, which would in many respects decentralize economic and political power, with the demands of regime 'hardliners' based in Meles-own Tigrayan ethnic group, who for practical and ideological reasons sought to maintain centralized political and economic power in the hands of the TPLF. When Meles advanced a program named 'tedahiso' ('renewal') in 2001 designed to drive the EPRDF towards greater economic and political liberalization, hardliners resisted. He overcame this challenge by accusing leading hardliners of corruption and purging them from the party, enabling him to at least ostensibly continue to push for liberalizing reforms (Fourie 2015, 297–298). Such internal tensions encouraged Meles and his supporters to prioritize the issue of the country's overreliance on Western donors. This led the EPRDF leadership to adopt a hedging strategy – seeking to deepen its relations with non-Western 'emerging donors,' such as China and Russia, and secure alternative sources of assistance (Adem 2012, 145).

Ethiopia and China's emerging relationship was formalized in a series of high-level exchanges between Addis Ababa and Beijing, with Prime Minister Meles traveling to China in October 1995 and Chinese President Jiang Zemin visiting Ethiopia in early 1996 (Cabestan 2012, 54). In 2003, Ethiopia hosted the second meeting of the Forum on China–Africa Cooperation (FOCAC) – a Beijing-sponsored platform designed to facilitate dialogue between China and African partners across the continent (Taylor 2011). At this point, Meles Zenawi established himself as a critical ally in China's effort to deepen its relations across Africa, resulting in Ethiopia receiving particular attention from Beijing in its effort to expand its economic and political reach across the continent. However, as revealed in Fourie's interviews with EPRDF officials, while Meles did see China as a valuable source of economic and political support in the early 2000s, he did not at the time view China as offering an alternative governance model that might be emulated until around the year 2005 (Fourie 2015, 298).

After Ethiopia hosted the second FOCAC forum in 2003, high-level exchanges between Beijing and Addis Ababa became near annual occurrences, and in 2012, Beijing financed and constructed a new African Union (AU) headquarters in Addis Ababa (Cabestan 2012, 54). During this time period, Ethiopia has become one of Africa's leading recipients of Chinese infrastructure financing. Bräutigam and Hwang (2017) estimated that Ethiopia received US$12.3 billion from 2000 to 2014 – second only to oil-rich Angola (US$21.2) among African nations. These funds and more recent loans have been used to finance a number of high-profile projects developed by Chinese construction firms, including the Tekeze, Halele Werabesa, and Gibe IV (Omo River) hydroelectric dam projects, Addis Ababa-Djibouti railway line, the Addis Ababa metro rail system, and more than two-thirds of the country's roads, including the Addis Ababa ring road (Farquharson 2017).

Over the last two decades, Ethiopia has experienced the rapid expansion of its total trade and the deepening of its economic linkages markets to East Asia, South Asia, and the Middle East. In 1995, Ethiopia received US$1.42 billion in imports and exported US$538 million in goods. At the time, only 2 percent of imports (US$30.5 million) came from China and only 0.0019 percent (US$579,000) of goods were exported to China. Ethiopia's primary imports came from Europe (50 percent) and North America (13 percent) and a majority of its exports went to Europe (57 percent). By 2014, Ethiopia's trade relations had changed dramatically. Now, 25 percent of Ethiopia's imports came from China, 45 percent from Western, Southern, and Southeast Asia, and only 19 percent came from Europe and 3 percent from North America. In terms of its exports, 14 percent went to East Asia with 10 percent to China alone, 40 percent went to Western, Southern, and Southeastern Asia, 21 percent went to other African countries, and only 19 percent went to Europe (Simoes and

Hidalgo 2017). These figures indicate that Ethiopia has undergone substantial economic development and also increasingly redirected its trade relations away from Western, first world markets to Asian and African markets in the Global South.

According to both official Ethiopian sources and outside sources, Chinese companies have contributed substantially to addressing Ethiopia's infrastructure deficit by constructing roads, railways, and telecommunications projects at a fast pace at very affordable prices, allowing previously isolated Ethiopian consumers and producers to access global markets (Foster et al. 2008, 8). The arrival of Chinese loans and Chinese-constructed infrastructure has in fact coincided with an increase in Ethiopia's economic growth. The country has achieved annual growth rates in its per capita gross domestic product averaging 7.96 percent from 2004 to 2015 (World Bank 2018).

China and backsliding

In the elections of 2005, often understood as a watershed moment in Ethiopia's post-Derg political transition, the EPRDF faced the strongest opposition challenge against its rule. Two opposition coalitions, the CUD and UEDF, actively competed in the election, seizing nearly a third of the seats in parliament. After the election, the two opposition parties alleged voter fraud and organized mass anti-government demonstrations. The EPRDF responded with a violent police crackdown that killed nearly 200 people (BBC News 2006). The European Union (EU), one of Ethiopia's leading sources of development assistance and trade at the time, issued a report condemning widespread human rights violations in the post-election crackdown and announcing that the election fell short of international standards (Vasagar 2005). Meles Zenawi publicly confronted the EU criticism, stating, 'We shall in the coming days and weeks see what we can do to expose the pack of lies and innuendoes that characterize the garbage in this report' (Vasagar 2005). He also went on to question the value of maintaining the country's relationship with the EU and receiving its development assistance remarking, 'What the implications of this will be in terms of relations between Ethiopia and the European Union, we will have to wait and see but I don't think you will be surprised if Ethiopia were to insist that it should not be patronized' (Vasagar 2005).

While many Western donor states criticized the election violence and symbolically suspended assistance to Ethiopia, Chinese Prime Minister Wen Jiabao issued a message of congratulations to Meles shortly after his election victory (*Ethiopian Herald* 2005). In August 2005, a few months after Ethiopia's turbulent general election, Chinese Lieutenant General Zhu Wenquan met Prime Minister Meles and announced, 'Ethiopia and China shall forge mutual cooperation in military training, exchange of military technologies, and peacekeeping missions, among others' (Cabestan 2012, 54). Beijing also provided equipment and training to help the EPRDF establish a system run by Ethiopia's Information Network Security Agency to surveil Internet activity for content critical of the regime and jam uncensored TV and radio signals from the independent Ethiopian Satellite Station, Voice of America, and Deutsche Welle (Addis Neger 2010; ESAT 2011). Additionally, China's Exim Bank extended a US$1.5 billion loan to Ethiopia for the Chinese firm, Zhong Xing Telecommunication Equipment, to establish a national mobile phone network (Yewondwossen 2008; Bräutigam and Hwang 2017). China's total trade with Ethiopia also grew from US$543 million in 2005 to US$692 million in 2006 (Simoes and Hidalgo 2017).

This intensification of Ethiopia's relationship with China alongside the Meles administration's public defiance against Western partners in the wake of the controversial 2005 election, suggests that China may have served as a 'black knight' (Levitsky and Way 2010, 41) in Ethiopia's political development. By offering Ethiopia growing political and economic support at a time in which it was facing intense scrutiny from Western states for its repression of political opponents, Beijing helped Ethiopia establish leverage against international pressure to adhere to democratic norms of governance and constrain its use of force against opposition actors. As noted in a growing literature on asymmetric bargaining in the field of international relations (Lobell et al. 2015; Womack 2016; Long 2017), weaker states or 'hypopowers' such as Ethiopia can often overcome their deficiencies in power relative to 'preponderant powers' such as the United States, the European Union or China, enabling them to enhance their autonomy as they pursue their particular interests (Long 2017, 144–147).

In their interactions with China and Western powers, Meles and his successors have played a multiple-level game. They have bargained internationally with Western powers and China. Consistent with Putnam's (1988) 'two-level game' framework, they have also simultaneously bargained with influential domestic actors in an 'intra-national' or domestic game. In Ethiopia, the bargaining position of Meles and his successors was impacted by three factors commonly discussed in the bargaining literature: patience, outside options, and domestic constraints (Oh 2018, 538–540). During the 1990s, Meles was 'impatient' in that the EPRDF had a great and immediate need for development assistance from potential donor states. The country was recovering from years of civil war and recurrent famine, and the EPRDF was newly in power, necessitating a relatively rapid economic recovery to help legitimize and stabilize the new regime. Conversely, the US operated as a 'disengaged hegemon' in Sub-Saharan Africa (Lobell et al. 2015, 147), perceiving Ethiopia and its neighbors as being strategically peripheral. Meanwhile, assistance from non-Western powers such as China was limited in scope, increasing the bargaining position of Western states. Ethiopia lacked credible outside options to Western assistance. This situation severely weakened Meles' bargaining power; while Western donors could unilaterally break off development assistance at any time and incur relatively little material cost for doing so, the Ethiopian leader lacked a credible fallback position or 'threat point' (Oh 2018, 536–540) if positive relations with the West could not be maintained. In terms of domestic constraints, Meles had to grapple with a relatively unstable multiethnic coalition of former rebel organizations within the EPRDF, as well as TPLF hardliners who resisted the kind of liberalizing reforms desired by Western donor states. These domestic constraints led to a situation where Meles and the EPRDF publicly advocated for economic and political liberalization in Ethiopia and the country held formally competitive elections during the 1990s and early 2000s, but in practice used 'oppressive means to control the electorate' and 'prevent … the opposition [from] taking part on a level playing field' (Aalen and Tronvoll 2009, 193).

In the early 2000s in the run-up to the 2005 elections, two changes rapidly improved Meles' bargaining position with Western donors. First, the regional priorities of the United States, which had functioned as a 'disengaged hegemon' in Sub-Saharan Africa shifted (Lobell et al. 2015, 147). With the deterioration of stability in the Horn of Africa and the attacks on September 11, 2001, the US reemphasized Ethiopia's role as a key security ally in the War on Terror. The perceived importance of democracy promotion and economic reform declined and were quickly superseded by the country's new role as a bastion of regional stability and supporter in the War on Terror. Second, Ethiopia's deepening partnership with China provided Meles with a much improved fallback position in his interactions with Western donors. Despite intense criticisms of the post-election crackdown in 2005, the EPRDF leadership could calculate first, that in light of the altered security situation on the Horn of Africa, Western donors were unlikely to cancel their assistance. Second, even if that assistance were reduced or cancelled, China now offered an alternative source for Ethiopia heading forward. Notably, in its asymmetric interactions with China, Ethiopia made effective use of ideational resources to improve its bargaining position and improve its attractiveness as development partner. Unlike other leading recipients of Chinese assistance in Sub-Saharan Africa, Ethiopia was relatively resource-poor and unfit for an Angola-style 'infrastructure for natural resource' relationship. However, in a unique, 'infrastructure for diplomatic support' arrangement, Meles Zenawi positioned himself as 'China's spokesman in Africa' using Ethiopia's diplomatic clout and unique status as a 'symbol of black freedom and stimulator of pan-Africanism' to defend China's position as an effective development partner and model for governance to other African states in the face of Western criticism (Adem 2012, 147–148).

Importantly, as noted by Fourie (2015), the electoral crisis of 2005 in particular had an important impact on Meles' perception of China. While he had previously seen China simply offering an alternative source of aid and support to Western donors, Meles and other leading officials now began to speak openly about China as offering an alternative model of development and (illiberal) governance that might be emulated by Ethiopia.

A shift towards the emulation of China as model of governance was also indicated by the EPRDF's growing interest and involvement in 'lesson-sharing' initiatives offered by Beijing (Fourie 2015, 300). The EPRDF frequently engaged in direct inter-party exchanges with the Chinese Communist Party (CCP), granting its officials greater exposure to China's approach to development and governance (ERTA News 2011; Hackenesch 2011, 29, 33). Yun Sun commented that 'Ethiopia has been the most eager student [in Sub-Saharan Africa] of China's development and government experience' noting the frequent delegations of EPRDF senior and mid-ranking officials who visited China for training programs on topics such as poverty alleviation (2011), cadre management (2013), and domestic development (2016) (Sun 2016). EPRDF participants in such programs would typically visit Beijing or other locations in China, attend lectures at CCP training centers, such as the Central Party School, or institutions of higher education, participate in field visits to observe the operations of local governments and industrial zones, interact with local officials as well as businessmen and other private citizens, and complete cultural programs designed to introduce Chinese traditional culture (Sun 2016; Kuo 2017). For Beijing, such initiatives serve the function of establishing a network of partnerships within the political power structure of Ethiopia and other Sub-Saharan Africa states, improving local perceptions of China and the so-called China model of governance and development, and finally, enhancing the state capacity of key development partners, such as Ethiopia (Sun 2016; Kuo 2017).

Notably, Western trade and assistance did not decline with the emergence of China as an alternative partner; the suspension of Western assistance in the wake of the 2005 election was largely symbolic. As noted in World Bank data, the net Official Development Assistance received by Ethiopia from DAC members of the OECD (mostly Western, traditional donor nations) rose from US$687 million in 2000 to US$1.9 billion in 2005. Even after the controversial 2005 elections, development assistance from DAC countries continued to increase, from US$2.04 billion in 2006 to US$3.23 billion in 2015 (World Bank 2018). The growing assertiveness of the EPRDF leadership towards traditional donors since the mid-2000s and its willingness to boldly suppress the opposition and run largely choreographed single-party elections in 2010 and 2015 is a visible shift from the previous decade. China's emergence as an alternative source for economic support and partnership weakened the ability of Western powers to place pressure on the EPRDF to implement political reform and exercise restraint concerning its repression of political challengers. Additionally, Western concerns with deteriorating security conditions in the Horn of Africa eroded the motivation to press the EPRDF to create a more democratic and inclusive regime and improve its checkered human rights record.

Conclusion

Authoritarian backsliding in Ethiopia is reflective of the complex interplay between domestic and international dynamics that have shaped the country's recent political trajectory. As it consolidated power in the wake of the Ethiopian Civil War, the EPRDF operated in an international environment characterized by the American 'unipolar moment' (Krauthammer 1990, 23–33). After the Soviet collapse, the EPRDF had little option but to adopt liberalizing political reforms as it actively sought out Western development assistance and trade.

China's growing economic and political engagement would ultimately provide the EPRDF with an alternative source of foreign assistance, diminishing the regime's need to implement further political reform and exercise restraint when interacting with opposition forces. Beijing's role was compounded by Ethiopia's increasing role as a strategically important security partner on the Horn of Africa. Seeking to contain the influence of al Qaeda affiliates, the Islamic Court Movement and later its successor, al Shabaab, and secure Ethiopia's support in addressing deteriorating political conditions in Sudan, the United States softened its criticism of Ethiopia's political regime and human rights record and extended growing levels of military assistance and arms sales. Combined with Beijing's arrival as an alternative foreign source of economic aid and assistance, this shift further weakened the democratizing pressure placed on the EPRDF. This deleveraging of Western partners, allowed Ethiopia – a country that had previously existed in a political 'gray zone' (Carothers 2002, 9–11) – to transition into a state of full authoritarianism.

Since 2018, there have been some notable signs of change within Ethiopia. At the end of 2015, thousands of demonstrators protested against the seizure of land for development on the outskirts of Addis Ababa. Because the land seizures targeted a predominantly Oromo area, the protests tapped into ethnic grievances and a new organization, Qeerroo Bilisummaa Oromo (Oromo Youth Movement) emerged as a symbol for the protests. The government, then led by Hailemariam Desalegn, attempted to suppress the growing protests with a police crackdown, killing 700 people and arresting 23,000, and a declaration of a state of emergency (Weber 2018, 1–2). As the protests continued, Hailemariam then attempted to address the situation by reaching out to opposition parties to engage in a constructive dialogue about the demands of the protesters and ordered the release of political prisoners. These earlier efforts having failed to quell the unrest, Hailemariam announced his resignation in spring 2018, and was (surprisingly) replaced by Abiy Ahmed, chair of the Oromo Democratic Party, as chair of the EPRDF and soon thereafter prime minister. Since coming to power, Abiy has embraced a policy of reconciliation with Eritrea, openly advocated the need for political reform and a free press, condemned the repressive actions of his predecessors in the EPRDF, released many political prisoners, and called for term limits for the office of prime minister. Additionally, within the EPRDF, he has reshuffled the cabinet, removing many long-standing officials, mostly from the TPLF, and replacing them with a new generation of mostly Oromo leaders (Fisher and Gebrewahd 2018, 194–196; Weber 2018, 2–3). While the impact of these changes remains unclear, there is reason to believe that Abiy's efforts at political reform are closely connected to ethnically charged factional politics within the EPRDF. In his first year in office, Abiy was targeted in an apparent assassination attempt on June 23, 2018, which was followed by a state crackdown on current and former members of the Ethiopian security and intelligence forces. Meanwhile, in the first months of his tenure in power, Abiy made overtures to both Western powers and China, visiting the United States, Europe, and China. During his meeting with Xi Jinping at

FOCAC in Beijing, Abiy identified China as 'the leading development partner of Ethiopia,' praising the benefits of the country's 'One Belt, One Road' project and noting Ethiopia's interest in learning from China's governing experience (Borkena 2018). While it remains to be seen what direction Ethiopia's political development will take in the months and years heading forward, it is clear that the new leadership has embraced a posture of jointly reaching out to both Western and Chinese partners and is engaged in a hard-nosed process of consolidating power by marginalizing and cracking down on opponents within the EPRDF.

This case reveals the need to better realize the agency of African elites in their interaction with great power states. Both Meles Zenawi and his successors, Hailemariam Desalegn and Abiy Ahmed, actively and successfully engaged in asymmetrical bargaining with both China and Western powers. In such relationships, stronger actors seek to apply a 'take it or leave it' or 'take it or suffer approach,' while weaker actors will 'borrow power' from outside sources to improve their negotiating position (Zartman 1997, 238). After actively courting Western partners in the 1990s and early 2000s, the leaders successfully secured a second alternative line of support in the form of Beijing, in effect 'borrowing' power from this outside source. Moreover, in the post-9/11 era, Ethiopia has further improved its bargaining position by positioning itself as a critical partner in international counterterrorism efforts and regional stabilizing force in the Horn of Africa. Both these efforts strengthened the position of Ethiopia in its bargaining relationships with stronger powers, resulting in its emergence as a leading recipient of both Western and Chinese aid and assistance and a regime with a relatively free hand in its interactions with domestic political rivals. Researchers investigating the relations between African states and outside powers, such as China and the United States, should thus place greater emphasis on the agency of African elites. Despite their conventionally weak power position in relation to established and emerging great powers, leaders in Ethiopia and other African states are taking advantage of an increasingly multipolar international system to improve their bargaining position and pursue their particular foreign and domestic interests.

References

Aalen, L. (2006) 'Ethnic Federalism and Self-determination for Nationalities in a Semi-authoritarian State: The Case of Ethiopia', *International Journal on Minority and Group Rights*, 13(2), 243–261.

Aalen, L. and Tronvoll, K. (2008) 'The 2008 Ethiopian Local Elections: The Return of Electoral Authoritarianism', *African Affairs*, 108(430), 111–120.

Aalen, L. and Tronvoll, K. (2009) 'The End of Democracy? Curtailing Political and Civil Rights in Ethiopia', *Review of African Political Economy*, 36(120), 193–207.

Abbink, J. (2006) 'Discomfiture of Democracy? The 2005 Election Crisis in Ethiopia and Its Aftermath', *African Affairs*, 105(419), 173–199.

Addis Neger (2010) *China involved in ESAT jamming*, (www.addisnegeronline.com/2010/06/china-involved-in-esat-jamming/), accessed 29 July 2018.

Adem, S. (2012) 'China in Ethiopia: Diplomacy and Economics of Sino-optimism', *African Studies Review*, 55(1), 143–160.

Arriola, L. R. (2008) 'Ethnicity, Economic Conditions and Opposition Support: Evidence from Ethiopia's 2005 Elections', *Northeast African Studies*, 10(1), 115–144.

BBC News (2006) *Ethiopian protesters massacred*, (http://news.bbc.co.uk/2/hi/africa/6064638.stm), accessed 12 May 2017.

Bermeo, N. (2016) 'On Democratic Backsliding', *Journal of Democracy*, 27(1), 5–19.

Borkena (2018) *China is the leading development partner, PM Abiy Ahmed told Xi Jinping*, (https://borkena.com/2018/09/02/china-is-the-leading-development-partner-pm-abiy-ahmed-told-xi-jinping/), accessed 25 February 2019.

Bräutigam, D. and Hwang, J. (2017) *Johns Hopkins University's China Africa research initiative*, (www.sais-cari.org/data-chinese-loans-and-aid-to-africa/), accessed 3 May 2017.

Bunce, V. and Wolchik, S. (2009) 'Postcommunist Ambiguities', *Journal of Democracy*, 20(3), 93–107.

Cabestan, J. P. (2012) 'China and Ethiopia: Authoritarian Affinities and Economic Cooperation', *China Perspectives*, 10(4), 53–62.

Carothers, T. (2002) 'The End of the Transition Paradigm', *Journal of Democracy*, 13(1), 5–21.

Diamond, L. (2002) 'Thinking about Hybrid Regimes', *Journal of Democracy*, 13(2), 163–175.

Diamond, L. (2015) 'Facing Up to the Democratic Recession', *Journal of Democracy*, 26(1), 141–155.

DOS (US Department of State) (1996) *Ethiopia human rights practices*, (http://dosfan.lib.uic.edu/ERC/democracy/1995_hrp_report/95hrp_report_africa/Ethiopia.html), accessed 1 May 2017.

Dresden, J. R. and Howard, M. M. (2015) 'Authoritarian Backsliding and the Concentration of Political Power', *Democratization*, 23(7), 1122–1143.

ERTA News (2011) *EPRDF, Chinese Communist Party vows to strengthen existing relations*, (www.ertagov.com/erta/erta-news-archive/1141-eprdf-chinese-communist-party-vow-to-strengthen-existing-relations.html), accessed 15 July 2018.

ESAT (Ethiopian Satellite Station) (2011) *ESAT accuses China of complicity in jamming signals*, (http://ethsat.com/2011/10/08/esat-accuses-china-of-complicity-in-jamming-signals), accessed 29 July 2018.

Ethiopian Herald (2005) *Ethiopia: Chinese premier, Algerian president congratulate Meles on re-election*, (http://allafrica.com/stories/200510110262.html), accessed 12 May 2017.

Farquharson, M. (2017) *Chinese infrastructure investment in Ethiopia*, (www.borgenmagazine.com/chinese-infrastructure-investment-in-ethiopia/), accessed 2 May 2017.

Fisher, J. and Gebrewahd, M. T. (2018) '"Game Over"? Abiy Ahmed, the Tigrayan People's Liberation Front and Ethiopia's Political Crisis', *African Affairs*, 118(470), 194–206.

Foster, V., Butterfield, W., Chen, C. and Pushak, N. (2008) *Building Bridges: China's Growing Role as Infrastructure Financier for Sub-Saharan Africa*, World Bank, Washington, DC.

Fourie, E. (2015) 'China's Example for Meles' Ethiopia: When Development "Models" Land', *Journal of Modern African Studies*, 53(3), 289–316.

Hackenesch, C. (2011) *European Good Governance Policies Meet China in Africa: Insights from Angola and Ethiopia*, German Development Institute Working Paper no. 10, Bonn.

Huntington, S. (1991) 'Democracy's Third Wave', *Journal of Democracy*, 2(2), 12–34.

Krauthammer, C. (1990) 'The Unipolar Moment', *Foreign Affairs*, 70(1), 23–33.

Kuo, L. (2017) *Beijing is cultivating the next generation of African elites by training them in China*, (https://qz.com/africa/1119447/china-is-training-africas-next-generation-of-leaders/), accessed 15 February 2019.

Levitsky, S. and Way, L. (2010) *Competitive Authoritarianism: Hybrid Regimes after the Cold War*, Cambridge University Press, Cambridge.

Lobell, S. E., Jesse, N. G. and Williams, K. P. (2015) 'Why Do Secondary States Choose to Support, Follow or Challenge?', *International Politics*, 52(2), 146–162.

Long, T. (2017) 'It's Not the Size, It's the Relationship: From "Small States" to Asymmetry', *International Politics*, 54(2), 144–160.

Ministry of National Defense of the People's Republic of China (2017) *China opens its first army support base overseas*, (http://eng.mod.gov.cn/news/2017-08/02/content_4787596.htm), accessed 11 September 2017.

Obama, B. and Hailemariam, D. (2015) *Joint press conference in Addis Ababa, Ethiopia*, (https://obamawhitehouse.archives.gov/the-press-office/2015/07/27/remarks-president-obama-and-prime-minister-hailemariam-desalegn-ethiopia), accessed 11 September 2017.

OECD (Organization for Economic Co-operation and Development) (2017) *Development aid at a glance: Africa*, (www.oecd.org/dac/stats/documentupload/Africa-Development-Aid-at-a-Glance.pdf), accessed 11 September 2017.

Oh, Y. A. (2018) 'Power Asymmetry and Threat Points: Negotiating China's Infrastructure Development in Southeast Asia', *Review of International Political Economy*, 25(4), 530–552.

Putnam, R. D. (1988) 'Diplomacy and Domestic Politics: The Logic of Two-level Games', *International Organization*, 42(3), 427–460.

Simoes, A. and Hidalgo, C. A. (2017) *Observatory of economic complexity*, (http://atlas.media.mit.edu), accessed 1 May 2017.

Sun, Y. (2016) *Political party training: China's ideological push in Africa?*, (www.brookings.edu/blog/africa-in-focus/2016/07/05/political-party-training-chinas-ideological-push-in-africa/), accessed 15 February 2019.

Taylor, I. (2011) *The Forum on China-Africa Cooperation*, Routledge, New York.

Tronvoll, K. (2011) 'The Ethiopian 2010 Federal and Regional Elections: Re-establishing the One-party State', *African Affairs* 110(438), 121–136.

United Nations (2016) *UN missions: Summary detailed by country*, (www.un.org/en/peacekeeping/contributors/2016/aug16_3.pdf), accessed 11 September 2017.

Vasagar, J. (2005) *Ethiopia attacks poll criticism*, (www.theguardian.com/world/2005/aug/30/hearafrica05.eu), accessed 12 May 2017.

Weber, A. (2018) *Abiy Superstar-reformer or Revolutionary? Hope for Transformation in Ethiopia*, SWP Comments no. 26, Stiftung Wissenschaft und Politik, Berlin.

Womack, B. (2016) *Asymmetry and International Relationships*, Cambridge University Press, New York.

World Bank (2017) *Global Economic Prospects: A Fragile Recovery*, World Bank, Washington, DC.

World Bank (2018) *World development indicators*, (http://data.worldbank.org), accessed 1 May 2018.

Yewondwossen, M. (2008) *ETC raising network capacity, blocks VOIP*, (http://nazret.com/blog/index.php/2008/09/16/ethiopia_etc_raising_network_capacitybl), accessed 12 May 2017.

Zartman, I. W. (1997) 'The Structuralist Dilemma in Negotiation', in R. J. Lewicki, R. J. Bies and B. H. Sheppard (eds) *Research on Negotiation in Organizations*, Vol. 6, Emerald, Bingley, 227–246.

9 Dialectics of popular discontent and democracy in China's engagements in Zambia

Richard Aidoo

Introduction: China in Zambia's political economic development

China's relationship with Zambia is one that has received persistent scrutiny over the past few decades of increased Chinese engagements in Africa. Though engagements between the two states have produced both complementary and controversial outcomes, China's presence and activities (both political and economic) have led to some popular anger and disfavor, leading to various anti-China protests, demonstrations, and confrontations in the Southern African country. Based on the diplomatic history of the relationship between China and Zambia, this chapter highlights how Zambia's dependence on copper mining, labor issues, and its government actions in relation to China have contributed to diverse political contentions and popular discontent in democratic Zambia. To fully understand the role that China has played in different political contentions in Zambia, this introductory section of the chapter will first broadly highlight the post-independent nature of Zambia–China relations, especially under different democratic regimes. Similarly, it will also discuss China's main involvement in various political and economic endeavors over the post-independent decades.

Shortly after attainment of independence in Zambia in 1964, China established formal relations characterized by friendship and mutual respect, as well as the exchange of loans, infrastructure, and natural resources – elements that have largely shaped Zambia–China relations over the years. As featured in Kaunda's statement soon after his first post-independent visit to Beijing, he stated: 'I must admit I found them [Chinese] a very friendly people, not only in their enthusiastic welcome by hundreds of thousands of people, but also in their understanding of our problems in Zambia in particular, and Africa as a whole' (cited in Mutukwa 1979, 127).

Presently, like in many resource-endowed African political economies, the benefits of the Chinese loans, infrastructure, and copper as the fulcrum of Zambia's economy are often dulled by the painful accounts of anti-Chinese protests by disgruntled and maltreated workers along with other segments of the population, as well as by the sporadic but widely reported violence that is associated with such demonstrations.

How important is Zambia to China's expanding role in Africa? Besides the economic imperatives of China's engagements in Zambia, Beijing has often been blamed for generally doing business with rogue African leaders and pariah states. Consequently, its relations with Zambia help challenge this often referenced and almost entrenched myth, particularly in the West. Dambisa Moyo (2012) in a *New York Times* op-ed, offers a general framework that can help contextualize China's resource diplomacy and labor rights issues in Zambia, which have been a source of contention in its democratic politics. This is of particular importance given that in the example of Zambia individual rights to protest and vote have often shaped the support for Chinese activities (Lee 2017) and that after an era of significant upward trends of democratic advancement in regions like Africa has witnessed some reversals (Diamond 2015).

First, China's engagements in Zambia began with Kenneth Kaunda and the United Independence Party (UNIP) right after independence. The Chinese motives for this relationship were quite clear from the onset, when China extended an US$500,000 grant right after independence in 1964, and formed a strategic partnership with a Southern African state with an influential nationalist leader in Kenneth Kaunda (Shinn and Eisenman 2012). Evidently, this relationship was largely driven by economic imperatives as a series of Chinese loan facilities was extended to Zambia. These included an US$7 million loan and an US$17 million interest-free loan, mostly meant for infrastructure development, which was a national need right after independence (Shinn and Eisenman 2012, 324).

Amid these initial fraternal efforts was the monumental infrastructure development project that has come to define China's commitment to the African continent. In an era of struggle over geopolitical spheres of influence (that included the Soviet Union) in the developing world, the much-celebrated Tanzania–Zambia railway (TAZARA) represents a strategic move on China's part. In the evaluation of China's motivations for offering to finance and build the TAZARA, Kasuka Mutukwa (1979, 142–157) simply argues that Beijing's commitment was tied to four main objectives. First, it was supposed to secure Third World solidarity by essentially considering countries in Asia, Africa, and Latin America as vital allies with a foreign policy view that recognized an unfolding world revolutionary struggle in international relations, in which they would play crucial roles. The second objective was to underscore the revolutionary ambitions of China, as it contributed to Africa's liberation struggle and signaled confidence in Africa's political future by the gesture of a monumental investment such as the TAZARA project. Third, Beijing envisaged the TAZARA as an indicator of China's growing capabilities to accomplish massive undertakings of the size of the railway against the backdrop of skepticism in the West and Soviet Union. Hence, in the game of (great) power competition, the construction of TAZARA rivaled the Russian financing of Egypt's Aswan Dam, and US support of the Volta project in Ghana. Fourth, China pursued the economic objective to open up new trade opportunities and to gain access to African markets that were traditionally controlled by Western countries.

Second, Beijing continued its diplomatic overtures to Lusaka under Frederick Chiluba and the Movement for Multiparty Democracy (MMD). Zambia was one of the first African countries to encounter the effects of the post-Cold War democratic wave, as the seemingly insuperable Kenneth Kaunda was defeated in the 1991 multiparty election by Frederick Chiluba (a former labor union leader) and the MMD as both received immense popular support. This victory was particularly notable given Kaunda's initial resistance towards multiparty democracy as he continuously warned it would lead to ethnic factionalism (Appiah and Gates 2010). China continued its warm relations under the Chiluba administration through continuous loan agreements such as the unconditional loan of US$21.6 million, which included US$18 million as a soft loan for the reconstruction and recapitalization of the Mulungushi Textile joint venture. To facilitate financial transactions by Chinese businesses and investors, the state-owned Bank of China was established in Zambia in 1997 – the first Chinese bank in Sub-Saharan Africa. Such institutions served as support for major Chinese investments in the mining sector. In 1998, the China Non-Ferrous Metal Mining Company purchased the Chambishi copper mine for US$20 million (Shinn and Eisenman 2012). This led to an increased Chinese stake in the Zambian economy and amplified the visibility of Chinese investors and their labor practices in Zambia.

Third, China continued its cordial, but somewhat controversial relationship with the MMD even under the new leadership of Levy Mwanawasa. In 2001, when the political mantle changed hands from President Chiluba to Levy Mwanawasa (both from the MMD), the democratic frustrations among the opposition parties also mirrored the failures in the economy, which were supposed to be tackled by World Bank and International Monetary Fund sponsored neoliberal arrangements. This situation elevated the role of the Chinese state-coordinated diplomacy as well as the large band of small-scale Chinese businesses that helped rejuvenate large parts of the economic sector. So, as Zambia's electoral democracy matured given the emergence of different political parties and coalitions, and the surge of Michael Sata and the Popular Front (PF), the complementary nature of Chinese investments has been eclipsed by the palpable popular anger directed at the dominance of the Chinese in almost all sectors of the economy – from the cheap and competitive Chinese goods in the general trade sectors to unregulated and poorly managed Chinese mining concessions. The demise of Sata in 2014 gave way to Edgar Lungu to lead the PF and become the sixth president of Zambia.

As China continues to invest and support development efforts in Zambia, making this Sub-Saharan African country the third-largest recipient of Chinese foreign investment in Africa and the nineteenth-largest in the world (Carmody 2016, 72–102), three main themes remain dominant in the Zambia–China relations. First is China's unrivalled dominance in the mining sector as a result of its heavy investment and interest in the copper mines of Zambia. This also includes other investments in minerals like nickel and cobalt. Currently, China is responsible for about 40 percent of global demand in copper, which has remained comparatively sturdy despite recent fluctuations in the global resource market. The profit interest in the copper mines led the Chinese government's support for the development of an US$800 million Multi-facility Economic Zone in the Copperbelt (Carmody 2016, 72–102). Additionally, NFC Africa, predominantly owned by China Non-ferrous Metals Company Limited recently launched an US$832 million copper mine that will reportedly extend the firm's lifespan by over 20 years (Reuters 2018).

The second main theme is attempts by different democratically elected administrations to establish or strengthen state control over resources and markets in response to growing popular discontent, especially towards Chinese engagements in Zambia. Through the various electoral cycles, one significant twist in the Chinese investments in the Copperbelt has been a shift from an agenda of liberalization, which allowed Chinese companies almost unfettered control over the mineral resources, to allowing more Zambian government control. This initially began under President Kaunda whose nationalization of the copper mines was meant to raise more revenue for the government, and was also an attempt to alleviate economic hardships on the Zambian people (see Appiah and Gates 2010). This approach became particularly popular when President Sata attempted a renationalization of major sectors of the Zambian economy, responding to an anti-Chinese outcry over Beijing's resource diplomacy that swept across Africa and was particularly pertaining to the Zambian economy. Carmody (2016, 72–102) notes the contentiousness and extensive local anger towards Chinese traders in Zambia, particularly when one of the main markets in the capital of Lusaka was leased to Chinese management. For instance, local women trading in imported second clothes, 'saluala,' found it difficult to compete with cheaper new Chinese imports. Such circumstances fuel popular anger and resentment, as the Chinese are perceived as hogging local economic opportunities meant for local investors with the capital resources and advantages of a foreign investor.

Third and concurrent to the issue of Chinese dominance in the Copperbelt and other related economic activities are the prevalence of human and workers' rights abuses, which have been notoriously associated with most Chinese investments, especially in the mining industry. In Zambia, these reports typically range from the neglect of safety standards meant to safeguard workers in their workplaces like factory settings and construction sites, to the remuneration for local workers. One of the major incidents that received global attention is the 2005 explosion at Chambishi, which killed forty-nine people (Carmody 2016, 92).

The most devastating report was the 2011 Human Rights Report titled *You'll be Fired if you Refuse*, which compiled in detail the abuses that took place in Chinese state-owned and -operated Zambian copper mines (Human Rights Watch 2011). Closely linked to these reports of disregard for safety regulations and workers rights is the issue of wage discrepancies between the Chinese and Zambian workers, which is often noted as exploitatively distinctive as the local Zambian workers that risk life and limbs at these workplaces with poor safety conditions often receive 'slave wages.' This perennial wage issue was also addressed in a comparative perspective by Ching Kwan Lee (2017) as she examined conditions and remunerations in three selected mines in Zambia – Mopani Copper Mines, Konkola Copper Mines, and Non-Ferrous Metal China, Africa. Predictably, most of the workers protests and resistance resulted from wage issues, but unfortunately most of these incidents often ended in violent confrontations between Chinese managers who pick up arms for defense and local miners. In 2010, about thirteen miners were shot by Chinese managers who recounted that the shots they fired were meant to scare off striking Zambian workers but mistakenly struck and killed some of the workers (Bearak 2010).

These three dominant themes in the relationship between Zambia and China have significant political implications in Zambia. In a competitive electoral democratic system like Zambia, sometimes the differences in reactions between political elites and the masses with regard to Chinese investments and management can be exploited for further political purposes. This broadly describes the 'Michael Sata effect' in Zambia–China relations – a phenomenon of exploiting intense anti-Chinese popular resentment to achieve a political goal of winning a competitive election contest. Furthermore, the victory of Michael Sata's foments the conception that palpable popular anger has rule-based conduits in African democratic governance, and also challenges the often-perceived lack of African agency in the multifaceted and complex relationship with China.

Politicizing Zambia–China engagement: discontent in democratic development

Zambia's postcolonial relationship with China has been rather warm and increasingly focused on economic development, notwithstanding the challenge of ensuring a win–win relationship in such an asymmetric development partnership. In a McKinsey report titled *Dance of the Lions and Dragons* Zambia is considered an 'unbalanced partner' to China as compared to the three other types robust, solid, and nascent. This categorization is grounded in a narrow focus of the relationship that provides 'major private-sector investment but not enough oversight from regulatory authorities to avoid labor and corruption scandals' (Sun et al. 2017, 12–13). Thus, this relationship presents both challenges and opportunities, especially as 47 percent of Zambian respondents identify China as the greatest external influence in their polity in a recent survey (Lekorwe et al. 2016). According to Moyo (2012), good diplomatic ties between Zambia and China are generally corroborated by evidence gathered through diverse data samples on the acceptability and impact of China–Africa engagement. She therefore implicitly suggests that to construct a framework to help construe the current discourse of dissatisfaction with Chinese engagement, competition, and alleged abuses in the mining sector in Zambia, it is essential to also consider domestic actors as well, and not only focus on the external actor – China. This further diversifies the configuration of agency in the generation of discontent in

Zambia's democratic culture by the display of different Chinese and African (Zambian) actors.

Deliberations on the generation of political discontent and disfavor in Zambia include a complex combination of Chinese engagements as well as the activities and complicity of other domestic actors and processes that contribute to some of the social and political problems in Zambia. The state of Zambia is classified as a high-capacity democracy, according to a classification of some of China's African partners by Aidoo and Hess (2015). The classification considers Freedom House scores and the Failed States Index to determine the robustness and capacity of the democratic state to encourage social movements within its boundaries. This is fundamentally grounded in the political thought that 'modern liberal democracies are no less subject to political decay than other types of regimes' (Fukuyama 2014, 28). In this chapter, the development of diverse contentions and the attendant popular discontent is considered part of political decay. Consequently, the instances of popular protests, demonstrations, strikes, organized movements, deadly clashes, and confrontations all impact the political status quo. By Mueller's (2018) classification of waves of protests in Africa, the development and building of popular discontent against the Chinese in Zambia may be considered part of the third wave that seems to arise from popular discontent with features of democratic backsliding. In the case of Zambia, the opacity of government dealings with the Chinese and increasing government repression or quelling of anti-Chinese protests (see Matfess 2018) all contribute to the erosion of popular trust in the democratic institutions.

Given the underlying appeal for the review of domestic factors along with China's role in Zambia's domestic political challenges, what factors have contributed to popular discontent in Zambia as China has expanded its engagements in the country?

First, 'political institutions, irrespective of their geographical stations, are stable, valued, recurring patterns of behaviors' that persist beyond the tenure of individual leaders (Huntington 2006, 12), and are also historical constructs in response to the needs of particular moments or eras. However, with societies in transition, there is a tendency for social change to outpace existing institutions and as Fukuyama (2014) notes, such situations serve as sources of political decay. China has been an external diplomatic fixture throughout Zambia's postcolonial existence, however, in the past decade, Zambia has encountered a notable increase in its engagements with China, as the latter has gained more global economic and political stature. China consumes 40 percent of global copper production, most of which is exported from Zambia's Copperbelt, and which generally contributes to the current bilateral trade of US$4 billion – a gradual but appreciable increase from the total of US$100 million in 2000 (ZambiaInvest.com 2016). This surge in economic interest has been accompanied by an increase in Chinese migrants into this mineral rich landlocked African country. Howard French (2014, 43) recounts the 'gigantic movement' of the Chinese into Zambia, which started in the 1990s and may now have brought 100,000 Chinese to the country making it home to one of the biggest Chinese communities across the African continent. Other scholars, who argue for an overestimation of the numbers of emigrated Chinese to Zambia, particular for business, have disputed Chinese migrant estimates in Zambia like French's (2014) reported estimate. However, there is general agreement that the approximations reflect a continuous interest in Zambia's economy (Postel 2016).

Regardless of the migrant surge debate, the Zambian society has undergone transformative postcolonial changes as a result of the expansion of Chinese business interests. When such changes occur rapidly within five decades, as in the case of Zambia, and are not matched by growth and maturity in institutions, the results are often wide-ranging, particularly pertaining to the integration of Chinese migrants into the local communities. Though a catalogue of xenophobic excesses, crime, corrupt and illegal activities exists in several Chinese engagements in countries like Nigeria, Ghana, Angola, and South Africa, Mohan et al. posit that with these areas of tension and conflict between the Chinese and their African counterparts 'there is some evidence of negative, racialized stereotypes emerging, potentially creating a distinct and dangerous divide that could be exploited by politicians, as has been seen in Zambia' (Mohan et al. 2014, 178). When such divisions are further exacerbated by differences in language, wages, work culture, and general expectations, unencumbered by robust socio-political institutions, workplace conflicts often spillover into communities and produce series of deadly disagreements between migrants and hosts. In recent years, anti-China movements organizing major civil protests such as the social media fueled campaign 'sayno2China' have gained attention and some sense of urgency by challenging the logic of the seemingly endless loans extended to Zambia (Rosen 2018) and by sketching out a scenario of a debt crisis that may lead to recolonization of their country (Laterza and Mususa 2018).

Second, and beyond the function of political institutions, is the role of political leaders and elites in framing and fueling the different dimensions of contention that feeds popular resentment. Fukuyama writes, 'while modern political orders seek to promote impersonal rule, elites in most societies tend to fall back on networks of family and friends, both as instrument for protecting their position and as beneficiaries of their efforts' (Fukuyama 2014, 27). As one of Africa's examples of an electoral democratic regime, Zambia represents a challenge to maintain a stable democratic culture, which has eluded some known cases of African democracies that emerged from one-party rule or military dictatorship. Though the democratic political structures are set up to propagate and support impersonal rule, leaders and elites of these political organizations are yet to shed their old ways and consider the well-being of their populations. In Zambia, as in other parts of Africa, where personal rule or neopatrimonialism has featured in the political economic history of the state, relationships with external political and economic actors (like China) often serve to accentuate the preexisting and current weak links between political elites and the mass populace. After the defeat of Kenneth Kaunda and the UNIP in 1991, political contests in Zambia have been characterized by political party coalitions, brokered intra and inter-party political deals, and the political wittiness of finding loopholes in the legal system to silence opposition.

Acting on its increased appetite for natural resources like copper, China stepped up its economic engagements in Zambia's Copperbelt and in other sectors. Beijing – the 'all-weather-friend' – was also perceived to be meddling in the political process to advantage itself (along with the incumbent MMD) under the leaderships of Levy Mwanawasa and Rupiah Banda (see Hess and Aidoo 2015). Campaign sound bites like 'Zambia is becoming a province – make that a district – of China' captured the anti-Chinese resentment that propelled PF's Michael Sata to power in the 2011 presidential election. Between 2016 and 2018, popular protests and political violence saw a surge with about seventy-five riots and protest in 2016, often fueled by opacity of the government's dealings with the Chinese, rumor mongering, and politicization of Chinese investment in Zambia (Matfess 2018).

Another main source of political discontent in Zambia is the issue of elite capture of the state and a disregard for local grievances. With successive electoral victories and spurts of economic growth, the MMD grew less accountable to the population as a whole. Mueller (2018) harkens back to the popular resentment towards austerity measures in the 1980s and early 1990s that led to the voting out of seemingly entrenched one-party state president – Kenneth Kaunda – who initially was obstinately opposed to dealing with the effects of the structural adjustment program on Zambia until a late decision to abandon price increases in maize against the advice of the international financial institutions was made. This attempt to quell public anger and resentment was too little, too late for his political fate. The popular discontent in Zambia helped vote him out after over two decades in office. With globalization and liberalization, access to external economic resources and influence by the Chinese bolstered the MMD's rule as investments from China meant some economic relief for segments of the population. Such a scenario grants the incumbent some political capital to extend political dominance as it delegitimizes the opposition and its capacity to deliver economic well-being to the electorates. As the political party and elites entrench themselves after a few election cycles, accountability to the people wanes as the political elites grow detached from the challenges facing the masses.

After the shooting of striking workers at the Chinese Collum coal mine, then President Rupiah Banda was quoted as saying that 'everyday, people are shot by Zambians, are shot by white people, are shot by the Americans, they are shot by everybody' (Bearak 2010). As this case that had captured global focus was due to go to trial, the Director of Public Prosecutions entered a 'nolle prosequi' decision or unwillingness to proceed for lack of witnesses. Such instances show detachment from the realities facing the Zambian population and more commitment towards the Chinese – a definite source of anti-Chinese populism and popular revolt against the government.

Challenging Zambia's democracy: China's role?

Zambia is a prime example of the third wave of democracy that swept through the African continent in the 1990s (see Huntington 1993). The independent African state of Zambia went through democratic transformation with its pivotal election in 1991, which led to the end of the one-party-state regime under Kenneth Kaunda and the UNIP – one that started from independence in 1964. From 1991 onwards, the political landscape in Zambia has changed along with continent-wide major democratic transitional moments, which are equally notable in states like Ghana, South Africa, and Kenya. However, while the latter moved towards democratic consolidation Zimbabwe, Angola, and Ethiopia witnessed some retrogressive patterns in their democratic evolution. Given the diverse stages of democratic maturity, reactions or resentments towards Chinese economic and diplomatic engagements vary from one democracy to another, and even within the same region. Popular resentment ranges from the visible protests, strikes, and deportations in Kenya, Malawi, and Ghana to taking aim at the local ruling government officials or directly at the Chinese businesses and nationals (whether workers or individual tourists) in states like Zambia and South Africa.

Over the past decades, a variety of political and economic challenges have been mounted against Zambia's democratic culture with the visible manifestation of popular resentment across cities and towns like Kitwe and Lusaka. A notable political outcome has been the breaking of the MMD's hold on power by anti-China advocate Michael Sata of the PF whose current successor Edgar Lungu (also of the PF) continues to face popular discontent against China's engagements. This segment attempts to offer explanations and discussions for the different challenges to the democratic status quo in Zambia as domestic political actors interact with Chinese engagements.

Like many African states, the Zambian political economy is overly dependent on copper, which has helped its development struggles, but also hurt its democratic progress. As a mainstay of the economy, much is expected from the investments in this sector as well as from the roles played by the investors in the mining industry. Much of the anti-Chinese resentment that has continued to increase in the Zambian society has largely emanated from or been directed at investment in the mining sector. As the well-being of large portions of the population is linked to jobs and management of the copper industry, politics and political actors are forced to address and redress the contentions that are associated with Chinese mining firms and their treatment of local workers. According to Moyo (2012), this is what is often missing in the analysis of the impact of Chinese investments throughout Africa. Scholars and critics often turn to examining the role of China as an external actor, meddling in domestic economic and political affairs of the polities and put less emphasis on the political leaders and elites who are supposed to be responsible for ensuring that Chinese investments are positively harnessed to ensure the well-being of the local population.

Chinese investments in the copper industry have strongly shaped Zambia's democratic politics in two significant ways. First, it has infused a divisive political stance and rhetoric as local political actors are often forced to choose sides in the debate around Chinese investments and labor practices in the copper industry. While the MMD, its leaders, and their Chinese partners seemingly perceive Zambia–China engagements as a win–win situation, leaders from the PF are perceived as critical of the Chinese hold over Zambian natural resources and a culture of work that places Zambians in a disadvantage. Thus, when Michael Sata referenced the Chinese as 'infestors' rather than 'investors' (Mutesa 2010), it resonated with sections of the population. As concisely put by one Zambian contractor, 'Zambians are left to scramble for the scrap that is left at the master's table' (cited in Koyi and Muneku 2007). Ching Kwan Lee (2017) reports the fear that anti-Chinese rhetoric produced during Michael Sata's 2008 election campaign as locals shouted out 'Chinese Go' while rendering other practices of intimidation towards Chinese nationals living and working in Zambia. For a democracy that is often challenged by ethnic dynamics, any additional element of divisiveness definitely fosters or foments local discord and discontent. Second, Chinese investment in the copper industry has overwhelmingly positioned China as a political meddler in a growing democratic culture where the local political actors have limited resources and are often easily influenced by external donations and affiliations, even more so when the external actor controls the mainstay of the economy – copper. There was some uproar when the Chinese issued an implicit threat of diplomatic degradation should Michael Sata win the 2011 presidential elections and instead sided with the incumbent MMD (see Hess and Aidoo 2015).

The second manifestation of the government's weakened capacity to control internal actors, structures and processes to the benefit of its population is the inability to ensure adequate and sustained corporate social responsibility from Chinese companies operating in the country. As a developing country with a per capita gross domestic product (GDP) that is inextricably linked to the sale of its natural resources, the general well-being of the population is equally tied to the contributions of multinational corporations to social development. According to the World Bank (2017), the per capita GDP of Zambia in 2015 grew at –0.2 percent, which could be attributed to wilted world demand for copper, especially by China, Zambia's most prominent investor and buyer. This elevates the need for corporate investments to contribute to infrastructure, education, healthcare, and other social services to help improve the living conditions of the locals. This has not been sustainably achieved under the various government administrations.

An instructive case is the Chinese state-owned enterprise, the Non-Ferrous Metal Industries (operating as NFC Africa Mining plc. – Chambishi) which bought a struggling mine owned and operated by the Zambian government through the Zambian Consolidated Copper Mines (ZCCM) in 1998. Prior to the takeover, the ZCCM had inherited (from colonial period), improved, and implemented a culture of corporate social responsibility termed 'from cradle to grave policy' which catered for all the needs of the mineworkers and their families (Lungu and Mulenga 2005). This included provision of medical care, education, accommodation, utilities, and supplementary food supplies. ZCCM also built and maintained infrastructure like schools and hospitals. As the mines were privatized and taken over by NFC, most of these provisions were discontinued and passed on to municipal councils that were inadequately equipped to take over management. Frazer and Lungu (2006) report that for an average family this curtailed needed healthcare benefits and brought about severe socio-economic hardships for residents of the mine townships, which is especially more debilitating given the poor working conditions and wages. Evidently, the lack of governmental responsibility to help ensure the sustainability and continuity in corporate social responsibility has left embittered local residents with little faith in government and palpable resentment towards the Chinese who are perceived to be engineering their economic and social destitution.

The Chinese have been heavily criticized, especially by the West, for labor arrangements and practices in Zambia, though a link exists between these two actors. Sautman and Hairong (2014) argue that the poor labor conditions that are often associated with Chinese companies and used as political fodder to fuel anti-Chinese populism are outcomes of neoliberalism rather than a feature of these companies. Along this line of argument, Negi (2008) posits that popular resentment towards Chinese engagements in Zambia metaphorically represents resistance to neoliberal orthodoxy and Zambian government's willingness to turn over valuable national assets to foreign owners and acquiesce to the policies and arrangements.

Dealing with popular discontent in Zambia: the China approach

As China's relationship with Zambia has been driven by the dialectics of its mining interests and treatment of domestic workers, in the past decade, the complementary aspects of the relationship that counts China as a partner-in-development and financier of infrastructure projects are often drowned in alleged labor abuses, poor safety working conditions, unfair wages issues, and increased local protests. Nonetheless, the litany of abuses and references to neo-colonial exploitation tagged on Zambia–China relations has neither upended the process of democracy in Zambia nor Zambia's increasing diplomatic and economic engagements with China, albeit creating some fault lines of discord and discontent among local political actors and their constituents. In a 2009 survey of African students and faculty, almost 75 percent of Zambian respondents perceived China as a positive model for development (Sautman and Hairong 2009). Later on, in the 2016 Afrobarometer, Zambian respondents chose China as the best model for development over the United States by 32 to 23 percent respectively (Lekorwe et al. 2016). Consequently, as Moyo (2012) indicates in her comments, Beijing is either doing something right to garner this amount and consistency of support or most analyses ignore the broader picture (by excluding the impacts on local political actors). She is right with both assertions.

Howard French reflects on this broader picture through his encounters in Zambia and asserts that:

> [w]hen most people think about China's relationship with Africa they reduce it to a single proposition: securing access to natural resources, of which Africa is the world's greatest storehouse … But there is a more far-sighted motive, one overlooked in almost all speculation about China's ambitions in Africa: to cultivate, or perhaps even create, future markets for China's export-oriented industries, markets that could one day pick up the slack from the aging consumers and debt-ridden economies of the West and of Japan.
>
> (French 2014, 42)

As the African political landscape diversifies and evolves, how has Beijing continuously projected its agenda in specific democracies like Zambia amid the wave of anti-Chinese sentiment and populism propelled by natural resource politics, domestic competition with local business interests, and disparities in work ethic and expectations? In response to this puzzle, given the evolving interests, circumstances, and allegiances to a continent-in-transition-Africa, China has adopted a timeless approach that combines its geopolitical and geoeconomic ambitions (see Aidoo 2017), while distinguishing its African engagements from past Western engagements on the continent. For instance, on the heels of pervasive anti-China protests with chants of Chinese colonization, the Chinese ambassador to Zambia thoughtfully and defensively retorted that 'I feel strange when I hear we want to colonize Africa' as he also further denied that China was seeking to buy Zambia's publicly-owned companies (Times Live 2018).

First, Zambia–China relations have been largely subjected to China's continuous insistence on the non-interference doctrine, which has seemingly become indefensible in practice, yet remains a potent diplomatic rhetorical device used by Beijing to rebuff any claims of interference in domestic policies or affairs. China's brand of diplomacy linked to its non-interference doctrine in Zambia has often projected support for the incumbents and ruling regimes in their contests with opposition parties (Hess and Aidoo 2010, 375). While engagements based on non-interference have enabled Zambian leaders and elites to engage Beijing in more equal economic development partnerships based on the business-is-business mantra, the lack of transparency between relationships between MMD leaders and the Chinese often left the party open to allegations of improper and corrupt practices with Chinese officials and business interests (Hess and Aidoo 2015, 37; Sun et al. 2017). Additionally, to achieve sought-after development goals with its African partners like Zambia, China has persistently focused on building and sustaining partnerships, one infrastructure development at a time. This is uniquely the case in its relationship with Zambia as the two countries were bound by the adventures of the

2,000-kilometer-long TAZARA. This major piece of infrastructure stands as an enduring symbol of friendship between the Chinese and Zambians, but also serves as a starting point for several other infrastructure projects that China has supported over the decades. Apart from a debt annulment for US$211 million, which included the loan for the TAZARA during the 2006 Forum on China African Cooperation, Chinese investors also initialed an agreement to construct a US$220 million copper smelter (Shinn and Eisenman 2012). Other recently slated Chinese-related projects include the National Heroes Stadium, Kenneth Kaunda International Airport, Kafue Gorge Lower Power Plant, Kariba North Bank Power Plant Expansion, and Levy Mwanawasa Hospital Expansion just to mention a few. Most of these projects are often noted by civil society and watchdog groups as causes of a Chinese debt-trap and of Zambia's viscous cycle of debt and surrender-of-sovereignty (Zambian Watchdog 2018).

Over the past decade, China has endeavored to deflect criticisms or scrutiny of its engagements in Africa by drawing a distinction between its current diplomatic footprints in Africa from the past and present Western encounters on the continent. One of the clearest points of distinction is Beijing's infrastructure diplomacy – a narrative that is often used in response to Western critique of China-related exploitation and a looming debt crisis in Africa. In concurrence, most of China's African partners perceive investment in infrastructure as a major contribution to China's positive image in Africa. In the 2016 Afrobarometer, Zambia stood out among 35 countries surveyed as 74 percent of its respondents pointed to infrastructure as the main contributing factor for China's positive image in their country and, on the average, 48 percent of all the African respondents agreed with Zambia (Lekorwe et al. 2016). This is Beijing's preferred storyline for its engagements in Africa, as opposed to detailed accounts of unfortunate domestic encounters in a Zambian manufacturing plant (and elsewhere in Africa) that are often a source of embarrassment and vindication for Western distrust for Chinese interests in Africa.

Finally, China touts its unique aid and development assistance structure and delivery to African countries as an instrument that is attuned to the needs and development challenges of Africans. According to Deborah Bräutigam,

> China's aid and economic cooperation differ, both in their content and in the norms of aid practice. The content … is considerably simpler, and it has changed far less often. Influenced mainly by their own experience of development and by the requests of recipient countries, the Chinese aid and economic cooperation programs emphasize infrastructure, production, and university scholarships at a time when traditional donors downplayed all of these.
>
> (Bräutigam 2009, 11)

A share of 56 percent of respondents in thirty-five African countries surveyed for the 2016 Afrobarometer generally appreciates Chinese economic development assistance. In the same survey, 69 percent of Zambian respondents perceived China as having a good and helpful economic development assistance program (Lekorwe et al. 2016). As a beneficiary of all these various forms of Chinese aid and development assistance throughout the decades, Zambia has shown immense support for China, particularly in the face of Western critique of the impact of a no-strings-attached style of Chinese aid on African democracy.

Conclusion

The relationship between China and Zambia has often been characterized as 'all-weather friends' with a post-independence history of diplomatic and economic engagement. The relationship has also had deep economic development imperatives through China's extension of loans and development assistance to Zambia with the most significant contribution being the TAZARA – a railway that cemented the bond between both states and seemingly set the pace for an enduring relationship in spite of the odds of popular discontent as China's economic activities also reflected competition with the locals.

Apart from loans and economic aid, Zambia–China relations have been shaped by the mining and export of copper, as China represents a major part of global demand for copper, and copper also remains the mainstay of the Zambian economy representing about 60 percent of the country's exports (Trading Economics 2019). However, in the past decade, the relationship between Beijing and Lusaka has gained global notoriety for clashes between locals and Chinese businesses for poor wage structures offered by the later, abuse of Zambian workers by their Chinese employers, and utter disregard for safety standards in Chinese-managed businesses. Clearly, these bitter and deadly exchanges often propel popular local discontent, which impacts domestic politics. This ranges from simple exercise of freedoms of speech, association, and political participation to deadly public protests.

China is often criticized in Zambia for interference in domestic politics as Chinese officials and resources either find their way or are rumored to impact the process of elections. The resentment towards the Chinese has also shaped the outcome of elections, for example, Michael Sata's victory in the 2011 elections underscores the impact of anti-Chinese populism in Africa's democratic process. These signals of Chinese influences in Zambia's democratic culture were also accompanied by a disabling impression of what Stoner et al. (2013) recognize as the role of international dimensions in the democratization process. However, with some increase in the amount of anti-Chinese populism, and as some of Zambia's domestic political challenges have been partly blamed on China as a political meddler, fellow Zambian economist Moyo (2012) calls attention to the critical roles played by local political leaders and elites, widening the sphere and complexity of African agency. This nexus of local and foreign actors in the machinations of the democratic process allows for a much broader exploration of factors that engender popular discontent.

Though popular political discontent is not foreign to Zambia's democratic culture as accusations, counteraccusations, coup attempts, political witch hunts, and an attempted assassination of Kaunda characterize most of the post-independence decades, the past few decades also prominently featured China as an agent in Zambia's political development. The Chinese are tied to diverse malpractices in the copper mining sector (see Lee 2017), as well as to exploitation and disrespect of their local employees. Most consequential are anti-China popular protests and other China-related engagements and issues that manifest in Zambia's political processes and outcomes. The intriguing dimension of why China still remains relevant and formidably supported by the Zambian public could be attributed to its diplomatic astuteness in staving off the unpopular impacts of its engagements by projecting known values and norms that have shaped Beijing's endeavors in the past and may help frame future Zambia–China relations, weathering many waves of popular discontent that are bound to test this China–African engagement.

References

Aidoo, R. (2017) 'The Changing Geoeconomics of China's Diplomacy in Africa', in J. M. Munoz (ed.) *Advances in Geoeconomics*, Routledge, Abingdon and New York, 93–102.

Aidoo, R. and Hess, S. (2015) 'Non-Interference 2.0: China's Evolving Foreign Policy towards a Changing Africa', *Journal of Current Chinese Affairs*, 44(1), 107–139.

Appiah, K. A. and Gates, H. L. (2010) *Encyclopedia of Africa*, Oxford University Press, Oxford.

Bearak, B. (2010) *Zambia uneasily balances Chinese investment and workers' resentment*, (www.nytimes.com/2010/11/21/world/africa/21zambia.html), accessed 25 May 2017.

Bräutigam, D. (2009) *The Dragon's Gift: The Real Story of China in Africa*, Oxford University Press, Oxford.

Carmody, P. (2016) *The New Scramble for Africa*, 2nd ed., Polity Press, Cambridge.

Diamond, L. (2015) 'Facing up to the Democratic Recession', *Journal of Democracy*, 26(1), 141–155.

Frazer, A. and Lungu, J. (2006) *For Whom the Windfalls? Winners and Losers in the Privatisation of Zambia's Copper Mines*, Civil Society Trade Network of Zambia, Lusaka.

French, H. (2014) *China's Second Continent: How a Million Migrants are Building a New Empire in Africa*, First Vintage Books, New York.

Fukuyama, F. (2014) *Political Order and Political Decay*, Farrar, Straus and Giroux, New York.

Hess, S. and Aidoo, R. (2010) 'Beyond the Rhetoric: Noninterference in China's African Policy', *African and Asian Studies*, 9(3), 356–383.

Hess, S. and Aidoo, R. (2015) *Charting the Roots of Anti-Chinese Populism in Africa*, Springer International Publishing, Cham.

Human Rights Watch (2011) *You'll Be Fired if You Refuse: Labor Abuses in Zambia's Chinese State-owned Copper Mines*, Human Rights Watch, Washington, DC.

Huntington, S. P. (1993) *The Third Wave: Democratization in the Late Twentieth Century*, University of Oklahoma Press, Oklahoma.

Huntington, S. P. (2006) *Political Order in Changing Societies*, Yale University Press, New Haven.

Koyi, G. and Muneku, A. (2007) *The Social and Economic Impact of Asian FDI in Zambia: A case of Chinese and Indian investments in Zambia, 1997–2007*, Study commissioned by Friedrich Ebert Stiftung, Lusaka.

Laterza, V. and Mususa, P. (2018) *Is China really to blame for Zambia's debt problems?*, (www.aljazeera.com/indepth/opinion/china-blame-zambia-debt-problems-181009140625090.html), accessed 10 March 2019.

Lee, C. K. (2017) *The Specter of Global China: Politics, Labor, and Foreign Investment in Africa*, University of Chicago Press, Chicago and London.

Lekorwe, M., Chingwete, A., Okuru, M. and Samson, R. (2016) *China's Growing Presence in Africa Wins Largely Positive Popular Reviews*, Afrobarometer Dispatch No. 122, Afrobarometer.

Lungu, J. and Mulenga, C. (2005) *Corporate Social Responsibility Practices in extractive Industry in Zambia*, Catholic Commission for Justice Development and Peace, Development Education Project and Zambia Congress of Trade Unions, Ndola.

Matfess, H. (2018) *All politics are local: Chinese investment, speculation, and protests in Zambia*, (www.acleddata.com/2018/11/29/all-politics-are-local-chinese-investment-speculation-and-protests-in-zambia/), accessed 20 March 2019.

Mohan, G., Lampert, B., Tan-Mullins, M. and Chang, D. (2014) *Chinese Migrants and Africa's Development: New Imperialists or Agents of Change?*, Zed Books, London.

Moyo, D. (2012) *Beijing, a boon for Africa*, (www.nytimes.com/2012/06/28/opinion/beijing-a-boon-for-africa.html), accessed 25 May 2017.

Mueller, L. (2018) *Political Protest in Contemporary Africa*, Cambridge, New York.

Mutesa, F. (2010) 'China and Zambia: Between Development and Politics', in F. Cheru and C. Obi (eds) *The Rise of China and India in Africa*, Zed Books, London and New York, 167–178.

Mutukwa, K. S. (1979) *Politics of The Tanzania-Zambia Railway Project: A Study of Tanzania-China-Zambia Relations*, University Press of America, Washington, DC.

Negi, R. (2008) '"Beyond the Chinese Scramble": The Political Economy of Anti-Chinese Sentiment in Zambia', *African Geographical Review*, 27(1), 41–63.

Postel, H. (2016) *We may have been massively overestimating the number of Chinese migrants in Africa*, (http://africanarguments.org/2016/12/19/we-may-have-been-massively-over-estimating-the-number-of-chinese-migrants-in-africa/), accessed 30 May 2017.

Reuters (2018) *Chinese firm launches $832 million Zambia copper mine*, (www.reuters.com/article/us-zambia-mining/chinese-firm-launches-832-million-zambia-copper-mine-idUSKCN1L71P7), accessed 5 March 2019.

Rosen, J. W. (2018) *'China must be stopped': Zambia debates the threat of debt-trap diplomacy*, (www.worldpoliticsreview.com/articles/27027/china-must-be-stopped-zambia-debates-the-threat-of-debt-trap-diplomacy), accessed 2 March 2019.

Sautman, B. and Hairong Y. (2009) 'African Perspectives on China-Africa Links', *China Quarterly*, 199, 728–759.

Sautman, B. and Hairong, Y. (2014) 'Bashing "the Chinese": Contextualizing Zambia's Collum Coal Mine shooting', *Journal of Contemporary China*, 23(90), 1073–1092.

Shinn, D. H. and Eisenman, J. (2012) *China and Africa: A Century of Engagement*, University of Pennsylvania, Philadelphia.

Stoner, K., Diamond, L., Girod, D. and McFaul, M. (2013) 'Transitional Successes and Failures: The International-Domestic Nexus', in K. Stoner and M. McFaul (eds)

Transitions to Democracy: A Comparative Perspective, Johns Hopkins University Press, Baltimore, 3–25.

Sun, I. Y., Jayaram, K. and Kassiri, O. (2017) *Dance of the Lions and Dragons: How are Africa and China Engaging, and how will the Partnership Evolve?*, McKinsey & Company, Washington, DC.

Times Live (2018) *'Say no to China': Anger mounts in Zambia over Beijing's presence*, (www.timeslive.co.za/news/africa/2018-09-23-say-no-to-china-anger-mounts-in-zambia-over-beijings-presence/), accessed 25 February 2019.

Trading Economics (2019) *Zambia exports, trading economics, January*, (https://tradingeconomics.com/zambia/exports), accessed 12 March 2019.

World Bank (2017) *Zambia data portal: Central statistical office*, (http://zambia.opendataforafrica.org/mhrzolg/gdp-by-country-statistics-from-the-world-bank-1960-2017?country=Zambia), accessed 15 June 2017.

ZambiaInvest.com (2016) *Zambia among China main trade partners in Africa with nearly USD 4.0 billion*, (www.zambiainvest.com/economy/trade/zambia-one-of-china-main-partners-with-nearly-usd-4-billion-in-bilateral-trade), accessed 30 May 2017.

Zambian Watchdog (2018) *Why Chinese feel they own Zambia*, (www.zambiawatchdog.com/why-chinese-feel-they-own-zambia/), accessed 3 March 2019.

10 Emerging alternative?

China's developmental peace approach in South Sudan[1]

Chun Zhang

Introduction

With the rapid development of China–Africa relations since the beginning of the twenty-first century, China's role in the continent's peace and security has become a focus of both policy and academic communities (Condon 2012; Osondu 2013; Verhoeven 2014). There is a sharp contradiction between Chinese and foreign views in terms of the envisaged role that the country should play in African peace and security affairs, and regarding also how this role should be enacted (Li 2018; Wang, H. 2018; Wang and Qi 2018; Zhang 2018). For international observers, including African scholars, the question is quite simply: why has China not played the role that it should (Taylor and Williams 2004; Tull 2006; Alden et al. 2008; Bräutigam 2009; Southall and Melber 2009; Wu and Taylor 2011; Alden and Large 2013; Agubamah 2014; Benabdallah 2016; Alden et al. 2018)?

Given the heated debates arising, the so-called developmental peace concept provides a new analytical tool for scrutinizing China's role in African peace and security affairs. More specifically, South Sudan proves to be the best case for observing the normative evolution of that developmental peace, because China's involvement there has covered almost every stage of the concept's life cycle. While revealing the nature of China's engagements, developmental peace theory is still under construction and leaves rooms for learning from the liberal peace theory advocated mainly by the Western world.

This chapter is composed of five parts. After a short introduction, the second and third sections sketch the transitions occurring in China's attitudes and roles in Sudan and South Sudan peace and security affairs, hence outlining the background conditions to the framing and enactment of the Chinese developmental peace approach. The fourth section summarizes the key elements of the developmental peace concept. The fifth and final section concludes with some final thoughts about the evolution of developmental peace and especially on how to integrate it with liberal peace theory.

China's engagement in Sudan

Advocating the Five Principles of Peaceful Coexistence with other developing countries ever since the 1950s, China has a record of being involved in international peace and security affairs – namely, supporting revolutions in certain developing countries in the 1960s and 1970s including, for example, Algeria and Angola. However, China's role in international peace and security affairs turned serious only after the end of the Cold War and especially on entering the twenty-first century – with the country's rapid rise as a result of its ongoing reform and opening up policies. While international responsibilities call for the providing of more global public goods, domestic thinking still lags behind and advocates meeting domestic needs first – which is precisely the reason for China's reluctant international involvement under external pressure. China's role in Sudan's peace and security affairs, especially in the Darfur crisis and South Sudan's independence, have been fundamentally reactive responses. Therefore, before the independence of South Sudan in 2011, China kept strict adherence to the non-interference principle, without substantial progress made in terms of theory and practice vis-à-vis engaging in international peace and security affairs.

Sudan first established diplomatic relations with China in 1959, 3 years after its independence, making it among the first of the African countries to have such relations. Thereafter, bilateral relations helped maintain steady development. However, due to technical underdevelopment, geographical distance, and low-level economic development, China–Sudan exchanges were not very intense before the mid- to late 1990s – by and large a common feature of China's relations with almost all African countries at that time. The two countries' bilateral relationship was given new momentum with the energy/oil cooperation starting in 1995 however, when the China National Petroleum Corporation (CNPC) undertook an economic assistance project to and began making investments in the Sudanese oil industry (CNPC 2010). This cooperation was very productive, quickly transforming Sudan from an oil-importing to an oil-exporting country by 1999.

Before South Sudan became independent in 2011, CNPC had eight projects in Sudan including: Block 1/2/4 (now mostly in South Sudan), Block 3/7 (now in South Sudan), Block 6, Block 15 (Red Sea), Block 13 (Sudan), and the Khartoum refinery projects. China helped Sudan to build a complete petroleum industry chain (CNPC 2010). Led by oil cooperation, bilateral trade between China and Sudan has grown rapidly: bilateral trade volume was only US$351 million in 1998, and even dropped by nearly 20 percent to US$280 million in 1999. With oil imports from Sudan, however, bilateral trade volume tripled to US$890 million in 2000, eventually reaching US$11.5 billion in 2011–41 times as high as that of 1999 (Table 10.1).

Due to its only short history of rising, and that with a focus on economic development, China was not very sensitive to the security and governance spill-over effects of economic cooperation in its engagement with the international community in the early twenty-first century. Thus, the economically productive cooperation with Sudan had its side effects as well in the context of both existing and emerging clashes and conflicts within the African country, which made this bilateral relationship a controversial one in the early years of the new

Table 10.1 China–Sudan trade relations, 1998–2011, in US$ Million

1998	*1999*	*2000*	*2001*	*2002*	*2003*	*2004*	*2005*	*2006*	*2007*	*2008*	*2009*	*2010*	*2011*
351	283	890	1,158	1,550	1,920	2,522	3,908	3,354	5,708	8,200	6,388	8,627	11,536

Source: National Bureau of Statistics of China, available online at: http://data.stats.gov.cn.

millennium. As a result, China's role in Sudan's internal peace and security affairs quickly came under scrutiny from the international community, even though this was not fully picked up on by Chinese officials and scholars.

The Darfur crisis was the first challenge for China to engage with in Sudan's peace and security affairs, absorbing significant attention. However, the real issue here is not that China has any direct links with it, but two other factors indeed. On the one hand, with the signing of the Comprehensive Peace Agreement (CPA) between the North and South in 2005, the Sudanese government would afterward have energy to deal with other domestic conflicts, and so its eyes turned to the Darfur region. On the other, those non-governmental organizations (NGOs) – led by The Enough Project, an American NGO – who had gained reputation and resources from facilitating reconciliation between the North and South now had to find a new issue to continue on with, following the Sudanese government shifting focus to Darfur. With coercion tactics vis-à-vis Washington no longer being effective, international NGO networks instead created a new strategy called '2Cs,' – 'China + Celebrity' – to use celebrities to pressure China into using its economic influence to force the Khartoum government to change its behavior in the Darfur region (Abramowitz and Kolieb 2007).

Under the guidance of the '2Cs' strategy, many celebrities would become involved in these efforts to force China to be proactive. For example, Eric Reeves, a professor at Smith College in Northampton, Massachusetts, was the first to argue that 'now is the time to start humiliating China' (2007). Mia Farrow, a Hollywood actress who was a goodwill ambassador to the United Nations (UN) Children's Fund, called the 2008 Beijing Olympic Games 'the Genocide Olympics' meanwhile; more than this, she even targeted Hollywood director Steven Spielberg, who was set to be an artistic adviser to the opening and closing ceremonies of the 2008 Games, asking him to pressure the Chinese government – and threating to name him Leni Riefenstahl, the director who had made a promotional film for the Berlin Olympics in 1936 (Cooper 2007). This led Spielberg to write an open letter on Darfur to then Chinese President Hu Jintao on April 2, 2008 (NPR 2007).

For China, among both governmental and non-governmental actors, it was hard to understand why it had suddenly become the primary target of focus regarding the Darfur crisis. According to the UN report, the Darfur crisis was primarily caused by climate change (Ban 2007; Sachs 2007; United Nations Environment Programme 2007), with no direct links to China itself. Thus, the challenge for China at that time was not how to engage but how to even make sense of the situation. Despite this, China would gradually step in from 2007, with international pressure mounting. The first initiative undertaken was President Hu twice expressing concern to his Sudanese counterpart, President Omar al-Bashir, about the situation in Darfur and his hope of Sudan accepting the UN–African Union (UN–AU) hybrid peacekeeping operation proposal. This happened at the summit of the Forum on China–Africa Cooperation in November 2006 and again during his visit to Sudan in February 2007 (MOFA 2006, 2007c; Evans and Steinberg 2007).

Second, Beijing appointed a Special Representative for African Affairs (special envoy) in May 2007, focusing on the Darfur issue. This represented the first endeavor undertaken by China as part of it officially engaging with pressing issues internationally, here the Sudan Darfur issue. Third, China contributed peacekeepers to the UN–AU forces, and actively provided humanitarian assistance to the Darfur region (*Sudan Tribune* 2008a, 2008b). To use the first Chinese special envoy Liu Guijin's own words, even under unreasonable pressure Beijing has always been willing to act as a 'bridge' and 'messenger' between Sudan and the West and has made considerable efforts to mediate on the Darfur issue (Zaobao 2008).

It is safe to conclude, despite the relative passivity in its reactions, China did change its attitude and behavior regarding the Darfur crisis shortly after 2005, and that was the reason why such international pressures disappeared just after the opening of the 2008 Beijing Olympics Games. The experience gave China a chance to think about its role in international peace and security, which facilitated a slow transition from passive reaction to active engagement. Before choosing the latter in its South Sudan civil war mediation, China played a positive but ultimately limited role in the implementation of the 2005 CPA – mainly because it was concluded long before China's active engagement would fully take shape.

After 2010 the full and effective implementation of the CPA became of international focus, due to the deadline approaching for that; China's (potential) role once again became a global concern, albeit to a lesser extent than on the Darfur issue. This created room for China to play a bigger role herein. Adhering to the non-interference principle and respecting the choice of the Southern Sudanese to seek independence, China actively engaged with the international community vis-à-vis guaranteeing the full implementation of the CPA. From late 2010 up to the referendum of the following year, Chinese special envoy Liu had four in-depth exchanges with United States special envoy to Sudan Princeton Lyman. The Chinese government sent a team of observers to South Sudan during the referendum, monitoring the voting process and exchanging views with officials from both the North and South and consulting with other observers sent by the Arab League, the AU, and the UN among others (China News 2011). While moderate, China's role in South Sudan's independence was still quite constructive. As Ambassador Lyman noted,

> We've talked with China often about Sudan. I've met several times with my counterpart the Chinese special envoy, Ambassador Liu. I think the

> Chinese share a great deal of what we want in Sudan … I think that's the message they're conveying. That's the indications I have, and that's the right message. And so that's helpful in itself … So I think on the whole, it's been positive.
>
> (Lyman 2011)

It is important to note that even when pressured to engage in Sudan's peace and security affairs, as represented by the Darfur crisis and the CPA's implementation, China kept its emphasis on economic development. As Daniel Large has pointed out, to better deal with the Sudan People's Liberation Movement (SPLM), led by the Government of Southern Sudan (GoSS), China introduced the policy of 'one country, two systems' (2009, 621–622). Since 2005 China and the GoSS have established formal relations, with then President Hu and President Salva Kiir Mayardit meeting twice in 2007 (MOFA 2007a, 2007b). China later opened a new consulate in Juba in 2008, an example followed by many Chinese companies which would also build their headquarters in that South Sudanese city. As mentioned above, even despite significant security challenges China–Sudan economic ties kept growing, evidenced by the ever-increasing bilateral trade volume. Such facts prove that China puts development as its top priority as long as very basic security and governance conditions exist.

An emerging developmental peace approach: China's role in South Sudan civil war mediation

In January 2011 Southern Sudan held a referendum on independence, with 98.83 percent of voters opting for separation. This laid down the legal foundation for South Sudan's independence (Southern Sudan Referendum 2011). Independence did not come about easily, nor did it guarantee development, peace, and stability. In fact, the road to peace in South Sudan has been destined to be difficult since the very beginning of – and, indeed, even before – the independence process. The key factor herein remains the acute scarcity of power resources that has come to dominate South Sudan's economic, political, security, and social development in the post-independence era – and, indeed, is what pushed South Sudan into a civil war within only 2 years of its founding.

While the international community remained confident about South Sudan's development until autumn 2013 and focused on financing its economic growth, the outbreak of civil war in December 2013 demonstrated that the path to peace and development in South Sudan was far from assured. After hostilities commenced, the international community quickly launched mediation efforts; in these, the Inter-Governmental Authority on Development (IGAD) – a regional entity operating in the Horn of Africa – would play a central and leading role (ICG 2015, 3). This involvement was largely due to its successful experience in mediating in the Sudan civil war during the period from 1993 to 2005 and its direct impact on the independence of South Sudan.

To date, IGAD's mediation in the civil war in South Sudan has gone through three phases: the first, lasting from December 2013 to February 2015, can be described as one of independent IGAD mediation. The regional body responded quickly to the outbreak of civil war, convening an extraordinary summit to discuss the situation within 2 weeks. On January 3, 2014 the IGAD-led mediation process was officially launched. By January 23, the first ceasefire agreement had been reached – one that has never been respected, unfortunately. Despite IGAD's insistence on its mediation process being dominant, since then circumstances have actually switched between upholding the original ceasefire agreement, belligerence, and the establishment once again of a ceasefire (see Table 10.2). This movement back and forth is mainly because of a lack of enforcement mechanisms and also due to the absence of 'protection and deterrence forces' (ICG 2015, 12–16).

The second phase, running from March 2015 to June 2018, was the so-called IGAD Plus international partner period. In March 2015, at the call of Ethiopia, the IGAD Plus peace process was established. Its members include the AU, China, the European Union, IGAD Partners Forum (IPF), Norway, the United Kingdom, the UN, and the US.[2] The launch of the IGAD Plus process contributed significantly to helping reconcile the warring parties in South Sudan. In early June 2015 IGAD presented a 'Comprehensive Document,' which provided an important basis for the cessation of the South Sudan civil war – with key elements on power-sharing, the formation of a transitional government, and regarding a proposed framework for security arrangements. Under pressure from

Table 10.2 Mediation efforts in South Sudan civil war, 2013–2018

Time	*Content*	*Main mediator*
January 23, 2014	Ceasefire agreement	IGAD
May 9, 2014	End of conflict agreement	IGAD
August 25, 2014	Ceasefire agreement, establish joint government within 45 days	IGAD
October 20, 2014	Arusha Agreement	South Africa, Tanzania
November 8, 2014	Stop all conflicts without any conditions	IGAD
January 21, 2015	Both parties promise to apologize and establish ceasefire	IGAD
February 1, 2015	Ceasefire agreement, conclude peace agreement by March 5, and establish transitional government	IGAD
August 17, 2015	Agreement on the Resolution of Conflict in South Sudan	IGAD Plus
September 12, 2018	Revitalized Agreement on the Resolution of Conflict in South Sudan	IGAD Plus

Source: Author's own compilation.

all sides, the South Sudan conflict parties finally signed a peace agreement – namely, the Agreement on the Resolution of Conflict in South Sudan (ARCIS) – by the end of August 2015. However, the agreement was again broken shortly after its signing and violent clashes in July 2016 brought the peace process to a standstill – or even set it back (ICG 2016).

The third phase came about with attempts at revitalizing ARCIS, which began in about June 2018. As the US arms embargo against South Sudan began to take effect, and with the splits occurring within major parties over the past 2 years, IGAD has found both the urgent need and the opportunity to revive ARCIS. Along with a rather complex and comprehensive power-sharing proposal, as compared to that of 2015, a different IGAD Plus approach has been attempted by involving mainly regional powers – including, for example, Egypt, Ethiopia, Uganda, and even Sudan. After months of repeated negotiations, an agreement was finally reached in September 2018: the Revitalized Agreement on the Resolution of Conflict in South Sudan. Nevertheless, the peace process in South Sudan continues to remain uncertain and unpredictable.

For China, the South Sudan civil war has provided a total new opportunity to develop its approach when engaging in international peace and security affairs – namely, developmental peace. On the one hand, this civil war has no direct connection to China – although bilateral oil cooperation remains very important. The fact is that, since the independence of South Sudan, trade volumes between China and the two Sudans have been declining significantly: in 2017 China's total trade with both Sudan and South Sudan was just US$4.1 billion, slightly more than one-third of the 2011 amount (see Table 10.3). On the other hand, China has accumulated certain experiences from engaging in international peace and security affairs for almost a decade now.

Table 10.3 Trade relations between China and the two Sudans, 2011–2017

Year	*Trade volume in US$ billion*	
	Sudan	*South Sudan*
2011	115.3615	0.0132
2012	37.3289	5.34
2013	44.9846	25.4
2014	34.5	43.97
2015	31.229	24.82
2016	26.3455	15.12
2017	28.03	13.21

Source: National Bureau of Statistics of China, available online at: http://data.stats.gov.cn/easyquery.htm?cn=C01.

It is important to note that China acknowledged the relevance of conflict dynamics even during its early engagements with South Sudan. China lobbied all parties there to change their mindsets from focusing on war and conflict to focusing on collaboration and development instead. For example, when meeting President Kiir on April 22, 2012, then Chinese President Hu said that China supported South Sudan's 'efforts in developing its economy, improving people's livelihood, safeguarding stability and entering the international community,' and hoped that 'South Sudan and Sudan would adhere to a peaceful path based on the fundamental interests of both people and the overall situation of regional peace' (MOFA 2012).

From Beijing's perspective, in order for South Sudan to achieve national development, the whole of the newly founded state needs to act as one genuine entity and build a culture of collaboration – not of confrontation. Prioritizing development over governance and security, China and South Sudan have tried to broaden cooperation from its previous focus just on oil. After production of that fossil fuel was suspended in early 2012, China and South Sudan signed a number of deals – including on the renovation and expansion of Juba International Airport, with a total contractual value of US$158 million. Despite the South Sudan civil war significantly threatening construction, Chinese contractors started on the project in July 2014 – being finished and handed over to South Sudan in early 2017. This project has enabled South Sudan to own a truly modern international airport, which is of great significance in better linking the country with the international community. This would have been impossible without adherence to a developmental peace approach.

The outbreak of the South Sudan civil war pressed China to better balance conflict mediation and development promotion. After the commencement of hostilities, China quickly launched its mediation efforts. On December 4, 2013 Zhang Ming, then Chinese Vice Minister of Foreign Affairs, met with the special representatives of IGAD. At the same time, then Chinese special envoy Zhong Jianhua began his shuttle diplomacy in the AU, Ethiopia, IGAD, South Sudan, and Uganda (Ambassador Zhong in personal exchange with the author). With the conflict continuing, China introduced new measures for mediation – namely, dealing with both parties of the conflict at the same time. In July 2014 the Chinese government invited the South Sudan vice president and deputy chairman of the SPLM, James Wani Igga, to visit China in order to discuss the ongoing crisis. During the meeting, Chinese Premier Li Keqiang explained that China 'hopes South Sudan realize[s] national reconciliation, security and stability at an early date,' and stated '[we are] ready to continue to play a constructive role in promoting South Sudan and Sudan to achieve peace and development' (MOFA 2014). Two months later, in September 2014, the Chinese government invited the chairman of the External Relations Committee of the Sudan People's Liberation Movement-in-Opposition, Dr. Dhieu Mathok Diing Wol, to visit China. Many high-level officials within China's foreign policy team met with Dr. Dhieu and expressed similar expectations of a comprehensive, early, and proper settlement to the South Sudan civil war (Wang 2014).

More importantly, unlike other international partners who rapidly shifted their support for South Sudan from development to the security field after the civil war broke out, China did not stop its development support for South Sudan – while simultaneously strengthening mediation efforts. In fact, China has continuously strengthened its economic support, hoping to lay down solid foundations for post-civil war reconstruction. For example, China and South Sudan signed two agreements in November 2014 that 97 percent of the African country's exports to its Asian partner would enjoy zero tariffs. Furthermore, despite the high associated risks, in December 2014 it was announced there were plans to start work on the Juba–Terekeka–Ramciel–Yirol–Rumbek Road (CAITEC 2018, 33–34).

According to China's Ministry of Commerce, China's foreign direct investment (FDI) flows to South Sudan in 2016 were US$2.03 million; FDI stock was US$37.03 million by the end of 2016. Chinese enterprises signed thirty-three new construction contracts with South Sudan with a value of US$1.618 billion, and a turnover of US$160 million in 2016 (CAITEC 2018, 33–34). While it is difficult to access detailed information on FDI projects and volume, the rising number of Chinese workers in South Sudan proves that the Asian country puts development as its top priority as long as some very basic security and governance conditions exist. For example, the year 2015 witnessed significant improvement in security in South Sudan, being supported by the signing of ARCIS in August – with this, the number of Chinese workers in the African country went up dramatically (Table 10.4).

With conflict mediation and development support going hand in hand, China's approach to international peace and security affairs – named, as noted, as developmental peace – is taking shape gradually. Three particular characteristics are key: first, China adheres to the principle of non-interference, embodied as it mediating through local platforms – IGAD in the South Sudan case. The most prominent example of this was on January 12, 2015, when China held a consultation with IGAD and the South Sudan conflict parties in Khartoum to support IGAD's leading role in the mediation.

Second, China insists on the principle of equity. In diplomatic practice, there is no differentiation between so-called conflict-affected or peaceful countries in the Chinese lexicon. Third and finally, China adopts a development-first approach to all engagements, including in peace and security fields. It insists on continuing development support, not securitizing the situation of the target

Table 10.4 Chinese workers in South Sudan, 2011–2016

	2011	*2012*	*2013*	*2014*	*2015*	*2016*
Flow	148	N	386	504	2,445	211
Total (by the end of the year)	148	N	313	596	4,575	342

Source: National Bureau of Statistics of China, available online at: http://data.stats.gov.cn/easyquery.htm?cn=C01.

country. Such a developmental peace approach was embodied in the speech of Ambassador Wu Haitao, the deputy permanent representative of China to the UN, given at the Security Council meeting held on South Sudan in August 2018. Ambassador Wu stressed that the international community should continue to work together to support the mediation efforts of regional organizations and states, to help South Sudan maintain peace and security in the country, and to increase humanitarian assistance and economic support to the African country – with particular emphasis on agriculture, education, energy, healthcare, and infrastructure (MOFA 2018).

Developmental peace: theoretical construction

From passively being engaged in Sudan's peace and security under external pressure to actively being involved in South Sudan civil war mediation, China's developmental peace approach has been developed and practiced gradually. Meanwhile China also takes this approach in other countries like Cambodia or Mali and in other fields including development assistance. Despite still being under construction, the developmental peace approach has the theoretical and practical potential to ease both internal and external tensions in those places where China engages in international peace and security affairs.

Observing their country's involvement in South Sudan, Sudan, UN peacekeeping operations, and other fields besides, several Chinese scholars have contributed to the development and perfecting of developmental peace theory. He Yin, a professor from the China Peace-keeping CIVPOL Training Center, took the lead in putting forward the concept of developmental peace based on his personal practice within UN peacekeeping operations. While not offering an academic definition of developmental peace, he identifies the core elements of this approach as follows: first of all, it gives priority to economic development; second, development peace requires domestic political and social stability to exist as a prerequisite; and, third, on the premise of domestic political and social stability being satisfied, changing the political system itself is not a prerequisite for peace being achieved (He 2013, 2014a, 2014b, 2014c, 2017).

However, the developmental peace approach involves almost every aspect of economic, political, security, and even societal development. Such a fact forces He to broaden his research focus, and leaves room for other disciplines to contribute too. For example, Wang Xuejun from the Center for African Studies of Zhejiang Normal University puts forward the concept of 'independent developmental peace' in order to explore this phenomenon from a broader perspective. Wang not only expands developmental peace from the relatively narrow areas of UN peacekeeping and peacebuilding to include greater economic development, governance, and political construction, but also takes the host country into account – emphasizing ownership of and the historical and cultural backgrounds of different target countries. At the same time, Wang also makes greater efforts to explore the Chinese traditional philosophical and contemporary practice foundations of the developmental peace concept, thus improving its philosophical guidance and practical basis (Wang and Zhang 2018). Besides He and Wang, other scholars such as He Wenping (2015) from the Institute of West-Asian and African Studies of the Chinese Academy of Social Sciences, Zhang Haibing (2013) from the Shanghai Institutes for International Studies, and some others engaged in African studies, development assistance scholarship, and UN-related research illustrate China's concrete practice of developmental peace from different perspectives.

All existing endeavors reveal the fundamental differences to the developmental peace approach, but an overarching academic definition of it is still lacking – as are discussions about its strengths and weaknesses when compared with other related concepts. This chapter argues that developmental peace can be defined as making development the top priority and a self-sustaining condition for peace and security; it seeks the promotion of economic development as long as a minimum basis of security and governance exist. The approach can be said to have four distinct characteristics to it when compared with other similar concepts advocated by both domestic and international scholars.

First, it reveals the theoretical foundations of China's engagement in international peace and security. Looking back on the 40-year experience of China with reform and opening up, one can easily identify how it realized development, security, and governance simultaneously. This has significant implications for how conflict-affected countries can themselves realize sustainable peace. When adopting reform and opening up policies in 1979, China's governance and security conditions were far from ideal; more accurately, the country was on the brink of state bankruptcy in the late 1970s. Forty years later, however, China is now the second-largest economy in the world, and among the safest states globally. What is the secret? It lies in the fact that China always follows a development-first approach, despite the peace and security environment never being ideal.

Second, the approach also reveals the benign interactions and circles existing between development, governance, and security. In the process of reform and opening up, China always emphasized the balance between development, stability, and reform. It is important to note that such an emphasis is similar to or even the same as that of the international community, because the Chinese term 'stability' is something equivalent to the international one of 'security,' while 'reform' means to improve 'governance.' According to China's experience, even when security and governance conditions were not ideal the country still decided to push forward with economic development first. After economic measures achieve a certain early harvest, China tries to improve security and governance while promoting even higher levels of economic development. In this way, a laddering approach to self-sustaining peace and stability – with economic development playing a leading role, and governance and security closely following – can be gradually built. In the long run, a virtuous circle between development, security, and governance will form; this has profound implications for those countries that are afflicted by conflict.

Third, the approach has the potential to help avoid the non-interference dilemma faced by China when engaging in international peace and security affairs. Along with the international focus thereon, there are many domestic discussions about this traditional diplomatic guiding principle too. From the government angle, the new security concepts advocated by both President Jiang Zemin and President Xi Jinping as well as the approach to resolving pressing issues proposed by Foreign Minister Wang Yi (2015) are the most prominent ones. From the academic community, the concepts of 'creative involvement' – a 'new and positive attitude' and a 'new direction' that calls on China to play a more active role and to become voluntarily involved in international affairs, as advocated by Professor Wang Yizhou at Beijing University (2011, 2013, 2015, 2018) – as well as of constructive mediation or of protective intervention (Chen 2018) are, among others, the ones most intensely discussed. However, almost all existing concepts or theories do not resolve the dilemma between non-interference and 'indifference'; that is, the core reason why there is still no consensus on theoretical explanations for China's engagement in international peace and security affairs. In this context, with its emphasis on economic development and the creation of internal balance between development, governance, and security, the developmental peace approach encourages endogenous development. It does this through supporting local development as the starting point, thus showing the potential to avoid the dilemma between peace and security engagements and regarding adherence to the principle of non-interference.

Fourth and finally, the approach leaves room for theoretical integration with other relative concepts – especially liberal peace theory. The latter derives from the democratic peace theory of International Relations and holds that the building-up of the domestic political system and security governance are conducive to peace and stability. For conflict-affected countries, self-sustaining peace can accordingly be achieved only through political and market liberalization (Mac Ginty 2008; Kuo 2012, 2015).

From here, one can identify the commonality between the liberal peace theory and developmental peace concept. Both stress the preconditions of security and governance, and the importance of self-sustaining peace. However, the two theories propose totally different solutions to these issues: first, regarding how high the security and governance thresholds should be; second, regarding how to actually realize self-sustaining peace. For the developmental peace approach, on the one hand, ideal security and governance conditions are not necessary for development – unlike for liberal peace theory. Rather, the former seeks development as long as a minimum governance and security basis exists. On the other hand, the developmental peace approach also supports endogenous development as it is seen as laying down the foundations for self-sustaining peace, while liberal peace theory neglects the sustainability of resource needs vis-à-vis security and governance. The building-up of security and governance institutions in itself cannot produce new resources to relieve the existing resource-scarcity situation in conflict-affected countries, made worse by intense competition between rival parties – even if it may contribute to the better distribution of such scarce resources. By making bigger pies, developmental peace has the potential to effectively solve existing resource scarcity. Thus while liberal peace theory focuses on crafting security and governance institutions, the developmental peace approach favors the promotion of development – and hence offers longer-term solutions. Integrating these two concepts might, then, be a valuable starting point for securing effective, self-sustaining peace in conflict-affected countries.

Conclusion

Although still under construction, the developmental peace concept has the potential to better portray the theoretical and practical bases for China's engagement in international peace and security affairs. It can also address the challenges of realizing self-sustaining peace, or the sustainability of peace emphasized by liberal peace theory, by building a dynamic balance between development, reform (governance), and stability (security). China's engagement in Sudan's and South Sudan's peace and security shows how the Asian country has moved from passive responses to actively shaping a developmental peace approach – even if there is still a long way to go. As a latecomer to African peace and security affairs, it is too early to comprehensively evaluate the impacts of China thereon – let alone the ultimate feasibility of its developmental peace concept.

There are, indeed, still internal challenges in terms of the conceptualization of developmental peace: first, as the number of cases for testing the developmental peace approach in Africa is limited, it is too early to thoroughly review its effectiveness. Second, China is still on its way in terms of rising, without it having enough strength or capacities to emphasize global security public goods provision – which implies some uncertainties for developmental peace in the future. Third, given the unique nature of China's political system and its domestic development experience, it is hard to tell whether the therefrom-derived developmental peace approach can be successfully practiced in other places around the globe. Furthermore, it is hard to predict whether the target country will indeed agree to shift its focus from security to development. China's role options as a security provider in Africa are further limited and constrained by the perception and evaluation of its actions by other external powers, given that actor constellations in Africa remain dominated by 'position competition'.

Notes

1 I am grateful to Dr. He Yin, Dr. Steven C. Y. Kuo, and Dr. Guillaume Moumouni for their valuable comments. I am solely responsible for the chapter and its contents.

2 The IPF consists mainly of donors to IGAD, and comprises three levels of membership: ministers, ambassadors, and technical staff. Current membership includes: Austria, Belgium, Canada, Denmark, France, Germany, Greece, Ireland, Italy, Japan, the Netherlands, Norway, Sweden, Switzerland, the United Kingdom, the US, the European Commission, the International Organization for Migration, the United Nations Development Programme, and the World Bank.

References

Abramowitz, M. and Kolieb, J. (2007) *Why China won't save Darfur*, (www.foreignpolicy.com/story/cms.php?story_id=3847), accessed 5 June 2019.

Agubamah, E. (2014) 'China and Peacekeeping in Africa', *International Journal of Humanities and Social Science*, 4(11), 193–197.

Alden, C., Alao, A., Chun, Z. and Barber, L. (eds) (2018) *China and Africa: Building Peace and Security Cooperation on the Continent*, Palgrave, London and New York.

Alden, C. and Large, D. (2013) 'China's Evolving Policy towards Peace and Security in Africa: Constructing a New Paradigm for Peace Building?', in M. G. Behre and L. Hongwu (eds) *China Africa Relations: Governance, Peace, and Security*, Institute of Peace and Security Studies, Addis Ababa, 16–28.

Alden, C., Large, D. and de Oliveira, R. S. (eds) (2008) *China Returns to Africa: A Rising Power and a Continent Embrace*, Columbia University Press, New York.

Ban, K.-M. (2007) 'A Climate Culprit in Darfur', *The Washington Post*, 16 June, 15.

Benabdallah, L. (2016) 'China's Peace and Security Strategies in Africa: Building Capacity is Building Peace?', *African Studies Quarterly*, 16 (3–4), 17–34.

Bräutigam, D. (2009) *The Dragon's Gift: The Real Story of China in Africa*, Oxford University Press, Oxford.

CAITEC (Chinese Academy of International Trade and Economic Cooperation) (2018) *FDI Country Direction, South Sudan 2017*, Chinese Academy of International Trade and Economic Cooperation, Beijing.

Chen, M. (2018) 'China Constructively Participating in African Peace and Security Affairs: New Situations, New Practice, New Challenges, and New Measures', *Learning Weekly*, (13), 187–190.

China News (2011) *China hopes Southern Sudan to keep stable and order in referendum*, (www.chinanews.com/gn/2011/01-11/2780649.shtml), accessed 11 January 2019.

CNPC (China National Petroleum Corporation) (2010) *CNPC in Sudan*, (www.petrochina.com.cn/hdipad/gbbg/201404/b1fc7e59279449af9ac78f527cd9c293/files/0e539fe82dee4212a8f5e0ea6850fa9d.pdf), accessed 11 November 2018.

Condon, M. (2012) 'China in Africa: What the Policy of Nonintervention Adds to the Western Development Dilemma', *The Fletcher Journal of Human Security*, 27(5), 5–25.

Cooper, H. (2007) *Darfur collides with Olympics, and China yields*, (www.nytimes.com/2007/04/13/washington/13diplo.html?_r=1&oref=slogin), accessed 13 April 2019.

Evans, G. and Steinberg, D. (2007) *Signs of transition*, (www.theguardian.com/commentisfree/2007/jun/11/signsoftransition?INTCMP=SRCH), accessed 11 June 2018.

He, W. (2015) 'Features of African Security Situation and New Perspectives on China-Africa Security Cooperation', *Asia and Africa Review*, 21(2), 1–14.

He, Y. (2013) 'China's Rising and International Normative System: A Case Study on UN Peacekeeping Operations', *New Strategy Studies*, (3), 37–42.

He, Y. (2014a) 'China EU Cooperation on UN Peacekeeping: Opportunities and Challenges', in F. Austermann, X. Wang and A. Vangeli (eds) *Europe and China in 21st Century Global Politics: Partnership, Competition, or Co-Evolution?* Cambridge Scholars Publishing, London, 43–61.

He, Y. (2014b) 'Normative Competition and Complementation: A Case Study on Peacebuilding', *World Economics and Politics*, 28(3), 105–121.

He, Y. (2014c) 'UN Peacebuilding and Protection of Human Security', *Journal of International Security Studies*, 32(3), 75–91.

He, Y. (2017) 'China's Doctrine on UN Peacekeeping', in C. de Coning, C. Aoi and J. Karlsrud (eds) *UN Peacekeeping Doctrine in a New Era*, Routledge, London, 109–131.

ICG (International Crisis Group) (2015) *South Sudan: Keeping Faith with the IGAD Peace Process*, Africa Report no. 228, International Crisis Group, Brussels.

ICG (International Crisis Group) (2016) *South Sudan: Rearranging the Chessboard*, Africa Report no. 243, International Crisis Group, Brussels.

Kuo, S. C. Y. (2012) 'Beijing's Understanding of African Security: Context and Limitations', *African Security*, 5(1), 24–43.

Kuo, S. C. Y. (2015) 'Chinese Peace? An Emergent Norm in African Peace Operations', *China Quarterly of International Strategic Studies*, 1(1), 155–181.

Large, D. (2009) 'China's Sudan Engagement: Changing Northern and Southern Political Trajectories in Peace and War', *The China Quarterly*, 199, 610–626.

Li, W. (2018) 'China-Africa Military-Security Cooperation Steps to Higher Level' *World Affairs*, No. 15.

Lyman, P. (2011) *Briefing on the current situation in Sudan*, (https://2009-2017.state.gov/s/sudan/rem/2011/167495.htm), accessed 1 July 2018.

Mac Ginty, R. (2008) 'Indigenous Peace-Making Versus the Liberal Peace', *Cooperation and Conflict*, 43(2), 139–159.

MOFA (Ministry of Foreign Affairs) (2006) *President Hu Jintao meets with Presidents of Botswana and Sudan*, (www.fmprc.gov.cn/web/gjhdq_676201/gj_676203/fz_677316/1206_678526/xgxw_678532/t278557.shtml), accessed 2 November 2018.

MOFA (Ministry of Foreign Affairs) (2007a) *Hu Jintao meets with Sudanese First Vice President*, (www.fmprc.gov.cn/mfa_eng/wjb_663304/zzjg_663340/xybfs_663590/gjlb_663594/2883_663766/2885_663770/t343862.shtml), accessed 19 July 2018.

MOFA (Ministry of Foreign Affairs) (2007b) *President Hu Jintao meets with First Vice President Salva Kiir Mayardit and Vice President Ali Osman Taha*, (www.fmprc.gov.cn/web/gjhdq_676201/gj_676203/fz_677316/1206_678526/xgxw_678532/t294360.shtml), accessed 4 February 2019.

MOFA (Ministry of Foreign Affairs) (2007c) *President Hu Jintao meets with Sudanese President Al-Bashir*, (www.fmprc.gov.cn/web/gjhdq_676201/gj_676203/fz_677316/1206_678526/xgxw_678532/t294619.shtml), accessed 4 February 2019.

MOFA (Ministry of Foreign Affairs) (2012) *Hu Jintao holds talks with South Sudanese President Salva Kiir Mayardit*, (www.fmprc.gov.cn/mfa_eng/wjb_663304/zzjg_663340/xybfs_663590/gjlb_663594/sousu_663756/ssaa_663760/t926468.shtml), accessed 24 April 2019.

MOFA (Ministry of Foreign Affairs) (2014) *Li Keqiang meets with Vice President James Wani Igga of South Sudan*, (www.fmprc.gov.cn/mfa_eng/wjb_663304/zzjg_663340/xybfs_663590/gjlb_663594/sousu_663756/ssaa_663760/t1171075.shtml), accessed 1 July 2018.

MOFA (Ministry of Foreign Affairs) (2018) *Amb. Wu Haitao statement at UNSC open discussion on South Sudan issue*, (www.fmprc.gov.cn/ce/ceun/chn/hyyfy/t1597008.htm), accessed 18 September 2018.

NPR (National Public Radio) (2007) *Darfur activists push Spielberg to pressure China*, (www.npr.org/templates/story/story.php?storyId=12204096), accessed 24 July 2018.

Osondu, A. (2013) 'Off and On: China's Principle of Non-Interference in Africa', *Mediterranean Journal of Social Sciences*, 4(3), 225–234.

Reeves, E. (2007) *On China and the 2008 Olympic Games: An open letter to Darfur activists and advocates*, (www.sudanreeves.org/files/File/2008%20Olympics%20(Chinese).pdf), accessed 10 February 2017.

Sachs, J. D. (2007) *No development, no peace*, (www.project-syndicate.org/commentary/no-development-no-peace?barrier=accesspaylog), accessed 20 July 2018.

Southall, G. and Melber, H. (eds) (2009) *A New Scramble for Africa? Imperialism, Investment and Development*, University of KwaZulu-Natal Press, Scottsville.

Southern Sudan Referendum (2011) *Results for the referendum of Southern Sudan*, (http://southernsudan2011.com/), accessed 10 July 2018.

Sudan Tribune (2008a) *China makes constant efforts to resolve crisis in Darfur – envoy*, (www.sudantribune.com/spip.php?article25995), accessed 17 February 2019.

Sudan Tribune (2008b) *China provides more humanitarian aid to Darfur*, (www.sudantribune.com/spip.php?article26144), accessed 26 February 2019.

Taylor, I. and Williams, P. (eds) (2004) *Africa in International Politics: External Involvement on the Continent*, Routledge, London.

Tull, D. (2006) 'China's Engagement in Africa: Scope, Significance and Consequences', *The Journal of Modern African Studies*, 44(3), 459–479.

United Nations Environment Programme (2007) *Sudan: Post-Conflict Environmental Assessment*, United Nations Environment Programme, Nairobi.

Verhoeven, H. (2014) 'Is Beijing's Non-Interference Policy History? How Africa is Changing China', *The Washington Quarterly*, 37(2), 55–70.

Wang, B. and Qi, X. (2018) 'China-Africa Defense and Security Cooperation in New Era' *China Investment*, No. 16.

Wang, H. (2018) 'New Challenges for African Security and Impacts on China-Africa Cooperation', *International Studies*, No. 4.

Wang, X. and Zhang, J. (2018) 'China and Reconstruction of International Peace Norm System: Africa as Case Study', *Area Study and Global Development*, 3(3), 35–45.

Wang, Yi (2014) *China sincerely hopes for an early, comprehensive and proper settlement of South Sudan issue*, (www.fmprc.gov.cn/mfa_eng/zxxx_662805/t1194118.shtml), accessed 22 September 2018.

Wang, Yi (2015) *Explore effective solutions with Chinese characteristics to hotspot issues in Africa*, (www.fmprc.gov.cn/mfa_eng/zxxx_662805/t1322225.shtml), accessed 6 December 2018.

Wang, Yizhou (2011) *Creative Involvement: A New Direction in China's Diplomacy*, Peking University Press, Beijing.

Wang, Yizhou (2013) *Creative Involvement: The Transition of China's Diplomacy*, Peking University Press, Beijing.

Wang, Yizhou (2015) *Creative Involvement: The Evolution of China's Global Role*, Peking University Press, Beijing.

Wang, Yizhou (2018) *Creative Involvement: The Transition of China's Diplomacy*, Routledge, London.

Wu, Z. and Taylor, I. (2011) 'From Refusal to Engagement: Chinese Contributions to Peacekeeping in Africa', *Journal of Contemporary African Studies*, 29(2), 137–154.

Zaobao (2008) *Amb. Liu Guijin says China willing to be Sudan's external bridge*, (http://realtime.zaobao.com/2008/02/080224_35.shtml), accessed 8 February 2019.

Zhang, C. (2018) 'China-Africa Peace and Security Cooperation in the New Era: Providing International Public Goods through an Innovative Way', *Contemporary World*, No. 10.

Zhang, H. (2013) *Development-Oriented Aid: China's Aid Model towards Africa*, Shanghai People's Publishing House, Shanghai.

11 China and Rwanda – natural allies or uneasy partners in regime stability?

Sven Grimm and Christine Hackenesch

Introduction

During the past two decades, China has become a more influential global actor and a more important economic and political partner for African countries. The rise of a (nominally) communist, authoritarian regime has caused concern that China would be a particular challenge to weak states, weak democracies, and authoritarian regimes. In cases of weak statehood, the concern is that Chinese actors would exploit weak institutions and thereby contribute to further corruption and resource exploitation. In fragile democracies and authoritarian regimes, one could expect that China contributes to strengthening authoritarian institutions – either by providing economic resources 'with no strings attached' that help stabilize these institutions or by providing advice and assistance to non-democratic actors. Skepticism about China's influence on political regimes and institutions elsewhere has been nurtured with the announcement of President Xi Jinping during the last Chinese Communist Party congress in October 2017 that China is now going to promote its political model abroad.

This chapter explores the potential effect of China's cooperation on African authoritarian regimes and states, using the case of Rwanda. Rwanda is a small-sized, landlocked African country, situated in a region with substantial mineral wealth, but with little to no mineral resources of its own. Since the Rwandan genocide in the early 1990s, the country has seen a remarkable improvement of a number of development indicators. Yet, despite these improvements human development levels remain low, and developing the human capital of Rwanda requires substantial investments, for which finance needs to be sought.

At least partly based on its socio-economic development improvements, Rwanda has emerged as a donor darling. It has seen a large number of donors wanting to engage in the country, i.e., wanting to be part of this development success story. Rwanda's dependency on financial assistance is particularly high. At the same time, Rwanda's record with regard to political freedoms is less favorable. Rwanda is a country with a closed authoritarian regime, strong statehood and government. China's engagement with Rwanda is driven by political, strategic, and aid-policy interests (not too different from Western actors), whereas business interests do not play a prominent role in China's relation with Rwanda.

Within the spectrum of cases considered in this edited volume, Rwanda is clearly located at the side of strong statehood and closed authoritarian settings. It allows us to explore how China contributes, or does not contribute, to the stabilization of strong African states and authoritarian regimes. Rwanda combines a strong statehood and stable regime with strong agency in its international relations (Brown and Harman 2013; Grimm 2013). This gives opportunity to explore how African agency plays out in China–Africa relations and how African governments use their cooperation with China to further their domestic interests and ultimately regime survival.

In the first part of the chapter, we analyze domestic politics and characteristics of Rwanda's political regime. In the second part, we explore whether – and if so, how – Rwanda's regime characteristics matter for China's engagement in the country and to what extent economic cooperation with China helps Rwanda's regime survival (also compared to other international actors). The chapter is based on primary and secondary literature analysis and interviews with thirty-eight Rwandan and Chinese officials, experts and business representatives conducted in Kigali and Beijing in July 2013.

Domestic politics in Rwanda – authoritarianism with economic performance

Academic research on Rwanda is quite polarized and has caused controversial debates among scholars on how to assess the political and economic situation of the country. Some experts highlight the socio-economic performance, progress in poverty reduction, the effectiveness of the Rwandan state, the government's efforts to improve the business environment, and President Kagame's active engagement in international and continental organizations and debates (Booth and Golooba-Muthebi 2012). Others emphasize that Rwanda is a closed authoritarian, party-based regime where elections are not free and fair, political opposition parties are absent or harassed, and media and civil society organizations are not allowed to critically engage on political issues (Reyntjens 2013). Both of these descriptions of Rwanda are part of the same coin; they are specific features of Rwanda's authoritarian regime.

Domestic politics and political regime dynamics

The government of Rwanda has a strong interest in building an effective state that not only limits political opposition, but is at the same time geared towards poverty reduction and public goods provision (for the following see also Hackenesch 2018, 49–51). These specific features of Rwanda's authoritarian regime are at least partly influenced by structural factors: the core elite on which the Rwandan leadership relies to remain in power is relatively small and ethnicity based. Even though the leadership made efforts to include Hutu in prominent positions, the core elite remains composed of Tutsi, some of them refugees from Uganda who fought the war against Hutu extremists to end the genocide in 1994. Given the circumstances of how the ruling party, the Rwandan Patriotic Front (RPF), came to power and its narrow support group, the Rwandan leadership is confronted with a considerable security dilemma. A regime change or any major political opening could constitute a considerable security threat to the elite. This security dilemma has several implications: the Rwandan leadership has an interest to suppress any kind of opposition, but it has also a strong interest to 'deliver' public services and socio-economic opportunities for the broader population to develop output legitimacy. Rwanda has scarce domestic revenues and no direct access to natural resources that are easy to extract, require little manpower, and could be used for distribution as spoils and perks to regime supporters. The government thus has a strong interest in public goods provision, domestic resource mobilization, and attracting international investments to generate support. Finally, the fact that the international community has remained inactive and did not help Rwanda prevent the genocide probably contributed to the Rwandan leaderships efforts to remain independent and 'in control' of its relations with international actors despite Rwanda's aid dependence.

To address Rwanda's structural challenges, the leadership has developed a comparatively strong state; the state administration functions effectively throughout the country and the government has created a strong presence throughout the country down to the village level (Bertelsmann Stiftung 2016, 6). The level of corruption in Rwanda is very low. According to the Worldwide Governance Indicators, government effectiveness as well as control of corruption have improved since the mid-2000s and Rwanda is among the best performing countries across Africa in these areas. In the Mo Ibrahim Governance Index Rwanda features high in the category 'public management' (rank seven). The least impressive score for Rwanda is also one of the least relevant for engagement of Chinese actors: Rwanda ranks a mere thirty-sixth place on 'participation and human rights.' Improvements in this category were negligible over the last decade (Mo Ibrahim Foundation 2016).

Since the early 2000s, when President Kagame came to power, Rwanda has been relatively stable domestically and has not faced major security challenges within the region. Domestically, opposition towards the RPF-based regime has remained very limited. Some members of the security apparatus have defected and some of them fled the country (Reyntjens 2013). Yet, none of them made attempts to seriously challenge President Kagame. Externally, the Forces Démocratiques de Libération du Rwanda – a rebel movement active in the Eastern part of the Democratic Republic of Congo (DRC) and composed of former Interahamwe and génocidaire who fled to the DRC after the genocide – has caused some challenges for the Rwandan leadership in the early 2000s, but gradually lost relevance (Longman 2004, 75; ICG 2009). The Rwandan government has difficult relations with most of its neighbors at various times, but these disputes over influence within the broader region (particularly with Uganda), refugees (particularly with Burundi and Tanzania), or access to resources (particularly in the Eastern parts of the DRC) have so far hardly resulted in security challenges for Rwanda itself.

Rwanda's development ambitions – and its need for partners

Rwanda's development needs and ambitions require partners, not least private investments. Challenges for development additionally include some geographical features that need to be addressed. The country

- has no access to the sea and is hilly, which results in a geographically difficult setting for hard infrastructure, making transport often costly;
- has a small surface with dense, but scattered population (which makes agricultural change and expansion difficult and at the same time lacks the advantages of urban centers);
- has few geological resources;
- and has high poverty levels, which means that purchasing powers are very limited.

At the same time, positively speaking, Rwanda provides for a compact market with a large and young population and good record with regard to regulatory environment and effective government. Due to its geographical location, it can potentially provide easy access to (natural resource-rich) Eastern Congo and could serve as an entry point to an East African market with more than 120 million inhabitants, according to Chinese officials (Chinese officials, interviews, July 2013). East Africa has also been included in China's foreign relations narrative under Xi Jinping, the 'Belt and Road' initiative (Mukwaya and Mold 2018), and Rwandan President Paul Kagame, often criticizing donors, speaks more highly of China as 'more respectful' (Mugisha 2018).

Given the scarcity of resources for a small and densely populated country like Rwanda, and thus limited opportunities for its elite to engage in rent-seeking, the development-orientation of the government is tangible, and levels of ambition are high. Domestically the Rwandan leadership has clearly limited rent-seeking behavior (see also Bertelsmann Stiftung 2016, 24). In the words of Booth and Golooba-Muthebi (2012, 391): rather than buying off loyalty by distributing rents in a neopatrimonial system, the Rwandan governing elites 'are gambling on the "expensive" option of building support on a broad base by demonstrating an ability to provide more and better public goods.' However, a United Nations (UN) expert panel found that parts of the Rwandan elite including high-level government and military officials have been involved in (illegal) extraction of resources in the Eastern parts of the DRC (UNSC 2014).

The Rwandan government has made considerable investments to improve its regulatory framework and make its business environment attractive for foreign investors. Rwanda's ranking in the Doing Business report has improved considerably since the mid-2000s. However, creating favorable conditions for foreign investors does not directly lead to more investments – according to the World Development Indicators, foreign direct investment (FDI) as a share of gross domestic product (GDP) has been marginal and increased only slightly since 2008.

Beyond creating favorable conditions for business, the government – or rather the party – directly intervenes in the economy so as to grow the economy. With regard to investment activities, the holding Crystal Ventures Ltd (CVL, previously Tri-Star Investment) is a major economic actor in Rwanda. The company owns (or holds major shares of) enterprises in various sectors, ranging from enterprises in furniture via construction, housing, fruit processing, mobile communication to security services. In the company's own description, CVL engages in 'unexplored high-risk sectors that yield high returns but also present opportunities to have a high socioeconomic impact' (Crystal Ventures 2019). It is thus a key business instrument for development in Rwanda. Interestingly, 'with one exception, the competition they face comes primarily from either regional (usually Kenyan) or international (*including notably Chinese*) firms' (Booth and Golooba-Muthebi 2012, 388, italics added). Particularly in construction and telecommunications, Chinese enterprises are key players on the continent – and are also present in Rwanda. This exposure of a key development tool in Rwanda to Chinese competition adds an interesting flavor to the engagement between Rwanda and China, as it prevents an unequivocal embrace of Chinese actors in Rwanda.

Rwanda's overall mid-term development goals are formulated in the Vision 2020: the country aspires for per capita income to reach US$1,240 by 2020, which would make it a middle-income country (Republic of Rwanda 2012). Other targets are: halving the poverty rate from 60.4 percent in 2000 to 30 percent by 2020; to increase life expectancy to 55 years from 49 years in 2000. Overall, the original Vision 2020 had forty-seven indicators, of which twelve were achieved by 2012, and another sixteen were 'highly on-track' to be achieved, such as the average GDP growth rate, agricultural production, infant mortality rate, secondary school transitional rate, malaria-related mortality and admission rate to tertiary education. Consequently, the original targets were replaced by more ambitious ones and comprise forty-eight targets now. The Vision 2020 also included targets for growth rates in sectors of the economy (agriculture: 6 percent; industry: 12 percent; services: 11 percent) and a gross national investment target (30 percent of GDP).

Below the level of the Vision 2020, 5-year Economic Development and Poverty Reduction Strategies (EDPRS) are formulated. The period 2013/2014 to 2017/2018 is the period for the second strategy, EDPRS 2. The government's highly ambitious goals formulated in the Vision 2020 and in the EDPRS 2 demand a strong coordination with the Rwandan administration and clear target-orientation, including interactions with external actors. These goals can only be achieved – if at all – with substantial investment flows from outside Rwanda.

Despite all efforts, Rwanda remains an aid-dependent country. Aid accounts for a share 18–20 percent in a share of Rwanda's gross national income (IMF 2013), making Rwanda one of the most aid-dependent countries in Africa. For its relations with development partners, Rwanda has formulated an Aid Policy in 2006, which describes budget support as the highest preference in aid modality for the Rwandan government. Sector budget support is seen as an alternative.

All other forms of aid are appreciated, but described as less favorable options. In this regard, President Kagame has not only vocally contributed to shaping the international aid effectiveness agenda, but Rwanda has used the agenda to hold its external partners accountable. Despite its high aid dependency, Rwanda is therefore portrayed as a country with exceptionally strong 'ownership' that has considerably more control over its relations with traditional donors than other African countries (Hayman 2009; Whitfield, 2009). This overall framework also defines the goals to which cooperation with China should contribute and against which the tangible effects of interactions with China are measured by the Rwandan government.

China's cooperation with Rwanda – what implications for statehood and regime stability?

We will approach this question from two angles. First, we will discuss the interests of Chinese actors in engaging with Rwanda, and more specifically, to what extent statehood and regime type matter to Chinese actors. Second, we will analyze the interests of Rwandan actors in engaging with China, also compared to their interests in engaging with other external partners. In particular, we will investigate to what extent and under what conditions Chinese engagement helps Rwanda's regime survival and weakens or strengthens Rwanda's statehood. And is China any different than Western partners?

Chinese interests in engaging with Rwanda

Even though China's economic engagement with Rwanda has intensified in recent years, relations are mainly driven by China's political and development aid interests – similar to other international actors' interests in cooperating with Rwanda. Interests and perspectives on economic opportunities in African countries differ among the various Chinese actors. Overall, the variety of interests seems to be increasing on the Chinese side, making engagement less clear-cut and more flexible.

Among Chinese actors, one can roughly differentiate between state (and party) actors on the one hand and private enterprises on the other. Among the various state actors, many actors have a medium to long-term interest in cooperation and they also need to take into account China's broader political interests.

Chinese state actors

Within the Chinese state administration, various actors engage in relations with Rwanda – managed by the Chinese Ministry of Commerce. The Ministry of Foreign Affairs (MOFA) supervises (and manages some) funds committed at Forum for China Africa Cooperation meetings; but the MOFA has a very limited role in finance allocation decisions (Zhao 2008; Corkin 2011). State-owned funding institutions such as China Development Bank (CDB), the sovereign wealth fund China–Africa Development Fund within CDB and the Export–Import Bank of China are main providers of commercial and preferential finance (Grimm et al. 2011). Most of Chinese state actors' engagement follows a business rationale. Funding decisions seek returns on investment and seek to identify economic opportunities rather than mere needs in African countries. All Chinese investment activities that qualify for state support need to be viable, which means technically and financially feasible and commercially beneficial after 5 years. In this context, aid in a Western sense, i.e., grants and subsidized loans, are used as catalysts for Chinese projects in other regions. State-owned institutions appear to also put emphasis on sound management and proper planning in activities abroad; even without using the word and often discussed under the term 'investment climate,' governance structures in host countries become of interest (e.g., Houanye and Shen 2012; Huang and Ren 2013; *South China Morning Post* 2019). The Chinese government views socio-economic development as a 'virtuous circle,' in which stability leads to (economic) development, which creates peace and security (State Council 2016). The Chinese engagement therefore has a high interest in the stability of existing conditions also when engaging abroad.[1]

In this regard, Chinese officials see very similar advantages in engaging with Rwanda compared to Western donors, particularly when it comes to Rwanda's political stability, strong state institutions, and government agency: as aid effectiveness and 'results' have become more of a concern for China as well, Chinese actors value the fact that Rwanda uses foreign economic cooperation to promote socio-economic development for the broader population. The relatively strong and effective state institutions and explicit domestic 'development vision' are valued as they help to 'get things done' (Chinese official, interview, July 2013). In contrast to (most) Western actors, Chinese state actors – obviously – are not concerned that economic growth goes hand in hand with a closed authoritarian regime. The closed space prevents any option for critical debates in the Rwanda parliament, the media, civil society, or the broader public about China's engagement. Yet, Rwanda is also not one of those countries, where one would expect that China's engagement was very critically discussed if political spaces would allow for it: China has emerged as a medium size donor, but is nowhere near the size of other large Western donors; China has not provided commercial loans for large infrastructure projects that might lead to a debt-trap and cause fear of how China uses the strategic influence (unlike for instance in Tanzania or Ethiopia); Chinese trade has not crowded out local companies, caused unemployment for local labor or major controversies around cheap consumer goods. While Rwanda's authoritarian regime is no specific ethical or political concern of China's government, it also does not per se make it easier to cooperate.

Business and private actors

Within the private segment of investors, some entrepreneurs aim for long-term business opportunities whereas others are interested in quick-wins. The latter are arguably more prone to seek shortcuts in procedures and they see higher corruption levels not necessarily as a threat, but rather as an opportunity to operate in a 'flexible' manner – as is an option in the Chinese domestic setting. These actors are a concern to the Chinese officials, who present them as 'bad apples' (that spoil the barrel), i.e., as a threat to China's reputation (Chinese official, interview, July 2013). Yet, Chinese supervision of quality delivery by local representatives is patchy at best and leaves this task to often ill-prepared African administrations.

The strong public management is likely to make Kigali a rather difficult partner, as negotiating shortcuts for investors will be less easy than in settings with 'big man' personal rule, where benefits – in the form of 'kick-backs' – are easily distributed. Similarly, in a setting of fragmented government, loopholes between actors can be sought and exploited, allowing for a 'smoother' operation of investment from the investors' perspective. In a strong authoritarian state like Rwanda, these conditions are less present, making Rwanda a more difficult place for short-term, quick-win interested investors, including Chinese enterprises.

Private investment decisions are understood not to be much influenced by international rankings such as Ease of Doing Business or the like, thereby ignoring Rwanda's top performance as a business destination. Rather, for small-scale enterprises, it seems to be a word-of-mouth promotion and business linkages build substantially on trust in established relationships ('guanxi' is a key Chinese business term, describing this network of relations). Rwanda therefore has made efforts to engage directly with Chinese businesses, and the state is providing guidance for enterprises, e.g., with a leaflet by the Rwandan Development Board for potential business partner matching between Rwanda and China.

Rwanda's strategic engagement with China – claiming Rwandan gains

While the Rwandan government regards China as one development partner among others, China claims to provide cooperation of a different kind, alongside other Southern development partners. The distinct features of such South–South Cooperation and how it differs from North–South Cooperation is subject to debate.

Does Chinese aid have stabilizing effects?

While being called 'more respectful' by President Kagame, China does not provide more assistance than Western actors and does not engage in sectors or through aid modalities that would have a more regime-stabilizing effect than aid provided by other actors.

Reading the volume of Chinese aid to Rwanda from official statistics is difficult, as Chinese aid figures are not published on a country-by-country basis (Bräutigam 2009; Grimm et al. 2011). For African governments the volume of development assistance they receive from China is often difficult to estimate, as the financial value of technical or in-kind assistance is unknown or prices on which Rwandan estimates are based differ from prices indicated by Chinese project implementers (Chinese and Rwandan government officials, interviews, July 2013). Estimates suggest that between 2005 and 2012, Rwanda received roughly US$245 million in grants, interest-free, and concessional loans from China (Hackenesch 2018, 79–80). Chinese interlocutors claimed that, compared to other African countries, Rwanda's aid from China is in the mid-range, being comparatively higher than what could be expected given the size of the country and (very limited) bilateral trade volumes (Chinese researcher, interview, July 2013; government official, interview, July 2013). This statement suggests that the Rwandan government is quite successful in accessing Chinese assistance funds; yet, it also suggests that Rwanda is unlikely to experience significant increases in its assistance from China.

With regard to modalities, Chinese aid is not more supportive to the regime in place than other foreign assistance. The Rwandan government's preference for grants, and specifically for direct budgetary support, sits square with Chinese aid practice of turnkey projects and (concessional and interest-free) loans that are tied to delivery by Chinese enterprises. Calls for tenders are done in China rather than internationally. Budget support is not provided by China; it is associated with 'donorship,' which China (still) regards as contrary to its own principles.[2] Rather, Beijing speaks of win–win situations and thus highlights that business gains for Chinese actors are important.

Past Chinese aid projects in Rwanda included the building of Rwanda's Ministry of Foreign Affairs (around US$8 million), partial debt cancellation for Rwanda, and the establishment of a Confucius Institute at the Kigali Institute of Education (Shinn and Eisenman 2012, 298–299). The oldest interaction is the sending of a medical team to Rwanda's Eastern Province, staffed by a medical team from China's Inner Mongolia province. This traditional mode of engagement – dubbed the 'barefoot doctors' in the old days of Maoist engagement – has been complemented with more recent types of international health engagement. For instance, the Masaka Hospital was refurbished and engages in malaria-related research. As in other African countries, the Chinese government also grants scholarships for Rwandan students to study in China (Grimm et al. 2010).

In a rationale of increasing planning certainty, by July 2013, three African governments – including that in Kigali – had succeeded in committing the Chinese side to 5-year plans in development cooperation, i.e., provided a list of national priorities from which Beijing should choose its cooperation projects. This was meant as an attempt to rein Beijing into 'aid coordination' despite their official rejection of the discourse (Rwandan government official, interview July 2013).

Does China undermine Western conditionality?

China arguably plays a regime-stabilizing role when providing assistance in periods during which Western actors seek to use aid funds as a leverage for promoting political reforms. In Rwanda, one case in point would be the period after 2012, when Western donors were withholding direct budget support (see Hackenesch 2018, 83–86 for the following). When the UN expert panel accused parts of the Rwandan government of supporting rebel groups in Eastern provinces of the DRC, key development finance institutions and donors such as the World Bank, the African Development Bank, the European Union (EU), the United States, Germany, the United Kingdom, and the Netherlands partly suspended or at least withheld some of their aid funds. Aid levels eventually did not reduce, but donors started to shift aid funds from budget support to sector budget support and project aid.

The Rwandan government strongly criticized these decisions of using aid funds as a political leverage. In the short term, withholding of aid funds, particularly of budget support funds, generated considerable costs for the Rwandan government. According to the International Monetary Fund, the delayed budget support funds amounted to about 3 percent of Rwanda's GDP (IMF 2013). In 2013, growth figures halved to 4.7 percent, by far the lowest rate since 2000 (EIU 2013). Particularly in the short term, the Rwandan government had difficulties in paying civil servants, as aid modalities shifted beyond the Rwanda government's budget. Even if aid levels eventually did not drop considerably, the Rwandan government was put under serious pressure.

Cooperation with China helped to stabilize the Rwandan regime, but clearly did not replace Western donors (Hackenesch 2018, 83–86). In parallel to these disputes over Rwanda's engagement in the DRC, China increased its development funds to Rwanda. In September 2012, only a few weeks after donors withheld budget support, President Kagame visited Beijing and signed a US$25 million grant and interest-free loan agreement (*New Times* 2012). At the end of December 2012, China pledged two more interest-free loans amounting to US$35 million for infrastructure development in Rwanda (*New Times* 2012).[3] For the Rwandan government, these loans certainly came timely and were much welcomed. Yet, these grants and loans were small compared to the volume of aid used by Western donors to exert pressure on the Rwandan government and they were no direct substitute for the loss in budget support funds. Overall, China's support was therefore probably very welcome, and helped – practically and symbolically – in moments of financial need. Yet, it did not fully guarantee overall and long-term regime stability.

Do Chinese FDI and trade contribute to regime stability?

Beyond development assistance, Chinese FDI and trade also provide interesting access to resources that might contribute to stabilizing the political regime. Similar to Chinese development assistance, China's relevance might not be too different from Western economic cooperation with Rwanda. As Dollar (2016, 33) notes, Chinese investment in Africa is both big and small. Overall, China ranked fifth as country of origin of investment in Africa; yet, its FDI flows accounted for only 4.4 percent of the total to Africa in 2013 and 2014, and FDI stocks were at 3.2 percent in 2011 (Dollar 2016, 34). Given the enormous size of the Chinese market, agricultural and mineral commodities are often sought in large quantities. And this certainly is a challenge to a small and resource-poor country like Rwanda.

Investment data suggest that Rwanda has not attracted particularly high investments from China despite (politically supported) investments in a textile factory in 2014, which received considerable media attention. A state visit by Xi Jinping in July 2018 might help to put the country on the map for Chinese investors. Its motivation, however, will mostly have been political, as Rwanda's President was a critic of too close relations to any foreign partner, including China.[4] Overall, Chinese investment stocks by the end of 2011 were ranked twenty-ninth for Rwanda for Mainland China. Even when data for Hong Kong (twenty-fourth) and the People's Republic China are collapsed into one figure, investment stocks in Rwanda were still smaller than those of Cyprus, Tanzania, or Togo, accounting for roughly the same investment stocks as Malaysia and the United Arab Emirates, and being only one-tenth of the amount of FDI stock of each of the leading two countries South Africa and Kenya.[5] Shinn and Eisenman (2012, 299) report an overall value of Chinese companies' contracts of US$500 million, with, at the time, an estimated 700 Chinese citizens in Rwanda. These data, however, need to be triangulated. Specifically, private investment from China is chronically underreported in Chinese statistics, and thus requires inquiries into data from Chinese provinces and national data from Rwanda (Shen 2013).

The competition with Chinese enterprises, including in the construction sector, is subject to state regulation and insistence on development planning in Rwanda, not least due to interests by the ruling party in this sector. In some instances, much to the puzzlement of Chinese officials, aid-subsidized activities in construction have been rejected by the Rwandan government, even though they were suggested as grants (Grimm 2013, 93). This was justified with different priorities by the Rwandan government, but can be expected to have also been based on the understanding that Chinese enterprises seek market access – and will thus have to be directed with a view to local capacities, not least so regarding Rwandan companies that generate revenue for domestic development.

Rwanda's small size as a market could be understood as an advantage in a few instances, such as hotel construction or telecommunications, where Rwanda is considered a 'compact' market and has been an entry point for both a mobile phone producer and a TV provider. In a geographically small country with high population density like Rwanda, costs for infrastructure development (and maintenance) are much lower for a relatively large group of customers than in other, less densely populated areas (Chinese officials, interviews, July 2013). This makes Rwanda possibly more prone to receive Chinese government funding for infrastructure than its location and small size might suggest.

Whereas bilateral trade between Rwanda and China was close to zero in the early 2000s, since 2006 China's share in Rwanda's trade has grown rapidly until around 2010, when Chinese imports to Rwanda were at US$55 million and exports to China were worth US$39 million (Shinn and Eisenman 2012, 299). In 2011, China was the fifth-largest trading partner for Rwanda after Kenya, the EU as a whole, Uganda and the United States (UNCTAD, 2016) and has surpassed the EU to become the second-largest Rwandan export destination after exports towards the East African community. Since, however, the trade has not expanded and UN trade data is reporting an import volume of US$33 million from China and Rwandan exports to China at a mere US$4.8 million in 2016 (UN Comtrade 2018a, 2018b). While these figures do not include Hong Kong, which is listed separately, the message remains that the Chinese market is not creating a boost to Rwandan trade and no substantial additional opportunities that could have a particular effect on regime stability that is different from Western engagement.

China and Rwanda – natural allies or too similar to attract?

Both Rwanda and China are strong states with relatively stable, authoritarian regimes. Yet, for Sino-Rwandan relations, the relationship between the two 'development now, democracy later' proponents is less smooth than one might expect. Pragmatism prevails in Chinese foreign policy since the end of the Cold War, after some hurtful experiences with ideology-led policy (Fernandes 2012, 69; Shinn and Eisenman 2012, 343). As stability is a prevailing motivation for Chinese foreign policy, there is neither a revolutionary zeal vis-à-vis multiparty settings nor a motivation to strongly engage for more inclusive governance in authoritarian partner countries. However, hard economic interests have come to the fore since the Chinese economic reforms, and this entails difficulties for the Rwandan government and its primary aim to ensure its own regime stability: China will be of help if it serves China's own interests, but China is probably not reliable as an ally out of conviction. For a small country like Rwanda, this is not a comfortable setting, as the imbalance between the two partners is massive.

Active support for regime stability depends on immediate benefit for Chinese economic abilities to deliver for its own population. However, in the mutual business engagement, neither country can play its specific advantage: Rwanda's wealth is in very few agricultural commodities (coffee and tea, mostly) and potentially in its people. From a Chinese perspective, none of these features makes the country economically complementary to China. An exception might be the production of coffee, which is increasingly popular in China's urban middle-class. Yet, coffee is not a strategic commodity, but a (luxury) consumption good. In other words: the inequality of the relationship is bound to persist and Rwanda can provide no strategically important good or commodity that would propel it into Chinese focus. Nevertheless, from a Rwandan perspective, China has the potential to become a more important trade partner and country of origin of investment. China is thus an obvious partner to turn to when the relation to Western countries goes rough, not unlike other African states and their 'Look East' strategies.

At the same time, Rwanda's attempts to structure bilateral cooperation according to its own preferences are perceived as somewhat 'irritating' by China. The often-cited win–win rationale of cooperation (in a South–South context) expects considerable gains to be generated for Chinese actors. The similarity of the elites' mindset might rather be an obstacle than a facilitating factor, and from a Rwandan perspective, China holds a lot of disruptive potential to the Rwandan development path. In direct contacts, meeting an equally development-oriented government in Kigali makes discussions particularly difficult, as both Rwanda and China are first and foremost concerned with their respective national developments. In this encounter, Beijing presumably finds a true test to its potentially contradictory two claims of aspiring to a win–win setting and, at the same time, operating only demand-driven in its South–South-Cooperation. High institutional stability and low levels of corruption in Rwanda are positive, but for a number of Chinese actors, this is also a complicating factor. Bribing politicians in neopatrimonial states who operate according to the politics of the belly might be easier than organizing around Rwandan rules and their policing. The rules-based and competitive setting that the Rwandan state provides is often simply too small and has too few resources to lead to a sort of proverbial 'gold rush' of Chinese private investors.

In situations where political developments facilitate donors' collective action to put pressure on the Rwandan government, the fragility of the country's agency becomes obvious. Rwanda can thus be expected to have a strong incentive to grow out of aid in the longer run, but also to diversify the basis of development finance in the short term, so as to counter pressures from Western donors. The bigger threat to Kigali appears to be the giant size of China – and possible negligence of small partners, including possible involuntary effects of policy-making in Beijing on Rwanda. President Kagame's outspokenness can thus also be understood as an attempt to gain relevance to large external partners, and thus ensuring stability of his regime by being internationally 'punching above his weight.' For Rwanda, it thus seems that it should not be getting too close to Beijing, as that would increase the risk of being overlooked. Rather, an independent foreign policy role and an ability to pique the giant partner (without overly annoying it) seems thus crucial, thus limiting Beijing's direct influence on regime stability in Rwanda and Beijing's direct impact on Kigali's role in peace and security in the region.

Notes

1 According to the logic, Chinese investments contribute to development and thus create peace. The success of this economistic strategy without regard to identities can certainly be challenged with a view to Western China. In international relations, however, from this starting point, the engagement in authoritarian states is not a moral problem for the Chinese government. In the official view, this is not surprising. According to this narrative, the reference to the possibly low political sustainability of this commitment is not valid.

2 However, with recent fears of debt distress, Chinese actors have issued 'bridging credit,' e.g., to Ethiopia. At the same time, a discussion on debt sustainability has also emerged in China (Reuters 2018).

3 China's motivation for providing these funds at that specific point in time remains subject to speculation. It coincided not only with Western conditionality but also with Rwanda's membership in the UN Security Council. Permanent members of the Security Council usually step up their support for non-permanent members during their mandate.

4 At the time of Xi's visit to Kigali, Kagame was Chairperson of the African Union (January 2018 to February 2019). Paul Kagame, reportedly having criticized fellow African leaders for not having funded the African Union headquarters by African funds, 'endorsed' Chinese aid at the occasion of a visit to China in September 2018 (*Rwanda Today* 2018).

5 Information is based on figures provided to the authors by the Rwanda Development Board in July 2013.

References

Bertelsmann Stiftung (2016) *Bertelsmann Transformation Index: Country Report Rwanda*, Bertelsmann Stiftung, Gütersloh.

Booth, D. and Golooba-Muthebi, F. (2012) 'Developmental Patrimonialism? The Case of Rwanda', *African Affairs*, 111(444), 379–403.

Bräutigam, D. (2009) *The Dragon's Gift: The Real Story of China in Africa*, Oxford University Press, Oxford.

Brown, W. and Harman, S. (eds) (2013) *African Agency in International Politics*, Routledge, London.

Corkin, L. (2011) 'Redefining Foreign Policy Impulses toward Africa: The Roles of the MFA, the MOFCOM and China Exim Bank', *Journal of Current Chinese Affairs*, 40(4), 61–90.

Crystal Ventures (2019) *Our portfolio*, (www.cvl.co.rw/), accessed 15 May 2019.

Dollar, D. (2016) *China's Engagement with Africa: From Natural Resources to Human Resources*, John L. Thornton China Center at Brookings, Washington, DC.

EIU (Economist Intelligence Unit) (2013) *Country Report Rwanda – March 2013*, Economist Intelligence Unit, London.

Fernandes, S. (2012) 'China and Angola: A Strategic Partnership?', in M. Power and A. Alves (eds) *China and Angola: A Marriage of Convenience?*, Pambazuka Press, Cape Town, 68–84.

Grimm, S. (2013) 'Aid Dependency as a Limitation to National Development Policy? The Case of Rwanda', in W. Brown and S. Harman (eds) *African Agency in International Politics*, Routledge, London, 81–96.

Grimm, S., Höß, H., Knappe, K., Siebold, M., Sperrfechter, J. and Vogler, I. (2010) *Coordinating China and DAC Development Partners: Challenges to the Aid Architecture in Rwanda*, German Development Institute Studies no. 56, German Development Institute, Bonn.

Grimm, S., Rank, R., McDonald, D. and Schickerling, E. (2011) *Transparency of Chinese Aid: An Analysis of the Published Information on Chinese External Financial Flows*, Publish What You Fund and Centre for Chinese Studies, Stellenbosch.

Hackenesch, C. (2018) *The EU and China in African Authoritarian Regimes: Domestic Politics and Governance Reforms*, Palgrave MacMillan, Basingstoke.

Hayman, R. (2009) 'From Rome to Accra Via Kigali: "Aid Effectiveness" in Rwanda', *Development Policy Review*, 27(5), 581–599.

Houanye, P. and Shen, S. (2012) 'Foreign Direct Investment in Africa: Securing Chinese investments for Lasting Development, the Case of West Africa', *Review of Business and Finance Studies*, 3(2), 103–117.

Huang, M. and Ren, P. (2013) *A Study on the Employment Effect of Chinese Investments in South Africa*, Discussion Paper no. 5, Centre for Chinese Studies, Stellenbosch.

ICG (International Crisis Group) (2009) *Congo: A Comprehensive Strategy to Disarm the FDLR*, Africa Report no. 151, International Crisis Group, Brussels.

IMF (International Monetary Fund) (2013) *Rwanda: 2012 Article IV Consultation and Fifth Review Under the Policy Support Instrument and Request for Modification of Assessment Criteria – Staff Report; Staff Supplement; Public Information Notice and Press Release on the Executive Board Discussion; and Statement by the Executive Director for Rwanda*, IMF Country Report no. 13/77, International Monetary Fund, Washington, DC.

Longman, T. (2004) 'Obstacles to Peacebuilding in Rwanda', in T. M. Ali and O. R. Matthews (eds) *Durable Peace: Challenges for Peacebuilding in Africa*, University of Toronto Press, Toronto.

Mo Ibrahim Foundation (2016) A *Decade of African Governance 2006–2015: Index Report*, Mo Ibrahim Foundation, London.

Mugisha, I. R. (2018) *Rwanda's Kagame endorses Chinese investment in Africa*, (www.theeastafrican.co.ke/news/ea/Rwanda-Paul-Kagame-endorses-Chinese-investment-Africa/4552908-4742800-5brualz/index.html), accessed 15 May 2019.

Mukwaya, R. and Mold, A. (2018) *Modelling the Economic Impact of the China Belt and Road Initiative on East Africa*, paper for the 'African Economic Conference', Kigali, 3–5 December.

New Times (2012) 'China Pledges $25 Million Grant to Rwanda, Kigali', *New Times*, 12 September.

Republic of Rwanda (2012) *Rwanda Vision 2020: Revised 2012*, (www.minecofin.gov.rw/fileadmin/templates/documents/NDPR/Vision_2020_.pdf), accessed 26 November 2018.

Reuters (2018) *Ethiopia PM says China will restructure railway loan*, (www.reuters.com/article/ethiopia-china-loan/update-1-ethiopia-pm-says-china-will-restructure-railway-loan-idUSL5N1VS4IW), accessed 15 May 2019.

Reyntjens, F. (2013) *Political Governance in Post-Genocide Rwanda*, Cambridge University Press, Cambridge.

Rwanda Today (2018) *Kagame endorses China's engagements in Africa*, (http://rwandatoday.africa/news/Kagame-endorses-China-s-engagements-in-Africa/4383214-4741654-v9y-rgg/index.html), accessed 15 May 2019.

Shen, X. (2013) *Chinese Private Investments in Africa: Myth and Realities*, Policy Research Working Paper no. 6311, World Bank, Washington, DC.

Shinn, D. and Eisenman, J. (2012) *China and Africa: A Century of Engagement*, Pennsylvania University Press, Philadelphia.

South China Morning Post (2019) *China's vast investment in Africa hits a snag in Congo*, (www.scmp.com/news/china/diplomacy/article/3007998/chinas-vast-investment-africa-hits-snag-congo), accessed 15 May 2019.

State Council (2016) *The right to development: China's philosophy, practice and contribution*, (http://english.gov.cn/archive/white_paper/2016/12/01/content_281475505407672.htm), accessed 3 May 2019.

UN Comtrade Database (2018a) *Chinese imports to Rwanda, 2013–2017*, (https://comtrade.un.org/data), accessed 26 November 2018.

UN Comtrade Database (2018b) *Rwandan exports to China, 2013–2017*, (https://comtrade.un.org/data), accessed 26 November 2018.

UNCTAD (United Nations Conference on Trade and Development) (2016) *UNCTAD Statistics*, (http://unctad.org/en/Pages/Statistics.aspx), Accessed 5 October 2016.

UNSC (United Nations Security Council) (2014) *Security Council adopts Resolution 2136 (2014), renewing arms embargo, related measures imposed on Democratic Republic of Congo*, (www.un.org/press/en/2014/sc11268.doc.htm), accessed 26 November 2018.

Whitfield, L. (2009) 'Aid and Power: A Comparative Analysis of Country Studies', in L. Whitfield (ed.) *The Politics of Aid: African Strategies for Dealing with Donors*, Oxford University Press, Oxford, 329–360.

Zhao, S. (2008) 'The Making of Chinese Foreign Policy: Actors and Institutions', in K. Ampiah and S. Naidu (eds) *Crouching Tiger, Hidden Dragon? Africa and China*, University of KwaZulu-Natal Press, Scottsville, 39–52.

12 Zimbabwe and China

An all-weather relationship for development and stability?

Lloyd Sachikonye

Introduction

In April 2008, a Chinese container ship, the *An Yue Jiang*, arrived in Durban port in South Africa with a cargo of armaments destined for Zimbabwe. It carried seventy-seven tons of 3 million rounds of ammunition, 1,500 rocket-propelled grenades, 2,500 mortar rounds and small arms (Larmer 2008). The shipment sparked wide publicity in the context of an electoral stalemate in 2008 between the ruling Zanu PF and opposition Movement for Democratic Change (MDC). President Mugabe had lost in the first round of the election while the opposition movement gained a majority of the parliamentary seats. There was inevitably speculation that the purpose of the armaments was to replenish the arsenal of the Zimbabwean military and police that were preparing to resist a transfer of power should the opposition candidate have won in the second presidential round.

In the event, the *An Yue Jiang* was refused permission to dock and discharge its contents in Durban but also in other ports in Mozambique, Namibia and Angola in a regional gesture of solidarity with Zimbabwean voters (*The Times* 2008). Nevertheless, the Zimbabwean military and other state agencies went on to play a prominent role in buttressing President Mugabe's campaign in a second round riddled with intimidation and violence that ultimately deterred the participation of Morgan Tsvangirai, the opposition candidate. The *An Yue Jiang* incident was emblematic of Sino-Zimbabwean relations built on solidarity, pragmatism but also on repression to secure stability.

Zimbabwe and China often describe their ties as a historical, durable 'all-weather' relationship that has endured good and difficult times. Indeed the relationship began during the liberation era, and before the founding of the post-independence state in 1980. Yet there was a lull in the relationship for close to two decades before the adoption of a 'Look East' policy (LEP) by the Mugabe government in the early 2000s.[1] Following a strain in relations with the West, especially with Britain, from 2000, due to human rights transgressions and electoral irregularities penalized by targeted sanctions, the Mugabe government took a pragmatic if also opportunistic turn to strengthening bilateral relations with China. It is important to note that although the sanctions were targeted at the Zimbabwean leadership, and also involved restrictions to loans and grants from Western institutions, trade flows were not affected.

This chapter will explore the political and economic dimensions of the Zimbabwe–China relations during 2000 to 2018, a period that coincided with China's spectacular economic rise and growing footprint in Africa. It then assesses the dilemmas that the Chinese face in a country in which political and economic stability remains a protracted challenge. The broader context of these evolving relations is one in which Zimbabwe, due to its adverse human rights record, experienced difficult relations with the West until 2009, and one in which it has sought to delicately balance its relations between that West and China in the post-2010 period. The balancing act displays some agency on part of the Zimbabwean state that has been played out in conditions of domestic political volatility and a shaky economic trajectory.

In Zimbabwe, China has become one of the leading investors in mining, agriculture, and energy as well as infrastructure, on top of being one of its principal trading partners. The Chinese policy of 'non-interference' in internal matters has reaped economic dividends in Zimbabwe for China in the short and medium term. However, as the strongman Mugabe and party in power became more enmeshed in factional politics and an economic turbulence from 2014, the Chinese developed anxieties both about political succession and economic stability. For instance, some of their interests in mining have been directly affected by economic nationalist measures in recent years.

China and Africa in the context of Forum on China–Africa Cooperation

Relations between Zimbabwe and China cannot be fully understood outside the context of Forum on China–Africa Cooperation (FOCAC) launched in 2000, the key cornerstone of the latter's relations with the continent. A positive rendition of FOCAC is that it represents, through its ministerial meetings and summits, a comprehensive consultation and dialogue mechanism to advance China–Africa cooperation and manage mutually beneficial economic interdependence (Shelton 2015). According to this perspective, the FOCAC process was uplifting Africa, providing urgently needed infrastructure while Chinese loans and aid programs represented new opportunities for overcoming poverty and promoting prosperity. This uplift was reflected in China–Africa trade that had grown exponentially from US$10 billion in 2000 to over US$200 billion by 2015 (Shelton 2015).

At the FOCAC Summit in Johannesburg in 2015, President Xi Jinping pledged a total of US$60 billion over 3 years for ten implementation programs including areas of industrialization, agricultural modernization, infrastructure, financial services, trade and investment facilitation, and peace and security among others. Xi Jinping went on to suggest the upgrading of the China–Africa partnership to a 'comprehensive strategic and cooperative partnership' built on five major pillars of political equality and mutual trust, promotion of win–win economic cooperation, mutually enriching cultural exchanges, mutual assistance in security and commitment to solidarity, and coordination in international affairs (*South News* 2015).

The FOCAC Conference in September 2018 in Beijing pledged another set of large funds for Africa. It would provide African countries US$20 billion in new credit lines; US$15 billion in foreign aid in the form of grants, interest-free and concessional loans; US$10 billion in a special fund for development financing; and US$5 billion for a special fund focusing on imports from Africa (FOCAC 2018).

There is little doubt that the rise of China particularly in the last 10 years has witnessed a spectacular increase in economic and political relations with Africa. Its climb to an economic superpower status has enabled it to catapult its trade and investment in individual countries while contributing to the wider upsurge in growth rates of the continent till the slowdown in 2015–2016. The commodity boom from the 2000s was largely built on China's voracious appetite for African raw materials. As this chapter explains, Zimbabwe has steered Chinese investments into energy, agriculture, infrastructure, and mining among other areas of economic cooperation. By and large, however, Chinese interests have been concentrated in extractive sectors. How did the wider framework of China–Africa relations shape its bilateral ties with Zimbabwe, a medium-sized country of about 14 million? What are the Chinese concerns regarding economic and political stability for their various investments? These are key questions that we address in the next sections of the chapter.

Zimbabwe, the West, and China

The post-2000 relations between Zimbabwe and China cannot be fully understood without reference to the deterioration of its relations with the West especially the United Kingdom (UK), European Union (EU) and the United States (US) between 2000 and 2008. Condemnation of Zimbabwe's electoral violence and human rights violations in the 2000 and 2002 elections, and breakdown in rule of law during land reform in the same period, found expression in targeted sanctions and an arms embargo applied by the West. Development aid from the West was reduced together with infusions of loans and grants from the World Bank and International Monetary Fund (IMF) among other financial institutions. The impact on the Zimbabwean economy was severe. Between 2000 and 2008, the country's gross domestic product (GDP) contracted by almost half due to the ensuing crisis (IMF 2010, 2017).

This was the immediate context in which President Mugabe around 2003 molded his LEP that sought to fill a vacuum created by the West's targeted sanctions and political ostracism. There was little alternative to this shift for economic infusions and survival. As we observed elsewhere, that immediate political and economic conjuncture distinguished the imperatives behind the impetus of the bilateral relationship of Zimbabwe and China, in comparison to other African countries (Sachikonye 2008).

However, while the economic imperative was an important factor in the 'Look East' shift, the ideological affinity and solidarity between Zimbabwe and China were also important. Like Zimbabwe, China received criticism for its authoritarianism in relation to human rights and civil liberties. Despite China's successful development record, its tough image was symbolized by its ruthless crushing of Tiananmen Square protests in 1989 (Sachikonye 2008; Yang 2017). The major difference between the two countries was that while the authoritarian model had been accompanied by impressive growth in China, this had not been the case in Zimbabwe.

There remains an inconclusive debate whether the bilateral relationship has indeed been a 'win–win' one or not (Mudyanadzo 2017). What cannot be overlooked, however, are the immense opportunities that have been availed to both Zimbabwe and China since 2000. For instance, trade grew steadily in the 2000s between the two countries; it rose from US$191 million in 2002 to US$1.1 billion in 2013 (Zhang 2014). The expansion in bilateral trade signified that Zimbabwe had secured markets for some of its products. The increased growth of Zimbabwe's exports to China was driven by enormous Chinese demand for natural resources that reflected the phenomenal growth of the Chinese economy (Mudyanadzo 2017). On the other hand, most of China's bilateral aid was tied to the use of Chinese sourced materials, a conditionality that had the effect of promoting Chinese imports into Zimbabwe.

The expansion in bilateral economic relations was reflected in the growing number of Chinese firms from twenty-nine in 2005 to sixty-two in 2014; this was accompanied by an increase from 200 to 300 small Chinese companies (Zhang 2014, 17). China invested in at least 128 projects from 2000 to 2012. There was also a phenomenal increase in Chinese foreign direct investment (FDI) especially between 2009 and 2013 when it increased from US$11 million to US$602 million. While the international financial institutions (IFIs) were wary of financing development projects, the Chinese investors became prominent especially in mining, energy, infrastructure, information and communications technologies (ICTs) and in agricultural development (Zhang 2014, 17).

Examples of substantial Chinese investment include some US$670 million in a Kariba hydropower project, US$1 billion in a Hwange thermal power project, as well as in mining and agriculture. By 2015, Zimbabwe had become one of the three top destinations of Chinese FDI in Africa. Having poured such substantive resources into Zimbabwe, it was inevitable that China would be concerned about the security and returns from the investments, as we explore in a later section (Zhang 2014, 14).

Agricultural development was another important sector that experienced growth and change in the post-2000 period thanks to Chinese financing of smallholder production. After an initial period of decline following a chaotic spell of land reform, tobacco production expanded in this sector on the back of contract farming arrangements buttressed by the Chinese tobacco company called Tian Ze. As we observed elsewhere, expansion of loan facilities and other forms of finance for contracted small growers transformed the tobacco production and marketing system within a decade (Sachikonye 2016). China is now the destination of more than half of Zimbabwe's tobacco exports, which amount to over 200 million kilograms per year. Earning about US$900 million per year, tobacco is grown by over 100,000 small growers whose incomes enable them to live above the poverty line. While the environmental costs of the shift to tobacco production should not be underestimated, this is a major success story in Zimbabwe–Chinese bilateral cooperation.

Chinese investments in mining have been more extractive oriented and not without taint in graft and corruption. This appears to have been the case with diamond, gold, and chrome mining. The Chinese company, Anjin, invested about US$400 million in a joint venture with the Zimbabwe government to mine diamonds in the 2000s. As the eighth-largest diamond producing country in the world, Zimbabwe enjoyed tax revenues of about US$84 million in 2014 (Wang 2016). However, there were many leakages through smuggling and underpricing by companies that prejudiced the state of potentially larger revenues. There were similar leakages in gold and chrome mining while allegations persisted that some minerals like platinum had been mortgaged by the state for Chinese loans (Wang 2016). These charges resulted in the tightening of laws such as the Indigenization and Economic Empowerment Act that restricted space for mining companies including Chinese ones in 2015.

In sum, the diversification of its trade and sources of investment in the post-2000 period yielded positive dividends for Zimbabwe and the Chinese. Yet during the same period this did not necessarily lead to a decline in Zimbabwe's trade links with the West. As noted above, trade volumes remained steady and even increased with the West. For instance, the bilateral trade between Zimbabwe and the EU group of countries actually expanded from US$448 million in 2003 to US$1.7 billion in 2013 (Mudyanadzo 2017, 191). This strengthens the argument of those who argue that the Western restrictive measures were more of 'targeted sanctions' aimed at the ruling elite rather than aimed at disrupting the flow of two-way trade. But to what extent has the issue of stability in economic policy and politics been uppermost in the minds of Chinese investors and policy-makers? We turn to this issue in the next section.

Development and stability

Zimbabwe's trajectory of economic growth has been less than robust and consistent in the post-2000 period. As we have already observed above, the period between 2000 and 2008 witnessed unprecedented contraction in a context of hyperinflation and endemic shortages fueled by extravagant quasi-fiscal policies (Gono 2008). Almost half of the country's GDP was wiped out. Nevertheless there was a notable recovery between 2009 and 2013 that coincided with the existence of a Government of National Unity (GNU) that brought together the ruling Zanu PF party and the two MDC parties. There was a spurt of growth and inflows of investment as both domestic and external confidence in the economy and governance grew. However, this was short-lived. With the end of the GNU in 2013, and the restoration of Zanu PF government with a parliamentary two-thirds majority, the old habits of overspending and patronage returned (Kanyenze 2018). These were exacerbated by intense factionalism within the party whose roots lay in economic competition and political jockeying within the ruling elite.

Zimbabwe–Chinese relations have not been unaffected by this economic and political turbulence. Chinese companies have needed to adjust to an unsettled and volatile environment in which policy inconsistency has been a constant factor. As one study corroborated, China began to view the cost of doing business in Zimbabwe as high and risky due to:

> hyper-inflation, high debt-overhang and failure to service previous loans, lack of respect for property rights and failure to uphold bilateral investment promotion and protection agreements (BIPPAS), policy inconsistency, corruption and political instability … There were perceptions by Chinese financial institutions that Zimbabwe was a risky investment destination due to the failure to service her debt obligations.
>
> (Mudyanadzo 2017, 200)

There was general agreement among analysts that China had not fully invested in Zimbabwe due to the latter's inability to service debts, and lack of credible plans to resuscitate the economy (Bräutigam 2009). Furthermore, Zimbabwe was viewed as a potential liability that negatively affected China's image in the West. Analysts observed that China had learnt, with respect to Zimbabwe, that in countries where mal-governance was acute, opportunities for exploitation were limited and counterproductive with regard to its international reputation (Taylor 2009).

There are a number of economic areas where Chinese interests have been ring-fenced by favorable state policies but also others where they have been exposed to domestic regulations. Some examples of favoritism relate to non-application of the Indigenization and Economic Empowerment Act to Chinese enterprises. This Act requires domestic majority share holding of at least 51 percent for enterprises of a certain size. Until 2015, Chinese mining companies were generally exempt from this Act (Ramani 2016). These exemptions by the state had given them unparalleled access to Zimbabwe's mineral resources, and entrenched Zimbabwe further into China's economic sphere.

However, in the diamond-mining sector, Chinese companies were later affected by state-sponsored consolidation in ownership and control of mining in Eastern Zimbabwe (Ramani 2016). This created a rift between the two states. The nationalization of the diamond sector adversely affected the interests of Chinese joint-venture companies and caused 'particular alarm in Beijing,' and witnessed an unprecedented appeal to the Supreme Court by the Chinese Anjin diamond company (Ramani 2016). Suspecting opaque corrupt deals in the sector, the government had instituted an audit of diamond-mining companies including the Chinese ones. State seizure of property of these companies also irked the Chinese who had previously been aloof in earlier state seizure of private property in the form of land and wildlife conservancy areas.

The economic downturn in the post-2013 period was partly caused by the international commodity price slump but also by profligate spending and policy inconsistences. Growth slumped from over 5 percent per annum to slightly above 1 percent in 2016. Lack of clarity about indigenization policy (a policy that stipulated that new investment required 51 percent ownership by indigenous Zimbabweans) and about property rights such as private farmland ownership contributed to the decline in foreign investment during this period. Foreign currency shortages in 2016 onward were a symptom of a deeper malaise in the economy. Clearly, policy inconsistences and prevalence of corruption raised further levels of risk. In particular, the Chinese were worried about leakages in government caused by lack of controls and bad corporate governance; hence their reluctance to release funds without instituting measures to protect their investments (Zimbabwe Independent 2015).

This environment of policy inconsistency, mistrust and graft slowed the implementation of the various 'mega deals' signed between China and Zimbabwe. Thus, the full potential of bilateral economic cooperation was not being achieved in the current context. As an analyst observed:

> China's extensive investments in Zimbabwe's crisis-ridden economy and rhetorical support for the regime are crucial to its broader strategy for expanded influence in Africa. If China can engineer a marked improvement in political and economic conditions in Zimbabwe, it will be able to profit economically from a country that Western powers have very limited leverage over and set a precedent for other countries in sub-Saharan Africa to pivot towards China …
>
> (Ramani 2016)

This was more a hope than a reality. Chinese interests have been exposed to considerable risk through policy changes leading to stagnation and decline in the post-2013 period. However, as already observed above, Chinese investments are massive in some sectors like energy, mining and infrastructure making it difficult to disengage.

The hopes of Chinese investors are pinned on an improvement in economic policy and development strategy that promote consistent and predictable growth. To that end, the Chinese National Development and Reform Commission has worked closely with the Zimbabwe's Office of the President and Cabinet in prioritizing areas of cooperation in investment and development policies, and their implementation (*Herald* 2016). One common area of interest that was identified was the resuscitation of the concept of Special Economic Zones (SEZs). A law to establish such SEZs was signed early in 2017.

In sum, there have been significant benefits to both Zimbabwe and China from the 'Look East' policy shift (Zhang 2014; Mudyanadzo 2017). The shift enabled Zimbabwe to weather the economic storms and sanctions that buffeted the country especially in the early 2000s. China gained handsomely from its preferential entry into such sectors as mining and contract agricultural production. However, as a consequence of policy inconsistences, corruption, and mounting debt, huge risks remain for the large Chinese investments made in infrastructure and energy and other lending extended to the Zimbabwean state, as we indicate in the next section.

Debt and economic slowdown in 2016–2018

The size of Zimbabwe's debt has a direct bearing on economic performance and broad investment environment. The spiraling of debt between 2015 and 2018 has been worrying. The total national debt stood at US$17 billion of which about US$7 billion consisted of external debt in November 2018 (Government of Zimbabwe 2018). It was significant to note that slow growth has contributed to persistent arrears in the servicing of the debt. There was enormous pressure on Zimbabwe to pay up its arrears on a debt of about US$2 billion owed to IFIs before lending can be resumed. This is the wider context in which Zimbabwe has experienced difficulties in servicing Chinese loans that amount to over US$2 billion. In 2018, the arrears over loan repayment amounted to about US$300 million, and this made China reluctant to advance more loans (Zimbabwe Independent 2015). Despite several high-profile visits to Beijing to obtain more aid, the Chinese were reluctant to provide any unless there was tangible growth and improved loan servicing. There was even speculation that China sought natural resources like minerals as barter in repayment arrangements prompting an official denial that 'we will never seize assets from Zimbabwe, although there are arrears to China' (Kunambura 2018).

Nevertheless, a subsequent lecture by the same Chinese embassy official in Harare emphasized that loans should not be squandered on consumption but invested in productive projects: 'good investments will mean that you are able to repay the loans. We have full confidence that if you invest wisely and come up with good policies and bankable projects … you will be able to clear loans…' (Kunambura 2018).

The risk of Zimbabwe defaulting on Chinese loans was considerable. Like in a number of African countries such as Sudan, and Mozambique where such a risk exists, there was growing apprehension in China about the possible consequences of such defaults. China needed to pay special attention to projects that were guaranteed by the host countries and their governments' solvency, and if necessary a mechanism of insurance needed to be introduced to avoid default on debt (Were 2018).

The unsustainable debt issue now featured in Beijing's relations with some African countries like Zimbabwe, and could potentially lead to a souring of relations especially if defaults occurred. It was significant that Africa's cumulative debt-to-GDP ratio stood at 56 percent in 2016, and has since climbed higher, meaning that governments will have to assign more revenue to debt servicing, rather than to the provision of goods and services to their populace

(Were 2018). There might even develop some backlash among the population against Chinese loans (or its use of 'debt diplomacy') as there was against those of the IMF in the 1990s. There could grow resentment against corruption associated with Chinese loans; opacity of loan negotiations between African governments and Chinese institutions, and the cost of servicing the loans themselves. There was a growing chorus of concerns about such opacity, corruption and mortgaging of natural resources in loan arrangements with the Chinese in Zimbabwe (van Eyssen 2018).

The wider question on the economic front relates to agency on the part of the Zimbabwean government. The level of its autonomy is being affected by relatively high levels of indebtedness both to the IFIs and increasingly to China. It remains to be systematically explored to what extent economic policy-making could be hamstrung by that indebtedness. It is possible that the debt can provide the Mnangagwa government with leverage in future negotiations on repayment terms both with IFIs and China. The possibility of friction over debt also exists, and if it occurred it would temper earlier expectations on both sides for the so-called 'all-weather relationship.'

Authoritarianism and security cooperation

Zimbabwe is an authoritarian state. Ruled for 37 years by a strongman who craftily used a combination of coercion and populism since gaining its independence in 1980 till 2017, Zimbabwe has trappings of a mixed dictatorial and illiberal electoral system. The Zimbabwean liberation movement found inspiration and model in the Chinese struggle, its communist party and state. As we observed elsewhere, the solidarity and ideological affinities between the Chinese Communist Party (CCP) and Zanu PF were cemented through material and moral support by the former during the latter's liberation struggle in the 1960s and 1970s (Sachikonye 2008). Not only have fraternal ties between the two ruling parties persisted, but also they have been considerably strengthened in the post-2000 period.

Although there are significant historical, geopolitical, and cultural differences between the CCP and Zanu PF, there are several similarities between the two ruling parties. First, they preside over party-states that they dominate; such is the fusion between party and state structures and personnel that it is difficult to disentangle one from the other. The strength of the party is partly derived from its rootedness within the state. To its electoral and economic advantage, the ruling Zanu PF party uses state institutions including coercive elements. Second, the ruling parties extol 'development' as being far more important and consequential than 'democracy' or 'human rights.' Their priority is consolidation of their rule, and pursuit of policies that extend their longevity in power. China has therefore had few qualms about Zimbabwe's domestic politics with respect to democracy and human rights. In return, Zimbabwe has been a consistent vocal supporter of China in regional and international fora.

In this section, we explore how Chinese material and diplomatic support has cushioned Zimbabwe, and how anxiety over intra-party factionalism in Zanu PF festers. Political stability cannot be guaranteed in that context of factionalism and a growing emboldened opposition (*Daily News* 2016). Chinese support has included military supplies and repressive equipment as well as diplomatic support for Zimbabwe in the UN Security Council. In the post-2000 period, China has provided Zimbabwe with:

- 12 jet fighters, 6 trainer/combat aircraft;
- 115 military trucks;
- 20,000 AK-47 rifles; and
- 21,000 pairs of handcuffs (Mudyanadzo 2017, 188).

In addition, China has also provided a radar system and constructed a National Defence College worth US$13 million and about US$100 million respectively. These military supplies took on greater significance in the light of the arms embargo contained in the Western-inspired sanctions. China filled the gap thus ensuring that Zimbabwe remained militarily strong during the turbulent period from 2003 and 2008 despite the economic meltdown. Some of the equipment such as handcuffs and others were not necessarily for external defense but for internal repression should there be an insurrection. Indeed, in 2008, there was increased deployment of the security apparatus against the opposition particularly in April to June 2008 period of the presidential campaign.

This was the wider context of the *Au Yue Jiang* incident of thwarted armaments delivery in the midst of Zimbabwe's electoral crisis of 2008. The region-wide boycott and attendant publicity of the incident proved embarrassing to China in the run-up to the Beijing Olympics. This 'ship of shame incident' embarrassed China diplomatically. It then temporarily scaled down its military cooperation, placing Zimbabwe on its list of 'limited level military trading' till 2013 (Zhang 2014, 13).

However, full military cooperation was later resumed after 2014. A significant development in 2018 was a report that China installed a surface to air missile (SAM) system in Zimbabwe as part of an umbrella to defend its interests in the region (The Zimbabwean 2018). The SAM technology was believed to be similar to the one that China deployed on Woody Island in the South China Sea. Significantly, there was no public announcement by government of installation of this defense system. As highlighted above, military cooperation between the two countries has been close but the advent of missile technology would signal a shift to a more intense level of cooperation. Chinese economic interests in Zimbabwe and the region have expanded, and there is logic in the setting up of military preparedness in case it was needed to protect those interests.

A related development has been a deal between a Chinese firm and the Zimbabwe government to provide surveillance technology. Cloudwalk Technology, a firm based in Guangzhou in China, reportedly will provide a mass facial recognition program that would enable Zimbabwe to replicate parts of the surveillance infrastructure that have made freedoms so limited in China (Hawkins 2018). The deal would not only involve surveillance cameras but also smart financial systems, airport, railway and bus station security as well as a national facial database. By gaining access to a population with a racial mix different from China's, Cloudwalk would be better able to train racial biases out of its facial recognition systems, a problem that has beleaguered facial recognition companies around the world, and that would give China a vital edge (Hawkins 2018). China would stand to reap economic gain while Zimbabwe would be enabled to strengthen its authoritarian grip.

Chinese diplomatic support for Zimbabwe at the UN Security Council in the 2000s had provided it with a crucial lifeline. As an analyst observed, throughout the time that Mugabe faced intense criticism, China provided all the necessary backing ensuring that the country escaped UN sanctions (Alao 2014). China was joined by Russia in opposing sanctions against Zimbabwe at the UN. China argued that the situation in Zimbabwe did not constitute a threat to international peace and security; that the imposition of sanctions would severely hamper the mediation efforts of then President Thabo Mbeki; and that those regional organizations like the African Union (AU) and Southern African Development Community (SADC) should be given a chance to resolve the crisis (Alao 2014). Indeed, China went on to play an active role in persuading the Mugabe government to implement the Global Political Agreement (GPA) of 2008 that led to the formation of the Government of National Unity (GNU). Furthermore, some of the largest infusions of investment from China occurred during that interregnum of stability between 2009 and 2013 (Mudyanadzo 2017).

Factionalism and potential instability

Some of fiercest factionalism occurred after Zanu PF's handsome victory in the 2013 election. For a party that was returned to power with a landslide win in mid-2013, the intra-party squabbles that began at the end of that year and culminated in the expulsion of a rump of the party under Vice-President Mujuru in 2014 were a huge surprise. A party that had skillfully and ruthlessly exploited weaknesses in the opposition Movement for Democratic Change – Tsvangirai (MDT-T) and increased its parliamentary majority was soon beset with a fratricidal power struggle. The comfortable electoral victory became a pyrrhic one as the party split into two factions. The immediate context and precipitating factor was the issue of who would succeed the then 93-year-old Robert Mugabe. Easily the then oldest leader on the African continent, the autocratic Mugabe had ruled for 37 years.

There were two principal factions vying for power in Zanu PF. The first was centered on the then Vice-President Emmerson Mnangagwa. The second crystallized around Grace Mugabe, the president's wife, and the party's Political Commissar, Saviour Kasukuwere. She not only played a catalytic role in the ouster of Vice-President Joyce Mujuru but she was soon catapulted to the influential party position of Secretary of Women's League in 2014. Grace Mugabe's faction known as G-40 sought to contest the Mnangagwa's faction in a series of confrontations in 2015. The political witch hunting ignited by the contestation embroiled the powerful war veterans lobby, and raised apprehension that the uniformed forces also known as 'securocrats' would be drawn into the contest. It was a sign of the raised political temperature that the war veterans sought a summit on these issues with Mugabe in April 2016 (*Daily News* 2016).

Mugabe was acutely aware of the influence of the war veterans and 'securocrats.' Heeding their interests had been one factor for him remaining entrenched in power for many years. This approach enabled him to maintain the coercive levers of power, as one analyst observed:

> authoritarian leaders will always accord special treatment to the armed forces in order to maintain their essential loyalty; even if civil servants sometimes go unpaid, every effort is made to compensate the military. But because autocrats rely heavily on repression, they inadvertently strengthen the hand of the armed forces, who, in turn are able to claim a share of both economic bounty and political decisions.
>
> (Bratton 2014, 8)

The split and factions in Zanu PF were reproduced in state institutions including the bureaucracy as well as 'securocrats.' This was a dangerous development that could potentially get out of hand. It was not clear whether the G-40 and Mnangagwa factions fully understood the ramifications of their contest. Increasingly, Mugabe tilted to the G-40 faction associated with his wife thereby undermining his credibility as a referee in the inter-factional dispute over succession.

Ultimately, the catalyst of the damaging factionalism in Zanu PF was the reluctance of the incumbent president to give way after 37 years in power. To that extent, Mugabe was an archetypal African 'strong man' wary of competition and constitutional rule.

How did China view these ominous factional developments in Zimbabwe? There were several positions as expressed by Chinese analysts:

- with Zimbabwe's political future uncertain, China was walking a fine line to avoid taking sides with either political faction, and keeping China-sponsored assets safe from the threat of political turmoil (Wang 2016);
- the potentially worst-case scenario for China was a rudderless Zimbabwe with neither of the Zanu PF factions winning over each other, a weak opposition force, social turmoil, and the military stepping into politics (Wang 2016);
- if Zimbabwean opposition parties that had expressed opposition to what they termed Chinese 'economic hegemony' came to power, its economic interests in Zimbabwe could be jeopardized (Ramani 2016); and

- the future of Zimbabwe–China relations was heavily dependent on Zimbabwe's political situation, with the chances of the West's re-engagement with Zimbabwe as great as the chances of China's 'retreating' from Zimbabwe (Zhang 2014).

The large question was therefore the mode that the post-Mugabe transition would take, and whether it would result in political and economic stability.

Postscript: the 2017 coup and search for stability

Some of above questions and assessments proved academic when a coup was executed to remove Mugabe from office in November 2017. Immediately before the coup, there was the sacking of Mnangagwa from his vice presidency post and flight into exile for several weeks in November. The Lacoste faction linked to Mnangagwa cooperated closely with the military and war veterans to engineer the trajectory of the largely peaceful coup. A few days prior to the coup, the commander of the armed forces, General Chiwenga, had visited China and held meetings with Chinese authorities. There were also unconfirmed reports that Mnangagwa himself had secretly visited China soon after his escape from Zimbabwe (*Newsday* 2019). This was the context in which, although China denied knowing about the coup beforehand, it was nevertheless believed that it supported it tacitly. It had drawn closer to the Lacoste faction and the military, while Chinese companies Anjin and Jinan had enjoyed joint ownership of diamond interests with the latter.

The immediate aftermath of the coup was a delicate phase during which it had to be made to appear 'legitimate enough' to SADC and AU whose principles shun the use of coups as a method of change of government. Despite official rhetoric that it was a 'military assisted transition,' the November coup did not however silence a debate about its unconstitutional aspects, and the possible implications of its precedence. That there was resort to military intervention to bring about leadership succession in the ruling party showed weaknesses in the political system. It also raised wider issues about the stability of that system, and the potential threat of future intervention. Some legal scholars have raised these issues:

> Mugabe's removal was the first of its kind (in Zimbabwe) where a president was literally forced to resign by military action and a threat of impeachment by parliament. The framing of the removal as a coup matters because it sets a precedent with potential to haunt the nation. The fact that it was condoned keeps alive the possibility that it could happen again.
>
> (Magaisa 2018)

The weaknesses in the Zimbabwean political system, and especially the unstable checks-and-balances between different branches of state, were exposed. An additional worry would be the possibility of infighting over party leadership in the future. In short, possible rivalry between President Mnangagwa, and Vice-President General Chiwenga in future would stoke fears of another military intervention.

The stability of the constitutional and political order thus remains central to Zimbabwean politics. This was reinforced when the military used draconian methods to quell protests against alleged rigging of the presidential poll in the 2018 July poll. The use of naked violence that resulted in six fatalities raised a large alarm not only domestically but also internationally. That violence cast a dark pall over the legitimacy of that election. These developments prompted some analysts to argue that:

> to restore the constitutional order, it must be made clear that that there are only three arms of the state and the rest operate within these confines as limited by law. The alternative of allowing the military to assert itself as it did in November 2017 using section 212 of the Constitution poses a serious risk to the current and future governments and constitutional order…
>
> (Magaisa 2018)

The draconian militaristic approach to addressing civilian dissent was repeated during a national strike in January 2019. Some seventeen protesters were shot dead and hundreds detained. This is the broader context in which these debates about stability and about the role of the military in politics will continue. They reflect imperatives for both deeper political and economic reforms.

Notwithstanding, the challenges about legitimacy of political and electoral processes, China has proved consistent in its support of the new government. As a confirmation of the priority given to the relationship, the first country that Mnangagwa visited outside Africa after attaining power was China (Tiezzi 2018). There are higher hopes in Beijing that he would succeed where his predecessor failed. As one analyst observed, China continued to hold a high stake in Zimbabwean politics due to their close economic and political relations: 'those risks did not disappear with Mugabe … China is watching to see if Mnangagwa can deliver economic and political stability that Mugabe could not…' (Tiezzi 2018). The prospects for reform and stability remain mixed; there will be need for deft steering of both economic and political reforms for stability.

Conclusion

This chapter has explored the Zimbabwe–China relationship and enquired the degree to which it meets criteria of a so-called 'all-weather' partnership for stability, as sought by the leaders of the two countries. Building on foundations of solidarity forged during the liberation struggle, the two countries rediscovered the imperative for close political and economic cooperation and mutual support in global forums in the post-2000 period following a hiatus of about 20 years.

The new circumstances for increased cooperation were dictated by Western-targeted sanctions against the Mugabe government for bad governance on the one hand, and Chinese appetite for natural resources and markets on the other. The chapter explained how Zimbabwe's economic survival hinged on the bilateral relations with China that were mutually beneficial to the degree that it had become one of its large trade partners and destination of foreign investment. The diversification of its trade and investment links enabled Zimbabwe to be cushioned from sanctions, and thus provided some modicum of economic stability.

Similarly, Chinese support in various regional and international institutions such as the UN Security Council prevented Zimbabwe from being brought under a comprehensive economic and arms embargo. This political support provided a favorable environment for increased Chinese economic, military, and cultural ties. The chapter explained how these ties have continued to be consolidated.

At the same time, however, Zimbabwe has not put all 'its eggs in one basket' because it has maintained its links, including trade relations, with the West during the post-2000 period. The current discourse of 're-engaging the West' is a reflection of this interest by Zimbabwe to diversify its external relations. This is a demonstration of Zimbabwe's agency or relative autonomy in how it manages its bilateral and multilateral relations. This agency could be replicated in Zimbabwe's response on the large debt that it now has with China. Its indebtedness could ironically provide it with leverage with the Chinese in future negotiations over its repayment.

The chapter also observed that there are factors that are weakening stability in the economic and political spheres. They include economic policy inconsistences, uncertainty, and corruption that make investment risky and expensive both to the Chinese and other international investors. The crisis in the Zimbabwean economy from 2002 to 2008, and again since 2015, posed risks to sustainable development and growth in the country. Economic risks accompany the large Chinese investments whose security has been put into question following shifts in mining ownership policies. The considerable arrears on some Chinese loans are a source of anxiety to Chinese companies and government. The limits of 'debt diplomacy' could be reached if there are defaults or divergences on terms of servicing the debt. This could develop into a stern test of the so-called 'all-weather relationship.'

Finally, questions remain about political stability during the post-Mugabe era. Early signs point to the rise of factional competition that feeds on the political ambitions of former army general and later vice president, Chiwenga. The worst scenario would be that the Chinese at some stage might be forced to take sides in that contest. That could exacerbate the situation if another round of factionalism fuels a political crisis. The above-mentioned economic risks could be compounded by political risks. It would be the hope of the Zimbabwean and the Chinese governments that these risks do not escalate, but instead are carefully managed and resolved.

Note

1 Mugabe was quoted as stating: 'We have turned East, where the sun rises, and given our backs to the West, where the sun sets,' see Chun (2014).

References

Alao, A. (2014) *China and Zimbabwe: The Context and Contents of a Complex Relationship*, SAIIA Occasional Paper no. 202, South African Institute of International Affairs, Johannesburg.

Bratton, M. (2014) *Power Politics in Zimbabwe*, Lynne Rienner, Boulder.

Bräutigam, D. (2009) *The Dragon's Gift: The Real Story of China in Africa*, Oxford University Press, New York.

Daily News (2016) 'Pressure piles on Mugabe', Harare, 10 July, 1–2.

FOCAC (Forum on China–Africa Cooperation) (2018) *Forum on China–Africa Cooperation Beijing Action Plan, 2019–2021*, (www.focac.org/eng/zywx_1/zywj/t1594297.htm), accessed 20 May 2019.

Gono, G. (2008) *Zimbabwe's Casino Economy*, Zimbabwe Publishing House, Harare.

Government of Zimbabwe (2018) *Budget 2019 Statement*, Harare.

Hawkins, A. (2018) *Beijing's big brother tech needs African faces*, (https://foreignpolicy.com/2018/07/24/beijings-big-brother-tech-needs-african-faces/), accessed 15 April 2019.

Herald (2016) 'President signs Special Economic Zones Bill', Harare, 1 November, 2.

Kanyenze, G. (2018) 'Economic Crisis, Structural Change and Devaluation of Labour', in L. Sachikonye, B. Raftopoulos and G. Kanyenze (eds) *Building from the Rubble: The Labour Movement in Zimbabwe since 2000*, Weaver Press, Harare, 75–123.

Kunambura, A. (2018) *We won't seize Zim assets: China*, (www.theindependent.co.zw/2018/09/28/we-wont-seize-zim-assets-china/), accessed 15 April 2019.

IMF (International Monetary Fund) (2010) *Zimbabwe: Challenges and Policy Options after Hyper-inflation*, International Monetary Fund, Washington, DC.

IMF (International Monetary Fund) (2017) *IMF executive board concludes 2017 Article IV consultation with Zimbabwe*, (www.imf.org/en/News/Articles/2017/07/07/pr17267-imf-executive-board-concludes-2017-article-iv-consultation-with-zimbabwe), accessed 15 April 2019.

Larmer, M. (2008) 'The Zimbabwe Arms Shipment Campaign', *Review of African Political Economy*, 35(117), 486–493.

Magaisa, A. (2018) *How the coup impacted our constitutional order*, (www.theindependent.co.zw/2018/11/17/how-the-coup-impacted-our-constitutional-order/), accessed 15 April 2019.

Mudyanadzo, W. (2017) 'The Post-Colonial Challenges of Nation-Building through International Engagement: An Analysis of Zimbabwe's International Relations from 1980 to 2016', PhD Thesis, Midlands State University, Gweru.

Newsday (2019) *Chiwenga's coup strategy exposed*, (www.newsday.co.zw/2019/02/chiwengas-coup-strategy-exposed/), accessed 15 April 2019.

Ramani, S. (2016) *Is China ready for a post-Mugabe Zimbabwe?*, (https://thediplomat.com/2016/08/is-china-ready-for-a-post-mugabe-zimbabwe/), accessed 15 April 2019.

Sachikonye, L. (2008) 'Crouching Tiger, Hidden Agenda? Zimbabwe-China Relations', in K. Ampiah and S. Naidu (eds) *Crouching Tiger, Hidden Dragon? Africa and China*, University of KwaZulu-Natal Press, Scottville, 124–137.

Sachikonye, L. (2016) 'Old Wine in New Bottles? Revisiting Contract Farming after Agrarian Reform in Zimbabwe', *Review of African Political Economy*, 43, S1, 86–98.

Sachikonye, L. (2017) 'The Protracted Democratic Transition in Zimbabwe', *Taiwan Journal of Democracy*, 13(1), 117–136.

Shelton, G. (2015) *China's path to Africa paved with growth*, (www.iol.co.za/business-report/opinion/chinas-path-to-africa-paved-with-growth-1952431), accessed 16 April 2019.

South News (2015) no.99, 15 December.

Taylor, I. (2009) *China's New Role in Africa*, Lynne Rienner, London.

The Times (2008) *Dockers refuse to unload China arms shipment for Zimbabwe*, (www.timesonline.co.uk/tol/news/world/africa/article3772113.ece), accessed 15 April 2019.

The Zimbabwean (2018) *China places strategic ground to air missiles in Zimbabwe*, (www.thezimbabwean.co/2018/08/china-places-strategic-ground-to-air-missiles-in-zimbabwe/), accessed 16 April 2019.

Tiezzi, S. (2018) *China renews 'all weather friendship' with Zimbabwe's new president*, (https://thediplomat.com/2018/04/china-renews-all-weather-friendship-with-zimbabwes-new-president/), accessed 15 April 2019.

van Eyssen, B. (2018) *Double debt risk for African countries that turn to China*, (www.newsday.co.zw/2018/08/double-debt-risk-for-african-countries-that-turn-to-china/), accessed 15 April 2019.

Wang, X. (2016) *China's Zimbabwe risk*, (https://thediplomat.com/2016/12/chinas-zimbabwe-risk/), accessed 15 April 2019.

Were, A. (2018) *Debt Trap? Chinese Loans and Africa's development Options*, SAIIA Policy Insights no. 66, South African Institute of International Affairs, Johannesburg.

Yang, D. L. (2017) 'China's Developmental Authoritarianism: Dynamism and Pitfalls', *Taiwan Journal of Democracy*, 12(1), 45–70.

Zhang, C. (2014) *China-Zimbabwe Relations: A Model of China-Africa Relations?* SAIIA Occasional Paper no. 205, South African Institute of International Affairs, Johannesburg.

Zimbabwe Independent (2015) 'Cautious Chinese handhold Mugabe', Harare, 14 August.

13 China and Africa's peace and security

Examining China's role in Nigeria's insecurity

Efem N. Ubi

Introduction

The importance of Nigeria to China cannot be overemphasized. Today, Nigeria remains the largest market for Chinese construction companies in Africa and third-largest in terms of bilateral trade relations; such is the scale of this that Premier Li Keqiang opined: 'We're happy to see a fast developing Nigerian economy. It has become Africa's largest economy and keeps rising … I believe we'll become motivators of each other' (China Economic Net 2014). In spite of Nigeria's economic status, since the turn of the millennium the West African country has been battling with endemic security challenges, ranging from militancy and insurgency in the South South region, to the bid for self-determination in South East, to terrorism in North East. It is thus puzzling how China, irrespective of Nigeria's security challenges, has continued to thrive and do business in and with the country without giving tangible input to the remedying of this endemic insecurity.

This particular stance has raised skepticism about China having one sole aim in Africa. In fact, for some, the debate has often hinged on the opportunistic nature of Chinese economic encroachment into Africa. For others, it has been on the realities of a supposedly mutually beneficial relationship; some others further query the aloofness of China vis-à-vis Africa's security needs. How can China embrace a continent that is home to a catalogue of security challenges like wars, terrorism, insurgencies, mass upheavals, or refugees that have condemned many Africans to misery, and even threatened the very existence of states (Ubi 2013), and yet still maintain a policy of non-interference and non-intervention in the internal affairs of these countries?

Whether these concerns are real or imaginary, the fact remains that China's economic presence in Africa is unequivocally preponderant. The future of China's participation in Africa's conflict resolution seems unavoidable, to the extent that its engagement with the continent is becoming more and more amplified. An analysis of China's foreign policy statements and documents brings to light a multifaceted modus operandi approach to African peace and security. Based on its policy of non-interference and non-intervention, China has tried to resolve Africa's insecurity by developing a distinct approach, one that is predicated strictly on economic development initiatives – the lack of which is, according to Chinese officials, a major instigator of conflict in Africa.

Being cognizant of the above and taking into consideration the amount of Chinese investment in Nigeria, this chapter will ask which role the Asian country has assumed in preserving and safeguarding its West African partner's peace and security. And, what does peace and security cooperation even mean for both China and for Nigeria? Answering these questions is critical to driving forward our understanding of the dynamics of Chinese–African peace and security relations.

Whither China–Africa security policy?

Contemporary China–Africa relations first emerged in the 1950s, with the 1955 Bandung Conference[1] of Asian–African states playing an important role in defining the China–Africa relationship. It gave China the impetus to gradually increase its link with countries in Africa. At the time, though, it offered only relatively low-level economic, technical, and shadowy military assistance to the continent – in the form of arms and training to African countries and liberation movements (Ubi 2011a).

During the 1960s and 1970s China's support to African countries was an attempt to restrain the dominant Western powers' influence on the continent and a way to offer an alternative political model to the newly independent states – as well as help them win their fight against enduring colonial rule and Apartheid (Van de Looy 2006). During the late 1990s the relationship was redefined and later brought about the creation of the Forum on China–Africa Cooperation (FOCAC) in 2000 and the establishment of the China–Africa 'New Strategic Partnership.' China's understanding of a new strategic partnership with Africa covered initially economic, social, and cultural issues (Ubi 2014, 246).

Under this new partnership, China foreign policy strategy became more inclusive and holistic in approach. Two issues have remained paramount since the conception of the new strategic partnership and the establishment of FOCAC. The first is that, beginning with the second FOCAC in 2003, FOCAC outcomes and its Action Plan have given some credence and priority to China–Africa peace and security cooperation. And, second, all FOCAC documents have also consistently agreed that regional conflict, insecurity, terrorism, and non-traditional security issues are both a threat to international peace and security as well as a major problem to Africa – and therefore must be eliminated through close and effective cooperation at the international level.

For instance, the FOCAC–Addis Ababa Action Plan (2004–2006) noted the importance of this cooperation when it stipulated that China would henceforth intensify its participation in peacekeeping operations in Africa as well as strengthen the capacity of the continent's states to undertake their own peace operations through logistical, financial, and material assistance and relevant training to be given to the Peace and Security Council of the African Union (AU) (FOCAC 2006). As a follow-up, in 2006, the Chinese government for the first time issued a China–Africa white paper, which took cognizance of four pertinent areas of security in which it wanted to cooperate with Africa. These included military cooperation, conflict settlement and peacekeeping operations, judicial and police cooperation, and non-traditional security cooperation (State Council 2006). The document stated that China would promote high-level military exchanges and actively carry out military-related technological exchanges and cooperation, as well as help train Africa military personnel, support defense, and bolster the capacity of African countries' militaries to cater for their own security (Shinn 2008, 162).

At the time, China–Africa peace and security cooperation consisted more or less of mere principles and rhetoric, rather than of a series of practical ways to help Africa mitigate its security problems. That notwithstanding, the China–Africa relationship gained momentum when in the first quarter of 2006 senior Chinese officials – including President Hu Jintao and former Chinese foreign minister Li Zhaoxing – visited fifteen different African countries. During the April 2006 state visits to Morocco, Nigeria, and Kenya, President Hu put forward concrete proposals that were intended to drive the new strategic partnership (Ubi 2011b). A key element in these proposals was the strengthening of cooperation with Africa on security, as also laid out in the white paper.

With the fifth FOCAC in 2012, China made Africa's peace and security one of the five priorities of cooperation and introduced a new dimension of African security. This led to the launching of the Initiative on China–Africa Cooperative Partnership for Peace and Security in the same year. This program was intended to provide financial and technical support to the AU, support peace operations, and further develop the African Peace and Security Architecture, inter alia through personnel exchanges and training given in the areas of peace and security (SIIS 2001; FOCAC 2006, 2009; SAFPI 2012).[2]

China's Second Africa Policy Paper (2015) is also of the utmost importance here, since it raised a number of important elements vis-à-vis safeguarding the continent's peace and security. First, the policy paper noted that China would support Africa in achieving peace and security by promoting African solutions to African problems, but that based on Chinese characteristics – predicated on its principles of non-interference and non-intervention in the internal affairs of other countries. This would involve constructive engagement, dialogue, and consultation with African countries and regional organizations. China seems thus to hold tenaciously to its policy of non-interference. Beijing has traditionally had reservations about the use of force – both for ideological reasons, but also out of considerations of risk avoidance. Chinese officials have thus argued that the deployment of combat troops to protect civilians does not compromise the principle of non-interference, so long as it is within the ambit of a multilateral framework of United Nations (UN) peacekeeping (Duchâtel et al. 2016). China currently contributes 10.25 percent of the UN peacekeeping budget and is the eleventh-largest contributor of its peacekeepers (CGTN 2018; Pauley 2018).

Second, the 2015 Africa Policy Paper further pointed out that the Chinese government would strengthen and deepen military exchanges and cooperation with African countries through related technological cooperation, joint training and exercises, and through the training of African military personnel according to each respective country's needs. And, third, it stipulated that China would support Africa in confronting non-traditional security threats by strengthening cooperation with the continent through intelligence-gathering and -sharing, and through capacity-building too (*China Daily* 2015). China also committed itself to supporting the efforts of individual African countries and regional organizations in improving their counterterrorism capabilities, and to further helping them develop their economies – and thereby nullifying the root causes of terrorism. In this regard, China also prefers multilateral platforms – that is, working through regional, continental, and global ones (Wei 2010; FOCAC 2015).

China's policy statements and actions show that its role in Africa's peace and security is determined by the vast amount of economic investment and trade therein and therewith. For instance, China's huge investments in East Africa and the Horn of Africa might be one reason why it established a military logistics base in Djibouti – specifically, to curtail piracy in Somalia and the Gulf of Aden. Its extensive investments in Nigeria and West Africa might, meanwhile, be the reason for the US$800 million deep-sea transshipment hub (port) that China is building in São Tomé and Principe – namely, to fight insecurity in the Gulf of Guinea (Global Security 2016). Irrespective of the purpose of the port, according to Sao Tomé's former Prime Minister, Patrice Trovoada: 'Everybody has to be together to fight the threat of piracy, terrorism. If China comes to protect what I call "common interests", then fine. If there is not a proportion between what they bring in terms of military force, then we need to question that' (Voice of America 2015).

Thus, China's recently built military logistics base further supports David Shinn's argument that the Asian country's military diplomacy – in Africa and elsewhere – emphasizes 'the conduct of foreign military relations by the People's Liberation Army (PLA) as a strategic-level activity in support of the larger foreign, diplomatic, economic, and security agenda set by China's leadership' (2008, 162). According to him, since the PLA is not an independent actor, it does not engage in freestanding military initiatives conducted by military professionals for military reasons. Rather, its activities must be in line with the Communist Party and with the Chinese state bureaucracy.

It is no gainsaying to note that China is yet to enter into any formal military alliance with a single African country. That notwithstanding, China–Africa military cooperation has seen the Asian country appoint military attachés to fourteen of the continent's states including Nigeria. The latter is also one of the six African countries that have a reciprocal defense attaché stationed in Beijing (McDowell 2012).

China's preemptive peace and security approach

As noted earlier, the influx and activities of China in Africa have created much debate about the Asian country's roles and actions in nations suffering from violence and prone to conflict. While in terms of policy pronouncements China has – as outlined above – shown great concern for Africa's insecurity, this rhetoric is often not matched with concrete action. This is a result of two dynamics. First, there exists no astute China–Africa security policy; second, China's role in addressing Africa's insecurity has often been defined solely as promoting economic growth as a remedy to the continent's problems.

It has been suggested that China is constructing a new paradigm for peaceful interventions in Africa, the 'sovereignty plus development' model, which according to Wang (2018) is primarily shaped by China's developmental peace concept. This approach to peace and security is somewhat different from the conventional ways in which the West has over time waded into Africa's conflicts. While agreeing with this scholar, this chapter also argues that China's role in the issues of peace and security in the developing world is anchored on what could be labeled as China's 'preemptive peace and security approach' (PPSA) (for further elaboration, see Ubi 2008).

Therefore, while China's approach takes into consideration a development–security nexus, which revolves around the interconnectedness of a nation's stability and its level of economic development (New Era 2015), the PPSA is seen as a method of prevention and protection vis-à-vis insecurity. This it does by anticipating what might cause these conflicts even before they occur and by preventing their escalation when they do erupt, using therein an economic growth and development strategy. In that light, therefore, and disregarding military intervention, China prefers that security issues everywhere are addressed by broad means – ones involving economic, development, and diplomatic initiatives.

Invariably, from China's viewpoint, the root causes of conflicts and insecurity in both Africa and elsewhere are poverty and a lack of access to basic services. Therefore, anticipating and preventing threat scenarios must, first, take into consideration long-term economic planning that should lay the foundations for any nation's economic growth and development and, second, the catalyzing effect of economic growth and development on the individual's development as a unit of analysis. China pursues these ends through common, cooperative, comprehensive, and sustainable security (*China Daily* 2015), which best captures the Asian country's conceptualization and operationalization of the PPSA in Africa and the developing world.

In defining each of the above concepts in May 2014 in Shanghai, President Xi Jinping opined that 'common security' revolves around the fact that insecurity in any country is bound to have knock-on effects in another country or region elsewhere – whether directly or indirectly. Therefore, there is the need to respect and ensure the security of each and every country around the globe. 'Comprehensive security' for China means providing security both from a traditional and non-traditional perspective, that by adopting a multipronged and holistic approach enacted through regionally coordinated security governance mechanisms. In other words, while tackling the immediate security challenges facing the region, plans should be made to address potential threats too – which means avoiding a fragmented and palliative approach that only treats the symptoms (Zhan 2016).

On the other hand, 'cooperative security' is about promoting the robustness of both individual countries and the region as a whole through dialogue and cooperation. In other words, dispute settlement should be achieved through peaceful means and not through the arbitrary use or threat of force. According to President Xi, for peace and security to be achieved each country should be allowed to search for solutions from within, with special consideration given to development and economic issues in order to address related inequalities and disparities (Zhan 2016).

Based on these concepts, China has often suggested that African countries should address poverty alleviation first and foremost, and thus focus on development in order for peace and security to reign. And in those African countries where there are violent conflicts, China has deemed it necessary to provide development assistance as part of its efforts to extend security to the target state, as well as to its overseas population and investments there (Tazoacha 2016). That notwithstanding, it is important for China to note that, while the provision of economic and development initiatives could indeed significantly forestall conflicts or help resolve existing ones, not all of them are – as the Chinese often speculate – the result of economic factors or of poverty.

The evolution of Nigeria–China relations

Nigeria–China relations cannot be dichotomized out from the wider China–Africa relationship. Since the normalization of diplomatic relations in February 1971, the two countries have had a connection spanning over four decades now. The 1990s saw a specific boost in Nigeria–China relations. Under the regime of General Sani Abacha, which began in 1993, Nigeria was a pariah state and ostracized by some Western countries. The only option left for Nigeria, then, was to look East, particularly by encouraging Chinese state-owned companies to conduct business in the country.

This period was further characterized by relatively good economic and diplomatic ties, typified in Nigeria's support for China's 'one country, two systems' policy as well as its repossession of Hong Kong. Abacha's 'Look East Policy' of 1995 culminated in the China Civil Engineering Construction Corporation securing a contract worth US$529 million for the rehabilitation of Nigeria's railway system (Bukarambe 2005). The period also saw a high-level visit by the former premier of China's State Council, Li Ping, to Nigeria in 1997, which culminated in the two countries signing various agreements (Utomi 2008).

Of importance to this chapter is the Nigeria–China Strategic Partnership, signed in 2006. This strategic partnership revolves around a four-point plan to improve bilateral relations, which includes addressing:

- expansion of trade;
- investments in agriculture;
- telecommunications, energy;
- and, infrastructure development (Ubi et al. 2017).

The 2006 agreement remains the foundational one around which other, newer accords and memoranda of understanding (MoUs) revolve. Within the strategic partnership, preeminence is given to economics, science and technology, and infrastructural development. This is because China thinks that weaknesses in those three areas are part of the reason why countries are underdeveloped and find themselves in an economic quagmire – as well as face many problems of insecurity. Although in the document no consideration is given to peace and security cooperation, these issues started to find resonance in the actual exchanges between the two countries (McDowell 2012).

With a population of over 170 million people and a gross domestic product of US$481 billion, Nigeria's huge market is seen as a highly attractive opportunity for trade and investment by China. Little wonder that Chinese officials stated:

> Nigeria is an important partner of China and the biggest economy and most populous country in Africa. China will firmly implement the policy of 'sincerity, real results, affinity and good faith' towards Nigeria and Africa put forward by President Xi Jinping.
>
> (Gu 2016)

Thus, the growth in Nigeria–China relations over the years is most visible in the two countries' trade cooperation which has boomed exponentially, from a low base of US$178 million in 1996 to the whopping sum of US$18.1 billion in 2014, before scaling down to US$13.78 billion in 2017 as a result of the recession that hit Nigeria (Ubi 2018). In fact, estimates show that the Nigeria–China trade volume constitutes 8.3 percent of China's total trade with Africa and 42 percent of Chinese trade with the Economic Community of West African States (ECOWAS) or, put another way, with one-third of the entire population of the ECOWAS region (Blackseagrain 2016). That notwithstanding, their trade relations are still beset with problems of imbalance.

In terms of investment, as of 2017, Chinese involvement in the Nigerian economy was worth some US$45 billion in total. A breakdown hereof reveals that China has invested in and completed projects with an overall value of US$22 billion, while ones worth a further US$23 billion are still ongoing at present (*The Nigerian Guardian* 2017). Hence, Nigeria's share of Chinese investment in Africa has increased by over 30 percent. There are about forty officially identified Chinese development projects in Nigeria, ranging from a US$2.5 billion loan to the Nigerian Railway Corporation to power and telecommunications projects (Liu 2015; *People's Daily* 2016). This makes Nigeria, as noted earlier, China's third-largest investment destination in Africa. The year 2015 saw the volume of newly signed Chinese engineering contracts in Nigeria amount to US$4.36 billion, while contracts worth US$1.6 billion have already been completed in projects related to railways, roads and highways, water supply and sanitation, communications, drilling, and the like (Xinhua 2016). Given this considerable Chinese investment in Nigeria, one should reasonably expect the Asian country to play a decisive role in its West African partner's endemic security problems.

The nature of Nigeria–China security cooperation

Defense or security cooperation is the provision of financial and technical assistance, the transfer of related goods, training, and services to allies, as well as the further promotion of military-to-military exchange. This includes also foreign military sales and international military education and training (Bartles 2012). While many countries in the West have inscribed security cooperation documents with countries in Africa, there has been no such documented defense cooperation between China and African countries to date.

Policy documents relating to peace and security cooperation between China and Africa are to be found – for example within FOCAC, AU, and ECOWAS agreements – as are bilateral statements. In fact, many of China's activities in the field of military and defense cooperation are shrouded in secrecy. This lack of data has led scholars to often work only with policy documents, public statements, and what little is made known in the media.

That notwithstanding, Nigeria–China security cooperation falls within the wider ambit of China–Africa peace and security cooperation as enshrined in FOCAC documents and the policy papers discussed earlier. Since the 1980s, Nigeria and China have had various forms of military cooperation in place. Today, the broad areas thereof mostly focus on reciprocal visits by senior military officers for the promotion of mutual understanding and trust, the training of military personnel, sales of arms and weapons, and on the upgrading and development of Nigeria's defense industries (Gambo 2018).

In terms of military exchanges, the first such ones were established when the Nigerian Defense Academy sent a number of delegates to China in the 1980s. Beginning with Nigeria's transition to democracy in 1999, there have since been several high-level military visits and exchanges between the two countries (Embassy of the People's Republic of China in in the Federal Republic of Nigeria 2004; *China Daily* 2006). For instance, in 2001, 2002, and 2004 the Nigerian defense minister visited Beijing to discuss areas of military cooperation. As a result of the signing of the 2006 strategic partnership, both sides agreed during a 2007 meeting in Beijing to enhance military cooperation between Nigeria and the PLA (Shinn 2008, 162). And, since then, the two countries' military cooperation has shown remarkable progress – especially in the areas of training of personnel and weapons sales.

Technical training and human capacity-building have remained core to China–Africa relations. The Nigerian military has benefited immensely. Over the years the PLA has further increased the number of courses and placement offers to those from the ranks of junior officers up to colonels to go for training in China (*The Nigerian Guardian* 2012, 2015). Every year, more than forty Nigerian officers are sent to various Chinese military institutions for training; according to Gambo (2018, 270), no less than 390 individuals from the Nigerian armed forces have received training in China to date.

In the areas of weapon sales and the acquisition of arms and military equipment, China has become an important supplier to Nigeria. In 2001 China granted Nigeria US$1 million to upgrade its military facilities (Shinn 2008, 162). Nigeria–China military cooperation gained further momentum when in September 2004 the Chinese arms producer Poly Technology announced that it would enter into partnership with the government-owned Defense Industries Corporation of Nigeria in Kaduna to modernize the West African country's domestic arms industry (Volman 2015, 311). China thus helped support the Nigerian government's dream of indigenous arms manufacturing. In 2005 the Chinese government also donated equipment, materials, gadgets, and uniforms to the Nigerian military (senior military officer, interview, May 4, 2017).

The Nigerian Air Force in 2005 also negotiated a contract with the China National Aero-Technology Import and Export Corporation to purchase twelve F-7M Airguard multipurpose combat aircraft (to replace aging MiG-21s) and three FT-7NI dual-seat fighter trainer aircraft, which were supplied in 2008 at a total cost of US$252 million (Shinn 2008, 162). In fact, this contract is said to have been Nigeria's most expensive military acquisition ever (McDowell 2012). The deal included training on runway-denial missions and the training of twelve Nigerian pilots in China to man the aircraft.

In addition to the above, China also delivered 120 Poly Technology CS/VP3 armored personnel carriers, thirty AR-1 anti-tank missiles, and five CASC CH-3 unmanned aerial vehicles (News Rescue 2016) to help the Nigerian government in its campaign against Boko Haram. The armed CH-3 UAV bought from China was for the first time used by the Nigerian Air Force on February 2, 2016 to destroy a Boko Haram logistics base in the Sambisa Forest. This represented the first ever occasion on which the Nigerian military used a drone in its fight against terrorism (Ventures 2016).

Regarding the Nigerian Navy, Nigeria–China peace and security cooperation saw an arms sales contract concluded in 2012 in which the West African country ordered two P-18N offshore patrol vessels for a sum of US$42 million, the NNS Centenary and NNS Unity, to be built by China Shipbuilding and Offshore International Co., Ltd. (Vanguard 2016b). These two vessels are a variant of the Chinese Type 056 corvette deployed by the PLA Navy (*Naval Today* 2016). *NNS Centenary* is the Nigerian Navy's first Chinese-built P18n Stealth Offshore Patrol Vessel, which arrived in Lagos in February 2015. This was followed by the *NNS Unity*, which can stay at sea for 20 days at a time. In appreciation of the warship (*NNS Centenary*) that Nigeria bought from them in 2015, the Chinese government donated a military vessel (*NNS Sagbama*) to the Nigeria Navy and also sent a nineteen-man Chinese team to the country for 4 months to train the personnel set to work aboard the vessel (*This Day* 2015). Finally, Nigeria also bought 200 patrol boats from China for use in tackling maritime security challenges (Gambo 2018, 269).

It is important to note here that this growing military cooperation between Nigeria and China has never operated on the understanding that the latter is obliged to play a critical role in the former's fight against insurgency and terrorism. However, the support with regard to sales and gifted weapons came at a time when Nigeria seriously needed to protect its territorial integrity both in

North East and in South South – in the latter, specifically its oil installations and the Gulf of Guinea. Those weapons thus helped considerably in defeating the Boko Haram insurgency in North East and also secured Nigeria territorial waters from piracy and illegal bunkering.

Nigeria's security quagmire and China's latent role

Incidences of insurgency and terrorism across Nigeria have brought the country into the international spotlight. It faces many security challenges, ones that have undermined the ability of the government to develop an inclusive citizenship that could lead to unity and nationhood (Ubi and Wapmuk 2016). Nigeria's insecurity is complex and multifaceted. For some the causes of conflict are poverty, unemployment, and a lack of development. In the South South region, Nigeria is faced with incidences of militancy and insurgency, which have resulted in the bombings of oil installations and the kidnapping of high-profile citizens and of expatriates – including some Chinese citizens (Taylor 2015).

China has been a critical stakeholder and investor in the Nigerian oil sector since the year 2000, with the then recent coming to power of President Olusegun Obasanjo (1999–2007). During his administration, many MoUs were signed between Nigeria and China relating to the downstream and upstream sectors of the Nigerian oil and gas industry. For instance, in 2005 Nigeria agreed to supply PetroChina with 30,000 barrels a day of oil in exchange for US$800 million. And in 2006, Nigeria allowed the China National Offshore Oil Corporation (CNOOC) to purchase a 45 percent stake (for US$2.3 billion) in the OML130 oil exploration block – a deepwater project comprising four oilfields, Akpo, Egina, Egina South, and Preowei – owned by Nigeria's former defense minister. In 2010, meanwhile, Nigeria and China signed another MoU worth US$8 billion that would permit the China State Construction Engineering Corporation to build three refineries and a petrochemical complex in the West African country (Nkagigieme 2005; Ubi 2011a). This deal, however, never actually materialized.

Notwithstanding that, China's investment in the Nigerian oil sector stood at over US$14 billion. In 2018 CNOOC also agreed to invest an additional US$3 billion in the country's offshore oil and gas operations (*The Nigerian Guardian* 2018; *The Punch* 2018), bringing total Chinese investment in the Nigerian oil sector to US$17 billion. As a result of these investments, and protracted militancy and insurgency in South South, in 2012 the Chinese government called for international collaboration with Nigeria to keep safe the Gulf of Guinea specifically by playing a positive and constructive role in enhancing West African security capabilities (Gambo 2018, 270).

In North East, the country is troubled by terrorism orchestrated by Boko Haram. Since 2011 this organization has grown from being a local nuisance to representing a new frontier of international terror (Ubi and Wapmuk 2016). Two events in 2011 announced its arrival on the international terror scene. For the first time in Nigeria, on June 16 the terrorist group detonated a vehicle-borne improvised explosive device (VBIED) manned by a suicide bomber at Nigerian police force headquarters in Abuja. Then on August 26, it carried out another VBIED attack on UN headquarters in Abuja, marking a major shift in the scope of its attacks to include international targets and making the group now a potent threat to both national and international security. Its rapid rise to international terror group status has been marked by unabatedly audacious and brutal terror attacks, with the problem of terrorism persisting ever since in Nigeria.

More worrisome is the inability of the Nigerian government, especially under President Goodluck Jonathan (2010–2015), to contain Boko Haram. The country's security forces have faced a lack of finance, logistics, and necessary materials, which over time has undermined Nigeria's ability to contain the various security problems existing in all of its regions. As it was difficult for the Nigerian government to fight the problem alone, it had to seek the help of some Western countries – especially with regard to weapons. Such support was not forthcoming, however. For instance, the US and other Western powers declined to provide more military aid to Nigeria to fight Boko Haram. They had grown frustrated with the way in which former President Jonathan was handling the issue of Boko Haram. Even when the Nigerian government resorted to buying arms from Israel, Washington persuaded the latter to call off its planned sale of Cobra helicopters on the grounds that they would be used in reckless operations affecting civilians and breaching human rights. In retaliation, the Nigerian government thereafter cancelled a US Army Special Forces training mission in Nigeria (de Luce and O'Grady 2015).

Reacting to the hesitation of the US and other Western nations to provide military aid for the fight against insurgency and terrorism, the only option left for the Nigerian government was to develop closer military cooperation with China. The latter had, as noted, been supplying arms, equipment, training, and technology to the Nigerian armed forces (Embassy of the People's Republic of China in the Federal Republic of Nigeria 2004) even before the advent of Boko Haram. However, China's role in the fight against insecurity in Nigeria is minimal in the sense that there has not been any official declaration made regarding military assistance, finance, or logistical support being given. The only exception is regarding intelligence-gathering and sharing. This is a further indicator that Nigeria's military cooperation with China is not synonymous with a defense pact that would establish the grounds for the latter's intervention, if need be. It also proves that, irrespective of its huge investments in Nigeria as discussed above, China will not renege on its principles of non-interference and non-intervention. Rather, it will stick to the policy stance of China–Africa peace and security cooperation and the traditional focus on intelligence-gathering and sharing, the training of military personnel, and to providing development aid.

For instance, in 2013 the president of the Chinese parliament, Zhang Deijiang, during a courtesy call to the president of the Nigerian Senate, David Mark, pledged Chinese support to help Nigeria in the areas of the training and retraining of security personnel on how to tackle terrorism and on disaster-response capabilities (*The Nigerian Guardian* 2013; *The Punch* 2013). In 2014 China and Nigeria then reiterated that they would work together so as to mitigate the activities of Boko Haram as part of a comprehensive plan to fight insurgency in Nigeria (*The Punch* 2014). This same gesture was repeated in December 2015 by the Chinese ambassador to Nigeria, Gu Xiaojile, during a courtesy visit to the Nigerian chief of defense staff, General Gabriel Olunisakin.

Thus, while China's role has remained a rhetorical one – even despite Chinese citizens, businesses, and interests being themselves affected by insurgency and terrorism – the Asian country has always insisted that the one way to prevent conflict is by addressing its root causes. Hence it gives significant amounts of aid to Africa, thereby framing insecurity as an exclusively economic issue. For the Chinese government, harmony and peace can only be attained when people are free from hunger and starvation. That is why official Chinese rhetoric has always hinged on addressing poverty alleviation, the building of infrastructure, and economic development to boost social progress.

Looking at the situation overall, we can conclude that China has not made any meaningful contributions to mitigating Nigeria's insecurity when one considers the amount of investment made and the close ties between the People's Republic of China and the Federal Republic of Nigeria. On the contrary, as Page (2018) argues, the practices associated with some Chinese enterprises – especially bribery and involvement in illegal mining, logging, and fishing – are problematic and potentially even destabilizing. Although these activities rarely spark violence themselves, they exacerbate homegrown conflict drivers such as resource competition, misgovernance, and policing failures.

Since Muhammadu Buhari took over the reins of government in 2015, the Western powers have, on the contrary, eventually extended assistance to Nigeria to help it fight insurgency and terrorism. The US, for instance, on January 7, 2016 donated twenty-four mine-resistant and ambush-protected vehicles valued at US$11 million to the Nigerian Army (Gordon 2015; Vanguard 2016c). This is a major step in the battle against the terror group. The UK in 2016 also made available £32 million in aid for Northeastern Nigeria (Vanguard 2016a).

Conclusion

It has become obvious that the analysis and evaluation of the role of China in addressing Nigeria's endemic security challenges is a somewhat difficult task. This is mainly due to four factors: first, cumulative data is difficult to collect. Second, China's role herein falls within the wider responsibility of China–Africa peace and security cooperation, which in itself is opaque when it comes to dealing with the individual nations of the continent. Third, there seems to be little synergy between established instruments of Nigeria–China military cooperation and Nigeria's own ongoing fight against insecurity. This is because the military cooperation between Nigeria and China is not primarily geared towards tackling Nigeria's security issues, but reflects predominantly the self-interest of the two governments. Fourth and finally, while China has had a major impact on many African economies, remedying the continent's entrenched insecurity does not actually seem to be a genuine priority in China–Africa relations. If it was, there would have been a tangible shift away from China's policy hitherto of non-interference and non-intervention. Therefore, there has actually been an absence of policy pragmatism in China's pledges to extenuate Nigeria's insecurity; 'words and deeds do not match.'

Notes

1 The Bandung Conference hinged Chinese aid on the 1964 Eight Principles for Economic and Technical Assistance to Developing Countries. The core content of this included: equality, mutual benefit, and no strings attached.

2 The latter source was compiled by the South African Foreign Policy Initiative to provide interested parties with an easily accessible document on the two major outcomes of FOCAC.

References

Bartles, C. K. (2012) *Understanding security cooperation: A comparison of the US and Russian systems of security cooperation*, (https://community.apan.org/wg/tradoc-g2/fmso/m/fmso-monographs/200408), accessed 15 February 2017.

Blackseagrain (2016) *Nigeria, China trade hits $101 billion in 11 years*, (www.blacksea-grain.net/novosti/nigeria-china-trade-hits-101-billion-in-11-years), accessed 1 April 2016.

Bukarambe, B. (2005) 'Nigeria-China Relations: The Unacknowledged Sino-dynamics', in U. J. Ogwu (ed.) *New Horizons for Nigeria in World Affairs*, Nigerian Institute of International Affairs, Lagos, 231–256.

CGTN (2018) *China-Africa in numbers: Peacekeeping operations*, (https://news.cgtn.com/news/3d3d774d7763444f79457a6333566d54/share_p.html), accessed 12 May 2019.

China Daily (2006) *Sino-Nigerian relations*, (www.chinadaily.com.cn/china/2006-04/17/content_569613.htm), accessed 12 May 2019.

China Daily (2015) *Full text: China's second Africa policy paper*, (www.chinadaily.com.cn/world/XiattendsParisclimateconference/2015-12/05/content_22632874.htm), accessed 25 May 2017.

China Economic Net (2014) *China and Nigeria sign landmark deals*, (http://en.ce.cn/subject/li14/li14n/201405/08/t20140508_2779848.shtml), accessed 28 August 2014.

de Luce, D. and O'Grady, S. (2015) *U.S. to boost military aid to Nigeria for Boko Haram fight*, (http://foreignpolicy.com/2015/07/16/u-s-to-boost-military-aid-to-nigeria-for-boko-haram-fight/), accessed 5 March 2017.

Duchâtel, M., Gowan, R. and Rapnouil, M. L. (2016) *Into Africa: China's Global Security Shift*, Policy Brief no. 179, European Council on Foreign Relations, London.

Embassy of the People's Republic of China in the Federal Republic of Nigeria (2004) *China-Nigeria relations*, (http://ng.china-embassy.org/eng/zngx/cne/t142490.htm), accessed 12 May 2019.

FOCAC (Forum on China-Africa Cooperation) (2006) *Forum on China-Africa Cooperation Beijing Action Plan, 2007–2009*, (www.fmprc.gov.cn/zflt/eng/zyzl/hywj/t280369.htm), accessed 12 May 2019.

FOCAC (Forum on China-Africa Cooperation) (2009) *Forum on China-Africa Cooperation Sharm El-Sheikh Action Plan (2010–2012)*, (www.fmprc.gov.cn/zflt/eng/dsjbzjhy/hywj/t626387.htm), accessed 12 May 2019.

FOCAC (Forum on China-Africa Cooperation) (2015) *The Forum on China-Africa Cooperation Johannesburg Action Plan* (2016–2018), (www.fmprc.gov.cn/mfa_eng/zxxx_662805/t1323159.shtml), accessed 23 May 2019.

Gambo, A. N. (2018) 'Nigeria-China Peace and Security Cooperation', in W. O. Alli (ed.) *Nigeria's Diplomacy of Economic Development and China*, Center for Inter-African and Human Development Studies, Abuja, 255–278.

Global Security (2016) *São Tomé e Principe-China relations*, (www.globalsecurity.org/military/world/africa/stp-forrel-prc.htm), accessed 6 June 2017.

Gordon, M. R. (2015) *U.S. signals willingness to expand military cooperation with Nigeria*, (https://mobile.nytimes.com/2015/05/30/world/africa/us-signal-willingness-to-widen-role-in-fighting-boko-haram-in-Nigeria.html), accessed 7 March 2017.

Gu, X. (2016) *Speech at the reception celebrating the 45th anniversary of the establishment of diplomatic relations between China and Nigeria & the Chinese Spring Festival by H.E. Gu Xiaojie, Chinese Ambassador to Nigeria*, (http://ng.china-embassy.org/eng/zngx/cne/t1338991.htm), accessed 12 May 2019.

Liu, K. (2015) *Speech from Consul General Liu Kan in 66th Chinese National Day reception*, (http://lagos.chineseconsulate.org/eng/xwfb/zxhd/t1302192.htm), accessed 11 May 2019.

McDowell, M. A. (2012) *China in Nigeria*, report for the Naval War College, Naval War College, Newport.

Naval Today (2016) *China-built Nigerian Navy ship NNS Unity arrives to Lagos*, (http://navaltoday.com/2016/11/07/china-built-nigerian-navy-ship-nns-unity-arrives-to-lagos/), accessed 27 May 2017.

New Era (2015) *Political stability vs economic development*, (www.newera.com.na/2015/03/13/political-stability-economic-development/), accessed 19 March 2015.

News Rescue (2016) *Flashback: Nigerian military acquisitions by The Goodluck Jonathan and late Yar'Adua administrations*, (http://newsrescue.com/flashback-nigerian-military-acquisitions-goodluck-jonathan-late-yaradua-administrations/#axzz4je7N5z7b), accessed 19 May 2017.

Nkagigieme, U. (2005) *The Challenges of Building a New Refinery in Nigeria with Limited Energy Infrastructure and Regulated Petroleum Products Market*, paper for the conference '18th World Petroleum Congress', Johannesburg, 25–29 September.

Page, M. T. (2018) *The Intersection of China's Commercial Interests and Nigeria's Conflict Landscape*, United States Institute of Peace Special Report no. 428, United States Institute of Peace, Washington, DC.

Pauley, L. (2018) *China takes the lead in UN peacekeeping*, (https://thediplomat.com/2018/04/china-takes-the-lead-in-un-peacekeeping/), accessed 13 May 2019.

People's Daily (2016) *Forty-Five years of Nigeria, China relations*, (www.peoplesdailyng.com/forty-five-years-of-nigeria-china-relations/), accessed 3 October 2016.

SAFPI (South African Foreign Policy Initiative) (2012) *Outcomes of the Fifth Ministerial Conference of the Forum on China-Africa Cooperation*, (www.safpi.org/publications/outcomes_fifth_ministerial_conference_forum_china_africa_cooperation/), accessed 4 May 2017.

Shinn, D. H. (2008) 'Military and Security Relations: China, Africa, and the Rest of the World', in R. I. Rotberg (ed.) *China into Africa: Trade, Aid and Influence*, Brookings Institution Press, Washington, DC, 155–196.

SIIS (Shanghai Institutes for International Studies) (2001) *China-Africa cooperative partnership for peace and security*, (www.siis.org.cn/Research/EnInfo/1700), accessed 12 May 2017.

State Council (2006) *China's African Policy*, (www.gov.cn/misc/2006-01/12/content_156490.htm#1), accessed 18 April 2019.

Taylor, I. (2015) 'The Good, the Bad, and the Ugly: Agency-as-Corruption and the Sino-Nigerian Relationship', in A. W. Gadzala (ed.) *Africa and China: How Africans and their Governments are Shaping Relations with China*, Rowman and Littlefield, London, 27–44.

Tazoacha, F. (2016) *China's security concerns in Africa: Another imperialistic 'mise en valeur'*, (www.friendsofeurope.org/security-europe/chinas-security-concerns-africa-another-imperialistic-mise-en-valeur/), accessed 7 February 2017.

The Nigerian Guardian (2012) 'China Wants to Partner Nigeria on the Gulf of Guinea', *The Nigerian Guardian*, 3 August.

The Nigerian Guardian (2013) 'China Offers to Assist Nigeria Institutions', *The Nigerian Guardian*, 19 September.

The Nigerian Guardian (2015) 'China Reiterates Commitment to Support Nigeria's Military', *The Nigerian Guardian*, 31 July.

The Nigerian Guardian (2017) 'China Plans $40b Investment in Nigeria', *The Nigerian Guardian*, 11 January.

The Nigerian Guardian (2018) 'China's Investment in Nigeria's Oil Sector to hit $17 billion', *The Nigerian Guardian*, 16 July.

The Punch (2013) 'Terrorism: China Pledges Military support for Nigeria', *The Punch*, 19 September.

The Punch (2014) 'Nigeria, China Agree to Share Intelligence, says Mark', *The Punch*, 19 May, 13.

The Punch (2018) 'Chinese Oil Firm to Invest $3bn in Nigeria', *The Punch*, 16 July.

This Day (2015) 'Nigeria, China deepen strategic Bi-lateral Ties', *This Day*, 10 September, 47.

Ubi, E. N. (2008) 'Nigeria and the Challenges of Human Security: A Case Study of the Niger-Delta Region', Nigerian Institute of International Affairs, unpublished.

Ubi, E. N. (2011a) 'China's Foreign Aid to Africa: An Examination of Infrastructure Development in Nigeria', PhD Dissertation, School of International and Public Affairs, Jilin University.

Ubi, E. N. (2011b) 'China's "New Strategic Partnership" with Africa: What's in for Africa?', *Journal of China and the World*, 1(1), 128–141.

Ubi, E. N. (2013) 'African Conflicts and the African Standby Force as a Desideratum', in B. Akinterinwa (ed.) *Organisation of African Unity/African Union at 50: Challenges and Prospects of Self-Reliance in Africa*, Vol. 1, Nigerian Institute of International Affairs, Lagos, 481–512.

Ubi, E. N. (2014) 'Foreign Aid and Development in Sino-African Relations', *Journal of Developing Society*, 30(3), 243–272.

Ubi, E. N. (2018) *Addressing Nigeria's trade disparity with China*, (www.financialnigeria.com/addressing-nigeria-s-trade-disparity-with-china-blog-317.html), accessed 13 May 2019.

Ubi, E., and Ibonye, V. (2017) 'An Examination of Nigeria-China Academic Relations', in P. A. Gwaza and E. N. Ubi (eds) *Nigeria in Global Governance, Peace and Security: Essays in Honor of Professor Joseph Habila Golwa*, Okoye Honeybees Ltd, Lagos, 29–81.

Ubi, E. N. and Wapmuk, S. (2016) *Nationhood Crisis and Violent Extremism as a Poverty Issue*, Centre for Humanitarian Dialogue and United Nations Development Programme, Geneva and New York.

Utomi, P. (2008) *China and Nigeria*, (https://csis-prod.s3.amazonaws.com/s3fs-public/legacy_files/files/media/csis/pubs/080603_utomi_nigeriachina.pdf), accessed 13 May 2019.

Van de Looy, J. (2006) *Africa and China: A Strategic Partnership?*, ASC Working Paper no. 67, African Studies Centre, Leiden.

Vanguard (2016a) *Insurgency: UK gives Nigeria £32m aid for north east devt*, (www.vanguardngr.com/2016/04/uk-gives-nigeria-32-million-energy-humanitarian-needs/), accessed 11 June 2019.

Vanguard (2016b) *Nigerian Navy acquires new vessel from China*, (www.vanguardngr.com/2016/09/nigerian-navy-acquires-new-vessel-china/), accessed 12 May 2017.

Vanguard (2016c) *US donates $11m mine resistant vehicles to Nigerian army*, (www.vanguardngr.com/2016/01/us-donates-11m-mine-resistant-vehicles-to-nigerian-army/), accessed 13 May 2019.

Ventures (2016) *Nigeria adopts the 'drone war' approach in the fight against Boko Haram: Here are other modern warfare options they can take on*, (http://venturesafrica.com/nigeria-joins-the-drone-wars-in-its-fight-against-boko-haram-here-are-other-weapons-they-could-use/), accessed 6 May 2017.

Voice of America (2015) *New Chinese port in Sao Tome has economic, not military aims*, (www.voanews.com/a/new-chinese-port-in-sao-tome-has-economic-not-military-aims/3025362.html), accessed 6 June 2017.

Volman, D. (2015) 'China, India, Russia, and the United States: The Scramble for African Oil and Militarization of the Continent', in T. Young (ed.) *Readings in the International Relations of Africa*, Indiana University Press, Bloomington, 309–321.

Wang, X. (2018) 'Developmental Peace: Understanding China's Africa Policy in Peace and Security', in C. Alden, A. Alao, Z. Chun and L. Barber (eds) *China and Africa: Building Peace and Security Cooperation on the Continent*, Palgrave Macmillan, London, 67–82.

Wei, W. (2010) *China and Africa envision new security cooperation*, (www.hiiraan.com/news2_rss/2010/July/china_and_africa_envision_new_security_cooperation.aspx), accessed 13 May 2019.

Xinhua (2016) *Roundup: China, Nigeria eye more fruitful results in bilateral ties*, (http://news.xinhuanet.com/english/2016-01/05/c_134980429.htm), accessed 6 October 2016.

Zhan, S. (2016) *The '3c' principle of sustainable security in Africa: For a common, comprehensive, cooperative and sustainable security*, (www.focac.org/eng/zxxx/t1347435.htm), accessed 4 July 2016.

14 'We are black Chinese' – making sense of APC's pro-China campaign in Sierra Leone's 2018 elections[1]

Patricia Rinck

Introduction

On March 7, 2018, Sierra Leone held presidential, parliamentary, and local elections. As President Ernest Bai Koroma from the All People's Congress (APC) had to step down after serving two 5-year terms in office, the ruling party was under pressure to be re-elected and the presidential election was the most competitive in at least a decade (EU EOM 2018, 8). The ruling APC won the majority of seats in the parliamentary elections on March 7, 2018, but the opposition candidate, Julius Maada Bio from the Sierra Leone People's Party (SLPP), won the presidential elections in a postponed run-off on March 31 with 51.8 percent over the APC's candidate, Dr. Samura Kamara. Maada Bio was sworn in as Sierra Leone's new president in the evening of April 4. As only the second peaceful transition from one elected leader to another in the country's history, the elections were an important milestone. International and local observers lauded the National Electoral Commission (NEC) for its commitment to a transparent and inclusive election (e.g., EU EOM 2018, 3; NEW 2018, 4; The Carter Center 2018, 4).

However, the months before the elections as well as the weeks between the two rounds of presidential elections were quite turbulent. Pushing for a third term for President Koroma, the government had repeatedly postponed the elections, which were due in 2017, and only announced an election date following sustained pressure from civil society organizations (CSOs) and the international community. Preparations for the elections were complicated due to a late disbursement of funding by the government as well as an overcrowded electoral calendar, and the NEC faced political pressure from the government throughout the electoral cycle (EU EOM 2018, 4, 12).

In the months before the elections, the ruling APC attracted attention by using its close relations with Chinese actors in its preparations for the elections: President Koroma and his party claimed that the Chinese Communist Party (CCP) had donated funding for the construction of a new regional APC headquarter in Freetown, which was later denied by the Chinese embassy. Chinese companies allegedly supported the construction of another APC office in the party's stronghold region and sponsored giveaways for the campaigns, and some

Chinese businessmen made it into the news openly campaigning alongside APC supporters.

While it is difficult to assess how substantial Chinese support for the APC really was, it was perceived as an unusually open and partisan involvement in the elections and led to vehement criticism and worries by opposition parties, journalists, civil society activists, and Sierra Leoneans from all walks of life whether China had given up its policy of non-interference and was now involved in Sierra Leone's national politics.

Overall relations with China and especially economic ties to the People's Republic have become an important factor in election campaigns in a number of African countries; most prominently in Zambia in 2011, where the 'anti-China card' helped Michael Sata win the presidency. Interestingly, the public response to Chinese economic involvement does not seem to be primarily linked to the respective level of Chinese investment, but determined by whether or not political elites have chosen to place anti-Chinese sentiment on their political agendas (Hess and Aidoo 2014, 144). In other words, the elites' decision to make relations with China a topic in the campaign matters. Against this background, the period leading to Sierra Leone's 2018 elections presents an interesting case since the government, different from Sata in Zambia, rather played a 'pro-China card,' using its good relations with Chinese actors in the campaigns to mobilize support. Given that Sierra Leoneans' perceptions of Chinese involvement are somewhat ambivalent, this was all the more surprising.

The chapter attempts to unravel the APC's role in using its relations with China and Chinese actors in Sierra Leone to mobilize support in the run-up to the elections, thus contributing to the debate on African agency, or more precisely the agency of political elites during elections. The episode demonstrates how China, through the APC's conduct, has become a part of political competition within Sierra Leone, showing that China's growing influence – intended or not – can shape domestic political dynamics and affect stability. Since the academic literature on China–Sierra Leone relations so far is scarce, the chapter additionally draws on newspaper articles covering relevant events as well as field research. In May and June 2018, sixteen interviews were conducted with Sierra Leonean academics, entrepreneurs, staff of non-governmental organizations, including National Election Watch (NEW), staff of the NEC, the Political Parties Registration Commission, politicians or lawyers of the two main parties APC and SLPP as well as the new National Grand Coalition (NGC) party. Interviews with foreign donor agencies or diplomats included United Kingdom (UK) Department for International Development, Irish Aid, United States Agency for International Development, European Union (EU), staff of United Nations (UN) agencies and private foundations. The chapter is informed by some interviews and conversations with Chinese academics and entrepreneurs in Freetown. Since it was unfortunately difficult to get interviews with any official Chinese actors, their perspectives could not be included.

In the following, after a short overview of Sino-Sierra Leonean relations, developments in the run-up to and during the elections as well as reactions to these will be reconstructed. The chapter will then attempt to make sense of the APC's use of the Chinese in the forefront of the elections and give a tentative appraisal of China's role in this. Subsequently, an explanation for the outcome of the elections is offered before the chapter closes with some conclusions on what this episode reveals about China's role in Sierra Leonean politics.

China's relations with Sierra Leone – the history of a 'very good marriage'?

China's diplomatic relations with Sierra Leone date back to 1971, when Sierra Leone shifted from supporting Taiwan and voted in favor of UN General Assembly Resolution 2758, which recognized the People's Republic of China as the only legitimate representative of China in the UN. From this period dates a special relationship between the CCP under Mao Zedong and the APC under Siaka Stevens, Sierra Leone's autocratic leader, who skillfully 'masqueraded' as an anti-capitalist, 'manipulating ideology for domestic and international gain in his nation-building efforts' (Bräutigam 1994, 332). He thus made sure to maintain Chinese support despite Sierra Leone's relative unimportance, even if Chinese support was just a small portion of its overall external assistance, most of which came from the former colonial power UK and other Western countries (Bräutigam 1994, 342).

Until today, Sierra Leone has been highly aid-dependent, and Sierra Leonean elites have always relied on external actors – most heavily, but not only on Western donors – in a strategy of extraversion (Bayart 2000). The small country has mineral resources – most notably diamonds, but also gold, iron ore, and oil to name but a few – but due to its size, its economic, political, and strategic importance cannot be compared to other resource-rich African countries like Angola or Nigeria.

Both in its self-understanding and perception by others, the APC has been closely connected to the CCP because of their shared communist background – although this alleged communist background is not really reflected in actual APC policies. Sierra Leoneans refer to the APC–CCP relationship as 'a very good marriage,' one interviewee even said the 'APC is like the offspring of the CPC party of China' (registrar, PPRC, interview, May 24, 2018). And indeed, China's support has been 'very responsive to the needs of Sierra Leone's leaders, in particular, the All People's Congress (APC) party' (Bräutigam 1998, 55), which was in power throughout most of Sierra Leone's post-independence history, including during its time as a one-party state. China has sent medical teams to Sierra Leone since the early 1970s, started trade relations in the 1980s, and has supported infrastructural development in Sierra Leone ever since. For instance, in the 1970s and 1980s the Chinese built several key buildings, among them the Youyi ('friendship') ministry building, as well as the national stadium, the parliament, police headquarters, bridges, as well as some agricultural promotion stations across the country (Bräutigam 1994; 1998, 211–213; Corkin and Burke 2006, 37).

Relations with China slowed down during Sierra Leone's armed conflict (1991–2002) and were slowly revived during the early post-conflict phase under the administration of President Ahmad Tejan Kabbah from the SLPP. In 2005, the construction of a new office complex for the Ministry of Foreign Affairs and a new stadium in Bo, the SLPP's stronghold, were negotiated (Bräutigam 2009, 138). Relations intensified after Ernest Bai Koroma of the APC had won the 2007 presidential elections. During his two terms, some new infrastructure projects were added, among them the renovation of some of Freetown's most important roads, the construction of the 'Sierra Leone-China Friendship Hospital' at Jui, just outside Freetown, and the clock tower landmark in the APC's stronghold of Makeni.

Since its foundation in 2012, the Confucius Institute at Fourah Bay College (FBC) has supported people-to-people and cultural exchanges through language courses, martial arts classes, and job fairs with Chinese companies. Sierra Leonean graduate and PhD students can study in China on scholarships (professor, Confucius Institute, interview, May 24, 2018).

With regard to development assistance, it is clear that Western donors still provide much more resources, although it is difficult to put an exact number on China's contributions. According to AidData, Chinese total official commitments to Sierra Leone between 2000 and 2014 amounted to US$670.7 million, including US$247 million Official Development Assistance (ODA) (Dreher et al. 2017). Put in a comparative perspective, this is only a fraction of what other African countries received from China; e.g., Côte d'Ivoire received about US$4 billion in ODA, and Tanzania, Nigeria, Ethiopia, Cameroon, Zimbabwe, and Ethiopia between US$3 and US$3.7 billion each. And even with decreasing ODA flows, Sierra Leone still received US$537.6 million in net ODA from OECD–Development Assistance Committee donors in 2017 alone (OECD–DAC n.d.). The Chinese also supported Sierra Leone's response to the 2014 Ebola outbreak; yet again it is difficult to estimate the size of China's contribution, even for international donors in Freetown.

While there were not too many Chinese investors a couple of years ago (Corkin and Burke 2006, 44; Datzberger 2013), this has changed in recent years, when Chinese companies secured a number of important contracts. In early 2015, the Chinese state-owned company Shandong Iron and Steel Group bought the Tonkolili mine, which is currently not in operation but considered to have some of the largest iron-ore resources in Africa, from Frank Timis' London-based African Minerals. Due to its complicated business environment and high levels of corruption, Sierra Leone is not considered an easy environment for high-quality investors. Since many of the Chinese companies in Sierra Leone are state-owned, they seem to be less risk averse and tend to be able to outbid Western competitors (Taylor 2006, 942; Hess and Aidoo 2015, 137).

In recent years, there were several scandals around controversial and unpopular infrastructure projects the former government had granted to Chinese companies, including the extremely overpriced maintenance of Wilkinson Road in Freetown, the road from Freetown to Masiaka with three toll gates and the

Mamamah International Airport project (Datzberger 2013, 3; Elcoate 2018; Inveen and Maclean 2018).

On an international level, Sierra Leone usually publicly supports China's political position, for instance siding with the Chinese on the South China Sea issue, which led Ambassador Zhao Yanbo to call Sierra Leone a 'bosom friend' (Zhao 2016). He described the Chinese–Sierra Leonean relations as 'win–win cooperation and common development,' saying that 'China has provided persistent and enormous support to infrastructure construction and human resources building with no political strings attached' (Zhao 2016). As in other African countries, China's engagement in Sierra Leone reflects a 'patterned process' involving a range of actors: national officials establishing or deepening bilateral relations with government counterparts via aid and trade agreements; state-owned companies implementing construction projects; and a group of largely independent actors such as independent entrepreneurs or laborers (Hess and Aidoo 2015, 137).

Perceptions of the Chinese are somewhat ambivalent in Sierra Leone. On the one hand, China's importance in Sierra Leone's economy and especially infrastructural development is generally acknowledged. On the other, people often criticize Chinese companies for particularly poor working conditions, suspect Chinese actors of being interested only in Sierra Leone's resources, not its democratic governance and development, and assume that China benefits more from bilateral deals than Sierra Leone (professor, FBC, interview, May 11, 2018; director, Institute for Governance Reform, interview, May 14, 2018).

Chinese support for the ruling APC in the 2018 elections

The 2018 elections were the first post-war elections entirely run by the Sierra Leonean government, after the UN had run the 2007 and monitored the 2012 elections. International actors, such as the EU, UK, or US, were strongly involved in making the elections possible, putting pressure on the government to have elections at all, supporting critical areas via a multi-donor project managed by United Nations Development Programme, funding the ballot papers, voter register, and tally center infrastructure; they were present in meetings, supported the NEC, and expressed their support for the whole process on the radio or in press releases (diplomats, interviews, May 17, 2018, June 1, 2018; program specialist, UN organization, interview, May 21, 2018; spokesperson, NEC, interview, May, 16 2018). The Chinese government did not officially support the electoral process and also did not participate in the steering committee set up to manage efficient mobilization and utilization of international assistance to the electoral process, where other embassies and donor agencies were present.

However, during the election campaigns, several Chinese men were seen supporting the ruling APC party in their rallies in the provinces in January 2018, sitting next to APC candidates, marching with them and wearing APC clothing. Pictures and videos of such incidents were sent around on WhatsApp and were hotly debated in the media. Other videos, whose backgrounds are not always clear, were circulated on WhatsApp featuring APC supporters commending the Chinese for their involvement, for instance a video showing the president's brother praising the Chinese (see Thomas 2018).

Campaigning materials and merchandise such as T-shirts, cups, fans, and banners were produced in China and allegedly sponsored by Chinese companies (The Carter Center 2018, 38; Inveen and Maclean 2018). Chinese companies had also allegedly supported the APC by furnishing their new office complex in Makeni with furniture made in China, as well as by sponsoring the motorbikes that were used to campaign (professor, FBC, interview, May 11, 2018). How much Chinese support the APC received is unclear. The APC had access to more funding than other parties – much of this, however, is likely to stem from its party members, many of whom held top positions in corporate entities (spokesperson, NEC, interview, May 16, 2018).

The impression that China was financially supporting the APC seems to have been received very positively among APC supporters: at an APC rally about a week before the first election round, APC presidential candidate Samura Kamara was greeted by supporters chanting 'We are Chinese! We are Chinese!' (Inveen and Maclean 2018), which was considered an 'expression of support for the country that has poured vast amounts of resources into Sierra Leone' (Elcoate 2018).

The background: the controversy over the 'APC/CPC Friendship Building'

Among the opposition, but also civil society activists and journalists, these incidents sparked a lot of public criticism, reviving memories of an earlier episode of perceived open involvement by Chinese actors into Sierra Leone's politics. In May 2017, several senior APC officials, among them the Minister of Information, Mohamed Bangura, had claimed in several radio programs that the CCP was partly funding a new seven-story office building for the APC (Cambayma 2017). The APC had published a similar statement on its Facebook page on February 8, 2016. At the sod-turning ceremony for the building in Pultney Street in the center of Freetown on May 17, 2017, President Koroma was reportedly recorded saying, in the presence of Chinese Deputy Ambassador Wang Xingming, 'that China's years of well-built relationship with the ruling APC is but the cause for the construction of a seven storey APC/CPC Chinese Friendship Building' (*Salone Today* 2017a).

The news, dispersed by the APC, that funding for the new APC building came from the CCP led to protests by opposition parties and CSOs and was a major topic in Sierra Leonean media for weeks. It was heavily criticized because any external party funding is illegal: The Political Parties Act 2002 (paragraph 19 (1)) foresees that party funding 'shall be limited to contributions or donations, whether in cash or in kind, of persons who are entitled to be registered as voters in Sierra Leone.' Sierra Leone is relatively restrictive when it comes to granting citizenship – many of the Lebanese born and raised in Sierra Leone have not been granted citizenship and are therefore not allowed to vote. In addition, this episode took place at a time when the government decided to bar Sierra Leoneans with dual citizenship from contesting in the elections based on a stipulation in the 1991 constitution, which had not been enforced until then (Jakwa 2018), but was now used to prevent some political opponents, most prominently Dr. Kandeh Yumkella[2] from the NGC, from contesting.

Due to its partisan nature, the alleged donation was criticized as contradicting China's foreign policy of non-interference in the internal affairs of other countries. It was seen to be linked to the contracts the APC government had granted to Chinese companies (Thomas 2017; chairperson, NEW, interview, May 21, 2018).

Interestingly, the Chinese ambassador denied any official Chinese support for the building. After protests by the main opposition party SLPP, Ambassador Wu Peng met with SLPP officials twice and

> assured the SLPP that contrary to widespread media reports and claims by the leadership of the APC, neither the Chinese Government nor the Communist Party of China (CPC) is involved, directly or indirectly, in the financing of the construction of said office building.
>
> (SLPP press release, cited in Gooding 2017)

The Chinese ambassador reportedly claimed that 'it was in fact the APC that had approached the CPC' and informed them about their plans to construct a new office building which 'as a symbol of their long-standing relationship they would like [...] to be named as the APC-CPC Friendship Building' (cited in Gooding 2017).

Under pressure to disclose the source of funding for the building built by the Chinese SKM Construction Company (SL) Limited, the APC submitted a document to the Political Parties Registration Commission (PPRC), stating that the new party office would be funded by the APC, not the Chinese (Salone Today 2017b). Still, many Sierra Leoneans doubted this (see Cambayma 2017).

Consequently, when Chinese men were seen campaigning together with APC officials in 2018, for many Sierra Leoneans, this seemed to confirm Chinese support for the APC in the elections. Even after the elections, in May and June 2018, many people still believed the building was financed by Chinese actors – not only people in the streets would say so, but also civil society activists, journalists, academics, and even Sierra Leoneans working for international donor agencies (professor, FBC, interview, May 11, 2018; governance specialist, development agency, interview, May 15, 2018; registrar, PPRC, interview, May 24, 2018). Many of them did not distinguish between the Chinese government and the communist party, arguing that these were basically synonymous to each other within the communist system. This extends to Chinese companies as well since they are often state-owned.

Diverging assessments of China's role in Sierra Leone's politics

Thus, although it is unclear how substantial Chinese support for the APC in terms of campaigning materials or funds really was and how much they potentially did or did not spend on the two APC buildings in Makeni and Freetown, their closeness to the APC has been perceived as an unusually open and partisan involvement and has led to sharp criticism and worries about China's role in Sierra Leone's national politics.

While the Chinese embassy denied their involvement in funding the APC headquarter in Freetown, they did not officially comment on Chinese support for and involvement in the APC campaigns. For many Sierra Leonean observers, it is hard to imagine that Chinese investors – in some cases of state-owned companies – could openly support the APC party against the wish of the Chinese embassy in Sierra Leone (chairperson, NEW, interview, May 21, 2018). Since the general impression is usually that the Chinese do not interfere in the internal affairs of other countries, many Sierra Leoneans were all the more surprised and worried (lawyer, interview, May 30, 2018). The incidents were interpreted as a sign that China had given up its principle of non-interference to let various Chinese actors get openly involved in Sierra Leone's national politics, attempting to support the ruling party in the elections in order to maintain the established business relations.

Non-Sierra Leonean staff of embassies or development agencies were more cautious about their assessment, saying that there probably was some support by Chinese companies for the APC before the elections, 'but not too massive' (diplomat, interview, June 1, 2018), and not by the government, since the Chinese embassy never got officially involved (diplomats, interviews, May 17, 2018, May 24, 2018, June 1, 2018). Inveen and Maclean (2018) cite officials at the Chinese embassy in Freetown saying that China was 'apolitical' towards Sierra Leone and that its companies did not represent the Chinese state. Indeed, as Hess and Aidoo (2015, 137–138) point out, the Chinese government sometimes struggles with independent Chinese nationals abroad whose (legitimate or illegitimate) activities can contribute to anti-Chinese sentiments in African countries. For many Sierra Leoneans, Chinese companies and the state are synonymous, as the interviews showed (see also Inveen and Maclean 2018).

Another event that in the eyes of many Sierra Leoneans seemed to underline the APC's close relations with the Chinese was the launching ceremony of the planned new airport: on March 1, 2018, only 6 days before the elections, President Koroma launched, in the presence of Chinese Ambassador Wu Peng, the construction of the highly controversial Mamamah International Airport. The project, which was to be built by China Railway Seventh Group, had been planned since 2012, but was on hold because of the Ebola crisis and a disagreement with the International Monetary Fund and the World Bank over whether such a project was prudent while Sierra Leone was still recovering from an economic crisis. China supported its launch with a loan at a time when other donors did not disburse any funds anymore because of the proximity to the elections (governance specialist, development agency, interview, May 15, 2018). The EU Election Observation Mission rated the ceremony as an abuse of incumbency: it was set in APC colors, rather than the national flag; it was attended by the APC's presidential and vice-presidential candidates, who did both not hold official government positions; and it took place just before the elections (EU EOM 2018, 22). The construction of the airport was stopped by the new government in June 2018.

Making sense of both the APC's and China's behavior

The APC seems to have been trying to use its good relations with China in its campaigns to mobilize support for the elections, which would be difficult to imagine in other African countries. Given that China's standing in Sierra Leone is quite ambivalent, as outlined before, the APC's behavior did surprise many Sierra Leoneans and international observers and needs explanation.

'APC is black Chinese' – the APC's attempt to court the Chinese

To start with, the Koroma government had strengthened relations with the Chinese from the beginning. While the bulk of development assistance continued to come from Western donors, the government always also used Chinese support to implement their agenda, and with the focus on visible infrastructural development, they shared similar interests. Implementing projects other donors did not support, like building or improving roads in the countryside, the Chinese have certainly filled a gap, which was acknowledged in the interviews by Sierra Leoneans and Western donors alike.

At the same time, Sierra Leonean interviewees suspect that the APC government's narrow focus on the Chinese might be explained by the lack of conditionality and the consequence that Chinese money may be more easily used for patronage than Western funding. As Dreher et al. (2016, 5–6) show, a disproportionate share of Chinese official financing goes to the birth regions of African leaders. For instance, one could question whether the school Chinese actors constructed in President Koroma's small village of birth Yoni in 2010 was built where it was most needed. More problematically, deals for large infrastructure projects, in Sierra Leone as in other African countries, often use natural resources as collateral for Chinese loans (Bräutigam 2009, 145) or involve the accumulation of debt (regional director, development agency, interview, May 16, 2018).

As a consequence of their close relationship, China's role in Sierra Leone's economy and political settlement has grown over the last years – although the Lebanese continue to be the most important business community. It seems likely that the APC was trying to capitalize on these close relations in the pre-elections period to sway voters, both by 'showcasing' their own achievements especially in infrastructural development (professor, FBC, interview, May 11, 2018), and by highlighting the future development potential linked to Chinese investments which would become reality if they were to win the election.

Focusing the campaign on their successes in terms of infrastructure projects achieved with Chinese support certainly made sense for at least two reasons: first, the government did not have a good record before the elections. Its popularity had suffered from the economic crisis, the Ebola outbreak and the mudslide in Regent in August 2017 with over 1000 fatalities. Moreover, President Koroma was deeply unpopular for his decision to sack Vice President Samuel Sam-Sumana, which according to a ruling of the Economic Community of West African States (ECOWAS) violated article seven of the African Charter on Human and Peoples' Rights (ECOWAS Court 2017). Second, relations with Western donors and diplomats had been strained for some years because of the government's record regarding governance and corruption. In the run-up to the 2012 elections, there had been some commotion when the UN abruptly removed the head of its UNIPSIL mission, Michael von der Schulenburg, after pressure by the president (Akam 2012; *The Economist* 2012). Von der Schulenburg, a respected diplomat who had voiced his concerns regarding some non-transparent deals with several mining companies before and who had been trying to create a level playing field for the elections, was accused of meddling in Sierra Leone's affairs (Gberie 2012; see also US Embassy Freetown 2012). A particular stumbling block in relations with Western donors and diplomats in the years before the 2018 elections was the president's attempt to extend the number of constitutional presidential terms. During that period, when Sierra Leone was hotly debating his 'more time' campaign, a visit by a delegation from the CCP and government officials' announcement that the new APC office was funded by the CCP were suspected to be potential signs of the CCP's endorsement of the 'more time' quest (Thomas 2016; Gooding 2017). Many Sierra Leoneans were concerned about this potential Chinese support for President Koroma's ambitions, given that he was at the same time trying to increase presidential powers through a constitutional review process, which many perceived as a danger to Sierra Leone's democracy (Thomas 2017). In the end, the attempt to abolish the two-term limit was not successful and President Koroma handpicked a successor, Samura Kamara, who had held two ministerial posts before and had been a consistent advocate for Chinese investment in Sierra Leone (Inveen and Maclean 2018).

In the view of the APC leadership, 'the Chinese have never been involved directly in our politics,' while others have (APC running mate Chernor Bah, interview, May 30, 2018). Several APC officials heavily criticized international observers during the elections. For instance, on state broadcaster SLBC radio, Deputy Minister of Information and Communication Cornelius Deveaux accused the international community of 'an international conspiracy to steal our victory [...] led by [the] British High Commissioner [and] implemented by [the] former Ghanaian President' (APA News 2018).[3] This was generally regarded as an attempt to blame the international community in case the APC would lose the elections, since the party did not provide any evidence for their claim that internationals were trying to meddle (director, Institute for Governance Reform, interview, May 14, 2018; see also NEW 2018, 54).

To sum up, the APC's attempt to use its relations with the Chinese can be explained by a combination of factors: the wish to highlight previous achievements in infrastructure and construction as well as the future development potential linked to being on good terms with the Chinese; the attempt to court a business partner whose terms are quite beneficial – not least because of the opportunity for patronage and personal profit they offer – and a diplomatic partner who does not mind one's more autocratic political aspirations, while other international donors and diplomats do.

From non-interference to helping a 'bosom friend'? An interpretation of China's role

As mentioned before, the Chinese government did not support the electoral process, which is, for ideological reasons, not surprising. The public perception is that Chinese companies were openly entangled in the process because they wanted to secure their previous investments, which could explain why they were more involved in 2018 than in 2012 (governance specialist, development agency, interview, May 15, 2018; diplomats, interview, June 1, 2018). In addition, one could argue that there was also more at stake in the 2018 elections than in 2012, when it had been likely that the sitting president was to be re-elected.

Relations with the Chinese remain limited to a relatively narrow group of people in Sierra Leone around the president, namely those in power and in charge of granting contracts. A case in point is that the new airport was approved without a feasibility study by the Minister of Foreign Affairs, who later became the presidential aspirant of the APC (IGR 2018a). While China has tried to establish ties to various important political parties in more democratic African regimes like Ghana and South Africa (Hess and Aidoo 2015, 152, 154), in Sierra Leone, they have concentrated more or less exclusively on the APC.

Throughout his campaign, Julius Maada Bio often criticized President Koroma's government for being too close to the Chinese, arguing that Sierra Leone did not benefit enough from the infrastructural projects, and promising that he, if elected, would improve relations with Western donors again. During Sierra Leone's first presidential debate, aired on TV in February 2018, Maada Bio said he would revise contracts of planned and ongoing Chinese projects, including the toll road and airport project. Other candidates criticized these projects as well. However, none of the presidential candidates used anti-Chinese sentiment in their campaigns to the extent seen in Zambia in 2011 (see Hess and Aidoo 2014).

To sum up, it seems that the APC was willing to use and display Chinese support to mobilize voters. Chinese businessmen obviously went along in the campaigns, and Chinese government officials supported their partner government in the months before the elections, including at events and ceremonies that Western actors regarded as abuse of incumbency. However, all in all, Chinese support does not seem to have been a concerted exercise to push through an APC victory.

Tensions before the run-off presidential elections and results

After the first round of elections, the NEC was heavily, and in the EU EOM's view unjustifiably, criticized by all main political parties, which failed to produce any evidence of fraud. The ruling APC in particular was creating serious tensions, questioning the procedure for the tallying process. Police and the High Court got involved in this already tense situation, and the Attorney-General/Minister of Justice and the Inspector General of Police sent letters that were understood to increase the pressure on the NEC (EU EOM 2018, 12–13). Particularly the court injunction on preparations for the run-off election, granted few days before the scheduled date, was perceived as a moment of acute crisis (spokesperson, NEC, interview, May 16, 2018; also see NEW 2018, 10–12).

This impasse was finally overcome through international mediation efforts, in particular by the four African ex-presidents leading the observation missions, John Dramani Mahama (Ghana, Commonwealth), Prof. Amos Sawyer (Liberia, ECOWAS), Kgalema Motlanthe (South Africa, African Union), and Dr. Goodluck Jonathan (Nigeria, EISA). As a compromise, the tallying process was slightly changed (EU EOM 2018, 6; NEW 2018, 48) and the run-off was held on March 31 instead of March 27.

Julius Maada Bio's narrow victory can be seen as the result of 'a combination of [his] popularity and former President Ernest Bai Koroma stepping on many toes' (Fofana 2018). To begin with, Koroma's handpicked successor, Samura Kamara, was not the most popular candidate. In addition to the administration's corruption record, the economic situation, the response to the Ebola crisis, and the 2017 mudslide, a major factor mentioned in all interviews is President Koroma's sacking of Vice President Samuel Sam–Sumana as well as of Saa Emerson Lamina, the mayor of Koidu town in Kono district (see also IGR 2018b, 4). Compared to the 2012 presidential elections, the APC candidate lost votes in the party's heartland in the North and massively in Kono.

International diplomats were surprised to see how far the APC was willing to go to try and claim victory. According to them, the presidential candidate and running mate were pressured to challenge the results by 'the old guard in the background,' referring to senior APC officials around the president (diplomats, interviews, May 17, 2018, June 1, 2018). Owing to local civil society organizations and initiatives such as NEW or the Women's Situation Room, international observers and donors, the NEC could carry out the turbulent elections despite the incumbents' attempts of interfering with the process, and the situation on the ground remained relatively peaceful, albeit not without fatalities.[4]

Conclusion

The episode reported above suggests that the APC leadership was trying to use Chinese support to stay in power, first during their 'more time' campaign to avoid or at least postpone elections, and then to win the elections, emphasizing infrastructure projects realized so far and highlighting the future development potential linked to Chinese support. With reference to the debate on African agency, the case shows how actors in the APC government tried to use Chinese investments and support to their own (political) benefit as well as that of the party, with the lines between the government and party being traditionally blurred. APC elites around the president seem to have been trying to use the Chinese in their strategy of extraversion, as a buffer against Western donors, relations with whom had deteriorated. With Chinese loans, the government was less dependent on Western support and conditionalities.

The way in which APC elites had roped in Chinese actors for the run-up to the elections irritated opposition and civil society alike. China thus became part of political competition in the campaigns, with the ruling party trying to capitalize on its relations with China and the opposition party condemning this close relationship. Celebrated by APC supporters, the behavior of various Chinese actors – among them the Chinese ambassador, visitors from the CCP, Chinese companies and individual businessmen – was perceived by parts of Sierra Leonean society as exactly the opposite of the proclaimed Chinese 'brand' of non-interference (Hess and Aidoo 2015), namely: open interference in Sierra Leone's domestic affairs.

Throughout the tense elections, the incumbent government acted in a way that could have threatened the country's stability. The role of the Chinese in this tumultuous period should, however, not be overrated. Official Chinese support was always directed at the elected government, and the Chinese embassy made clear that it was not responsible for the doings of Chinese businesses. Still, many Sierra Leonean observers were very critical of their role – not necessarily because of their business activities in the country, but because of their disinterest in democratic governance and support for a government that was trying to rule in increasingly more authoritarian ways.

While the picture that develops from the behavior of the different Chinese actors in Sierra Leone may look a little unclear, it actually shows that China approaches its non-interference policy quite pragmatically, as Aidoo and Hess (2015, 109–110) point out, supporting incumbents and avoiding confrontations with powerful opposition forces, but courting new leaders once they have won elections, all in order to maintain stable economic and diplomatic relations with African partners.

This strategy seems to work. A few days after President Maada Bio had been sworn in, the spokesperson of the Chinese Ministry of Foreign Affairs, and later President Xi Jinping, congratulated him on his election. In the immediate post-election period, according to rumors, there had been some uncertainty in the Chinese business community about the future relationship with the new SLPP government because of President Bio's comments during the campaigns that he would revise some controversial contracts. His administration did indeed stop the contentious airport project, but contracted a Chinese company, PowerChina International Group Ltd., to build a bridge to the old airport in Lungi instead (State House 2018). Other bilateral agreements were signed when President Bio officially visited President Xi Jinping in August 2018 shortly before the 2018 Forum on China-Africa Cooperation. While it remains to be seen where President Bio's 'New Direction' will lead the Sierra Leone–China relationship in the future, it looks like they have managed the transition of power relatively smoothly.

Notes

1 The author would like to thank the editors, Adam Sandor, Sigrid Quack, Anne Stemmer, Janina Rinck, and the participants of the research colloquium of the Centre for Global Cooperation Research for their constructive comments as well as Saina Klein for careful proofreading of the chapter. Special thanks go to all interview partners in Sierra Leone. The title is derived from a newspaper article from *The Sierra Leone Telegraph* of March 18, 2018 titled 'We are black Chinese,' which claims that APC officials called themselves and their supporters 'black Chinese,' referring to a video circulated on WhatsApp and newspapers websites, in which the brother of President Koroma says 'APC is Black Chinese.'

2 Kandeh Yumkella had the US citizenship which he renounced in 2017.

3 ECOWAS, the AU, the Commonwealth, the EU, the Electoral Institute for Sustainable Democracy in Africa (EISA) sent election observation missions, as well as The Carter Center for the first round of elections. The former Ghanaian president was involved in mediating between APC and SLPP as the head of the Commonwealth mission, and the British High Commissioner – according to an interviewee – may have got the blame because 'it's easier to put the blame on the ex-colonial power than to say something about your own next-door neighbors,' i.e., the other ex-presidents heading the African missions (diplomat, interview, May 17, 2018).

4 Several people were killed in violent attacks related to the elections. Among them journalist Ibrahim Samura, who I had met only few days before his death on June 6, 2018. Samura, together with another colleague, had been beaten by 'very senior members of the APC party' (NEW 2018, 40) and security personnel on the day of the presidential run-off, while monitoring and reporting on the elections in Lumley, Freetown. The APC condemned the attack and apologized to him as well as the Sierra Leone Association of Journalists. An autopsy showed that he died of a heart attack caused by a fractured skull that left blood dripping into his organs (Sankoh 2018).

References

Aidoo, R. and Hess, S. (2015) 'Non-Interference 2.0: China's Evolving Foreign Policy towards a Changing Africa', *Journal Of Current Chinese Affairs*, 44(1), 107–139.

Akam, S. (2012) *Sierra Leone president forced out U.N. envoy: Letter*, (www.reuters.com/article/us-sierraleone-un-envoy/sierra-leone-president-forced-out-u-n-envoy-letter-idUSTRE81C27420120213), accessed 5 February 2019.

APA News (Agence de Presse Africaine) (2018) *Britain accused of interfering in S/Leone elections*, (www.apanews.net), accessed 25 September 2018.

Bayart, J. F. (2000) 'Africa in the World: A History of Extraversion', *African Affairs*, 99(395), 217–267.

Bräutigam, D. (1994) 'Foreign Assistance and the Export of Ideas: Chinese Development Aid in The Gambia and Sierra Leone', *The Journal of Commonwealth & Comparative Politics*, 32(3), 324–348.

Bräutigam, D. (1998) *Chinese Aid and African Development: Exporting Green Revolution*, Palgrave Macmillan UK, Basingstoke.

Bräutigam, D. (2009) *The Dragon's Gift: The Real Story of China in Africa*, Oxford University Press, Oxford.

Cambayma, B. (2017) *Sierra Leone News: APC 7-Floor: A case of incumbency immunity?*, (www.awoko.org), accessed 5 July 2018.

Corkin, L. and Burke, C. (2006) *China's Interest and Activity in Africa's Construction and Infrastructure Sectors. A Research Undertaking Evaluating China's Involvement in Africa's Construction and Infrastructure Sector Prepared for DFID China*, Centre for Chinese Studies, Stellenbosch.

Datzberger, S. (2013) *China's Silent Storm in Sierra Leone*, SAAIA Policy Briefing no. 71, South African Institute of International Affairs, Johannesburg.

Dreher, A., Fuchs, A., Hodler, R., Parks, B. C., Raschky, P. A. and Tierney, M. J. (2016) *Aid on Demand: African Leaders and the Geography of China's Foreign Assistance*, Working Paper no. 3, AidData, Williamsburg.

Dreher, A., Fuchs, A., Parks, B. C., Strange, A. M. and Tierney, M. J. (2017) *Aid, China, and Growth: Evidence from a New Global Development Finance Dataset*. AidData Working Paper no. 46, AidData, Williamsburg.

ECOWAS Court (2017) *Court orders government of Sierra Leone to pay former Vice President remuneration and entitlements*, (www.courtecowas.org), accessed 21 September 2018.

Elcoate, A. (2018) *'We are Chinese': How China is influencing Sierra Leone's presidential election. China is playing an unusually direct role in Sierra Leone's presidential campaign*, (www.thediplomat.com), accessed 13 June 2018.

EU EOM (European Union Election Observation Mission) (2018) *European Union Election Observation Mission Sierra Leone. Presidential, Parliamentary and Local Council Elections 2018. Final Report*. June 2018.

Fofana, U. (2018) *A hard road ahead*, (www.bbc.com/news/world-africa-43653098), accessed 10 February 2019.

Gberie, L. (2012) *The dignity and prestige of the UN were under attack: Schulenburg had to go*, (www.thesierraleonetelegraph.com), accessed 5 February 2019.

Gooding, O. (2017) *Sierra Leone News: Chinese Embassy denies funding ... SLPP calls for APC to account for $3m building project*, (www.awoko.org), accessed 5 July 2018.

Hess, S. and Aidoo, R. (2014) 'Charting the Roots of Anti-Chinese Populism in Africa: A Comparison of Zambia and Ghana', *Journal of Asian and African Studies*, 49(2), 129–147.

Hess, S. and Aidoo, R. (2015) *Charting the Roots of Anti-Chinese Populism in Africa*, Springer International Publishing, Cham.

IGR (Institute for Governance Reform) (2018a) *Divorcing Wealth from Power: How Successive Regimes Fail Sierra Leone*, Critical Perspectives of Governance Vol. X, April 2018, Institute for Governance Reform, Freetown.

IGR (Institute for Governance Reform) (2018b) *Presidential Election Results 2018: Lessons Learnt and Implications for the Runoff and Democracy Building*, Policy Brief Vol. 4, Institute for Governance Reform, Freetown.

Inveen, C. and Maclean, R. (2018) *China's influence looms as Sierra Leone goes to the polls. Beijing has been a close ally of outgoing president and is seen as a powerful player in an unusually open election*, (www.theguardian.com), accessed 11 June 2018.

Jakwa, T. (2018) *Making Sense of Sierra Leone's Dual Citizenship Fiasco*, Australian Outlook, 12 February 2018, Australian Institute of International Affairs.

NEW (National Election Watch) (2018) *Observation Report of the 2018 Electoral Cycle in Sierra Leone*, National Election Watch, Freetown.

OECD–DAC (OECD Development Assistance Committee) (n.d.) *Aid at a glance*, (www.oecd.org/dac/financing-sustainable-development/development-finance-data/aid-at-a-glance.htm), accessed 31 January 2019.

Salone Today (2017a) *Provocation ... APC 7 storey building costs 7,413,725,000 billion*, (www.salonetoday.com), accessed 5 July 2018.

Salone Today (2017b) *State capture ... APC building, army contract and Chinese SKM*, (www.salonetoday.com), accessed 5 July 2018.

Sankoh, A. (2018) *Amnesty International demands police probe into journalist Ibrahim Samura's death*, (www.slconcordtimes.com), accessed 12 October 2018.

State House Media and Communications Unit (2018) *President Bio engages PowerChina on the construction of Lungi Bridge*, (www.statehouse.gov.sl), accessed 30 January 2019.

Taylor, I. (2006) 'China's Oil Diplomacy in Africa', *International Affairs (Royal Institute of International Affairs)*, 82(5), 937–959.

The Carter Center (2018) *March 7, 2018 Presidential and Parliamentary Elections in Sierra Leone, Final Report March 23, 2018*, The Carter Center, Atlanta.

The Economist (2012) *Sierra Leone and the UN. Turning tables*, (www.economist.com/middle-east-and-africa/2012/02/18/turning-tables), accessed 5 February 2019.

The Political Parties Act (2002) *Supplement to the Sierra Leone Gazette Vol. CXXXIII*, No. 8, dated 21 February 2002.

Thomas, A. R. (2016) *Sierra Leone ruling APC realigns its politics with the Chinese Communist Party*, (www.thesierraleonetelegraph.com), accessed 14 June 2018.

Thomas, A. R. (2017) *China is meddling in Sierra Leone's party*, (www.thesierraleonetelegraph.com), accessed 11 June 2018.

Thomas, A. R. (2018) *We are black Chinese – says the ruling APC as they seek re-election*, (www.thesierraleonetelegraph.com), accessed 5 July 2018.

US Embassy Freetown (2012) *Local press summaries*, (https://photos.state.gov/libraries/sierraleone/452467/Info_%20Assist%20Desk_%20AVSM/Local%20Press%20Summaries%2026-27%20January%202012%20final.pdf), accessed 5 February 2019.

Zhao, Y. (2016) *Building on past achievements and joining hands to make an even brighter future of China-Sierra Leone friendship. In commemoration of the 45th anniversary of the establishment of China-Sierra Leone diplomatic relations*, (www.fmprc.gov.cn/mfa_eng/wjb_663304/zwjg_665342/zwbd_665378/t1386491.shtml), accessed 14 June 2018.

15 Conclusion

China and Africa's complex security challenges

Nele Noesselt and Christof Hartmann

The contributions compiled in this volume undertake a theory-guided evaluation of the 'China factor' in the evolving security challenges in Africa – before the backdrop of the still ongoing readjustment process of the People's Republic of China's (PRC) foreign strategy and the therefrom-deriving strategic opportunities (as well as challenges) for African actors. This final chapter seeks to connect and discuss the contributions' core findings along the lines of the three paramount research puzzles outlined in the introduction: (1) Chinas national images and (re-)definitions of its Africa strategy in the shadow of shifting global power constellations; (2) China's perception(s) of and contribution to political stability in Africa; (3) African agency in the quest for stable political settlements within Africa–China relationships. Finally, the chapter will address the implications of these findings for future research on African peace and security in connection with China's global ambitions. In addition, given the transformation of the actors involved as well as the changing regional and global power constellations, it will also take up the obvious need to finetune and update the related theoretical frameworks of analysis, and outline ways to assess the complexity of these multidimensional dynamics from an interactionist perspective.

National images and changing threat perceptions

The Maoist 'Three World Theory' had operated with a rather ideology-based classification of Africa as belonging to the 'third world' (Yee 1983, 239) and thus being a potential ally of the PRC in its struggle for spheres of influence to counterbalance the two superpowers, the US and the Soviet Union. During the years of the Cold War, the PRC covertly contributed to the training of the guerrilla opposition movements, inter alia in Angola and Zaire (Snow 2006, 295). Defining itself as an advocate speaking on behalf of the interests of this group of (developing) states, the Maoist PRC launched an image campaign to stress its symbolic support for the ongoing national liberation movements occurring across the African continent (Yu 1988, 852–857). In 1964, the PRC's Premier Zhou Enlai proclaimed the 'Eight Principles of Chinese Aid,' which centered on the provision of low-interest (or, under certain conditions, even interest-free loans and credits) as well as technical assistance including the sending of Chinese engineers and construction teams. Beijing, despite the PRC's domestic economy being in a severe crisis, decided to supply Tanzania with the financial and technical backing needed to realize the very ambitious Tanzania-Zambia railway project during the 1970s (Snow 2006, 287). Nonetheless, Beijing's active promotion of African liberation movements and the perceived atrocities of the Cultural Revolution (1966–1976) led to severe reputational losses among those African regimes maintaining close ties with (Western) Europe or the US – forcing the PRC to refine its relationship with its African counterparts. During the high tide of the Cold War, Beijing finally managed to win the support of the majority of African states to launch a shift of the permanent seat in the UN Security Council from the Republic of China (with its government retreated to the island of Taiwan) to the PRC represented by the Chinese Communist Party (CCP) government in Beijing (Ismael 1971, 529).

The post-Maoist PRC, following a more pragmatic approach to foreign affairs and mainly focusing on trade benefits, turned from the ideological interpretation of the world as being composed of 'two camps' added by 'intermediate zones' – later on further extended to Mao's tripartite division of the globe into 'three worlds' – to the idea of a unipolar interim period transitioning towards multipolarity. But it did not give up its self-defined role identity as being a 'developing state' engaged in 'South-South cooperation.' However, the rising anti-Chinese sentiments and the instrumentalization of these negative emotions during electoral campaigns in select African states somehow evidence the widening gap between China's self-proclaimed role identities and the roles and images associated with the PRC by the targeted (African) governments (and their societies). The soft power campaigns launched by Beijing as well as the local cultural activities initiated by Chinese entrepreneurial communities and associations in Africa seek to appease and defuse the lurking threat perceptions deriving from the global rise of the PRC in terms of economic and financial power. Beijing actively relates to Africa's historical memory of asymmetric relations, dangerous overdependencies, and vicious debt spirals by continuously stressing its peaceful ambitions and highlighting the 'win–win' dimension of Chinese investment and infrastructure projects across Africa, imagined as being opposed to colonial practices. While the official data compiled by Afrobarometer indicate a rather positive China image (Lekorwe et al. 2016), the large-scale entrepreneurial and street vendor migration to Africa has created rising tensions and competition at the micro-level of the African economies (inter alia Hess and Aidoo 2014).

Beijing's resteering of the PRC's domestic development model and the strategic inclusion of the domestic–global nexus in its strategic economic planning are the main drivers behind its New Silk Road project – which involve the further intensification of economic and financial activities in Africa. While the PRC's large-scale infrastructure projects are mainly undertaken by state-owned companies and financed by China's state-owned banks, the activities of local traders and private entrepreneurs are beyond the direct reach of the Chinese party-state. African societies' perception of 'China' can hence easily be distorted by the misbehavior of single individuals (see Chapter 5 by Haifang Liu), which explains the national government's efforts to crack down on corruption and illegal activities of Chinese nationals abroad.

Apparently, Beijing is no longer passively observing the deterioration of the China image(s) in Africa and the speculations regarding the assumed assertive, neocolonial turn along the PRC's New Silk Road corridors. It seeks to position itself as a promoter of African agency in terms of economic modernization (and global competitiveness) as well as domestic and regional security.

The deployment of Chinese peacekeepers and combat forces to Africa officially follows the principle of 'responsible protection' as opposed to the notion of 'responsibility to protect,' the latter being criticized as Trojan horse of the 'West' to facilitate the interference into the internal affairs of sovereign states and the overthrow of their heads of states in the name of democracy and human rights (Ruan 2012, 36–39). Over the past few decades, the PRC's political elites did learn that non-interference and the abstention from international peace missions can all too easily result in reputational losses and weaken the trust and support of groups regarded as strategic allies to counterbalance the predominant power position of the US – the African Union as well as the Arab League.

Furthermore, the PRC's official view on 'Africa' has become more differentiated and now includes critical evaluations and risks assessments of the empirical reality. Over the past 10 years, Beijing had to respond to the threats and risks deriving from local rebellions, civil wars, as well as radical religious movements in Africa. This explains the gradual shift from traditional to non-traditional security issues in Beijing's foreign strategy towards Africa. 'Human security' has likewise become a major concern for the PRC's political decision-makers; the realization of the New Silk Road implies that the number of Chinese businesspeople and engineers deployed to the African continent will most likely continue to increase.

One explanation for the recent changes regarding China's reluctant willingness to contribute to African peace and security operations might be a perception change among China's political elites and rising unease among Chinese state-owned companies involved in infrastructure-building activities along the African corridors of the New Silk Road. Earlier already, starting around the year 2004, kidnappings and/or killings of Chinese workers had occurred in Sudan, Pakistan, and Afghanistan. This had triggered several readjustments to the state institutions and departments in China responsible for coordinating the PRC's foreign affairs, economic and trade relations, as well as public security. In 2010, new regulations were passed prescribing that Chinese companies operating abroad would have to improve their 'risk-assessment capabilities.' Responding to the worsening security constellations in Libya (2011), these regulations were further amended, prescribing the preparatory training of workers regarding 'basic self-defense, crisis response techniques, first-aid procedures (even for gunshot wounds).' Since 2010, Chinese private security companies have extended their services to Africa and the Middle East, the main target regions of Chinese state-owned companies in the oil sector (Ghiselli 2018). In addition, the PRC is also engaged in training local police and security forces in Africa, and Chinese private security companies have intensified their cooperation with local and multinational security companies (Shinn 2015).

Furthermore, the resteering of the Chinese development model in 2013/2014 and the launching of Beijing's New Silk Road Initiative have added some novel dimensions to Beijing's strategic foreign policy calculations. In late 2013, the Chinese state President, Xi Jinping, officially proclaimed the building of a 'New Silk Road,' consisting of overland trade corridors and maritime passages. At the 19th Congress of the Chinese Communist Party in autumn 2017, the 'Belt and Road Initiative' (BRI) was officially anchored as a core principle of China's foreign strategy (Xinhua 2017). Since then, more states and regions have been actively invited to join this global connectivity network. The Chinese naval and logistical base in Djibouti is officially presented as an important nodal point of this network. At the Forum on China–Africa Cooperation (FOCAC) Summit 2018 in Beijing, Xi Jinping framed the Belt and Road Initiative as a complement to 'the AU Agenda 2063, the UN 2030 Agenda for Sustainable Development and the development programs of African countries' and declared that 'fifty security assistance programs (would) be launched to advance China-Africa cooperation under the Belt and Road Initiative, and in areas of law and order, UN peacekeeping missions, fighting piracy and combating terrorism' (Xinhua 2018a).

Highlighting the concept of 'developmental peace,' the PRC positions itself as offering an alternative to good governance-based conditional credits and prioritizes development over developmental 'aid.' Beijing's main concern remains stability at home as well as along the New Silk Road corridors – and it stresses the idea that access to development will decrease both the likeliness of an outbreak of local rebellions as well as the spread of religious extremism in other world regions. Nevertheless, despite these narratives of peace and harmony, the PRC has reportedly strengthened its surveillance approach and is using AI-based steering solutions. The extension of the New Silk Road to Africa might, in the long run, also catalyze the export of 'Chinese' governance concepts and steering mechanism, as the New Silk Road also includes a digital dimension. Besides telecommunication and IT infrastructure, some African states have reportedly started to resort to 'smart' and 'safe city' solutions as advanced by Chinese companies (see Chapter 2 by Nele Noesselt).

In sum, even though the PRC is not actively promoting and exporting any 'Chinese Model,' it is selling its high-speed rise to the status of the world's second-largest economy and its successful fight against absolute poverty as a universal blueprint of 'non-Western' modernization (on the most recent Chinese reflections on the 'Chinese Model,' see Zhao 2017).

Grand strategy versus muddling through

The astonishing speed of the PRC's rise to global power status has triggered speculations about Beijing's long-term (geo)strategic ambitions. While Wang

Jisi (2011) had once bemoaned the absence of a 'grand strategy,' hence implying that the PRC has been pursuing an experimental muddling through without any related risk assessment, predictions about future global power constellations put forward by US-based analysts sketch a rather gloomy scenario of a battle for global hegemony and Beijing's strategic push for setting-up an 'illiberal order.' In the run up to the PRC's changing of the guard in 2012, Chinese think tanks had been engaged in a heated debate about whether or not to give up Deng Xiaoping's formula of 'keeping a low profile' (*taoguang yanghui*), but finally concluded that a continuation of the basic foreign policy patterns would suit China's overarching development goals (Noesselt 2015). Since the formal launching of the Chinese BRI in 2013, international observers did, once again, assess the potential future global positioning strategy of the PRC assuming that the BRI would have to be backed by the coining of a formal 'grand strategy' deviating from China's previous rather passive observer status (Leverett and Wu 2016, 120). Some scholars have looked at China's 'new neighborhood diplomacy' towards Central Asia to identify elements of an emerging 'grand strategy' (inter alia Fallon 2015; Zhang 2016). Given that the economic reforms, as Xi Jinping proclaimed in 2014, did formally enter 'deep waters' (Xinhua 2014), an uncoordinated muddling through approach seems no longer appropriate. There are obvious efforts to professionalize and update China's foreign and security strategy, which implies that theory frames and core terms designed to describe Maoist and post-Maoist reform politics might no longer be able to catch and categorize the most recent developments.

While there have been various reports on the PRC's resteering of its domestic economic development roadmap, official statements present the country's foreign politics as being a continuation of the axiomatic principles laid down by the previous leadership generations. There are, however, visible efforts to institutionalize foreign relations with select countries or groups of states and to constitutionalize bi- and multilateral agreements. Along these lines, Ferdinand (2016, 949) identifies three core foreign policy add-ons devised by China's fifth generation: the formula of a 'new type of great power relations,' mainly addressing the PRC's interactions with the US, the concept of 'new neighborhood diplomacy,' and the BRI. Likewise, Aoyama argues that Xi Jinping's foreign strategy deviates from the PRC's previous positioning in two points. First, its 'geographical scope' has been extended to cover the whole world and not just the PRC's regional cooperation partners. Second, the BRI intends to simultaneously explore land-based and maritime passages. While the previous development idea had been to boost the economy in the less developed Western provinces, the revised development roadmap seeks to pursue a joint development of China's backward West and the flourishing coastal provinces in the East (Aoyama 2016, 8–9). Friedberg (2018) identifies a three-step evolution of China's post-Maoist 'grand strategy' characterized by a transition from the patterns of 'hiding and biding,' 'binding and hedging,' to, finally, 'shaping and restructuring' (of the international system and its institutions).

Africa is only indirectly covered by these strategy debates and continues to fall into the 'South–South' cooperation cluster. Beijing's symbolic positioning towards African countries and regional organizations is skillfully staged as 'win–win' opportunity as opposed to the US' updated Africa strategy, which, according to Chinese media analyses, is driven by the principle of 'America First' (Xinhua 2018b). The PRC's Africa strategy is, hence, similar to the BRI which is contrasted with the US Marshall Plan and conditional development aid programs (see, Wang 2016), defined *ex negativo*, i.e., by ascribing other players (neo)colonial ambitions and the intention to limit African states' autonomous and self-defined development. The PRC's *White Paper on Foreign Aid* (State Council 2014) contains a comparatively long chapter entitled 'Promoting a New China-Africa Strategic Partnership' that refers to infrastructure and investment projects which are central to Beijing's BRI – and thus rather fall under the category of trade and financial cooperation than conventional development aid (State Council 2014). Taking the Chinese narratives and strategy reflections into account, this is quite in line with Beijing's claim to pursue a distinct approach to cooperation with the states of the 'Global South' beyond conditional aid programs. While the Marshall Plan is referred to by Chinese scholars as having consolidated the division of the world into a Western capitalist and a (Soviet) socialist camp, the BRI is generally presented as facilitating the integration and interconnection of all players involved. Instead of 'aid' the main offer for the 'Global South' consists of trade and investment opportunities to catalyze local development. This might, in the long run, also support Africa's quest for redefining its independent African cultural identity (on this issue, see Senghaas 2019) or even facilitate the deepening of regional coordination mechanisms among Africa's rising economies and trigger the formation of joint security mechanisms.

African agency

The country chapters nicely reflect how China–African relationships offer a growing diversity of interaction patterns, which both display different structural environments in terms of economic basis and regime and state trajectories, and the more contingent spaces for agency used by African elites. Take the cases of Rwanda and Ethiopia discussed by Grimm/Hackenesch and Hess. These countries share many properties. They will not be courted by investors for mineral resources, and China might be interested in these economies only as a potential location for industries and as a market for own export products (Ethiopia more than Rwanda given market size, but Rwanda as an entry towards the common market of the East African Community). Both Rwanda and Ethiopia have invited China to invest, but both countries have also maintained very good relationships to the West and the international donor community. Both countries have a legacy of mass violence and civil war, and authoritarian regimes. Their governments gained legitimacy as political movements, which created a new regime committed to development and that makes a difference to the lives of ordinary people, although starting from very low levels of human development.

Yet, despite all these similarities, Rwandan elites have adopted a quite different strategy in dealing with Chinese influence compared to Ethiopia. The late Ethiopian Prime Minister Meles Zenawi actively promoted his country's image as China's gateway to Africa, or a spokesperson of China in Africa. He explicitly referred to China as a model of governance to be emulated by African countries. Rwanda's Paul Kagame, on the contrary, has certainly hailed China for its capacity to better understand African realities than the 'West,' but did not openly refer to China as a reference for the management of Rwandan governance. As highlighted by Grimm and Hackenesch in their chapter, Rwanda might be a real test case for China's claim to initiate win–win partnerships that are also demand-driven. Rwanda's development–authoritarian regime has a clear vision about future economic development, and is likely to accept support only under conditions, which are indeed mutually beneficial, while it remains unclear which economic benefits China might really draw from a more intense cooperation with Rwanda.

We can also have closer look at the examples of Sierra Leone and Zambia, discussed by Rinck as well as Aidoo in this volume. They also share a specific economic context, as both countries depend on the export of mineral resources, with China being a major investor in resource extraction in both cases and a history of controversial deals, whether in mining (Zambia) or infrastructure (Sierra Leone). While the economic structure presents unfavorable frame conditions for competitive politics, both Zambia and Sierra Leone have attempted a transition towards liberal democracy. In both countries, the population has voted out incumbent governments, and there is thus some functioning political accountability of rulers, while other dimensions of a democratic order seem more fragile. The massive economic presence of China led to the politicization during electoral campaigns, with China being accused of partisan support for incumbent parties in their attempt to secure re-election in a competitive environment with open electoral races.

Again, in similar environments, elites made different choices. In Zambia, it was the opposition, which mobilized against the Chinese and claimed the ruling party was making opaque deals with China and not defending Zambian workers' rights, promising voters to critically assess all Chinese investments once elected. In Sierra Leone, on the contrary, the ruling party was playing a 'pro-China card,' using its good relations with Chinese actors in the campaigns to mobilize support, in the absence of any evidence for an actual material support of official Chinese agencies to the electoral campaign of the ruling party. The Chinese ambassador did, however, not decline to launch the construction of a Chinese-financed international airport during a public ceremony with the incumbent President in the midst of the electoral campaign, 6 days before the presidential elections, not vetoing against the whole event being framed as a ruling party achievement. The newly elected President of Sierra Leone eventually stopped the construction of the airport in 2018, while Zambian President Sata did not seriously rediscuss the terms of Chinese investments in the country after his elections, despite all contrary rhetoric.

These examples reveal that African elites have some agency in shaping Chinese–Africa policies, notwithstanding the asymmetrical nature of the bilateral relationship and the inherent structural dependence from China as powerful investor, trade partner and 'donor.' The cases also illustrate that the growing use of Bayart's extraversion concept in the sense of a short-term strategic, cynical manipulation of external actors to the advantage of individual African power-holders, reflects a distorted perspective of African politics and of China–African relationships. As indicated in Hartmann's chapter in this volume, such agency should be dominant only in one category of African regimes, such as Angola or Zimbabwe, where personalistic and clientelist networks shape governance. The examples of Sierra Leone and Zambia, however, do clearly illustrate, how China cannot avoid being drawn into domestic political games.

Theory implications

The combined observations regarding the transformation of the PRC from being an observing bystander to becoming a proactive player and norm-maker of world politics (see Alden and Large 2015, 125) imply that both the theory-based frameworks of analysis to assess the PRC's foreign policy as well as the empirical databases on Chinese foreign and security strategy need to be refined and updated.

The contributions to this volume have considered the discursive dimensions and role theory approaches to the decryption of Chinese relations with Africa. This means looking at 'international roles' as 'social positions (…) constituted by ego- and alter-expectations regarding the purpose of an actor in an organized group' (Harnisch 2016, 5). The PRC's international positioning has so far been analyzed by applying overarching role frames, often centering on the assumed power competition and global struggle for hegemony (or leadership) between China and the US, and with regard to role ascriptions and role-taking. Less attention has been paid to the framing and communication processes related to role claims, especially in constellations where role articulations collide with the role ascriptions and role perceptions within the targeted audiences (see Chapter 3 by Julia C. Strauss).

As the case studies examined in this volume show, roles and positions are not only created through interactions but are actively coined and communicated in order to win support and to generate followers. The often-identified gap between Chinese role elements and concrete behavior should, in this vein, be the logical result of the coexistence of various slightly contradicting role elements of which the PRC's official role is composed. Depending on the group of significant others addressed, some role elements, those that seem to be dysfunctional in these specific actor constellations (Turner 1990), might (silently) be deactivated, while others might be reconfirmed. The PRC is obviously not sticking to one unified strategy to communicate with 'Africa' but simultaneously speaks to multilateral frameworks (e.g., FOCAC), regional organizations (e.g., the African Union), subgroups of like-minded African states as well as individual strategic cooperation partners. Moreover, it is following a quite pragmatic strategy to address both the ruling elites as well as influential societal actor groups.

Besides, the case studies presented illustrate that roles are linked to a specific (group) identity and (relative) status positions of the players involved. Recognition of position and role claims by other actors thus become a decisive factor that might determine a state's strategic room of maneuver in world affairs. If states are seen as 'assertive' players, 'revisionist' powers, or 'enemies,' this will trigger the formation of alliances engaging in containment actions. The coining of the BRI and the construction of maritime New Silk Road corridors integrates the various Africa activities of the multitude of 'Chinese' actors and presents them as following a coherent, top-down coordinated roadmap that promises tangible benefits for everyone involved. This displays certain core features of the strategy of 'purposeful framing,' i.e., the endeavor to counter negative images, as 'an attempt by leaders and other influential actors to insert into the policy debate (...) organizing themes that will affect how the targets themselves as well as the public and other actors (e.g., media) perceive an issue' (Mintz and Redd 2003, 194). Framing is closely linked to persuasion. It provides the target audience with a coherent story line and seeks to establish certain world views and normative values (see, van Hulst and Yanow 2016,101).

Socio-constructivist approaches to world politics ascribe ideas a central meaning in the (re-)making of institutions (Lieberman 2002; Zittoun 2009). Ideas 'help to construct the problems and issues that enter the policy agenda [...], shape the assumptions that impact the content of reform proposals [...], can become discursive weapons that participate in the construction of reform imperatives' (Béland 2009, 702). This might explain the PRC's active engagement in setting up novel multilateral fora and taking part in the rebargaining of the basic norms and values underlying peacekeeping missions and reconstruction operations in Africa.

The recognition of the PRC's status and role claims (Deng 2005, 2008) – i.e., the acceptance as an equal partner in the coordination of world politics and economics – by significant others increases the legitimacy of the PRC's 'developmental state' approach at home. Symbolic actions and rhetoric statements are, however, not the only drivers of the PRC's refined Africa strategy. Beijing's noticeable interest in African states' domestic politics and the anticipation of their potential implications for Chinese infrastructure and investment plans clearly evidences that the Chinese leadership does neither operate with fixed role frames nor does it take role ascriptions and role recognition statements by significant others as static and unchangeable. It is hence operating before the backdrop of risk uncertainty and seeks to establish long-term stable structures via the formal constitutionalizing of bi- and multilateral interactions. Hence, Beijing does not support movements that might destabilize its strategic cooperation partners and central nodal points of the African branch of the New Silk Road. Instead, it has turned to prioritizing legal robustness as well as the installment of checks-and-balances to secure a stable and secure environment for Chinese state-owned enterprises as well as private companies operating across Africa. There is thus still much to learn, not only for Chinese policy-makers but also researchers, from a more systematic analysis of these differing contexts, whether analyzed from a more institutional or political economy perspective.

Further research is also required regarding the effectiveness of alternative Chinese 'models' of peacebuilding in Africa. 'Developmental peace' is an interesting concept in terms of Chinese attempts to act as a global norm-maker and as a reflection about how Chinese leadership interprets its own history, but it is still unclear how the concept can be further operationalized, and how it might represent a departure from more conventional attempts at international peacebuilding. The more proactive engagement of China in African peacebuilding (in Mali or South Sudan) has been supportive of existing multilateral diplomatic efforts and interventions. Whether China manages to contribute towards the stabilization of these countries, does not depend on the success or failure of a specific Chinese approach but, at least for the time being, on the fate of the UN-led multilateral interventions. As these missions have rarely attempted to promote a comprehensive liberal peacebuilding and rather prioritized the stabilization of incumbent governments over the last years, China does not need 'developmental peace' in order to protect its economic interests and to pursue its broader geopolitical strategy.

References

Alden, C. and Large, D. (2015) 'On Becoming a Norms Maker: Chinese Foreign Policy, Norms Evolution and the Challenges of Security in Africa', *The China Quarterly*, 221, 123–142.

Aoyama, R. (2016) '"One Belt, One Road": China's New Global Strategy', *Journal of Contemporary East Asia Studies*, 5(2), 3–22.

Béland, D. (2009) 'Ideas, Institutions, and Policy Change', *Journal of European Public Policy*, 16(5), 701–718.

Deng, Y. (2005) 'Better than Power: "International Status" in Chinese Foreign Policy', in Y. Deng and F. Wang (eds) *China Rising: Power and Motivation in Chinese Foreign Policy*, Rowman and Littlefield, Lanham, 51–72.

Deng, Y. (2008) *China's Struggle for Status: The Realignment of International Relations*, Cambridge University Press, Cambridge.

Fallon, T. (2015) 'The New Silk Road: Xi Jinping's Grand Strategy for Eurasia', *American Foreign Policy Interests*, 37(3), 140–147.

Ferdinand, P. (2016) 'Westward Ho-The China Dream and "One Belt One Road": Chinese Foreign Policy under Xi Jinping', *International Affairs*, 92(4), 941–957.

Friedberg, A. L. (2018) 'Globalisation and Chinese Grand Strategy', *Survival*, 60(1), 7–40.

Ghiselli, A. (2018) 'Market Opportunities and Political Responsibilities: The Difficult Development of Chinese Private Security Companies Abroad', *Armed Forces & Society*, online first: DOI: 10.1177/0095327X18806517, 7–9.

Harnisch, S. (2015) 'Role Theory and the Study of Chinese Foreign Policy', in S. Harnisch, S. Bersick, and J.-C. Gottwald (eds) *China's International Roles: Challenging or Supporting International Order*, Routledge, New York, 3–21.

Hess, S. and Aidoo, R. (2014) 'Charting the Roots of Anti-Chinese Populism in Africa: A Comparison of Zambia and Ghana', *Journal of Asian and African Studies*, 49(2), 129–147.

Ismael, T. Y. (1971) 'The People's Republic of China and Africa', *The Journal of Modern African Studies*, 9(4), 507–529.

Lekorwe, M., Chingwete, A., Okuru M., and Samson, R. (2016) 'China's Growing Presence in Africa Wins Largely Positive Popular Reviews', *Afrobarometer*, 122, https://afrobarometer.org/sites/default/files/publications/Dispatches/ab_r6_dispatchno122_perceptions_of_china_in_africa1.pdf.

Leverett, F. and Wu, B. (2016) 'The New Silk Road and China's Evolving Grand Strategy', *The China Journal*, 77, 110–132.

Lieberman, R. C. (2002) 'Ideas, Institutions, and Political Order: Explaining Political Change', *American Political Science Review*, 96(4), 697–712.

Mintz, A. and Redd, S. B. (2003) 'Framing Effects in International Relations', *Synthese*, 135, 193–213.

Noesselt, N. (2015) 'China's Foreign Strategy after the 18th Party Congress: Business as Usual?', *Journal of Chinese Political Science*, 20(1), 17–33.

Ruan, Z. (2012) 'Responsible Protection: Building a Safer World', *China International Studies*, 34, 19–41.

Senghaas, D. (2019) 'Afrika: Weiterhin auf der Suche nach einer Leitkultur?' (Africa: Still looking for a (unified) cultural identity?), *Soziologie Heute*, 29–30.

Shinn, D. H. (2015) 'China's Growing Security Relationship with Africa: For Whose Benefit?', *African East Asian Affairs* (China Monitor), 3(4), 124–143.

Snow, P. (2006) [1994] 'China and Africa: Consensus and Camouflage', in T. W. Robinson and D. Shambaugh (eds) *Chinese Foreign Policy: Theory and Practice*, Clarendon Press, Oxford, 283–321.

State Council (2014) *China's foreign aid (2014)*, (http://english.gov.cn/archive/white_paper/2014/08/23/content_281474982986592.htm), accessed 15 March 2015

Turner, R. H. (1990) 'Role Change', *Annual Review of Sociology*, 16, 87–110.

van Hulst, M. and Yanow, D. (2016) 'From Policy "Frames" to "Framing": Theorizing a More Dynamic, Political Approach', *American Review of Public Administration*, 46(1), 92–112.

Wang, J. (2011) 'China's Search for a Grand Strategy: A Rising Great Power Finds its Way', *Foreign Affairs*, 90(2), 68–79.

Wang, Y. (2016) 'The "Belt and Road Initiative" is Not China's "Marshall Plan"', *Qiushi*, (http://english.qstheory.cn/2016-03/08/c_1118036249.htm), accessed 15 March 2017.

Xinhua (2014) *Xi Jinping: Gaige yi jinru shenshuiqu (Xi Jinping: Reforms have entered deep waters)*, (http://finance.sina.com.cn/china/20140330/014018656114.shtml), accessed 15 March 2017.

Xinhua (2017) *Secure a decisive victory in building a moderately prosperous society in all respects and strive for the great success of socialism with Chinese characteristics for a new era* (Speech by Xi Jinping at the 19th Party Congress), (www.xinhuanet.com/english/special/2017-11/03/c_136725942.htm), accessed 11 January 2019.

Xinhua (2018a) *Full text of Chinese President Xi Jinping's speech at opening ceremony of 2018 FOCAC Beijing Summit*, (www.xinhuanet.com/english/2018-09/03/c_137441987.htm), accessed 11 January 2019.

Xinhua (2018b) *Mei tui xin Feizhou zhanlüe: Qiangdiao Meiguo youxian (The US put forward a new Africa strategy: Stressing the America First principle)*, (www.xinhuanet.com/world/2018-12/14/c_1123852984.htm), accessed 11 January 2019.

Yee, H. (1983) 'The Three World Theory and Post-Mao China's Global Strategy', *International Affairs*, 59(2), 239–249.

Yu, G. T. (1988) 'Africa in Chinese Foreign Policy', *Asian Survey*, 28(8), 849–862.

Zhang, Y. (2016) 'China and its Neighbourhood: Transformation, Challenges and Grand Strategy, *International Affairs*, 92(4), 835–848.

Zhao, S. (2017) 'Whither the China Model: Revisiting the debate', *Journal of Contemporary China*, 26(103), 1–17.

Zittoun, P. (2009) 'Understanding policy change as a discursive problem', *Journal of Comparative Policy Analysis*, 11(1), 65–82.

Index

Page numbers in **bold** denote tables.